W9-ADP-859

THE FIN-DE-SIÈCLE
CULTURE OF
ADOLESCENCE

JOHN NEUBAUER

The Fin-de-Siècle
Culture of
Adolescence

YALE UNIVERSITY PRESS

NEW HAVEN & LONDON

Published with assistance from the Kingsley Trust Association Publication Fund established by the Scroll and Key Society of Yale College

Portions of chapter 1 originally appeared as "Identity by Metaphors," in *Neverending Stories: Toward a Critical Narratology,* ed. by Ann Fehn, Ingeborg Hoesterey, and Maria Tatar. Copyright © 1991 Princeton University Press. Reprinted by permission of Princeton University Press. Portions of chapter 7 originally appeared as "Psychoanalysis and Female Identity: The Adolescent Diaries of Karen Horney," in *Essays in European Literature for Walter A. Strauss,* ed. by Alice N. Benston and Marshall C. Olds. Studies in Twentieth Century Literature, Monograph Series no. 1. Lincoln: University of Nebraska Press, 1989. 215–227.

Designed by Nancy Ovedovitz and set in Perpetua type by Brevis Press. Printed in the United States of America by Edwards Brothers, Ann Arbor, Michigan.

Library of Congress Cataloging-in-Publication Data
Neubauer, John. 1933–
    The fin-de-siècle culture of adolescence / John Neubauer.
    p.   cm.
    Includes bibliographical references and index.
    ISBN 0-300-05103-4 (alk. paper)
    1. Literature, Modern—19th century—History and criticism.   2. Literature, Modern—20th century—History and criticism.   3. Adolescents in literature.
I. Title.
PN761.N48   1992
809'.93352055'09034—dc20   91-35085
                                                    CIP

The paper in this book meets the guidelines for permanence and durability of the Committee on Production Guidelines for Book Longevity of the Council on Library Resources.

1   3   5   7   9   10   8   6   4   2

For Eva and Nicole who mastered the age faster and better

Contents

Contents

Contents

Illustrations

8. Erich Heckel, *Girl (Fränzi) with Doll,* 1910. © Erich Heckel 1991, c/o Beeldrecht, Amsterdam, Netherlands. Photo: Kunsthistorisch Instituut, Universiteit van Amsterdam.

9. Erich Heckel, woodcut after Kirchner's 1910 Brücke poster. © Erich Heckel 1991, c/o Beeldrecht, Amsterdam, Netherlands. Photo: Brücke Museum, Berlin.

10. George Minne, *The Fountain of Kneeling Boys,* 1901? Museum voor Schone Kunsten, Gent, Belgium. Photo: Piet Ysabie.

11. Oskar Kokoschka, *The Girl Li and I,* from *The Dreaming Boys,* 1908. © Erich Heckel 1991, c/o Beeldrecht, Amsterdam, Netherlands. Photo: Kunsthistorisch Instituut, Universiteit van Amsterdam.

12. Egon Schiele, *Nude Girl with Arms Crossed in front of her Breast,* 1910. Graphische Sammlung Albertina, Vienna, Austria. Photo: Graphische Sammlung Albertina.

13. Egon Schiele, Sketch for the *Self-Seer I,* 1910. Graphische Sammlung Albertina, Vienna, Austria. Photo: Graphische Sammlung Albertina.

14. Egon Schiele, *Two Girls Embracing Each Other,* 1915. Szépmüvészeti Múzeum, Budapest, Hungary. Photo: A. Szenczi Mária.

15. Hermann Pfeiffer, illustration from *Der Zupfgeigenhansl,* 1909. Photo: Musikverlag B. Schott's Söhne, Mainz.

Preface

My book explores historical and cultural aspects of adolescence, but these were not my original concerns, nor are they the central issues for me today. Adolescence is an intense, unique personal experience that remains an active influence throughout one's life, whatever shape it may acquire in different periods, cultures, and academic discourses.

I grew up during the time of Hitler and Stalin, and I was an idealistic, introverted, and isolated adolescent, for whom preoccupation with myself was the anchor in life. Once I emerged from adolescence and the shadow of dictatorships, I found other anchors, and my broadening horizons led me to a skeptical, at times even cynical, attitude with respect to my intense former self. And yet, the recurrent images of my adolescence often fill me also with a sense of loss.

Although I can no longer reconstruct the original motives for embarking on this project, and I certainly cannot claim that it was a conscious mid-life effort to retrace my steps, looking back I do recognize in it an effort to recover a more intensely personal engagement both with respect to myself and towards others. I conceived this project for teaching, and carried it out partly while watching my own children passing through adolescence. On the way, it led to a great many lively interchanges with students, friends, and colleagues, for it is a topic that instantaneously engages everybody's imagination. The original course on literature and adolescence grew into a historically specific research project with scholarly and formal concerns that mercifully screened out self-indulgence, but it remains a more personal matter to me than most of my earlier publications, in part because it has provided a link with my own past, a reconnecting, however tenuous, with my former self.

The complete list of those persons and institutions that helped me along the way would be too long to be included here; I can therefore name only the most important ones. The first course I taught was assisted by a grant from the National Endowment for the Humanities to the University of Pittsburgh to find new ways of teaching the humanities. Ben Bart, then director of the comparative literature program at Pitt, warmly supported the project from the very beginning, and I treasure the intellectual stimulation as well as the friendship he offered me throughout the years. During the gestation of the idea I also had lengthy discussions with the late Donald Gordon, who was at the time finishing his book on Expressionism and thus preoccupied with similar questions of identity.

Teaching the course for the first time at Harvard is almost as memorable for me as my adolescence, and discussions with students then stimulated me to carry the project further. Since then I have profited from teaching similar courses at the University of Pittsburgh, the University of Amsterdam, and the University of Essen. One of my most constant and reliable dialogue partners was, of course, my wife, Ursel, and I only hope that those discussions and the finished book will be a small consolation to her for the long hours I spent secluded, facing the computer screen.

The greatest help in completing the research project came from the Netherlands Institute for Advanced Study, which allowed me to work there undisturbed during the academic year 1987–88. It was a delightful year, and I am happy to acknowledge my debt to its staff and its director, Professor D. J. van de Kaa.

The last phase of my work meant cooperation with Yale University Press. Ellen Graham was as kind, encouraging, and helpful with this book as with my previous one. At the occasion of her retirement I would like to acknowledge once more how enjoyable it has been to work with her over the years. Jane Hedges did a splendid job of correcting my mistakes and calling my attention to passages where the argument was muddled.

I am grateful to Princeton University Press and *Twentieth Century Fiction* for permissions to reprint revised versions of texts that appeared earlier.

A NOTE ON THE TRANSLATIONS

I quote from standard English translations named in the bibliography whenever these stay close to the original. I have translated all the remaining foreign texts myself; my debt to existing translations is acknowledged in the footnotes. The original texts are provided in footnotes for my translations of literary texts.

Introduction

> It is as if, to every period of history, there corresponded a privileged
> age and a particular division of human life: youth is the privileged
> age of the seventeenth century, childhood of the nineteenth,
> adolescence of the twentieth.
> —Philippe Ariès, *Centuries of Childhood*

SPRING AWAKENING

In the opening scene of Wedekind's *Frühlings Erwachen* (*Spring Awakening,*
1891) Wendla Bergmann refuses the long "penitential robe" that her mother
has sewn for her fourteenth birthday and clings to her old *Prinzesskleidchen.*
She also rejects Frau Bergmann's offer to lengthen the old dress. She would
prefer a sudden leap to age twenty.[1]

The perennial problems of growing up appear here in the idiom and social
situation of the 1890s. Frau Bergmann finally consents to her retaining the
old dress because she too would prefer prolonging Wendla's childhood. The
"robe" was made long, she claims, only in anticipation of Wendla's growth.
Later, she fails in her attempt to communicate to Wendla the facts of puberty
and sexuality. The unenlightened girl becomes pregnant, undergoes an abor-
tion arranged by her mother, and dies.

As a late twentieth-century audience we read and view Wedekind's tragicomic satire and cautionary tale about education as a historical document.
Frau Bergmann's timidity and Wendla's naïveté when confronting sexuality

seem to us attitudes of yesterday. Like the girl in Munch's *Puberty* (fig. 1), Wendla experiences her changing body as a foreboding of death. Unlike her counterparts a century later, she would prefer to remain a child.

Does Wedekind's play accurately document turn-of-the-century (German) attitudes and values? The scene discussed is ambiguous. The *Prinzesskleidchen,* we learn, was a dress with a tight waistline, introduced by Princess Alexandra of England around 1865. Does Wendla perhaps want to retain it because it displays her budding femininity better than her mother's sacklike robe? And are we to accept Frau Bergmann's word that she sewed a "penitential garment" only to economize? Medical and pedagogical authorities like Max Wolf, author of *Die physiche und sittliche Entartung des modernen Weibes* (*The Physical and Moral Degeneration of the Modern Woman,* 1892), recommended that teenagers not be given thick, tight garments lest they stimulate sexual desire and lead to masturbation. Frau Bergmann would surely have followed their advice— but she would seem too old-fashioned, untutored, and timid to read such books.

Though Wedekind's text is no unequivocal social and historical document, its language and its problems reveal a mentality that differs as much from earlier approaches to adolescence as it differs from ours. Its scenes of sadomasochistic lovemaking (1.5), masturbation (2.3, 3.4), and pubescent homosexuality (3.6) were considered so provocative at the time that *Frühlings Erwachen* could not be staged until 1906, and even then it had to be toned down by Max Reinhard. Yet in the 1890s it spawned a wave of novels and plays depicting how German secondary education led to adolescent miseries and even suicides.[2] In this sense, time was ripe for *Frühlings Erwachen.*

A social historian of German education has recently remarked that "if as many schoolboys killed themselves as do in these novels and plays, the schools would have run out of pupils" (Albisetti 44). Undoubtedly. But I am not much interested in the statistical correctness of the literary image. Rather, I ask whether it expressed broader public concerns, whether others have shared Wedekind's criticism and his plea that adolescents be granted greater freedom.

Wendla's opening dress rehearsal and the subsequent events show that she knows no adolescence. She wishes to be catapulted into the adulthood of twenty, but mentally and emotionally she remains a child, only sexually does she become precocious. She needs a period of transition to learn about her sexuality and to coordinate the development of her mental, emotional, and physical capabilities.

In his monumental, pioneering study *Adolescence: Its Psychology and Its Relations to Physiology, Anthropology, Sociology, Sex, Crime, Religion, and Education,* G. S. Hall (1844–1924) pleaded for just such a transitional period: "We are progressively forgetting that for the complete apprenticeship to life, youth needs repose, leisure, art, legends, romance, idealization, and in a word humanism, if it is to enter the kingdom of man well equipped for man's highest work in the world" (xvi–xvii).

Ludwig Gurlitt, a German teacher, educational reformer, and popular author of, for example, a book on suicide among school children, devotes a chapter of his book on German schools to "More Repose." Citing Emerson's dictum that it is vulgar to hurry, he chastises modern "unculture" for leaving no space for "peace and concentration" (*Der Deutsche* 201). Germany has too little trust in the healthy, normal development of its children and overeducates them: "We fashion them too much and always want them different from the way they really are" (218). Gurlitt seeks to emancipate youth by relaxing education. This, he believes, "would agree with the scientific knowledge of the soul's whole development and growth, and with the new teaching that all ages in life have the same life-value and that adulthood is by no means the model of youth but relates to it like fruit to flowering."[3]

THE ANTHROPOLOGY AND HISTORY OF ADOLESCENCE

Hall and Gurlitt, a psychologist and an educator, share Wedekind's concern about youth. Like him, they plead for recognizing the special problems of an age we have come to call adolescence. Were these problems new to turn-of-the-century Western culture?

Seeking an answer, we are led into the thickets of cross-cultural and historical debates. The anthropological debate can be traced back to Hall himself, who was the first American to receive a Ph.D. in psychology (from Harvard University in 1878) and the founding president of Clark University (1889). The group of remarkable young social scientists he hired during the first years of his presidency included Franz Boas, who went to Columbia in 1892 and became a leading opponent of biological determinism. For Boas, the cultural anthropologist, culture was the decisive determinant of human behavior.

It was Boas who suggested to Margaret Mead to investigate whether the pains and conflicts of adolescence in America were "absolutely inevitable" (Mead 2). Were "these difficulties due to being adolescent or to being adolescent in America?" (Mead 5). As we know, Mead's *Coming of Age in Samoa* concluded that female adolescence in Samoa was more joyful and less stressful. Adolescence was therefore not universal but culturally specific, and the pain of American adolescence could be eased, though not, of course, by following the Samoan example. Recently, however, Derek Freeman has shown that Mead's picture of Samoa was too rosy. Contrary to Mead, Freeman found a chastity cult, stress, and crime among the adolescent Samoan girls.[4]

The debate among historians was partly motivated by renewed societal preoccupations with adolescence in the early 1970s. Ariès suggested as early as 1960 that "adolescence," a vague and rare term in the Middle Ages and early modern times (43), was born only around 1900 (*L'Enfance* 49–50). Following him, Demos, Gillis, Kett, Keniston, and other social historians marshalled impressive evidence showing that adolescence emerged, was even invented, in the course of the nineteenth century.

Counterarguments have meanwhile appeared. Natalie Zemon Davis has suggested in her remarkable article "The Reasons of Misrule" that "Abbeys of Misrule" existed in France during the Middle Ages and the sixteenth century. These "organizations of the unmarried men in peasant communities who have reached the age of puberty" (104) originally had important, officially sanctioned social roles, and "functioned rather like *rites de passage*" (107). In the cities, where they no longer included the urban elite and ceased being age-specific, they assumed the function of organizing charivaris, carnivals, and parades. However, according to Davis, "medical literature, religious manuals, and popular prints" continued to distinguish and recognize adolescence "as a period of sexual maturation" (112).

Although I cannot muster new weapons to enter these debates, I shall clarify my own position with respect to them. If Freeman's critique of Mead is true, Samoa will not support Mead's hypothesis that adolescence is culturally relative. But by Freeman's own standards this does not falsify the hypothesis, for less stressful adolescence may well exist in other cultures. It can never be proven definitively that the adolescent experience is the same everywhere.

The French youth-abbeys raise the questions of Samoa within Western history rather than cross-culturally. At issue here, as far as I know, are not Davis's findings, only whether they are similar enough to modern patterns to warrant the term *adolescence*. Davis (108–9) does not seem to have given as yet a satisfactory answer to Ariès's objection (*L'Enfance* 14) that her rural abbeys were organizations of mostly postadolescent bachelors.

Shall we ever have enough evidence to substantiate the analogy? Actually, Davis proposes to apply the term *adolescence* to young people in all societies from the onset of puberty to the full assumption of adult roles. One might then "examine systematically the different ways in which it is defined, valued, and organized" (108). Several recent studies on adolescence from the fifteenth to the nineteenth centuries have started to undertake this task and point towards certain historical invariables. But how generally can the term *adolescence* be applied? Is this just the historian's choice? Lawrence Stone, who sides with Davis, thinks that the terminological debate has little to do with social "realities": "The dispute seems to be more about boundaries and definitions than about concrete realities, and the difference between 'youth' and 'adolescence' to be mainly one of terminology" ("Family History" 69).

But is this so? Is the historical usage of the term *adolescence* itself not part of what Stone calls "reality"? I answer affirmatively, not out of a pedantic insistence on historical accuracy but rather because I believe that "concrete realities" do not fully come into existence until they became conceptualized. Important social changes undoubtedly occur "underground," yet their full "reality" involves inclusion in discourse, for only then can they be discussed and acted upon.

Did people of earlier ages think and speak of "adolescence"? The evidence is admittedly inconclusive, partly because words shift their meaning and earlier terms may have covered the semantic field of today's "adolescence." Nevertheless, it is important that "adolescence" has only recently entered the major western languages. Though it descends from Latin, it was rarely used in the Middle Ages and the Renaissance, and it was only occasionally included in the traditional "ages of man." The earliest entries in the *Oxford English Dictionary* and in the Littré date from the fourteenth-century, but examples remain sparse until the late nineteenth century in both languages. "Adoleszenz," a recent foreign import into German, was not included in Grimm's nineteenth-century dictionary. Its niche was partly taken in the eighteenth and nineteenth centuries by terms like *Lümmeljahre* ("lubber-years"), *Flegeljahre* ("cubhood"), and *Backfisch* ("bobby-soxer"), which have pejorative and ironic connotations.[5]

Ariès claims that age-designators tended to be vague until the eighteenth century. In the sixteenth century, for instance, *puer* and *adolescens* were interchangeable, and the ages were usually distinguished by social functions rather than biological phases. Davis answers that this in itself does not prove "that a period of adolescence was not recognized," for terms like *boys* and *kids* today are equally vague age-designators (305)—but her riposte is unconvincing: what matters is that today we do have more precise age-designators next to these vague ones and, if Ariès is right, *only* vague ones existed in the sixteenth century.

I propose, then, that adolescence "came of age" in the decades around 1900, not only because the term itself had little currency earlier, but, as I shall show, because interlocking discourses about adolescence emerged in psychoanalysis, psychology, criminal justice, pedagogy, sociology, as well as in literature. Adolescence may have been used sporadically earlier, but the appearance of the interlocking discourses testifies that human life was perceived in terms of a new category by the end of the nineteenth century.

THE PSYCHOLOGY OF ADOLESCENCE

What precisely was that phenomenon that emerged at the end of the nineteenth century? We must distinguish it from later as well as earlier formations, for although the phenomenon is still with us, its changed aspects may make relating it to our world rather complex. For example, contemporary definitions, analyses, and descriptions of adolescence ill fit Wendla's case.

With this caveat in mind, let us start with the contemporary view that adolescence stretches from the onset of puberty until the time that the individual is sexually mature and reasonably integrated into adult society, assuming or working towards professional and family responsibilities. It covers, roughly, the years from twelve or thirteen to eighteen or twenty, the years of secondary school rather than college or university. Whereas puberty depends on physiological changes that vary only slightly with climate, diet, and health, adolescence knows no physical determinants and depends on the way societies structure their families, education, and institutions of labor.

Industrialization, urbanization, nationalism, imperial expansion, accumulation of wealth, the growth of the middle class, and the need for extended career training are among the factors that generated the nineteenth-century institutions for young people. The most important of these institutions is the secondary school. For the present context, adolescence can therefore be defined as a middle-class social formation in industrial societies generated by the expansion of secondary education. Traditionally, adolescent children were educated at home or in apprenticeship, within an adult environment. In early nineteenth-century America, for instance, they were not yet "institutionally segregated from casual contacts with a broad range of adults," even if they attended school beyond age fourteen (Kett, *Rites* 36).

In the course of the nineteenth century, education shifted away from the home, and a growing proportion of adolescents came to spend ever longer years in schools: "As technological advances put more and more time between early school life and the young person's final access to specialized work, the stage of adolescing becomes an even more marked and conscious period and, as it has always been in some cultures in some periods, almost a way of life between childhood and adulthood" (Erickson, *Identity* 128). The intermediate zone of the secondary school allowed for a *moratorium* (literally a delay in payment), a "psychosocial stage between childhood and adulthood" (Erikson, *Childhood* 262–63).

To be sure, the late nineteenth-century institutions of adolescence varied from country to country and certainly from those of the later twentieth century. The adolescents of 1900 differed from those that Erikson clinically observed in the 1950s, and from the rebellious adolescents of the late 1960s and early 1970s. But the emergence of a late nineteenth-century discourse about adolescence was the product of long-term changes in social institutions and habits (improvements in health, the growth of science and technology, and the reorganization of family structures) that constitute the progress of civilization in Norbert Elias's sense. The price of progress, Elias holds, has been the imposition of self-control and suppression of instincts. Precisely this control and suppression was one of the germinating concerns of Hall's study: "Civilization with all its accumulated mass of cultures and skills, its artifacts, its necessity of longer and severer apprenticeship and specialization, is ever harder on adolescents" (*Adolescence* 1: 321).

Hall, Gurlitt, and others demanded that the pressures of civilization on adolescence be relaxed and adolescents be given a space of their own. The various youth-organizations that emerged institutionalized the moratorium and furthered the development of an adolescent subculture, which, to be sure, came to manifest as many "faddish attempts" (Erikson, *Identity* 128) as "repose, leisure, art, legends, romance, idealization" (Hall, *Adolescence* 1: xvii). Actually, the advocates of adolescence seldom seriously considered its total emancipation, which would also have meant its total segregation. In practice, adolescents remained legally under age, under parental and school supervision, and without independent means to support themselves. The semi-independent adolescent subculture around 1900 was larger and more cohesive than earlier adolescent-age societies and differed also from the affluent, sexually much more liberated teenage subculture of the later twentieth century.

Yet some of Erikson's insights into the individual's position within the peer group are applicable to pre–World War I European youth, exposed to rising chauvinism and anti-Semitism. In Erikson's view, adolescents temporarily over-identify "with the heroes of cliques and crowds"; they can be "remarkably clannish, and cruel in their exclusion of all those who are 'different,' in skin color or cultural background, in tastes and gifts, and often in such petty aspects of dress and gesture as have been temporarily selected as *the* signs of an in-grouper or out-grouper." Such conformance and intolerance are a "defense against a sense of identity confusion" (*Childhood* 262). Erikson's insight (with the hindsight of Hitler, Stalin, and Mussolini) that "simple and cruel totalitarian doctrines" may appeal to adolescents (*Childhood* 262), had been anticipated by Musil, Lacretelle, and some educators and psychologists at the beginning of this century. Adolescents may yield to the lure of ideologies, not only because of their eagerness to conform and to be affirmed by their peers, but also because they search for "social values which guide identity" (*Childhood* 263). They are inclined "to install lasting idols and ideals as guardians of a final identity" (*Childhood* 261), and to fervently acclaim "men and ideas in whose service it would seem worth while to prove oneself trustworthy" (*Identity* 129), although they can also mock them by sudden turns.

METHODOLOGY AND THEORY IN CULTURAL STUDIES

Questions about identity interconnect the personal, historical, and theoretical dimensions of my topic. Contemporary challenges to the notion of autonomous and enduring selves, whether they come from structuralists, sociologists, Marxists, or deconstructionists feed on Nietzsche and the fin-de-siècle questioning of personal identity that also motivated the first interest in the diffuse identity of adolescence. Such challenges also question two other forms of identity: the autonomy of literature, which became for me a major issue as I gradually turned to broader cultural and social areas, and the identity of historical periods, such as "turn-of-the-century." I wish to emphasize these interlocking theoretical questions of cultural studies, of which I now give a preliminary sketch.

The relationship between literature and its surrounding world was unproblematic within some older models: economic and social laws of history produced adolescence, and literature, subject to the same laws, mirrored the changes. Such a model would have demanded that my presentation move from social history to its literary products, and that brownie points be awarded to writers who best portrayed "reality."

Such models have been justly criticized in recent decades. I need to indicate only why they do not suit my purposes and what alternatives I seek. As I have already suggested, socioeconomic "realities" are constantly affected by mental attitudes, by the linguistic and semiotic conceptualizations that people impose upon their otherwise chaotic impressions. The mental structures offered by the arts, psychology, education, law, and other fields are not merely imprints of the socioeconomic conditions but constructions that follow their linguistic and other inner mechanisms. As constructs they interact with those conditions.

Literature participates in this conceptualization, and its images become active in "the social construction of reality." Thus, for instance, secondary schools grew gradually in the nineteenth century whereas the literary thematization of adolescence started, at least in France and Germany, rather late and suddenly around 1890. Wedekind, Barrès, Kipling, and others had waves of followers, whose treatments of adolescence were written within literary traditions. These writers responded not merely to social issues but also to the narrative forms, plots, metaphors, and characterizations of their predecesssors, which they imitated, parodied, varied, or undermined. Literature is as much a product of previous writing, fictional as well as nonfictional, as of social experience. More precisely, previous writing is part of the social experience.

Similarly, discourse is a constructive force in shaping adolescent identity. If the latter became the subject of turn-of-the-century discourses, it is equally true, inversely, that language, literature, and artistic self-expressions guided identity forming and socialization within the peer group. Adolescents experiment with discourses, for instance with diaries and poetry, both of which appeared rather suddenly on the public scene around 1900. As Eduard Spranger notes, such expressions attempt to record a self-image, and to liberate the self by means of this self-objectification (67); similarly, Erikson remarks that adolescent love is to a considerable extent "an attempt to arrive at a definition of one's identity by projecting one's diffused self-image on another and by seeing it thus reflected and gradually clarified. This is why so much of young love is conversation" (*Identity* 132). Furthermore, adolescents assume their peer-group position by telling stories and playing roles. Before the advent of film and television their scripts and models were usually taken from the books they read during their "reading craze."

Looking from another angle at the relationship between adolescence and the cultural climate around 1900, I note that literary adolescence and literary modernism developed in a symbiotic relationship, for characteristic traits of adolescence, such as the blurring of identity, rapid role changing, and the merging of the individual into a group, can only be represented by means of those shifting narrative perspectives that literature had been developing since Flaubert. They became the hallmark of literary modernism, brought to a peak in Gide's *Les Faux-monnayeurs* (*The Counterfeiters,* 1926), a key work of literary adolescence as well.

Broadening the context, I suggest that the age focused on adolescence because it found therein a mirror of its own uneasiness with its heritage, its crisis of identity, and its groping for a new one. The diagnosticians of this crisis were Dostoevsky, Nietzsche, and Freud, its centers fin-de-siècle Vienna, as well as Dresden, Berlin, Munich, and Paris.

But is it justified to speak in such general terms? I realize how problematic it is to personify "the age," and I agree with recent cultural studies (such as Stephen Greenblatt's *Shakespearean Negotiations*) that question monolithic portrayals of historical periods, be they in terms of a Zeitgeist, an *epistème,* or a paradigm. I do not mean, as Hall actually did, that turn-of-the-century culture was mankind's adolescence, nor do I imply that one can reduce the whole age to a common code or common themes like decadence and adolescence.

As does New Historicism, I seek to identify mutual affinities and exchanges between literature and sociocultural phenomena, but my model and my method differ. Greenblatt consistently relates somewhat obscure nonliterary Elizabethan texts to Shakespeare's plays in order to arrive at a general characterization of Renaissance England. By focusing on a small corpus of paradigmatic texts he partially negates his theoretical distrust of totalizing. As Jane Howard writes, Greenblatt's *Renaissance Self-fashioning* "continues to use the language of representativeness and to speak of certain figures (those people, inevitably male, upon whom a great deal of critical attention has already been focused) as epitomizing or crystallizing the period's characteristic strategies for self-fashioning" (28). Studies in the mode of New Historicism tend to "begin with the painstaking description of a particular historical event, place, or experience and from that supposedly paradigmatic moment sketch a cultural law" (Howard 29).

In contrast to this method I start with the study of literary structures and narrative modes, not as an exercise in formalist criticism but rather because I believe that they encode social and historical issues. This way, it should be possible to acknowledge the quasi-autonomous nature of literature, which

New Historicism affirms in theory but, as Edward Pechter charges, silently negates in practice. Distrusting the notion that single texts can reveal central attitudes of an entire age, I try to achieve reasonable comprehensiveness by discussing a large number of literary and nonliterary, canonized and noncanonized texts. I end up with a large but inhomogeneous corpus that, spanning a variety of ideologies, discourses, and national cultures, is interlinked primarily by the common theme.

My sifting of this large body of texts led me to question two interrelated canonized views of the adolescents around 1900: that they were first and foremost engaged in a generational conflict, and that they were heroic rebels fighting for the emancipation of the individual.

We are accustomed to think of nineteenth-century childhood in terms of the authoritarian family and school structures of Victorian England, Prussian Germany, Puritan New England, and imperial France, which extended themselves into the twentieth century and led to the generational and Oedipal conflicts dramatized by Freud, Kafka, and the expressionists. But the flare up of generational conflicts around 1970 may have conditioned us to overestimate the role of such conflicts around 1900 and underestimate the role of the peer-group culture. The latter, in my opinion, played a far more important role in maturation than conflicts with parental authorities. As Spranger suggested already, studies of youth ought to focus on the "cohort movement" rather than on attitudes toward the parental world (161).

The canonized view that the adolescents were rebels and revolutionaries struggling against the suppressive parental orders of family, church, and state originated with turn-of-the-century self-images of youth. Such self-fashioning are evident in Joyce's *A Portrait of the Artist,* expressionist art, and the youth movement, but, I suggest, their heroic and emancipatory posture was largely hollowed out psychologically and socially. Psychologically, because the outer-directed verbal and physical violence was usually accompanied by fits of self-doubt; and sociologically, because of the sudden sprouting of organizations (whether founded by adults or initiated by youth itself) that forced the individual back into bonds. The military formations of World War I, in which most of the adolescents ended, are in my view the ultimate symbols of broader, profoundly antiliberal and anti-individualist trends in the preceding decades.

ORGANIZATION

I have tried to incorporate these views both in the overall structure of my book and the manner in which I approach individual texts. Instead of starting with the social and historical context, I begin in chapters 1 and 2 by examining how narrative forms were used to deal with problems of adolescent identity. From there I move in chapters 3 and 4 to the social context of the individual, the portrayal of adolescent groups and spaces in literature. I close the literary part of the book in chapter 5 with questions of genre, history, and the reading public, which take us from inside the books to the social context of literary institutions.

In the second part I move to other areas of turn-of-the-century culture: first to cultural artifacts (fine arts in chapter 6, psychoanalysis in chapter 7, psychology in chapter 8) and then to social institutions and movements (chapters 9 and 10). In the course of offering representative accounts of each field, I focus on the ways in which literary elements like narration, dialogue, metaphors, and rhetoric contributed to the construction of nonliterary discourses and social institutions. The final chapter shows that the "social construction of reality" involved not just literary procedures and forms but the social and institutional uses of concrete literary texts as well.

My story ends there though much more could still be said. Tackling problems of history, culture, and literature is an endless task, just as mastering adolescence is.

CHAPTER ONE

(Metaphoric) Identity

Like adolescents, modern third-person narrators tend to have diffuse identities. Traditionally, though certainly not in all cases, they have been regarded as their authors' mouthpieces, but Henry James, Virginia Woolf, James Joyce, and other modernist followers of Gustave Flaubert dissociated themselves from their narrative voices and often muzzled them.

What are we to do then with third-person narratives that clearly incorporate elements of the author's biography into the protagonist's story? If we resist reading them as autobiographies, the knowledge that they elaborate on the *author's* experiences will continue to press us to read the story as the *narrator's* autobiographical reflection, even if the protagonist is addressed in the third-person. What are the character and function of a narrator, who is not the author's mouthpiece even though he narrates the story of a protagonist who in some respects resembles him?

Joyce's *A Portrait of the Artist as a Young Man,* Thomas Mann's *Tonio Kröger,* and Robert Musil's *Die Verwirrungen des Zöglings Törless (The Confusions of Pupil Törless)* are such third-person stories involving adolescent protagonists. They elaborate on their authors' experiences in terms of an interplay between the narrator and the protagonist, although they employ altogether different narrators and resolve the protagonists' adolescent crises in opposing manners. I wish to examine the ways narrators and protagonists employ metaphor in their discourses. This approach will allow us to characterize the narrators, the protagonists, and their relationships without recourse to authorial biography and intention, although, as *A Portrait* will show, we may ultimately have to transgress the textual boundaries by appealing, not to *authorial* biography and intention, but to the broader artistic and societal discourses from which these works emerged.

Third-person narratives may foreground the protagonist's or the narrator's discourse. In earlier novels like Henry Fielding's *Tom Jones,* the narrator had total insight into the minds of his fictional characters. Modernist narratives tend to restrict this insight. The narrative genre about adolescents that emerged at the end of the nineteenth century usually reveals only the adolescent minds (frequently only that of the protagonist), leaving the adult ones unilluminated. The narrators nevertheless continue to offer commentary and judgments, in spite of modernist injunctions against this practice. Mann's *Tonio Kröger* and Musil's *Törless,* for instance, are full of narratorial comments, and these constitute the heart of the text's narrative irony. To be sure, Joyce's *A Portrait* is told by a "chameleonic" narrator who blends with the protagonist (Cohn 30), but even he is active, too busy to "pair his fingernails"—a privilege of the dramatist according to Stephen Dedalus himself (*Portrait* 215).

In the discourse of these narrators, intellectual condescension, irony, and retrospective nostalgia intermingle so ambiguously that their attitude with respect to their protagonist may become, as in the case of *A Portrait,* a matter of interpretive dispute. The adolescent protagonist is naive and confused but more intense and authentic than the adult narrator, and he matures to gain wisdom and insight often at the cost of authenticity and freedom. The narrator may ridicule the protagonist's discourse, adopt it, or sentimentally portray it as a mode irretrievably lost for him: the attitude fluctuates between irony and compassion.

A PORTRAIT OF THE ARTIST

Critics concerned with "aesthetic distance" in *Portrait* have traditionally asked what *Joyce* thought of his adolescent protagonist, Stephen Dedalus,[1] but they usually answer by referring to the Stephen-figures in *Stephen Hero* and *Ulysses* rather than biographical facts or authorial commentary.

Such intertextual evidence is, however, no more reliable than authorial commentary, for we cannot assume that the narrators and the Stephen-figures of the three texts are coherent. How could the narrator's view of Stephen in *Ulysses* or *Stephen Hero* shed light on the Stephen in *A Portrait* if, as critics frequently claim, the narrative perspective on the protagonist changes even within the latter? In fact, such approaches to Stephen are hardly "intertextual" in the contemporary critical sense, for they tacitly postulate a teleological development from early to "mature" works that is incompatible with Joyce's own notion of temporality and excludes the possibility of breaks, inversions, and multiple perspectives. Critics usually appeal to such a development in order to overcome ambiguity. Wayne Booth, for instance, acknowledges that the evidence of *Stephen Hero* is tenuous, yet falls back upon it, for he cannot believe, short of retreating "into babbling and incommunicable relativism," that *A Portrait* is "*both* a portrait of the prisoner freed *and* a portrait of the soul placing itself in chains" (328). Although *A Portrait* is "a better work because the immature author has been effaced," Booth turns to the "immature commentary" of *Stephen Hero* in order to decipher "the ironies of the later, purer work" (333).[2]

John Paul Riquelme decided to discard such tenuous extratextual evidence and focus on the "text itself," but he imposes another unwarranted identity on the narrator by regarding him as the older protagonist, now engaged in writing his autobiographical retrospective.[3] Since the narrator never literally identifies himself with the protagonist, Riquelme can merely suggest that by the end of the book Stephen has reached a level of artistry that enables him to write the novel: the closing pages, passages from his diary, indicate that he can now retell his childhood and adolescence. In this view, the writing of *A Portrait* begins where the action of the story ends, Stephen-the-protagonist matures into Stephen-the-narrator. Better even, the protagonist fathers the narrator who will recreate him as a fictional protagonist: in a truly Joycean manner father and son, Daedalus and Icarus, are conflated.

First-person narratives like Hölderlin's *Hyperion,* which ends with the protagonists' decision to recollect and record his experiences, may well contain such transformations from protagonist into narrator. But Stephen's story is told in the third-person, and much of its narrative subtlety would disappear if the loose tie between narrator and protagonist were to be hardened into a lifeline. Nevertheless, this is what Riquelme actually wants. Like Booth, he wishes to stabilize the novel's meaning and hopes to eliminate narrative irony by making Stephen the narrator. Yet contradicting this desire to extract a stable focus on Stephen, Riquelme speaks of "oscillating perspectives" in the subtitle of his book, and he regards the "subtle intermingling of third- and first-person perspectives" as the most significant stylistic change between *A Portrait* and *Stephen Hero* (48).

The most prominent stylistic marker of this intermingling is the "narrated monologue" (*erlebte Rede, style indirect libre*) (Cohn 104–5). In contrast to "psycho-narration," where narrators integrate the thoughts of fictional characters into their own (third-person) discourse, and "quoted monologues," which are introduced with marking phrases (for example, "he thought") and told in the first person, "narrated monologues" continue the third-person discourse without quotation marks but indicate (by means of style and content) that we are actually privy to the thoughts of a character. Witness, for instance, Stephen's ecstatic vision and his anointment as a poet that concludes chapter 4 of *A Portrait*:

> His soul had arisen from the grave of boyhood, spurning her graveclothes. Yes! Yes! Yes! He would create proudly out of the freedom and power of his soul, as the great artificer whose name he bore, a living thing, new and soaring and beautiful, impalpable, imperishable. . . .
>
> A girl stood before him in midstream, alone and still, gazing out to sea. She seemed like one whom magic had changed into the likeness of a strange and beautiful seabird. Her long slender bare legs were delicate as a crane's . . . Her bosom was as a bird's soft and slight, slight and soft as the breast of some darkplumaged dove. . . .
>
> . . . A wild angel had appeared to him, the angel of mortal youth and beauty, an envoy from the fair courts of life, to throw open before him in an instant of ecstasy the gates of all the ways of error and glory. On and on and on and on! (170–72)

"His soul had arisen from the grave of boyhood" and "a girl stood before him in midstream" are narratorial, but style, content, and the conditional "he would" urge us to attribute such ecstatic words as "Yes! Yes! Yes!" to Stephen, even if spoken in the third person. We read them "as if" he uttered them, just as Stephen sees the girl "as if" she were an angel: "By leaving the relationship between words and thoughts latent, the narrated monologue casts a peculiarly penumbral light on the figural consciousness, suspending it on the threshold of verbalization in a manner that cannot be achieved by direct quotation" (Cohn 103).

Riquelme rightly notes that in *A Portrait* "the style shifts from psycho-narration narrowly conceived toward narrated monologue" (54), but it is difficult to see why this should signal a rapprochement and final merging of the protagonist and the narrator. Although narrated monologues interlink narrators and fictional figures,[4] they relate differently to each, and this gives a unique, "hovering" quality to the relation. Riquelme acknowledges that narrated monologues are *temporary* alignments and complex mixes (58) but uses them to combat "hovering" ambiguity, to stabilize the novel's meaning, and to polemicize against readings "that dwell on the problem of irony, or aesthetic distance, and on the impersonality of the narration" (51). There can be no irony if Stephen is the narrator.

But surely, autobiographical reflections may be full of irony. The narrated monologues of *A Portrait* link but also distance the narrator and the protagonist; they indicate both affinity and distance between two different selves, whether these be different persons or mere temporal stages of the same self. Compare a narrated monologue from the mentioned seaside scene with the closing words in Stephen's diary:

> He would create proudly out of the freedom and power of his soul, as the great artificer whose name he bore, a living thing, new and soaring and beautiful, impalpable, imperishable.
>
> . . . I go to encounter for the millionth time the reality of experience and to forge in the smithy of my soul the uncreated conscience of my race. (170, 252–53)

The "hovering" indirection of the first passage contrasts sharply with the decisive thrust of Stephen's unmediated voice in the second. The third-person form in the first passage indicates the narrator's presence and his separateness from Stephen. Does he share the verbal extravaganzas of his adolescent protagonist or does he merely smile at them? Do we receive no internal "processing instructions"? Does the narrator not reveal his hand?

It is generally assumed that he adjusts to "the age and mood of his hero" and is barely perceptible as a "separate entity within the text" (Cohn, 30–31). *A Portrait*'s opening is a favorite illustration of a "vanishing narrator." At the seaside scene, however, the narrator does not fully blend into Stephen, for this poetic initiation becomes credible only if Stephen is the inventor of the similes "seabird" and "wild angel." In this story, becoming a poet means to envision the world by means of similes.

Standing in the water, Stephen is baptized to become an artist, and the logic of his new identity requires that he not *receive* a name but manifest his "profane" creative force by *endowing* things with metaphors. If, as Hugh Kenner writes, "it is through their names that things have power over Stephen" (116), in such scenes it is Stephen who acquires power over things and people by "rebaptizing" them with metaphors: his consecration implies that henceforth he himself will baptize girls to become "seabirds" and "wild angels." Stephen can now endow his dim perceptions with ecstatic metaphors that the narrator eschews. The gradual dominance of Stephen's (public and private) thoughts in the latter parts of *A Portrait* reveals that he is mastering his adolescence by learning to verbalize his perceptions and experiences.

Stephen's growing verbal sophistication also sheds new light on the narrator: the protagonist's shift from mimetic to metaphoric language, the efflorescence of Stephen's creative discourse in the later chapters of the book, highlights the narrator's continued adherence to mimicry. The narrator's consistent *mimesis* makes the emancipation of Stephen's *creative* discourse, its transmission without paternalistic narratorial intrusions, possible. Whether that creative discourse nevertheless retains mimetic elements is something I shall consider later.

TONIO KRÖGER

Thomas Mann's *Tonio Kröger* shows some evident analogies to *A Portrait*: both narratives are heavily autobiographical accounts of adolescent crises by postadolescent authors, both tell how the resolution of those crises leads to the birth of an artist, both use narrated monologues to portray the protagonist's (and only his) thoughts. Stephen's concluding diary corresponds to Tonio's concluding letter.

Yet Tonio is suspicious of the aesthetics that Stephen embraces and he finds a fragile modus vivendi with the bourgeois-civic world that his uncompromising fellow writer rejects. The differences are evident at the outset. Whereas *A Portrait* opens with the narrator's self-effacing presentation of Stephen's infantile memories, *Tonio Kröger* starts with a more traditional indication of setting: "The winter sun stood only as a poor reflection [*Schein*], milky and wan behind layers of cloud above the confined spaces of the city. It was wet and windy in the gabled streets, and a sort of soft hail, neither ice nor snow, drizzled occasionally."[5] The scene is a well-crafted image of the protagonist's adolescent state of mind: the faint sun, the misty air, the mixed state of slush, the street that is a mere conduit between home and school—

all these vague images of transition and diffusion anticipate Tonio, who enters the scene with a hesitant gait, walking "carelessly and unevenly, whereas Hansen's slender legs in their black stockings marched along elastically and rhythmically . . ."[6]

Tonio's arhythmic, offbeat gait—so different from Hans's self-assured march with the civic order—becomes a leitmotif. In the dancing lesson of the second scene, the sixteen-year-old Tonio is supposed to imitate the inimitably "elastic, swinging, weaving, royal" ("elastisch, wogend, wiegend, königlich" 285) steps of the grotesque dancing master, but literally loses his way and lands amidst the girls. The hesitant movements in the street and the blunder on the dance floor reveal Tonio's disorientation, which was the kernel of the story according to Mann's first notebook entry for the novella from 1899: "Tonio Kröger. Some stray with a full awareness of its necessity, because a right path does not exist for them."[7] The narrator's concluding commentary to the adolescent sections of the story appropriately recalls the descriptions of Tonio's gait, "carelessly" and "unevenly":

> He went the way he had to go, a bit carelessly and unevenly, whistling to himself, gazing into the distance with head tilted, and if he went astray this happened only because for some there is no right way. Asked what in the world he thought to become, he provided various answers for he used to say (and he had already noted it in writing) that he carried in himself possibilities for thousands of different forms of existence, together with the secret knowledge that they were basically all impossibilities.[8]

Like the story's opening passage, this summary shows the narrator's superiority. Tonio's habit of recording self-observations indicates his mental development, the deepening of his self-knowledge, and his sharpening ability to verbalize it, but his observations and metaphors have been anticipated in the narrator's discourse. In the last sections of the story, events happening to others replicate Tonio's adolescent experiences and provide him with an opportunity to generalize upon them. When in the penultimate scene he watches a group of young dancers that remind him of his adolescent infatuations, he too can articulate the story's core idea: "For some go necessarily astray because there is no right path for them."[9] When a girl of "his type" slips during dancing, he helps her get up and suggests that she stop dancing.

The heart metaphor is another index to the trajectory of Tonio's growth, his gradual appropriation of narrative insight. It appears for the first time in the narrative comment concluding the Hans Hansen episode: "His heart was alive then; there was longing in it, and melancholy envy, a faint disdain and an altogether chaste bliss."[10] The following episode of the dancing lesson concludes by developing this into an elaborate simile of Tonio's cooling adolescent ardor: "And he cautiously circled the sacrificial altar upon which the pure, chaste flame of his love was glowing; he knelt before it, tended and nourished it in every way because he wanted to be faithful. And after a while, imperceptibly, without stir and noise it went out nevertheless."[11] During the following period of success as a writer Tonio's "dead and loveless heart" oscillates between "icy intellect and consuming sensual fire" ("eisiger Geistigkeit und verzehrender Sinnenglut" 292), but he rekindles his adolescent fire at the end, becomes conscious of his position, and masters the narrator's metaphor by reaffirming his love for the Hanses and Inges: "There is yearning in it and melancholy envy; a tiny bit of disdain and an altogether chaste bliss."[12]

The "gait" and "heart" motifs show then that the novella justifiably ends with Tonio's words in a concluding letter: having mastered the metaphors he can outline a permanent, though precarious, "hovering" position. Like Stephen, Tonio gradually masters his initial confusion by means of language and finally reaches a state where he can "speak for himself." But the acquired identities totally differ. Stephen defiantly departs from the Ireland of his childhood and adolescence, whereas Tonio, at thirty, reconsiders his departure and metaphorically returns (not to childhood but) to an adolescent state of mind that is more open and hospitable to others than Stephen's departing aesthetic egotism: [I am] "a bourgeois who strayed into art, a bohemian with a nostalgia for the proper upbringing, an artist with a bad conscience. . . . I stand between two worlds without being at home in either, and have it somewhat difficult therefore."[13]

Traditional critical preoccupation with the moral and aesthetic questions of Tonio's double homelessness has diverted attention from their narrative presentation, which is as much a matter of substance as of form. The novella's irony results from the initial knowledge differential that gradually vanishes. In the middle, for instance in the passage that follows Tonio's bungling of the dance, distancing irony and interlinking narrated monologue are coupled:

> Tonio Kröger stole away, went unnoticed out into the corridor and stationed himself there, with hands behind his back, in front of a window with the blind down, without realizing that one could see nothing through this blind and that it was ridiculous to stand in front of it as if one were looking out.
>
> But he was looking inward, where there was so much pain and longing. Why, why was he here? . . . No, no, after all, his place was here, where he

felt close to Inge, even though he stood lonely and aside, trying to recognize her voice that carried notes of warm life amidst the buzzing, clattering, and laughter in there. Your narrow, laughing blue eyes, you blond Inge![14]

Tonio's standing in front of a blind (no pun in German!) provides one of the rare passages in the story where the narrator's paternalistic benevolence tips over into direct irony. The narrator is superior because he knows more than the ridiculous Tonio. Yet the narrated monologue that immediately follows the ridicule reveals the narrator's sustained identification with his hero by means of his adoption of Tonio's familiar form of address to the girl ("du blonde Inge"). The scene's emotional empathy is replaced at the end of the story by an association through shared intellectual insight, which reconfigures Tonio's relation to the narrator: by then, Tonio will have as much insight into the narrator's mind as the narrator in this scene has into Tonio's heart. The shift reflects Tonio's growth and minimizes irony by the end.

STEPHEN AND TONIO

Not only are Stephen and Tonio different artists, they develop in different ways and acquire different identities. Stephen gained an autonomous voice in the baptismal scene by *inventing* metaphors to name things. By *adopting* the narrator's metaphors, Tonio internalizes prior knowledge and perceives already existing connections. For the reader, he is an imitator rather than an autonomous creator. The difference in metaphor usage anticipates the incremental difference between Stephen's and Tonio's final emancipation. Stephen, the sovereign creator of metaphors, cuts his ties with family, church, and nation, whereas Tonio, an "adaptor" of metaphors, reassumes older emotional ties with the bourgeois order. Would Tonio's adoption of the narrator's language offer a better communicative position than Stephen's striving for an autonomous personal language?

The contrast is all too neat and forces me to reconsider matters I initially passed over in my discussion of *A Portrait*. We know that Joyce went on to write about his common countrymen, just as Tonio promises to do in his closing letter to Lisabeta. But we need not turn to Joyce's biography and other extratextual evidence to resist Stephen's rhetorical stylization of the book's closure into a glorious emancipation: we can find the evidence inscribed in the text itself if, paradoxically, we are willing to step outside it and look at the discourses in which it was historically embedded.

Stephen's symbolist aesthetics speaks of an original creation, of forging "in the smithy" of his soul the "uncreated conscience" of his race (253)—as if his language contained no mimesis and represented an absolute new departure. Yet Stephen's language is by no means original. When in the final chapter he struggles to emancipate himself from the domination of British English, he seeks to find a native dialect rather than a private idiolect. His discussion with the dean (185–90) and his subsequent reflections on language reveal the dilemma. When he finally understands that the dean's "funnel" means "tundish" in the native dialect of Lower Drumcondra, he concedes with wounded pride: "The language in which we are speaking is his before it is mine. . . . His language, so familiar and so foreign, will always be for me an acquired speech. I have not made or accepted its words. My voice holds them at bay. My soul frets in the shadow of his language" (189). The final diary entries record Stephen's delight at having discovered in the dictionary that "tundish" was "good old blunt English too" (251)—but this merely shows that having emancipated himself from the dean's language he is content to forge the "uncreated conscience" of his race with the "blunt" English of Lower Drumcondra. His rhetoric of creativity masks his debt to a native linguistic tradition.

Furthermore, Stephen's "poetic" discourse—the language of his epiphanies, his villanelle, and his concluding diary—is dependent on *poetic* conventions. Kenner rightly claims that Stephen writes "purple prose" and that the language of his seaside ecstasy beats "again and again the tambours of a fin-de-siècle ecstasy" (131). Whether Joyce shared Stephen's ecstatic language or merely mimicked it smilingly and whether we readers can appreciate that "purple prose" is not at issue here. Suffice to note that readers familiar with fin-de-siècle artistic discourses will recognize that Stephen's originality is "forged" of certain contemporary conventions in representing ecstasy and writing poetry: his rhetoric of "free" creation is undercut by his reliance on "prepatterned" language. Such conformance is inevitable because language predates the individual. At best, it can be enriched in adoption for personal use, be transferred from alien spheres by means of metaphors. Since the "uncreated conscience" of the race, pace Stephen, always preexists, what is "forged" in the smithy of the soul cannot avoid being "forgery" as well.

By recognizing that Stephen, no less than Tonio, internalizes prior language, we gain a critical perspective on his rhetoric of creativity. To be sure, the metaphors of Stephen's Irish forefathers and the "poetic" conventions of his age function as *silent* subtexts to his utterances, whereas Tonio's subtext is contained in the narrator's explicit scenario. The difference in articulating the subtexts affects the protagonists' self-consciousness: Tonio is aware of and satisfied with the mimeticism of his ethics and aesthetics, whereas Stephen rebelliously tries to shake it off. It is the reader's task to recognize that his rebellious credo is negated by his practice, that his self-image as absolute creator is undermined by his adoptive rather than purely creative use of language.

The identity of fictional figures depends, then, not only on their own discourses and that of the narrator, but also on the various embedding discourses outside the text. The conventional figures of language compel us to sacrifice part of the text's autonomy and seek the subtexts beyond its boundaries. This legitimate transgression of textual boundaries is the shaping contribution that readers must bring to the "fuzzy" identity of *texts* and a corrective they must provide in contemplating the identity of *protagonists*. It may be added in anticipation that precisely this kind of criticism will have to be applied in the following chapters to similar claims to originality and authenticity in manifestations of turn-of-the-century adolescence.

YOUNG TÖRLESS

Like *A Portrait* and *Tonio Kröger,* Musil's *Die Verwirrungen des Zöglings Törless* thematizes adolescence as a problem of articulation.[15] However, the story of cadet Törless's brief homosexual involvement with a thieving boy, Basini, and his complicity in Basini's sordid torture by Beineberg and Reiting, is condensed into a few weeks of his life at sixteen. The brief passages in which Törless recalls scenes of his childhood and the narrator anticipates his adulthood fall outside the temporal limits of the story.

Musil excludes long-range development by confining the story to an adolescent episode. Although some critics claim that Törless will become a writer, the matter is left open, and, significantly, the story does not end with a text by him. The narrator remains in control. The "psycho-analogical" narration in Musil's *The Perfecting of a Love* (*Die Vollendung der Liebe,* 1911) may fuse "the narrating and the figural consciousness by blurring the line that separates them" (Cohn 43), but that line is sharper in *Törless* than in *A Portrait* and in *Tonio Kröger.* The narrator, who momentarily even appears in the first person (*Young Törless* 9), not only reads the minds of Törless's mother (8), Beineberg's father (22 f.), Beineberg (23), and Basini (61 f.), he also anticipates Törless's adulthood (30, 127 ff.), and complements, corrects, explains, and generalizes

Törless's thoughts and actions, revealing himself as an emotionally under-standing but intellectually condescending interpreter. In short, he is anything but a "vanishing" narrator.

Indeed, he assumes an attitude of intellectual and verbal superiority. When Törless anxiously asks himself why he had associated the prostitute Božena with his mother in a daydream, the narrator comments that his questions barely touched the heart of the matter, "were something secondary, something that occurred to Törless only afterwards. They multiplied only because none of them pointed to the real thing" (39–40).

At other times, the narrator condescendingly remarks that Törless's "dis-torted relationship to philosophy and literature" unhappily effected his de-velopment (96) and that he had no inkling of "the intuition of great artists" (113). Out of eagerness to minimize the impact of Törless's brush with homosexuality, he suggests that although Törless debased himself "it would be entirely wrong" to believe that Basini had aroused a deeper, genuine desire in him. His desire preceded the encounter and "was never satisfied by him" (134). Basini only triggered Törless's hitherto suppressed feelings to fling open "a gate, a way ahead into life," and Törless could mistake this for love only in his first surprise and confusion (135). "It was all the result not of perversity, but of a psychological situation in which he had lost his sense of direction" (140). With Basini's removal from school one phase of Törless's development came to an end, "the soul had formed another annual ring, as a young tree does" (162). Like Basini's torturers, the narrator reduces the unhappy boy to an implement.

Downright irritating are the frequent generalizations and pontifications appended to Törless's words and deeds. It may be appropriate to comment that "youthful, upsurging energies" in military schools "filled the imagination with random voluptuous images that caused some to lose their head" (139–40, revised), but it is pompous sermonizing to remark that "ludicrous" ad-olescent writings have a subjective value (14), that "every fine moral energy" will encounter a fear of fantasy (29 f.), that adolescents have strange motives in choosing a profession (96), or that art is a bore for the young that grew up "in the open air" (121). The narrator's discourse is studded with gra-tuitous adages introduced by phrases like "such young people generally" (36), "it is said" (55), "it is always of such a nature" (79), "strange how it is with thoughts" (168). Specific experiences usually occasion platitudes: "What in the distance seems so great and mysterious *comes up to us always* as something plain and undistorted in natural, everyday proportions" (130, revised).

Typical narratorial "correctives" explicate ideas and feelings that are still obscure and inarticulate in Törless. When Törless waits for something that his words could not as yet say (20), the narrator fills the gap with his own extended metaphors. When Törless feels an obscure physical attraction to Basini, the narrator interprets this with an indelicate simile and a gratuitous moral judgment: "A fascination such as comes from sleeping near a woman and knowing one can at any instant pull the covers off her body. It was the same thing that often drives young couples into orgies of sensuality far beyond the bodies' real demands" (115). In yet other cases the narrator merely underlines his hero's confusion: questions in Törless's mind "loomed up, obscurely, tight-lipped, cloaked in some vague, dull feeling . . . weakness . . . a faint dread" (56); "Törless was dreaming rather than thinking" (74); a feeling in him was "as yet wordless, but overwhelming" (162).

The theme of confusion is announced in the novel's motto from Maurice Maeterlinck, which states that "we devalue things as soon as we give utterance to them." But these devalued words are partially redeemed by their metaphoric restatement: "We believe we have dived to the uttermost depths of the abyss, and yet when we return to the surface the drop of water on our pallid finger-tips no longer resembles the sea from which it came" (5). The motto depreciates language but reaffirms the communicative efficacy of metaphors.

The subsequent story may be described as Törless's search for metaphors and similes that could serve as "some bridge, some connection, some means of comparison, between himself and the wordless thing confronting his spirit" (79–80).

Like Tonio, the adolescent Törless is "torn between two worlds." But whereas the former is suspended between the bourgeois and the bohemian, the ethical and the aesthetic, Törless, living in the parental world of the superego, experiences an invasion by chaos, the unconscious. His "solid bourgeois" order, in which "everything happened in an ordered and rational way, just as he knew from home," is threatened by forces "of adventure, full of darkness, mystery, blood, and unsuspected surprises" (50, revised). The sexual, moral, and epistemological foundations of his parental world give way.

Epistemological certainty crumbles when Törless discovers what calculating with imaginary numbers entails: "Such calculations begin with ordinary solid numbers that may represent length or weight or some other tangible item—at any rate, they're real numbers. At the end you have similar real numbers. But these two are connected by something that simply doesn't exist.

Isn't this like a bridge that has nothing but piles at the beginning and the end and which one crosses just as surely and safely as if it were complete?" (90, revised)

As a child, Törless had learned from his parents how to construct a coherent world view with rational discourse. His adolescent experience bursts this order and forces him to seek a metaphoric discourse capable of accommodating the irrational without rationalizing it. Like mathematical deductions and rational discourse, metaphors bridge different realms, but they reemphasize the abyss by forcing a jump. The frequently noted saturation of Musil's text with extended metaphors serves as a double indication of Törless's adolescent identity crisis: his groping for understanding is a search for metaphors, and that search itself is represented by the specific metaphors of walls, doors, and bridges.

These metaphors may be "real" objects in the fictional world, figures in the narrator's and the protagonist's discourse, and unverbalized images in Törless's mind. Whereas in *A Portrait* Stephen is the principal creator of metaphors and the narrator remains silent, in *Törless* it is the narrator who manufactures elaborate similes, and he does so in order to lay bare time and again the boy's inarticulateness. Metaphor use differentiates adolescence from adulthood, protagonist from narrator in both works, but the specific character of that differentiation requires that the metaphors be produced by the protagonist in one case and by the narrator in the other.

We have already seen how Musil's narrator supplies figures that Törless does not as yet have at his disposal. If, for instance, something stirs in Törless "like a crazy whirl that immediately folded Basini's image in most unbelievable contortions and tore it then asunder in unheard-of dislocations, so that he himself grew dizzy," the narrator adds: "These were, to be sure, only figures of speech that he invented later. Right then he merely had the feeling that something like a wildly spinning top, the feeling of his dizziness, whirled upwards from his tightened breast to his head" (111, revised). Young Törless sees the erotic contortions of Basini's image and feels dizzy, the narrator provides the simile of the spinning top to relate the contortions to the feeling. The right figures of speech are granted Törless only proleptically.

Doors have a subtler function in the text, as their elaborate introductory simile shows: when by day "he remembered that he would write his letter in the evening, it was as though he were wearing, hidden on his person, fastened to an invisible chain, a golden key with which, as soon as no one was looking, he would open the gate leading into marvellous gardens" (9).

The passage is initiated by Törless but soon becomes grammatically independent of the introductory "he remembered" and seems to be the narrator's discourse, because it expresses Törless's inarticulate yearning for the parental edenic garden with adult sophistication. Only adults can evoke the myth of childhood so poetically. The garden that Törless himself first encounters in the story is an empty one. While sitting in the bakery and conversing with Beineberg he stares at it through the window (21) without perceiving it metaphorically. It is there as a counterpart to his "paradise lost" in the narrator's web of symbols.

The edenic myth is soon desacralized, for Törless's mathematics teacher, who carries about his knowledge "like a key to a locked garden" (91), leads him into the "desert" of Kant's *Critique of Pure Reason*. The teacher "stressed the word 'mathematics' as though he were slamming some fateful door once and for all," and ever since Törless "had heard that door slam it had seemed to him the words were moving farther and farther away from him" (94).

Real doors lead to more dangerous terrains. Early in the story we are told that when Beineberg's father read he "did not want to reflect on opinions and controversies but, from the very instant of opening the book, to enter as through a secret portal into the midst of some very exclusive knowledge" (22). This uncritical reader, who enters books as if they were enchanted gardens, fathers a son who seeks to draw on his father's arcane knowledge to hypnotize Basini and learn to gain power over others. Törless listens inattentively to his friend's muddled ideas, but the image of a door in his castration fantasy shows his dangerous proximity to the Beinebergs:

> At this moment he had no liking for human beings—for all who were adults. He never liked them when it was dark. He was in the habit then of cancelling them out of his thoughts. After that the world seemed to him like a sombre, empty house, and in his breast there was a sense of awe and horror, as though he must now search room after room—dark rooms . . . until in one room the doors would suddenly slam behind him and before him and he would stand confronting the mistress of the black hordes herself. And at the same instant the locks would snap shut in all the doors through which he had come; and only . . . outside the walls, would the shades of darkness stand on guard like black eunuchs, warding off any human approach. (29)

Soon after this fantasy Törless excitedly fumbles his way in the dark towards the door leading to the prostitute Božena; hesitating in the doorway he "greedily" devours her with his eyes (34–35). Once more, the sexual excitement generates in his mind a series of door metaphors that lead to closed interior spaces instead of gardens. He is tortured by the question whether the world of his "calm and irreproachable" parents is separated by doors from the "mysterious joys" of Božena's night world (41), but the laughter in his mind seems associated with a sexual act between his parents, and the door is closed to keep him out: "And that laughter of his mother's? . . . as though she were going, with quiet steps, to shut all the doors" (43, ellipses in original).

In the following key simile, as in the previous examples, the door separates as well as connects. Basini, a "normal" fellow pupil, stole money and has become a "fallen" creature, falling from the world of the "irreproachable" to the depths of "mysterious joys":

> Yesterday Basini had been the same as himself. Now a trap-door had opened and Basini had plunged into the depths. . . . Then it was also possible that from the bright diurnal world, which was all he had known hitherto, there was a door leading into another world, where all was muffled, seething, passionate, naked, and destructive—and that there was not just a bridge between those people whose lives moved in an orderly way between the office and the family, as though in a transparent and yet solid structure of glass and iron, and the others, the outcasts, the blood-stained, the debauched and filthy, those who wandered in the labyrinthine passages full of roaring voices, but that the borders of their lives secretly met and could be crossed at any moment. (56, revised)

These simple bridge and door metaphors of Törless's moral landscape differ profoundly from the narrator's subsequent elaborate simile, which compares Törless's tender awakening with the spirit "such as reigns in a house at Christmas-time, when the children know the presents are already there, though locked away behind the mysterious door, and all that can be glimpsed now and then is a glow of light through the chinks" (108). When Törless subsequently attempts to write (108–13), first about "The Nature of Man," then, more modestly, about his own feelings, the sight of Basini distracts him and finally extinguishes his desire to write. The narrator takes recourse to the door metaphor to signal Törless's failure at articulation: "It was as if he had already felt in his hand the knob of the door that would open into the further realm, and then it had slipped from his grasp" (114). Here, too, is a contrast with *A Portrait*: Stephen asserts his articulateness with metaphors, whereas Musil's narrator uses the clever simile of the "slipping" doorknob to show that his protagonist cannot as yet "grasp" his experience. Since the use of that metaphor shows that the speaker has grasped the situation, this cannot be Törless's voice. The reverse is true in Stephen's case.

However, the usage of the wall metaphor changes the relation between narrator and protagonist. The wall first appears as a "real" obstacle, as the "immense, long wall" of the military school seen by Törless's departing parents, supposedly separating the school's "healthy" world from the surrounding meanness, depravity, and chaos. But Törless soon encounters behind an attic door in the school experiences that the wall was supposed to exclude, and he subsequently grasps the "porosity" of obstacles by staring at the school wall from within: "His glance happened to pass over the grey, windowless wall behind him: it seemed to have leaned forward over him and to be looking at him in silence. From time to time a faint trickling sound came down, and an uncanny life awakened in the wall" (80, revised).

This trickling sound in a dead wall keeps haunting Törless until he succeeds at figurative language, and during the great concluding confrontation with his teachers he is inspired, like Stephen, to speak in metaphors. The narrator underscores the rarity of the event: "These words and these figures of speech, which were far beyond what was appropriate to Törless' age, flowed easily and naturally from his lips in this state of vast excitement he was in, in this moment of almost poetic inspiration" (170).

Törless can now capture the experience of the living wall in a figure of speech, and, even more important, he can recognize the figure as his own metaphoric "construct": "I wasn't wrong when I couldn't turn my ear away from the faint trickling sound in the high wall . . . I—I don't mean it literally—it's not that these things live . . . but rather there was in me a second life that did not look upon all this with the eyes of reason" (169–70, revised).

The passage is doubly remarkable. It indicates Törless's understanding that metaphors do not merely designate with the "eyes of reason" but emerge from "a second life" that operates by intuition. This time Törless goes beyond the narrator, who has used the wall metaphor as a vehicle for Törless's adolescent breakthrough: "It was the secret, aimless, melancholy sensuality of adolescence, a sensuality attaching itself to no person, and . . . like dark, subterranean waters that need only some chance occasion to break through their walls" (134–35, revised).

The narrator's notion of a breakthrough is a hardened metaphor of adolescence, all but a commonplace. Törless's live wall metaphor remains productively disturbing, for we cannot read it literally, only as a figure, although it accurately reflects his experience. The walls that separated his moral and social landscape into upper and lower, good and bad, gardens and buildings, have by no means crumbled fully, they only became "porous," as indicated by the subtle wall image, integrated into his departing wisdom that "there were fine and easily effaced boundary-lines around each human being, that feverish dreams prowl around the soul, gnawing at solid walls" (173, revised).

The narrator routinely adds that "he could not quite have explained this" because of "his inability to find words for it" (173). Perhaps, but if so, if those metaphors were uttered by the narrator himself, then he must have redefined his own previous hardened wall metaphor of adolescence in light of Törless's talk about "porous" walls. And this, perhaps, is how it should be if metaphors are to be taken seriously, both in general and as images of adolescence. For metaphors have a split identity and remain effective only if they do not harden into a logically firm meaning but readily renew themselves. Similarly, the personality that emerges from adolescence must erect walls that are tentative and "porous," retaining thereby a readiness for change. Metaphors as well as people must remain free to redefine themselves—this perhaps is the metaphoric meaning of the similes that emerge from the field of tension between Törless and his narrator. Indeed in all three novels discussed, the identity achieved by using metaphors must necessarily remain loose due to the protean nature of metaphors.

CHAPTER TWO

The Other

Contrary to children, who can be only the subject of narration, adolescents can write about themselves, and adolescent diaries began to interest the public at the end of the nineteenth century. But *fictional* representations of adolescence were usually written from an adult perspective and seldom assumed the form of fictional diaries and letters comparable to *Clarissa* or *Werther*.[1] The modernists preferred polyperspectival and distanced representation to confessional "close-up." As André Gide wrote in his notebooks accompanying *The Counterfeiters*: "Intimacy, insight, psychological investigation can in certain respects be carried even further in the 'novel' than in 'confessions'" (*Counterfeiters* 415). Representing adolescence from the distance of adulthood created distance, tension, irony, and perspective and provided an important testing ground for the modernist narrative. Form and stance revealed that the modernists were skeptical that a "true" self exists and that we can discover it through the language of confessional sincerity.

Perspectival representation is particularly evident in a new early twentieth-century genre of adolescent fiction, the "peer-group narrative," in which fictional narrators recall their adolescent friendship with the protagonist named in the title. The genre employs a "first-person" narrator who is part of the fictional world and seems to be always male. Instead of writing "confessionally" about himself, this narrator offers a portrait of an adolescent friend he admired. The resultant narrative provides a perspective on both the protagonist, who is seen only through the eyes of the narrator and not "from within," and the narrator, whose perception of and friendship with the protagonist offers an indirect portrait of himself. We may speak therefore of a "double-portrait," a third-person representation of the protagonist, and a self-portrait of the narrator that avoids the "confessional" style by characterizing himself through the friendship. This modernist technique is well suited to represent the fluctuations and divisions of the adolescent mind, its search for camaraderie, and its embeddedness in the peer group.

Such "peer-group" narrators, who were apparently not used before 1910, appear in Valery Larbaud's *Fermina Márquez* (1910), Alain-Fournier's *Le Grand Meaulnes* (1913), Hermann Hesse's *Demian* (1919), Jacques de Lacretelle's *Silbermann* (1922).[2] The form was still so little known in 1919 that the public readily accepted the fictional narrator of *Demian* as its author.

FERMINA MÁRQUEZ

Larbaud was probably the first to use a "peer-group" narrator, though he made "improper" use of it in *Fermina Márquez*[3] by allowing his internal narrator insight into his peers' minds. The unnamed narrator and the protagonist, a beautiful sixteen-year-old Colombian girl, who is living temporarily with her aunt and sister near her brother's boarding school, are not befriended. They remain enigmatically closed figures: Fermina seldom speaks, although her inner thoughts are revealed in one short passage (132–37), and the narrator does not refer to himself in the first person until the very end of his story. He prefers the plural "we," meaning the pupils of the boarding school who become infatuated with Fermina. The center is therefore largely empty and silent: the protagonist is characterized by the impact of her beauty and aura on the boys, and the narrator remains self-effacing. Since this indistinct center is encircled by portraits of Fermina's adolescent admirers, we may characterize the book using Heinrich Böll's later title, "Group Portrait with Lady." Only glimpses are given of teachers, parents, and the outside world.

Santos Iturria (22–30, 130–31), Camille Moutier (101–8), and, above all, Joanny Léniot (35–100, 108–30, 139–47) are members of the group. They serve as mirrors of Fermina, but their own inner lives are of intrinsic interest as well and are made transparent. Since Larbaud does not explain how his narrator can read the minds of his fellow pupils, this narrator seems to arrogate the powers of a traditional "omniscient" narrator throughout most of the book. This formal misuse of the "first-person" narrative convention allows the reader to peek into the inner lives of the group members. The collective portrait emerges as Larbaud's narrator weaves his way in and out of the minds of his fellows.

Yet Joanny Léniot, whose story constitutes more than half of the book, is so much in the foreground that he (and his reactions to Fermina) is arguably the true focus. The fifteen-year-old Joanny, the school's ambitious model student, decides to test his prowess by seducing a woman, and Fermina becomes the target of his desire to play Don Juan. By helping and protecting Fermina's little brother, he gains the confidence of Fermina, her sister, and her aunt and is allowed to accompany them on afternoon walks in the park. At first he tries merely to impress Fermina, but he soon becomes genuinely infatuated with her, loses some of his egotism, and yearns to confide to her "all his secrets and all his hopes" (71). He now looks back upon his former values and behavior, including his grandiose seduction plan, as foolish and worthless: "These projects of seduction seemed so remote! . . . my God, what childishness! he was ashamed of it now" (73).[4] When Fermina chides him for his pride and questions his faith, Joanny concludes that she is too pious to love (83) and gives up the idea of ever winning her. Yet he still wants to impress her with his pet idea that European unity must be reestablished by means of a hegemony comparable to the Rome of Constantine and Theodosius (87)—Joanny's version of the adolescent dream of "leadership, victory, and splendor amid the plaudits of an admiring world" (Hall, *Adolescence* 2: 302).

Predictably, Fermina understands nothing of his lengthy, impassioned speech, and Joanny despairs, this time for having sought her company: "And he, who thought to find if not a mistress, at least a friend, a comrade to whom he could tell everything as an equal! *An equal!* OK! he fell back again upon his theories about the stupidity of mankind. She did not like him, and that's all" (97).[5]

Joanny has to swallow the most bitter pill when he discovers that Fermina is not unresponsive to Santos Iturria and even meets him secretly. Joanny bows out of the afternoon walks (claiming that he started lessons in aquarelle painting) and leaves the field to the macho charmer, the "man of the world" who used to climb the walls of the school in the evenings to savor the night life of Paris. As a concluding demonstration to Fermina of what she has lost,

Joanny delivers a rambling but carefully prepared encomium of his genius and his inevitable fame to come: "In sum, all his eloquence amounted to this: 'You chose between Santos Iturria and myself. That's all right. But you must know then whom you have rejected, and feel sorry!'" (125).[6]

Joanny's story is so dominant in *Fermina Márquez* that Brown (99) has come to associate Joanny with Larbaud. But the brilliant tragicomic portrait is written with remarkable detachment. At best, the text suggests an affinity between Joanny and the narrator, who terminates Joanny's story by referring to himself for the first time: "This was the time when I reviewed the year and congratulated myself for not having merited a single punishment; for I too was a very good pupil" (146).[7]

The epilogue's retrospective on adolescence softens the ironic portrait of Joanny's pride, braggadocio, and illusions of grandeur: when the narrator returns to the closed-down school, he learns from the concierge that Joanny Léniot died in an epidemic four months after he had been drafted. Joanny's death and the school's closing both point to the conclusion of adolescence.

AUGUSTIN MEAULNES

Alain-Fournier's thirty-year-old narrator starts with a retrospective on adolescence that resembles Larbaud's nostalgic epilogue but also arouses excitement and expectation:[8] "He appeared at our house on a Sunday in November 189 ... I still say 'our' house though it is ours no longer; nearly fifteen years have passed since we left the neighborhood, and we shall not be going back to it" (11). Who is "he"? After tantalizing the reader throughout much of the first chapter, the narrator, François, finally reveals him to be a prospective boarder in François's home. While the conditions of his boarding are being negotiated below, he enters the attic, makes some mysterious noises there, and finally appears in the door, his face still barely discernible, as "a tall youth, about seventeen":

> "See what I found in your attic," he said. "Didn't it ever occur to you to have a look in there?"
>
> He held out a little wheel of blackened wood wound about with frayed fuses—the "sun" or perhaps the "moon" of last July's display.
>
> "There were two that hadn't gone off. We'll set them off just the same," he added placidly, as if this would do till something better turned up.
>
> When he threw down his hat I saw that he was close-cropped like a peasant. He was showing me the two fuses with paper wicks which the

flame had bitten into, seared, and then abandoned. He stuck the nave of the wheels in the gravel, produced a box of matches—this to my astonishment, for we were not allowed matches—and stooping carefully held a flame to the wicks. Then, taking my hand, he pulled me quickly back.

Coming out of doors with Madame Meaulnes—terms of pension having been discussed and agreed upon—my mother saw two great bouquets of red and white stars soar up from the ground with a hiss. And for the space of a second she could see me standing in a magical glow, holding the tall newcomer by the hand, and not flinching . . . (15–16)

François wants to evoke a momentary mood. Instead of describing Augustin Meaulnes directly, he sees him through his own mother's eyes and records her excitement at his deeds.[9] Meaulnes literally enhances his aura by producing magical fireworks with objects that lay forgotten in the attic. He finds "magic" where others pass inattentively.

Subsequently, Meaulnes stumbles into a larger adventure. He rides a stolen carriage in order to be the first to meet François's grandparents, loses his way, arrives by chance at a wedding that fails to materialize because there is no bride, briefly encounters the desolate bridegroom, and falls in love with a girl. Once back in François's village, he vainly tries to retrace his steps to the "lost domain." A bandaged vagabond appears and becomes the leader of the pupils opposing Meaulnes, but he soon befriends Augustin and makes him swear to come to his aid should he ever ask for it. Just when he is revealed to be Frantz de Galais, the former bridegroom, he must flee because he is suspected of theft. Meaulnes goes to Paris to seek the girl of the "lost domain," and François sees his adolescence "born away in that old-fashioned carriage, for ever" (116).

Somewhat later, François accidentally locates Meaulnes's lost love, who turns out to be Yvonne, Frantz's sister. He reunites the lovers at an outing, but the inexplicably irritated and unhappy Meaulnes insists that the past cannot be revived:

Fatally, with an obstinacy of which he was certainly unaware, Meaulnes kept going back to the past and all its marvels. And at each evocation the tortured girl could only repeat that everything had vanished: the strange and complicated old house pulled down; the lake drained and filled in; the children and all their gay costumes dispersed. (155)

When Meaulnes nevertheless marries Yvonne, Frantz reappears on their wedding night and demands that Meaulnes help him find Valentine, his lost bride.

Meaulnes leaves, François becomes Yvonne's confidant and assumes the care for her daughter when she dies. From a diary that Augustin left in the attic François learns that Meaulnes befriended another women while in Paris and reluctantly became engaged to her, only to discover that she was Valentine, Frantz's fiancée. Augustin's sense of guilt, as well as his oath to Frantz, forced him to abandon Yvonne in search of Valentine.

A year later, Meaulnes returns with Frantz and Valentine and reinstates them in Frantz's little childhood house. The melancholy François surrenders Yvonne's and Augustin's daughter with undiminished admiration for his friend: "I could see that the child had at last found the companion she had been unconsciously waiting for . . . I could see that *le grand Meaulnes* had come to take back the one joy he had left me, and I already pictured him, in the night, wrapping his daughter in a cloak, to carry her off with him on some new adventure" (206).

The closing lines suggest that in François's eyes Meaulnes has developed from an adventurous adolescent into some latter-day tragic hero, whom fate had maneuvered into an engagement with his friend's fiancée. Indeed, several indices suggest that the action is motivated by fate and by Augustin's guilt for having unknowingly betrayed Frantz. When François tells Augustin that he has found Yvonne, Augustin is on his way to redeem his "sin" (148) and ask Frantz's pardon (170). The news of Yvonne's reappearance rekindles his dedication to the old adventure, but "unable to act or to confess" he falls "prey to remorse, regret, and sorrow" (202) for the sin he committed.

Yet Meaulnes's motivation is overdetermined and allows for alternative interpretations. He is a tragic hero atoning for his innocent mistake, as well as a victim of his own imagination. He hesitates to meet the rediscovered Yvonne, not only because he has meanwhile met Valentine, but also because the encounter with Yvonne in the "lost domain" has acquired mythic dimensions for him. Having "once strayed into Heaven" and realizing that he cannot permanently bring "Heaven" to earth, he rejects the humdrum life that earth can offer. Since only death can recapture the peak of perfection and purity in that brief encounter (148), Meaulnes self-destructively devalues the present and the promise of an earthly future.

Seen this way, Meaulnes's tragedy lies not in his mature sense of responsibility for having snatched Valentine from Frantz, but in the failure of his adolescent imagination to submit to the "reality principle" of adulthood. Alain-Fournier's book exposes how this immature imagination can both express high idealism and manifest a prolonged narcissism.[10] According to Hall, this narcissism shows that the adolescent has not yet matured to adult altruism and sociability (*Adolescence* 2: 302–3). Augustin's insistence that the *real* Yvonne and world be measured against his *idea* of the "lost domain" is idealistic cruelty, whose inhumanity is best revealed by comparing him to Frantz, the figure whom he resembles more than François and whom he regards as his best friend and brother (198).

Frantz, Meaulnes's negative projection, displays the consequences of the indulgent education they both enjoyed. By the time of his engagement, his whims, his parties, and his amusements had already consumed his father's fortune (134). When he disappears, creditors assert their claims (156), the domain crumbles because of his extravagance.

The wedding fails because of Frantz's solipsistic imagination, his inability to project himself into Valentine's situation and state of mind. Valentine cannot marry him because she is a dressmaker, not a princess (71), and she believes that "he had made up all the wonderful things he described to her" (142). Frantz interprets this as a failure of *her* imagination and her "lack of faith" (69), but in fact it is his imagination that fails to understand Valentine from within. Her prosaic self-perception cannot be overcome by making her his idol. He sees her only in the colors of his own imagination, and this, as she rightly says, is childish (193, 197). It does not come as a surprise that after the failed wedding he wants to live just "like a child, like a vagabond" (95).

Meaulnes joins Frantz in blaming Valentine for the timidity of her belief (198), and the Yvonne-image of his own imperial imagination is as cruelly elevated as Frantz's image of Valentine (147–49). Both men are enamored with figments of their imagination rather than real women. When Frantz summons Meaulnes's help on his wedding night, expecting that Yvonne (who never refused him anything) will release him, the mature François rightly accuses him of being a petulant and egocentric child: "I'll take you to them. They'll welcome you like a child that was lost and has been found again, and your miseries will be at an end. . . . The time has gone by for all that abracadabra; we're grown-up people now" (165).

But Frantz refuses to be a prodigal son and Yvonne's continued defense of "her brother's follies" (173) reveals a fatal indulgence. François blames her for condoning Frantz's "extravagant fantasies," for remaining loyal to his "boyish caprices," and for trying "to preserve some vestiges of the dream world he had lived in up to the age of twenty" (173). He thinks she was similarly indulgent with Meaulnes, "made a great mistake out of generosity, in a spirit of self-sacrifice, to put him back on the path of adventure" (180). Instead of responding critically, she "would listen gravely, tenderly, almost maternally to detailed accounts of our trials and hardships as grown-up boys. None of our childish exploits, even the boldest and most dangerous, seemed strange to her" (173).

Upon closer inspection one notes that Meaulnes's unique experience at the "lost domain" was not the physical reality of the domain itself. The fête of the failed wedding (as filtered through François's retelling of Meaulnes's story) resembles a painting by Watteau, insubstantial, unauthentic, suspended in unreal space and time. Amid the guests, mostly children and older people in masks, Meaulnes loses "all sense of identity" (59), and his most intense experiences consist of daydreams that recall scenes of his childhood and anticipate his archetypal woman before meeting her (47 and 60). What he savors is neither the momentary reality of the "lost domain" nor even its world of "make believe," but recollections and anticipations.

The portraits of adolescence in *Le Grand Meaulnes* include not only the title hero but also the narrator, whose childhood ends with his friend's arrival: "Someone came and put an end to all these mild and childish pleasures. Someone blew out the candle which illumined for me the sweet maternal face bent over the evening meal" (18). François's life appears at first as a sequence of vicarious experiences, emblematized by the lengthy scene in which he watches through the classroom window as Meaulnes embarks on his adventure (23–25). On the wedding night, as he stands outside Meaulnes's house and looks at the windowpane that separates him from his adventurous friend now inside, François says to himself with self-effacing modesty: " 'Meaulnes is there at her side. To know that, to be sure of it, is enough to fill me with contentment, simple child that I am" (163). His temporary foster-fatherhood is his last vicarious experience: he hoped that Augustin's daughter would one day be "in a sense" his own (204), but Augustin reclaims her and effortlessly wins from her the affection she withheld from François, who now seems doomed to become a historian of his friend's exploits.

Yet François is no passive follower of Meaulnes. His injured knee improves during the friendship with Augustin, but he learns to bicycle only once Meaulnes is gone: by swooping down "from a hill-top into the hollows as if on wings" he can make his own dreams come true (139). He is the one to find and reunite Yvonne with Augustin, and although he sees himself as a child standing under the newlyweds' window, he is the one who negotiates with Frantz and urges him to grow up.

François's orchestration of the events is surpassed by his narrative shaping of the plot. Like Larbaud's narrator, François gains access to the mind of his protagonist-friend, but whereas the former temporarily becomes a mind reader, the latter possesses only information that need no telepathy. Alain-Fournier maintains the illusion of a genuine peer-group narrator, though at a price: Meaulnes's psychologically subtle experiences at the lost domain (39–75), which François recounts without having witnessed them, are implausibly said to be pieced together from conversations between the two. Even worse, Augustin's adventures after leaving François's home town are mediated by means of letters (120–23) and a secret diary that Meaulnes bequeaths to his friend (189–203). François reproduces its first part "word for word" (189) but "re-edits" and orders the later sections (194, 199), nurturing thus a second "child" of Meaulnes to grow into a book.

Alain-Fournier's followers, Hesse in *Demian,* Lacretelle in *Silbermann,* and, much later, Günter Grass in *Cat and Mouse* (1961) were able to use the peer-group narrator more consistently, by shrouding the mind and the unobserved deeds of their protagonists in full mystery, enhancing thus the aura around them. Were the conversations, letters, and diaries just clumsy tricks of an inexperienced author to provide his internal narrator with the necessary information, or rather the product of conflicting tendencies in the text?

Until rather recently, *Le Grand Meaulnes* was usually read in terms of Alain-Fournier's life, above all his hopeless love for Yvonne de Quièvrecourt. Such biographical readings stressed the author's affinity with Meaulnes and the "confessional" aspects of the novel, for which the trip to the "lost domain" and the self-revelations in the letters and diaries are indispensable. Several recent studies have profited, however, from developments in narrative theory as well as from a greater sensitivity to the psychology of writing. Critical interest has shifted to the figure of François and the manner in which he constructs his story. The shift rectifies the earlier dominance of biography but threatens to lead to another kind of psychologism by suggesting that the modest François actually dominates his admired friend (he *does* have the last word) and manipulates his letters, diaries, and conversations for his own needs.

Could Meaulnes's "gigantic shadow" (35) be a projection of François's imagination to resolve his own problems? The suggestion is tempting, but ascribing such compensatory intentions would make him the author and a flesh-and-blood person.[11] Yet, like Meaulnes, he is only a fictional character, one to whom Alain-Fournier entrusted the role of narrator, and the narrative intentions ascribed to him ought to be seen within the text's broader narrative strategy. As I see it, the friend-narrator neutralizes the autobiographical and confessional impulse of a project that could have resulted in a psychological and symbolist work comparable to Gide's *Les Cahiers d'André Walter.* By means of François's construction and reconstruction of Meaulnes' diaries, letters, and conversations, Meaulnes appears in refracted light, not merely in the glow of his own "magical" fireworks. Employing such a narrator complicates the storytelling: the work as we have it thematizes not only a hero and an adolescent friendship but also their representation.

MAX DEMIAN

Like Meaulnes, Demian gains stature by the absence of a father; like Meaulnes, he is an older adolescent when he enters the life of the still childish narrator; like Meaulnes, he is considered different by his peers and accepted only grudgingly, out of a fearful respect. Like Meaulnes, finally, he reveals to his narrator at their first encounter something that the latter has overlooked in his own world: the heraldry of a strange bird hewn into the keystone of Emil Sinclair's house.

But Meaulnes's firecrackers illuminate his own "glittering" personality, whereas the heraldry calls attention to Sinclair's "home": Demian's main function will be to help Sinclair find his way to himself. "Cain," the title of the chapter containing the first meeting between Sinclair and Demian, reveals a further difference with respect to Alain-Fournier's novel. Demian shatters Sinclair's belief in the canonized interpretation of the biblical story, by suggesting that Cain's mark was not a consequence of murdering Abel but a sign of his otherness:

> Here was a man with something in his face that frightened the others. They didn't dare lay hands on him; he impressed them, he and his children. We can guess—no, we can be quite certain—that it was not a mark on his forehead like a postmark—life is hardly ever as clear and straightforward as that. It was much more likely that he struck people as faintly sinister, perhaps a little more intellect and boldness in his look than people were used to. This man was powerful: you would approach him only with awe. He had a "sign." ... So they did not interpret the sign for what it was— a mark of distinction—but as its opposite. They said: "Those fellows with the sign, they're a strange lot"—and indeed they were. People with courage and character always seem sinister to the rest. It was a scandal that a breed

of fearless and sinister people ran about freely, so they attached a nickname and myth to these people to get even with them, to make up for the many times they had felt afraid—do you get it? (24–25)[12]

Demian gives a Nietzschean interpretation of the murder by reversing the chronological relationship between the sign and the deed, and by showing how a psychological defense mechanism can turn fear into hateful contempt, subjective feeling into an "objective" sign. The sign did not result from the murder, it was a Nietzschean projection of the herdsmen's fear upon a master—a projection they self-defensively came to call a divine sign in order to eschew avenging Abel's murder. Now they could answer to those calling for revenge: "'You can't, he has a sign. God has marked him'" (25).

By suggesting that the herdsmen fabricated the "official" story to cover their own cowardice, Demian performs a Nietzschean "transvaluation of values": he questions the foundations of traditional morality by showing how values emerge from human weakness. By inverting the traditional reading, Demian reveals himself as a master, albeit one who is less egocentric than Meaulnes. By telling Sinclair a new version of Cain's story, Demian assumes the role of a Socratic mentor who jolts his pupil from his comfortable inherited beliefs. He figuratively kills the Abel in Sinclair, not in order to subjugate him but to awaken in him the strong, autonomous self of Cain. If, however, the Cain-chapter is read together with the preceding first chapter, Demian appears as a savior as well as a destroyer, and the plot can be read against a double biblical foil: the Cain story as well as the story of the prodigal son who leaves his parental home but returns to it repentantly.

The title of the first chapter, "Two Worlds," picks up the familiar theme of *Tonio Kröger* and *Törless* and sets the stage for a "Fall" from the clean, warm, and cozy nest into the world of maids, drunkards, prisoners, thieves, and murderers.[13] At age ten, Sinclair passes an afternoon with Franz Kromer, a rough, muscular thirteen-year-old pupil at a lower school and the son of a drunkard tailor. Franz impresses Sinclair and his fellows by accurately spitting at targets through a gap between his teeth. In order to keep up with him, the kids boast with "all sorts of schoolboy heroics and naughty pranks" (19). When Sinclair invents a story about stealing a sack of apples in a neighboring garden, Franz starts to blackmail him by threatening to tell the owner.

Thus Franz penetrates into Sinclair's childhood paradise and "contaminates" it, not unlike Božena and Basini soiled Törless's. Under the threat of denunciation, Sinclair desperately attempts to placate Franz, first with his pennies and later, like Basini, by performing demeaning tasks for his tormentor. He suffers for sinning against the parental morality and is often overwhelmed by "a fit of home-sickness as if for a lost paradise" (48). Yet he is occasionally proud to have a secret, and his father's ignorance of it desacralizes his "holy image" (28). In retrospect, the death of innocence turns out to be a rebirth, though not, as yet, as Cain:

> I was forced to observe with a chill in my heart how my world, my good, happy, carefree life, was becoming a part of the past, was breaking away from me, and I was forced to feel how I was being shackled and held fast with new roots to the outside, to the dark and alien world. For the first time in my life I tasted death, and death tasted bitter, for death is birth, is fear and dread of some terrible renewal. (15–16)

Franz is finally scared away by a new student in Sinclair's class, Demian, who shakes the foundations of Sinclair's moral convictions but also becomes his savior-peer. Once Sinclair is "saved," he flees from his "valley of sorrow" back "to where I had been happy and content, back to the lost paradise that was opening up again now, back to the light, untroubled world of mother and father, my sisters, the smell of cleanliness, and the piety of Abel." After confessing to his parents the story of Franz, Sinclair starts "the feast of my readmittance to the fold, the return of the Prodigal Son" (36–37).

Törless, like Sinclair, reunites with his mother after a descent into the underworld, but sniffing her perfume he can no longer clearly distinguish between the safe and clean world of his childhood and the fallen world of prostitutes, petty thieves, and sadists of his adolescence. Though he too returns home as a prodigal son, his adolescent experience has radically changed his vision of the parental world. Sinclair, on the other hand, reaffirms the parental values at the end of chapter 2, in spite of Demian's Nietzschean lesson. He returns to the safety of childhood because he lacks as yet the courage to shake himself free (37–39). In retrospect, however, he rejects the romantic notion of a paradisiacal childhood as a pernicious myth that blocks the formation of a genuine self: many people experience death and rebirth only when childhood slowly disintegrates "and they suddenly feel surrounded by the loneliness and mortal cold of the universe. Very many are caught forever in this impasse, and for the rest of their lives cling painfully to an irrevocable past, the dream of the lost paradise—which is the worst and most ruthless of dreams" (41).

As we shall see in the following chapter, the prodigal son will depart once more, this time irrevocably.

DAVID SILBERMANN

Like Meaulnes and Demian, Lacretelle's Silbermann enters the life of his anonymous narrator by exerting an irresistible charm and opening his senses to hitherto unknown beauties in familiar things. Augustin Meaulnes discovers firecrackers in the attic, Silbermann brings Racine's *Iphigénie* to life:

> I listened spellbound, struck by a sudden discovery. These assembled words, which I recognized for having seen them printed and having stored them mechanically from beginning to end in my memory—these words formed for the first time an image in my mind. . . . I did not believe until then that a classical tragedy could be so vividly and sensitively rendered . . . his yellow complexion and the black bonnet of his curled hair made me dream of a magician in some oriental story who keeps the key to all marvels.[14]

When Silbermann leaves, life appears as dismal and worthless to the narrator (111), as it did to François upon Meaulnes's departure.

But Lacretelle's story is more concretely rooted in its social and historical environment than *Le Grand Meaulnes, Fermina Márquez,* and the psychodrama in the opening chapters of *Demian.* The psychology of *Silbermann*'s opening scene is embedded in social tension. The narrator, son of a puritanical Protestant judge, recalls how he anticipated returning to school and renewing his friendship with Philippe Robin, son of an important Catholic lawyer. The reunion disappoints the narrator, but his mother encourages him to cultivate the friendship for it may further his father's career.

However, to his mother's disappointment, the narrator turns from the desirable Catholic Philippe to the undesirable Jewish Silbermann, who is a newcomer in the school and does not even appeal to him at first: "He was short and puny in appearance. His face . . . was very well shaped but very ugly, with protruding cheekbones and a pointed chin. . . . All this suggested the idea of a strange precocity; it made me think of child prodigies that make rounds in circuses."[15] Silbermann's intelligence and poetic sensitivity neutralize this initial impression, but the budding friendship gradually isolates the narrator. Some schoolmates envy Silbermann's superior intellect, Philippe avoids contact with him because he is under the influence of his anti-Semitic uncle, and the narrator's parents are taken aback by Silbermann's precocious table talk. Silbermann is fond of his family but has little in common with his father, who deals with art for pecuniary reasons (41–42). The Silbermanns' opulent home overwhelms the frugally raised narrator.

When Silbermann becomes the target of anti-Semitic attacks, the narrator enthusiastically swears to stand by him, and he takes this oath of loyalty with all the puritanical severity of his upbringing. Confronted with Philippe's demand to choose between Silbermann and himself, he is tempted by the expected "gentle and regulated feeling, the unproblematic and permitted pleasures" in Philippe's friendship, but he is swayed by the "arduous task" of taking Silbermann's side: "I foresaw a painful destiny, and, exalted at the perspective of sacrifice, I responded by exclaiming irresistibly: Him."[16]

Loyalty to Silbermann becomes the narrator's mission (50). Although he does not intervene when his friend is beaten, he comforts him at the price of being ostracized. Their friendship becomes impossible, however, when Silbermann's father is accused of fraud by the right-wing press, and the narrator's father is charged with the investigation. When, upon Silbermann's desperate request, the narrator attempts to sway his father, he is severely rebuked, suspected of an "abnormal attachment" (87), and told to drop the friendship. He disobeys, but his parents persuade the school to remove the "divisive" Silbermann, who departs for America to enter his uncle's diamond business.

Like *Le Grand Meaulnes* and *Demian, Silbermann* is, then, the story of the narrator's adolescent friendship with an outsider. But whereas Meaulnes and Demian are alienated only because of their personal qualities, in Silbermann's case being Jewish determines both his identity and his exclusion.

Whereas Meaulnes's inner life is revealed through his own diary and letters, Silbermann is fittingly seen only through the narrator, for his identity is also forced upon him from outside; his character is a role assigned to him by the confining circumstances. Initially, Silbermann has a weak Jewish identity: he is neither religious nor respectful of his father's commercial success, and his dream is to make a glorious contribution to French literary life by means of assimilation. But the attacks by his classmates stamp him a Jew, identify him with his father, and destroy his dream. By entering his uncle's diamond business he assumes an identity that befits his upbringing and conforms to the image of Jews. Having been addressed by his friend only as Silbermann, he assumes his full name in his bitter farewell: "I have left my dreams behind. In America, I am going to *make money*. Having the name I do, I was predestined for it. Eh? . . . David Silbermann is more fitting for the sign of a diamond merchant than the cover of a book!"[17] Lacretelle successfully portrays the powerful force of the milieu upon adolescent identity formation.[18]

The social image is equally formative in the *narrator's* struggle for identity, which is another version of the departure and return of a "prodigal son." When Silbermann departs, the narrator returns into the bosom of his family. To be sure, the returning son finds the nest no longer as cozy and unsullied as earlier, and he is eager to show that he can forget neither Silbermann's fate nor his father's refusal to be lenient with the art dealer. The hypocrisy of his father's refusal becomes apparent when the judge later does become lenient to please a powerful deputy. The narrator skillfully blends self-criticism with self-promotion in order to demonstrate that the return to the father's world does not imply endorsing his father's hypocritical puritan morality. He joins the celebration of his father's promotion (which was furthered by his leniency) by adopting the spirit of forgiveness and understanding of human fallibility: "Recognizing the fragile matter of that pure face [of my mother] I understood that however virtuous a soul may be and however it may aspire to sainthood, it cannot elevate itself above human imperfection."[19]

This, at any rate, is how the narrator justifies his reconciliation with his family. Though his account is full of self-chastisement, the rationale of the "humane" reconciliation is cast in a different light in the concluding scene, which depicts his reconciliation with Philippe:

> His face was gay and serene. He seemed to pursue a much simpler path, one that was provided with easy sideways and advantageous safeguards, skirting chasms without ever straying into them.
>
> I felt that my future happiness depended on the choice I was to make between the two paths I was facing. I hesitated . . . But suddenly the landscape on Philippe's side seemed so attractive that I relaxed and let a faint smile escape.[20]

The reconciliation occurs in front of a wall on which a crude and faded caricature of Silbermann is drawn. It symbolizes not just reconciliation but also the acceptance of the racial stereotype: "I turned to Silbermann's caricature and, after some effort, said in a slightly mocking tone, whose perfect ease disconcerted me internally: 'This is very true to life.'"[21]

The remark betrays Silvermann and marks a shift from sincere to hypocritical puritan ethics. Until now, the narrator saw his courageous defense of Silbermann as a mission, a puritan self-sacrifice.[22] Upon Silbermann's departure, "I fell into profound desperation. Neither his person nor the end of our friendship were the reason for it. I suffered from no longer feeling upon awakening each morning, with the first ray of the day, the inspiration of that glorious task."[23] When Silbermann departs, the narrator's Calvinist sacrificial service for the persecuted Jew comes to an end. By choosing the "attractive" landscape on Philippe's side and accepting the stereotypical caricature as truthful, the narrator adopts an attitude of expediency and social conformity.

The narrator and Silbermann redefine their identities by moving in opposite directions. Silbermann starts with a diffuse identity but is compelled by external pressure to rigidify it. The narrator begins with clearly affirmed beliefs and values, but these crumble through exposure to Silbermann and through the narrator's subsequent reconciliation with the surrounding world. Since the old values are not replaced by new ones, his final identity merely extends the parental one and does not constitute a creative resolution of adolescence. The concluding reconciliation with Philippe reverses the earlier choice between the difficult and easy paths and marks the emergence of a false consciousness. This time the narrator opts for the convenient path and the attractive landscape instead of the course of arduous service. His words undermine themselves; the hypocrisy of the compromise needs no commentary.

CHAPTER THREE

Groups

Literary texts exemplify the proposition that peer groups provide the primary context for adolescence and that education "by one's contemporaries"
outweighs all other influences (Forbush 65). This primacy of the peer group
implies that adult national, religious, and class divisions play only a secondary
role in adolescent identity formation, partly, of course, because the secondary
school population is already fairly homogeneous. Musil's and Deyssel's boarding schools form small states or republics that are semi-detached from the
adult world, and even day schools have powerful peer-group subcultures. In
Tonio Kröger, Le Grand Meaulnes, Fermina Márquez, and *Törless,* the adolescents
are essentially ignorant of the larger social and national issues; Catholicism
and Irish nationalism are important in *A Portrait,* but they enter Stephen's
education through his elders rather than his peers. Only in *Silbermann* are the
small world and the embedding larger one inextricably interlinked.

The works of Maurice Barrès that I shall discuss in this chapter provide
early examples of a preoccupation with the adult social context, a concern
that seems to have been particularly keen in French literature. However, as

Hesse's *Demian,* Jean Cocteau's *Thomas l'imposteur,* Raymond Radiguet's *Le Diable au corps,* and other stories indicate, social and political problems entered literary adolescence mainly after the war. More than anything else, the war had revealed how dependent adolescents were on adults.

CLIQUES

The peer group is both fascinated and frightened by the superiority of outsiders like Meaulnes, Silbermann, and Demian, and peer-group narrators are usually torn between their loyalty and attachment to the outsider and the fluctuating demands of the group.

Meaulnes, for instance, becomes the center of attention upon his arrival: the seniors stay in the classroom, the boys huddle around him, and "endless discussions, interminable arguments" begin, in which François participates "half delighted, half uneasy" (18).

But Meaulnes, usually silent, is no leader, and after the experience of the "lost domain" he loses all interest in his comrades, who turn against him and even plan a war on him (37). Meaulnes and François become isolated (79). Frantz becomes the ringleader of the clan that used to follow Meaulnes, but once he concludes a pact with Meaulnes and François, the balance of power shifts again. When Frantz and Meaulnes depart, François becomes "a village lad like the rest of them" (117) within the loose power structure of Jasmin, who aspires to fill the vacuum and assumes Meaulnes's heritage (127). François divulges Meaulnes's secret in order to pass beyond mere "counterfeit intimacy" with the group (117), but the story makes no impression, and François feels he betrayed his friend. Similar betrayals occur in Hesse's *Unterm Rad (Under the Wheel,* 1906), *Törless,* and elsewhere, most seriously, as we have seen, in *Silbermann.*

Betrayal means that the "friend" is too cowardly to take a public stand against the teasing, persecution, beating, or torturing of the outsider (be he superior like Meaulnes and Silbermann or "morally abject" like Basini), which, Hall notes, are common features of adolescent formations:

> It is perhaps almost normal at a certain stage of human life to take pleasure in hectoring, plaguing, pecking at, worrying, etc., often perhaps to test the temper or cry point. . . . The fighting instinct, which is so strongly reenforced by the dawn of sexuality; the egoistic assertion of tyrannical power; the appropriation of property; the compulsion of service, and obedience of those weaker by bullying and sometimes under awful threats of torture . . .

all these illustrate the strange teasing instinct often almost irresistible even in those incapable of rancor and who are overflowing with general good-will. (*Adolescence* 1: 358–59)

Stalky & Co.

Hall focuses on a main feature of Rudyard Kipling's classic portrayal of the adolescent clique, a work that curiously ignores other central features we have come to identify with adolescence such as identity crisis and sexuality. Kipling's boys are cocky, intermittently brutal, and lacking in tenderness and compassion, which may be associated with their suppressed or immature sexuality. The absence of women and heterosexual contact in *Stalky & Co.* was typical of the male public schools and perpetuated itself in the public school story (see chapter 5), but it is somewhat surprising that Kipling shows no interest in sports, the main substitute for sex in the public school. In *Stalky and Co.* male camaraderie and displays of prowess are exclusively limited to the clique's inexhaustible passion for challenging authority and doing mischief.

Kipling's title clearly indicates a group identity with an internal power structure. Although the members of the closed clique, Stalky, Beetle, and M'Turk, are excellently individualized, their identity as a group dominates. That identity is associated with the leader, Stalky, but the informal "Co." suggests a commercial rather than a military union and perhaps reflects something of the spirit at United Service College, which Kipling himself attended, a recently founded school with little prestige, educating primarily sons of those serving in the outlying areas of the empire.

The cohesiveness of the clique as well as the quasi-independence of the public school subculture is expressed through language. In contrast to Wedekind, whose adolescents adopt the highfalutin discourse of their elders (a sign of their continuing dependence), Kipling brilliantly and innovatively evokes a sloppy, irreverent, sophisticated, and creative adolescent idiolect.

Thus the housemaster Prout is nicknamed "Hoofer," on account of his large feet, and this metaphor becomes the source of endless phonetic distortions, including Heffy (with "fairy" feet), Hartoffles, Heffles, Hooplats, and Heffelinga. School slang of the type "likewise blow" (3), "pon my sainted Sam" (17), scrumptious" (7), "gloomy old ass" (16), and "libelous old rip" (25) are "redeemed" by a generous sprinkling of misused Latin and other foreign phrases such as "his rebus infectis" (3) "destricto ense" (3), "flagrante delicto" (20), "je vais gloater," and "nous bunkerons aux bunkers" (97).

The institutional limits of this talk become evident as soon as members of

the clique reenter the paternal order. Although Stalky and Beetle "had carefully kicked M'Turk out of his Irish dialect" (10), he instantaneously relapses
to assume its class privileges, when he encounters a landowner of Irish descent: "Forgotten was the College and the decency due to elders! M'Turk was
treading again the barren purple mountains of the rainy West coast, where
in his holidays he was viceroy of four thousand naked acres, only son of a
three-hundred-year-old house, lord of a crazy fishing-boat, and the idol of
his father's shiftless tenantry. It was the landed man speaking to his equal—
deep calling to deep—and the old gentleman acknowledged the cry" (10–
11). Similarly, whenever the situation requires it, Stalky can smoothly blend
into "the broad Devon," his *langue de guerre*" (20), and lash out in the drill
"with a blast of withering invective" learned from his father or uncle (203).

"Co." also implies that the clique's defiant challenge to authority can easily
be accommodated within adult formations, including the college, which is "a
limited liability company payin' four per cent" (166), founded to get a max-
imum of its graduates into the Royal Military College at Sandhurst and send
the rest into business and banking (170). The clique may have no pecuniary
interests, yet its opposition to authority is based on commercial as well as
intellectual and artistic values. Its fierce individualism is mostly intellectual
arrogance against stupidity and pomposity that readily submits to the "clever"
tyranny of the headmaster.

The relationship between societal and clique values is highly ambiguous.
When a visiting member of the College Board of Council mistakes a "de-
faulters" drill for a regular training exercise and proposes to establish a vol-
unteer cadet corps at the school, Stalky enthusiastically assumes command,
displaying what he had picked up from his father. But when a member of
parliament delivers a pompous pep talk about honor and glory, climaxing his
performance by unfurling the Union Jack, the cadet corps falls apart. Yet, the
epilogue, told by Kipling-Beetle, relates how Stalky distinguished himself in
the imperial army by employing clever ruses learned in the clique. His adventures are recounted at a cozy reunion of schoolmates, an evening of male
camaraderie that links the clique to the school's sociability and military male
bonding. Stalky & Co., for all its flaunting of independence, is part and parcel
of the larger world.

The Counterfeiters

Hall notes that a torturing child is merely "an extreme and abnormal"
teaser without compassion for his victim (*Adolescence* 1: 359). He could have

added that merciless torturing, adolescent or otherwise, needs a group that supports the torture by watching. Such is the case in *Törless,* in Marieluise Fleisser's works, and in Gide's *Les Faux-monnayeurs* (*The Counterfeiters*). The original impulses for the latter included two newspaper reports (reprinted in *Counterfeiters* 455–57): one from the September 16, 1906, issue of *Figaro* about a band (of mostly postadolescents) that brought counterfeit coins into circulation; the other one, which Gide called his "primary inspiration" (*Counterfeiters* 460), from the June 5, 1909, issue of the *Journal de Rouen* about a fifteen-year-old boy forced to commit suicide in a class at Clermont-Ferrand by "an evil society of youngsters."

Gide gave increasingly more attention to questions of form and perspective during the novel's long years of gestation, whereby the judicial "counterfeit" of the original news item acquired a broader moral meaning of "theatricality" and "inauthenticity" typical of adolescent behavior. But Gide retained the concern with bands, common to both newspaper stories, by fusing the two crime reports and turning the counterfeiters into the "evil society of youngsters" responsible for little Boris's suicide. Boris's life enters the book peripherally, but his death becomes its closure, bringing together Gide's concerns with masturbation, psychoanalysis, adolescent gangs, and suicide.

Boris lives with his widowed mother in Poland. He adores the somewhat older Bronja. At the age of thirteen, Boris is taken for a vacation to Switzerland by Bronja's mother, Mme Sophroniska, who treats Boris for nervous disorders. Edouard, one of the major characters of the book who is engaged in writing a novel entitled "The Counterfeiters," visits him there at the request of his paternal grandfather, La Pérouse, and Boris's story is pieced together from remarks made by Mme Sophroniska (mediated through Edouard's diary), Edouard, the grandfather, and the narrator.

Boris's story is preceded in Edouard's diary by the remark that the deep subject of his book will be "the rivalry between the real world and the representation of it which we make to ourselves" (*Counterfeiters* 205). This has direct relevance to what follows, for Mme Sophroniska claims that Boris's neuroses result from his habit of creating an imaginary world during masturbation. When he was nine, a schoolmate "initiated him into certain clandestine practices, which the children in their ignorance and astonishment believed to be 'magic'"—magic, because they thought they had discovered "a secret which made up for real absence by illusory presence" (206). The "talisman" that Boris carried around his neck and used as a "formula of incantation—the 'Open Sesame' of the shameful Paradise, into which their pleasure plunged them" (207) consisted of insignificant words on a parchment.

Mme Sophroniska believes that she has all but cured Boris through psychoanalysis[1] and she gives away the "talisman" she was able to extract from him. But when Boris comes to Paris the "talisman" suddenly reappears in the hands of the adolescents who just barely escaped prosecution for spreading counterfeit money.

Thus Boris's old habit of preferring "the possession of imaginary goods to the real goods" (208) makes him a victim of those who have experience in deceiving others with counterfeit. The analogy between masturbation and false coins becomes obvious, though one may ask whether Gide shared Mme Sophroniska's opinion that Boris's real cure lay in his heterosexual love for Bronja (180), and whether the correlation between the pretense of masturbatory self-deception, counterfeit coins, and literary fiction is meant to be a probing rather than a serious proposal.

When Boris is mysteriously reconfronted with his "talisman," he is embarrassed and relapses into his "ancient vice." The counterfeiters form a new clique called "The Brotherhood of Strong Men" and succeed in convincing Boris to join for he desperately wants to overcome his vice by proving himself. The rest follows the newspaper report: Ghéri, the leader of the brotherhood, decides that a member chosen by lot must prove its motto, The Strong Man Cares Nothing for Life, by shooting himself in front of the class. The rigged lot falls to Boris. Ghéri assures the others that the pistol is unloaded, although he knows that it is, and Boris heroically shoots himself. The clique manages to erase the traces of their criminal manipulation, and Edouard, unaware of what only the narrator told his readers, decides to omit the unfathomable suicide from his book. The narrator provides the facts of the background, but the unmitigated evil of the clandestine clique, all too real to be a counterfeit, remains incomprehensible.

THE GANG: MOLNÁR'S *THE PÁL STREET BOYS*

Street gangs became a judicial, psychological, and sociological concern towards the end of the nineteenth century. Puffer devoted an article to the subject in Hall's *Pedagogical Seminary,* and they play a prominent role in Riis's classic study of New York tenements. Forbush, himself the organizer of an "Order of the Knights of King Arthur" for boys (100–104), sanely advised parents and social workers to make use of the adolescent "gang-instinct" rather than suppress it (25, 132). But as a social phenomenon of the lower classes and the outcasts, gangs seldom appear in the literature of adolescence, which treats middle-class children.

Ferenc Molnár's bittersweet account of a fight between two high school gangs for a vacant lot (the "grund") on Pál Street, is probably the first modern story of teenage gangs.[2] The lot, situated in a lower-middle-class neighborhood of Budapest, is occupied by the Pál Street gang. It opens in the back unto a lumberyard where stacks of drying timber conveniently serve as fortresses. The rival gang of the Redshirts has its playground and headquarters on an island in the neighboring botanical garden, but since this cannot be used for ball playing, the Redshirts declare war in order to take the "grund" from the Pál Street gang. The two major figures of the story are János Bóka, the clever general of the Pál Street boys, and little Ernő Nemecsek, the only private in the gang, whom everybody bosses around. Boka's "brilliant" strategy notwithstanding, the defense of the "grund" is on the verge of collapsing in the crucial battle, when Nemecsek (who caught pneumonia during a scouting expedition) suddenly appears, captures the "giant" leader of the Redshirts, and leads the Pál Street boys to victory. It is a Pyrrhic victory: Nemecsek dies within a few days, and Boka, returning from his friend's deathbed to the scene of victory, learns that another tenement house will be erected on the "grund." Death and exile overshadow the glorious victory and force Boka to take his first step towards adulthood.

Such a summary reveals Molnár's undeniable penchant for sentimentality but fails to render the flavor of his humor and the evocative power of his descriptions. The narrator's attitude towards early adolescence is ironic but never condescending, and his adults are more differentiated than the consistently black figures in *Frühlings Erwachen* and expressionist drama.

Like Stalky & Co., the Pál Street gangs are seemingly unique adolescent cliques that actually replicate features of adult organizations. The gang war, for all its comedy, reflects disconcerting truths about the world at large. The Redshirts declare the war because, as one of them remarks, "We need a place to play ball, and that's all," upon which the narrator comments, "They decided on war for the same reasons that real soldiers usually fight. The Russians needed the sea, that's why they fought Japan. The Redshirts needed a playing field, and since there was no other way, they wanted to acquire it by means of war" (55). In turn, the Pál Street boys defend their territory with patriotic fervor: "They shouted 'Long live the grund' as if they were exclaiming 'Long live our country.'"[3]

Reflecting adult chauvinism and warfare, the adolescents imitate rather than oppose the adults, the small and big worlds resemble each other. Instead of being oppressive, as in *Frühlings Erwachen,* the school is irrelevant to matters that most concern the adolescents. The only teacher that enters the picture is "severe faced but meek-hearted" (126). The rest of the adult world consists of a Slovak guard at the sawmill, who sides with the boys, a street vendor of sweets, and parents who unfailingly identify with their children and split along class and ethnic lines. The only instance of social criticism concerns the callousness of the rich rather than the educational system: Nemecsek's father must serve a customer who insists on speedy delivery though he sees that the child is dying. In contrast, Leonhard Frank's *Räuberbande* (1914) tells the story of a gang that enacts Indian tribal rituals under the fortification of Würzburg in conscious opposition to a hostile adult world.

Molnár's adolescents do not fight, then, against adults but conduct an internecine war that replicates adult ones. The replica deviates inasmuch as the adolescents fight gallantly and their gangs do not split along adult divisions. Molnár hints at class differences by letting the Pál Street boys attend a classical gymnasium and the Redshirts merely a "realgymnasium" (126), but the contrast remains marginal. Similarly, Nemecsek is a private because of his timidity and physical weakness rather than his lower social standing, and Weisz is so much part of the group that one cannot be sure whether he is Jewish or not.

These relations within the Pál Street gang reflect Molnár's utopian and assimilationist Jewish attitude rather than the prevailing social conditions in turn-of-the-century Budapest. Nevertheless, the novel has a strong realistic strain that paradoxically becomes evident through its depiction of fiction's impact on reality: the gang's rituals and ethics are distilled from chivalric romances and Karl May's immensely popular novels about noble Indians. Molnár's Redshirts scout by putting their ears against the ground, use wooden tomahawks and lances for ceremonial purposes, and fight according to the rules of wrestling (139). The leader of the Redshirts "would not take over the grund when nobody is there," for he wants to conduct the war "in a proper way" (55). When their delegation delivers the declaration of war and agrees with the enemy about the weapons and the modalities of fighting, they also inquire about Nemecsek, who behaved so heroically when captured and forced to take a dip in the lake. On the way home they convey their get-well wishes to the sick boy. In a world rushing headlong into a ruthless war of bombing and chemical warfare, such gallantries in fighting could only be modelled after fiction. Molnár is most realistic when describing how adolescents imaginatively play out their readings. We shall see in chapter 11 that similar imitations of fiction structured the reality of the Boy Scouts and other youth movements.

ETHNIC BONDS: BARRÈS

The works of Maurice Barrès (1862–1923) differ in several important respects from the ones discussed so far. The title of his first trilogy, *Le Culte du moi* (*The Cult of the Self,* 1891) indicates that Barrès, like Joyce, Mann, Hesse, and others, was first concerned with the quest of the individual. But Barrès strove to overcome individualism and self-cultivation by seeking for ways leading back into a community and a shared tradition. Since his anti-individualism accorded with the general political shift towards a collectivism that psychologically prepared for war, Barrès is, his tedious style notwithstanding, a better guide to the social and national trends of the age than those who opposed them by insisting on the cultivation of the self in the manner of Stephen Dedalus or Tonio Kröger. Barrès was not just a secluded writer but also a journalist and a deputy in the French Assembly, which gave added weight and influence to his fiction. His works mirrored the growth of chauvinism and antidemocracy in prewar France and helped, in turn, to instill these qualities in the French adolescents growing up around 1900.

Like Barrès himself, the protagonist of *Le Cult du moi* rebels against a French situation that bears some resemblance to Weimar Germany. The republic that emerged in France after the defeat of 1870–71 was a beleaguered parliamentary democracy, held under steady fire by monarchists, opponents of capitalism and urbanization, and revanchists demanding the reannexation of Alsace and Lorraine.

The title of the first volume indicates that the cult of the self takes place *Sous l'oeil des barbares* (*Under the Eyes of Barbarians,* 1888) and is motivated by a rejection of the apparently bankrupt barbarian world. Barrès remarked about the conclusion of the first chapter: "I found that our morality, our religion, our patriotic feelings had disintegrated and could no longer offer rules for our lives. And waiting until our masters would rebuild certainties for us, it was proper to hold to the only reality, the self."[4]

Stephen Dedalus's belief that the self is the only reality represents just a point of departure for Barrès. In the second volume, *Un homme libre* (*A Free Man,* 1889) (dedicated to secondary school pupils), the adolescent protagonist,

Philippe, assumes the narration and develops a syllogism about maximizing the pleasure of self-cultivation: "The first principle: we are most happy in exaltation. Second principle: the pleasure of exaltation is greatly augmented by its analysis. . . . Consequence: we must maximize feeling by maximizing its analysis."[5]

Since Philippe is surrounded by "barbarians," self-cultivation must take place in semi-solitude. When he calls upon his friend Simon to "flee into solitude" and to "be born anew,"[6] the two retreat to a village southeast of Nancy in their native Lorraine, to contemplate and to rigorously execute the exercises of Ignatius Loyola. They reject active life in favor of constructing a true inner self in the romantic tradition: "What do I care about my *outer self*! Deeds do not count; the only thing that counts is my *inner self*! The God I am constructing."[7]

The God in construction becomes, however, a Proteus with many personalities and thus without character. Philippe, who thinks that he is becoming "a truly free man" by inducing "rarest emotions" with a perfectly controlled, "mechanized soul," soon realizes that he is splitting himself "into a great many souls." The outcome is pure hedonism: "The emotions we knew yesterday no longer belong to us. The desires, the passions, the yearnings are everything; the goal nothing."[8]

This exercise of disassembling (rather than constructing) the self cannot satisfy Philippe, who revolted against the "barbarians" precisely because they were lacking a center: "Since my first childhood reflections, I dreaded the barbarians who reproached me for being different; I cultivated the eternal in me, and this led me to develop a method for enjoying a thousand fragments of my ideal. That amounted to giving myself a thousand successive souls; for the birth of one, another had to die; I suffer under this dissipation. I yearn to rest in a plentiful unity amidst this succession of imperfections. Can't I reunite all these discordant sounds into a large harmony?"[9]

Loyola's exercises are supposed to coerce the discordant elements, but unlike many of Barrès's contemporaries Philippe remains an agnostic. The region of his retreat reawakens in him memories of different communal ties. Walking through old Nancy and its museums (181–97), he relives its history and concludes that the tradition and the racial stock seem dead (192), incapable of further unfolding (197). But with some effort he can discover in himself the soul of Lorraine (188) and the voice of all those dead ancestors who inform his sensibility (195). The quest for self-discovery that first led to a plurality of autonomous selves, each focused on momentary enjoyment without memory or anticipation, now moves into a phase of cementing by rediscovering a "racial" past and submitting to it. Thus Philippe terminates his retreat and bids farewell to his friend: "Individuals, however perfect one imagines them to be, are only fragments of a more complete system, which is the race, itself a fragment of God. Avoiding the sterile analysis of my own organization, I shall labor from now on to unfold the disposition of my being."[10]

In the final volume, entitled *Le Jardin de Bérénice* (*Bérénice's Garden,* 1891), Philippe sustains a platonic relationship with Bérénice, a delicate creature and former acquaintance who has been faithful to the memory of her dead lover. Upon Philippe's urging she finally marries somebody else, only to die shortly thereafter. Bérénice, her loyalty to the deceased, her garden, and the surrounding marshy Aigues-Mortes become in Philippe's mind a joint mystical symbol of the "dead soil" in which he has to take root again: "I am a garden where hitherto uprooted emotions flower. Will Bérénice and Aigues-Mortes be able to indicate to me the culture that would cure me of my instability? I am lost in roaming around, ignorant of the place where I could rediscover the unity of my life."[11] He surrenders the idea of a contemplative life and wages a successful election campaign against a "barbarian" engineer, who unsuccessfully wooed Bérénice and has no comprehension of the native tradition.

The allegory becomes somewhat heavy-handed towards the end, but it effectively, and disturbingly, traces the path of Barrès's adolescent from radical individualism to reintegration into a racially and geographically defined communal tradition. As Agathon commented in a survey of French youth conducted in 1911 (see chapter 10): "Cultivating oneself does not mean liberation, plunging into crazy adventures, but rediscovering in one's self the energies of one's race, of those who died, and expanding in this sense one's destiny."[12] Philippe's path in Barrès's novel became for Agathon the trajectory of French adolescents around 1900. Barrès both anticipated and encouraged the shift, one may even say that he helped an ideologically more coherent conservative adolescent generation to marginalize the cosmopolitan and liberal "barbarians." The fictional Philippe, without a peer group as yet, forged out of nothing the myth of a community of dead souls, which served as a rallying point for the peer group of the next generation. Seen from another angle, this is the story of Silbermann's exclusion.

Barrès returned to the themes of *Le Cult du moi* in *Les Déracinés* (*The Uprooted Ones,* 1897), by widening the focus into a group portrait of seven pupils from Nancy, framed by the events of French politics between 1879 and 1885. He subsequently extended the book into a trilogy of "national energy" (*L'Appel au soldat,* 1900; *Leurs Figures,* 1902), a commentated chronicle of France as seen from the perspective of a chauvinistic, anti-Semitic, and anti-intellectualist dogma that Barrès adopted in the course of the Dreyfus affair. *Les Déracinés* appeared just before the affair erupted and represents a midway point between the mystic-pantheistic regionalism that closes the earlier trilogy and the reactionary dogma of the anti-Dreyfusard.

The seven adolescents become "uprooted" by leaving their native Lorraine after graduation for the cosmopolitan and corrupt capital. They were encouraged to do so by Paul Bouteiller, the young and inspiring philosophy teacher of their senior year, who initiated them into adolescence (16). Bouteiller—modelled after Barrès's teacher Auguste Burdeau, a later finance minister and president of the Assembly—is a Kantian moralist who believes in universal moral principles.

The narrator's running commentary unequivocally condemns Bouteiller's philosophy and influence. The opening essay on the lycée in Nancy decries the coalescing of the peer group as a sign of loosening ties with the older people in whom tradition lives on: "Isolated from their communities of birth, and trained only to compete among themselves, adolescents take the most lamentable view of life, its conditions, and its aim."[13] Barrès is thus opposed to the "emancipation" and segregation of adolescents.

As a teacher of universal principles, Bouteiller is himself uprooted, a "nomadic philosopher" (31)[14] who urges the boys to break with their heritage. He is disinterested in the family, the tradition, and the region of his pupils, and unconcerned with their individual needs. Yet, the narrator says: "Each individual is constituted of realities that cannot be contradicted; a teacher who recognizes these has to proportion and distribute truth in such a way that each person carries home his own truth."[15] The remark seems to be a plea for recognizing individuality, but in the narrator's discourse "realities" generally refer to transindividual social and historical forces.

Bouteiller's example and teaching are to blame if the seven adolescents of Lorraine are cut off from the "soul" and the tradition of their native soil and depart for the Parisian university that "disdains or ignores most readily tangible realities" (33). Their own adolescent bond is the only tie they will carry with them.

These developments occur in what one may call the book's prologue. The remainder of the book presents the predictable consequences of this erroneous education, sprinkled with broad and satirical descriptions of the Parisian political and social scene. Each boy goes his own way first, but their common desire to achieve greatness, inspired by Napoleon's tomb, brings them together to start an idealistic newspaper. All too soon they have to confront the corrupt political and economic demands of the world. Some refuse to prostitute themselves, others are carried away by the current, and the two who are financially responsible for the enterprise commit an atrocious murder when the money finally runs out. One of them is hanged.

Sternhell's study of Barrès shows how the plot and the narrator's commentary reveal Barrès's reactionary, even protofascist, ideas. It shall suffice to point out here that *Le Culte du moi* and *Les Déracinés* delineate oppositely moving paths between identical poles: if the earlier work showed how self-examination ought to lead back to a racially and regionally conceived community, the new one depicts how without such a self-examination and reintegration adolescents will become uprooted "barbarians" in the corrupt world of the republic. The novels sharply attack two different resolutions to the adolescent identity crisis: one that affirms individuality, the other that surrenders the self to the reigning chaos of the commercial, corrupt, cosmopolitan-Jewish world. Only reintegration into the orderly chain of ancestors can shape a satisfactory new identity—and this leaves precious little free space for the individual and the peer group.

DEMIAN'S COMRADES IN THE TRENCHES

In *Törless, Demian, Silbermann,* and other stories, the first adolescent experience ends with the (temporary) return of the prodigal son into the bosom of the family. But the typical turn-of-the-century variants of this archetypal adolescent parable do not follow the biblical model. Rainer Maria Rilke's *Aufzeichnungen des Malte Laurids Brigge* ends with the young protagonist's rejection of the orthodox version, while Gide in *Le Retour de l'enfant prodigue* adds a younger brother who departs at the end with the blessing of the one returned. Hesse's Sinclair is a prodigal son who, in Gide's sense, turns into his own younger brother, he exits once more to embark on a quest of self-discovery, which ends, ambiguously, in World War I.

If "home" is the Eden of childhood in the first episode of *Demian,* it becomes the utopian inner sphere of the authentic self, the goal of Sinclair's striving, in the middle sections. In Hesse's metaphysics of the self, inherited from Novalis and the romantics, reaching that authentic self means overcoming alienation and returning home to one's "true self." Hesse departs from his romantic model by making the landscape of urban decay the scene of alienation: "It was like a bad dream. I can see myself: crawling along in my odious and unclean way, across filth and slime, across broken beer glasses and through cynically wasted nights, a spellbound dreamer, restless and racked. . . . I was condemned to become lonely, and I raised between myself and my childhood a locked gateway to Eden with its pitilessly resplendent host of guardian" (64).[16]

This romantic quest through unromantic landscapes is Sinclair's story. Its utopian character is projected already in the book's opening reflection: "Each man's life represents a road toward himself, an attempt at such a road, the intimation of a path. No man has ever been entirely and completely himself" (4).

Nevertheless, Sinclair and Demian believe that the authentic inner self exists and can reliably guide those who know how to listen to it (114), for they perceive an identity between the outer and the authentic inner world. "The things we see," says Pistorius, a musician and temporary friend of Sinclair's, "are the same things that are within us. There is no reality except the one contained within us" (96).

Although Pistorius disappoints Sinclair, his ideas find their way into Sinclair's philosophy, partly because of their kinship to Demian's ideas: "Each man had only one genuine vocation—to find the way to himself. . . . His task was to discover his own destiny—not an arbitrary one—and live it out wholly and resolutely within himself" (108).

These idealistic-romantic calls gain rhetorical power because the quest for the authentic self is set against the cowardly and easy ways of the masses. Finding one's way to oneself is the only "genuine vocation," everything else is "only a would-be existence, an attempt at evasion, a flight back to the ideals of the masses, conformity and fear of one's own inwardness" (108).

Accordingly, Sinclair joins the inner circle of "marked ones" in the coterie of Demian and his mother Frau Eva, which includes prophets and proselytizers. This elite sees itself as a nucleus of future mankind, as "the will of Nature to something new, to the individualism of the future" (122). The originally hesitant and groping search now becomes "duty," "destiny," and utter faithfulness "to the active seed which Nature planted within" (124)—a trajectory, whose ineluctability the organic metaphors ominously reflect, revealing a hidden analogy to the seemingly opposing ideology of *Le Jardin de Bérénice*!

Indeed, the message of radical and elitist Nietzschean individualism is negated in *Demian* from the outset by a somewhat heavy-handed Jungian archetypal symbolism of birth and rebirth, which first appears in the hatching bird in the heraldry of Sinclair's gate. The bird, initially a personal reference to Sinclair's "hatching" at "home," becomes an archetypal symbol of mankind in the final pages, where societal rebirth ironically reveals itself as a cataclysmic war. Demian's cullings from Nietzsche foreshadow the catastrophe:

> Everywhere, he said, we could observe the reign of the herd instinct, nowhere freedom and love. All this false communion—from the fraternities to the choral societies and the nations themselves—was an inevitable development, was a community born of fear and dread, out of embarrassment, but inwardly rotten, outworn, close to collapsing.
>
> . . . The community spirit at present is only a manifestation of the herd instinct. Men fly into each other's arms because they are afraid of each other. . . . People are afraid because they have never owned up to themselves. . . . No, what Nature wants of man stands indelibly written in the individual, in you, in me. It stood written in Jesus, it stood written in Nietzsche. (114–16)

The presentiments, visions, and dreams of a terrible natural catastrophe (130–31) come true as a man-made war. Demian knows better: he practices boxing and becomes a reserve lieutenant (135). The war scatters the elite group of the "marked ones" among the broader community of comrades in the trenches. Sinclair, the seeker of his authentic self, is swept along by the mass hysteria of the war:

> All men seemed to have become brothers. They talked of "the fatherland" and of "honor," but they gazed for a moment into the naked face of fate . . . I too was embraced by people whom I had never seen before, and I understood it and gladly responded. Intoxication, not the will to please fate, that made them do it, but the intoxication was holy for it resulted from their brief and unsettling glance into the eyes of fate. (137, revised)

Sinclair discovers in the trenches that the ideals for which people may readily die are communal and given rather than personal and freely chosen (138)—a wisdom that Barrès would have gladly conveyed to his "uprooted" adolescents seeking greatness. The laws of organic nature, whose metaphors foreshadowed the coming of war, now become historical destiny. History becomes a puppet show where fate pulls the strings and ceases to be a stage for individual initiative.

It is difficult to understand why the mass readiness to die for received ideals, the surrender of the self to become a weapon of impersonal forces, should raise Sinclair's opinion of humanity. And yet, he condones, or at least excuses, killing as an elemental urge expressing a great desire for renewal. Sinclair concludes an unreflected peace with war by gracing it with a beatific vision, the way revolutionaries and terrorists justify their inhumanity: "The most primitive, even the wildest feelings were not directed at the enemy; their bloody task was merely an irradiation of the soul, of the soul divided within itself, which filled them with the lust to rage and kill, annihilate and die so that they might be born anew" (138). Though Barrès's Philippe and Hesse's Sinclair are focalized differently and placed in different environments, their paths from self-cultivation to submergence into a community seem dangerously similar.

Hesse's novel has an ambiguous ending. Demian, the voice of the self, bids a Christ-like farewell to his disciple, Sinclair, who lies wounded in a makeshift hospital, enjoining him to harken to his inner voice whenever he seeks him. Sinclair's closing words suggest that he internalized the message: "When I . . . climb deep into myself where the images of fate lie aslumber in the dark mirror, I need only bend over that dark mirror to behold my own image, now completely resembling him, my brother, my master [*Führer*]" (141).

But what does it mean if Sinclair internalizes Demian, the voice of selfhood, after having surrendered to male camaraderie in the war? Ziolkowski interprets the closure as the climax of a triadic development that starts from childish innocence and passes through the world of doubt: the "original state of Paradise, the fall, and redemption through Christ" of Christian faith become for Hesse, in this view, the "triadic rhythm of humanization" subsequently outlined in the essay *A Bit of Theology* (1932). According to Ziolkowski, Sinclair cannot return to innocence: "His progressive stages of alienation represent the realization that the true goal, a mature and higher redemption, lies ahead of him on the third level of awareness and not behind, in childhood. In the final vision, when he realizes that the ideal, the justification of his life, lies within him and not in the external world, he has reached the chiliastic realm: the 'new kind of innocence'" (144–45).

Reading the story as a neat progression overlooks the problematics of war, which is a problematics of the self. Innocence, new or old, is "self-less," and the closing may thus be read as a double surrender of the self: a blending with the comrades in the trenches and a devotion to the internalized voice of a "brother" and "Führer." It is hard to say which one is meant to be taken more seriously. But whether we chose the one or the other (or a dialectic of both), it will be difficult to read the ending as a culminating synthesis, let alone as a "humanization," of Sinclair.

What does Demian's disappearance in the war signify? A symbolic death of the idea of elitist pursuit of selfhood, or, just its opposite, the internalization and rebirth of this idea in Sinclair? The narrator's sympathy with the mass hysteria and his humane compassion for the previously belittled herdsmen who are now his comrades-in-arms indicate an alienation from rather than an internalization of Demian's radical individualism. The closing offers no bridge, certainly no synthesis, between the embrace of the comrades and the internalization of the departed "Führer." As in Hesse's other novels, notably the *Glass Bead Game,* the choice between a self-centered and a socially engaged life is left open.

Seen as the story of an adolescent identity crisis, *Demian* offers not a resolution but two dead ends: in the reality of war, both the quest for authenticity as well as the desire for integration become meaningless. Hesse's personal view remains concealed behind the voice of his narrator. But *Sinclair*'s final view on identity and integration may be further illuminated if we turn from the closing pages of his story, which terminate only the plot but not his reflections, to the prologue and the narratorial commentaries scattered throughout the text, which represent his reflections on his experiences well after their occurrence. Like the commentaries, the chronologically ultimate prologue unequivocally reaffirms the quest for the authentic self: "I have been and still am a seeker, but I have ceased to question stars and books; I have begun to listen to the teachings my blood whispers to me. . . . Each man's life represents a road toward himself, an attempt at such a road, the intimation of a path" (4).

The comrades in the trenches have faded, and one may wonder how Sinclair's encounter with them has contributed to his becoming a narrator. Like "stars and books," the obscure message of the intoxicated herdsmen is no longer questioned. But if we conclude that only the personal quest matters, we are still left with two contrasting metaphors for the inner self: a dark interior mirror that reflects the double image of Sinclair-Demian on the last page of the book, and the whispering voice of blood in the temporally later prologue. The metaphors, like the self they reflect, are and remain split.

CHAPTER FOUR

Adolescent Spaces

The garden is the mythic habitat of the child. What are the spaces of the adolescent who has outgrown the paradise of childhood? Literary adolescence is full of nostalgic references to mythical gardens, but the "real" gardens of adolescence are in the city, and urban spaces represent its changing scenery. Unspoilt nature is an object of yearning; the often abhorred but irresistibly fascinating cityscape is where events take place.

At first sight, the romantic topos of unspoilt nature seems to have retained its magic. Wedekind's metaphoric title (as well as Franz Stuck's spring meadow frontispiece for the first edition) suggests that adolescence is natural awakening. In this play, woods, riverbanks, parks, and gardens seem to offer freedom to the young. Adult civilization is a stuffy conference room, where portraits of Jean-Jacques Rousseau and Johann Pestalozzi observe how teachers farcically debate whether to let in the fresh air (3.1).

And yet, nature is enigmatic in Wedekind's play. Melchior's and Wendla's first open-air love scene begins tenderly but ends with a sadomasochistic beating of the girl, and during their second encounter in a hayloft Melchior exclaims, "There is no love! Everything is self-interest, egotism! I love you as little as you love me!" (2.4). In bourgeois society, adolescent sexuality is taboo and its depiction lacks the poignant naturalness of Romeo's and Juliet's love. Wedekind ridicules the follies of *adult society* as mercilessly as Shakespeare, but he offers no moral antidote. Desperately searching for moral guidelines that would replace their parents' hypocrisy, Wedekind's adolescents find only Social Darwinism and Nietzschean skepticism. They are not heroes battling parental corruption in the name of healthy nature, merely bewildered and awkward children who no longer know how to act naturally.

THE GARDEN

What, then, remains of the garden? Of course, all gardens are products of civilization; but for adolescents, this mythic secluded place has fragmented into many different locales, none of them pure, all of them contaminated, cultivated, and dragged into the sphere of urban civilization.

To be adolescent means to be banished from the garden. Friedrich Huch's undeservedly forgotten novel *Mao* is the story of a child whose early years are illuminated by the blissful hours spent with his adored mother in their mysterious garden. The remembrance of that bliss prevents Thomas from entering adolescence. When he is thirteen, his ambitious and successful father decides to move to a larger, more representative house. Thomas conceals the wounds of this eviction from paradise by withdrawing completely. When he finally musters the courage to pass the old house he sees the trunk of his favorite tree being transported away, and his will to live collapses. He returns to the half-demolished old house in the dark, climbs to an upper floor, and is seized by a vision, in which "the leaves of an enormous tree blazed and roared above him, swung in circles of fire. Black fruits popped and burst asunder and shot the golden, glowing dust of infinite sparks upon the old home." And then: "a monstrous harp rang, snapped, and split. Next day, in the pale morning light, workers found him in the depth below, dead."[1]

Such alienations from pure gardens were rare. As Carl Schorske (*Fin-de-siècle* 279–360) has shown of Viennese culture, transformations of and explosions in the garden were more frequent. Indeed, transformed gardens of all varieties became spaces of adolescence. The major variety in England was the sports field that converted the green of the meadows into a scene of physical competition for the good of societal and national values. On the continent, fictional as well as real (see Blüher on "Veit's garden" in chapter

10) adolescents have imaginatively transformed urban plots of land for games. Such a transformation of a cityscape in the collective imagination of a group, which differs from the nostalgic evocation of imaginary gardens by solitary individuals, is, in fact, the subject of Molnár's novel. Time and again its narrator sings panegyrics of the "grund"—not of the plot of soil but of its transformation:

> Did we need for a more beautiful place for having fun? We city kids surely didn't need any other place. We could not imagine anything more beautiful, more indian-like. . . .
>
> You beautiful, healthy pupils of the plain, who need only take one step to be outside in the endless open countryside, . . . you have no idea what a vacant lot means for a kid in Pest. For a kid in Pest these are his lowlands, his plain, his open country. For him, this lot means boundlessness and freedom. A tiny plot of land, bounded on one side by crumbling planks and on all the others by tall buildings rising towards the sky. Today, a five-story building is brooding on top of the Pál Street plot, full of inhabitants, amidst whom perhaps nobody knows that this tiny earth was the youth of a few poor pupils in Pest. . . .
>
> This tiny, barren, uneven earth of Pest . . . which was American prairie in the morning, Hungarian plain in the afternoon, sea when it rained, north pole in the winter—it was their friend and turned into whatever they wished it to become just to entertain them.[2]

As in *Törless*, literary gardens assume symbolic values in narratives about adolescence. In one version, the paternal cultivated garden is consciously rejected in favor of an abandoned urban plot. When one of Wedekind's adolescents remarks that she wants to bring up her children "as weeds in our flowergarden" (1.3), the image captures her rejection of regimentation, utilitarianism, and even bourgeois aesthetics, but the desire for the rank growth of weeds complicates the notion of nature. In Thomas Mann's *Buddenbrooks* the consul's similar preference for a wild, uncultivated plot of land outside the city boundaries represents a "romantic" extravagance within the civic order that foreshadows the family's future decline and extinction.

In the opening chapter of Gide's *Counterfeiters,* entitled "The Luxembourg Gardens," a poetically inclined adolescent wants to write a story about a day in the life of a path in these gardens. His epilogue would show "the same garden path at night, after everyone has gone, deserted and much more beautiful than in the day-time. In the deep silence; all the natural sounds intensified—the sound of the fountain, and the wind in the trees, and the song of a night-bird" (8).

Thus Lucien's symbolist project would conclude with a stationary tableau of sounds, drained of human life and visual impulses. Other literary gardens serve as similar emblems. If the garden is infantile paradise in Huch's novel, and ancestral soil to revitalize Philippe's "hitherto uprooted emotions" in Barrès's *Le Jardin de Bérénice* (294), it is adult wisdom in Leopold Andrian-Werburg's novella, *Der Garten der Erkenntnis* (*The Garden of Knowledge,* 1895). In contrast to Huch's Thomas, who is driven from the garden before reaching adolescence, Andrian-Werburg's Erwin never matures to enter and cultivate it with adult Voltairean wisdom. He drifts along, passively registers his chance encounters, and dies finally in the city of Vienna. The motto of the story, "Ego Narcissus," accurately reflects Erwin's lack of involvement with others, but it does not imply its reverse, the cultivation of his self, for he dies as ignorant of himself as of the world. His passivity is skillfully reflected by a narrative mode that rigorously limits itself to his vision but always speaks for him in indirect discourse instead of letting him speak in his own voice— save the quoted phrase "Das Fest des Lebens" (the feast of life, 41) and a brief dialogue (51–52). Like Erwin, the narrator cannot fathom others, he only acts as a spokesman for his tongue-tied protagonist.

ROOMS

Gardens are the objects of reverie, but the daydreaming itself usually occurs within private rooms. The transition from garden to private room is a move from childhood into adolescence, or, rather, from childhood as seen from an adolescent perspective into the adolescent scene itself. Although the mystique of adolescent rooms in literature may be traced back to Raskolnikov's wretched room in Fedor Dostoevski's *Crime and Punishment,* the private room is, of course, a luxury of the affluent.

Tonio Kröger, reading, playing the violin, and dreamily contemplating the walnut tree and the fountain in his garden (276), is perhaps the archetypical adolescent in his room. But the role of the room in constructing an adolescent sense of self is best described by Anatole France's little Pierre. The closing chapter ("My Room") of *Le Petit Pierre* marks the end of childhood: "As soon as I had a room of my own, I became a different person. Overnight I turned from a child into a young man. My ideas and my values were instantaneously formed. I had a way of being, a proper existence. . . . I had an inner life. I was capable of reflection, of meditation. . . . My room separated me from the universe, and I rediscovered the universe in it."[3]

Psychologists at the turn of the century were divided on whether such privacy was advantageous. E. G. Lancaster thought that a penchant for solitude meant self-sufficiency (98), Hall considered the release of the imagination in solitude romance and freedom (*Adolescence* 1: 313), and Charlotte Bühler cited Anatole France to claim that the private room was "pedagogically and socially of highest significance" for introversion, the most important event in the postpubescent phase (*Seelenleben* 49). But Pierre Mendousse considered adolescent solitude dangerous "for the average precocious misanthrope," because it could lead to excessive pride and distorted conceptions of society, even morbidity (168).

By "pride," Mendousse may have meant concretely masturbation, for fin-de-siècle pedagogy and psychology emphatically warned parents against the danger of the "secret vice" (see chapter 8). Fiction voyeuristically spied on adolescent masturbation in private spaces. Joyce reveals metaphorically that Stephen Dedalus's villanelle emerges from a "wet dream" (217 ff.), and in one of the most outrageous scenes (2.3) of *Frühlings Erwachen* Hänschen Rilow "plays" Bluebeard in the toilet. Having "killed off" in previous sessions six reproductions of nudes, including Correggio's *Io* and Bouguereau's *Amor,* he now "sacrifices" Palma Vecchio's *Venus* by tearing it up and flushing it away. The sin he commits while gazing at them is masked with Bluebeard's extended metaphor: "You move in like the ancestral mistress into her abandoned castle. Unseen hands open gate and door, while the fountain down in the park begins to splash." Like Wedekind's other adolescents, Hänschen possesses a precocious wit and erudition, yet his aesthetic sublimation of the transgression is psychologically more credible and effective than Boris's tragic bout with masturbation in *The Counterfeiters.*

Cocteau's *Les Enfants terribles*

Although the private room gives Anatole France's Pierre inner support to grow into an adolescent, it is more often a crustacean defense against the outside world. For Hans Giebenrath in Hesse's *Unterm Rad (Under the Wheel,* 1906) the room, temporarily granted to prepare his exam, becomes a haven "in which he was lord and left undisturbed." Here he can enjoy "those few, magically rare hours full of pride, intoxication, and daring (*Siegesmut*), during which he rose above school, examination, and the rest, dreaming of and yearning to become part of a circle of higher beings."[4]

The epitome of this adolescent bower is undoubtedly Paul's and Elisabeth's *carapace* in *Les Enfants terribles* (1929). Aged fourteen and sixteen, respectively, at the outset, the siblings gradually turn their room into a shrine and a theater in which to act out their lives.

At first, the scenery does not seem to differ much from the chaos of familiar teenage dens: "Without the beds, one could have mistaken it for a storage room. Boxes, underwear, and towels littered the floor. . . . Pages of magazines, newspapers, and program booklets depicting filmstars, boxers, and murderers were thumbtacked everywhere onto the walls."[5] However, when Paul is forced to stay in bed, the aggravated disorder metamorphoses into imaginary land-scapes: "These vistas of chests, these lakes of paper, these mountains of underwear were the village of the sick and his décor. Elisabeth delighted in destroying the key lookouts, levelling the mountains under the pretext of a waiting laundress, and raising with her hands that storm temperature without which neither of them could live."[6]

When the children become orphaned, their autonomous adolescence and their room enter a symbiotic existence. Marietta, the new caretaker, admires the creative genius of the room and protects it, for, the narrator adds, "these children were creating a true masterpiece, one made of what they themselves *were*. Intelligence had no place in it, its charm derived from being without pride and purpose."[7] Hence the artistic power of the room does not derive (how could it?) from beauty, order, and cohesion, qualities that were tradi-tionally identified as intrinsic to works of art, but from its negation of the surrounding utility and rationality. The room embodies two other features that have been regarded as criteria of aesthetic objects ever since Kant, namely *purposelessness* and *autonomy*.

After a vacation (during which the children acquire the habit of stealing "for no particular purpose"), the room assumes the nautical metaphor of being put to sea: "Its sail was further unfurled, its cargo more dangerous, the waves higher. In the unique childhood world one could both float and be driven. As with opium, staying calm became as dangerous as breakneck speed."[8]

This foreshadows a tensing of nerves in confinement. After protracted fights with Elisabeth, Paul succeeds in draping a red rag around the lamp, mysti-fying the space and endowing it with a stagelike quality. Each night after eleven, ritual fights break out between the two, a theater of insults, teasing, offense, and reconciliation. Yet the narrator insists that all this occurs in-nocently and without malice, for the actors on stage were unaware of playing roles: "This primal simplicity endowed the piece with an eternal youth. They did not realize that their play (the room, if you wish) verged on myth."⁹

By calling the children "innocent," the stealing "purposeless," and the fighting "ritual," the narrator aestheticizes behaviors that would normally be judged on moral grounds, and he ascribes aesthetic qualities to acts rather than to objects. Indeed, the magic of the room and the theatrics in it depend on the children's imaginations, not on the physical space; it continues to exert its charm when they move to a palace they inherit from Elisabeth's tragically deceased bridegroom and Paul reinstalls his paraphernalia and his mountains of laundry in a useless room.

But the narrator cannot indefinitely aestheticize the events, and the aesthetic space around the siblings has never been completely autonomous. They are joined from the beginning by Gérard, who first admires Paul but later transfers his unrequited attachment to Elisabeth. Furthermore, Elisabeth decides at one point to start working, and although this proves to be short-lived she brings Agathe, another orphan, into the circle. The inevitable happens: Paul falls in love with Agathe. His declaration of love is intercepted, however, by Elisabeth, who maneuvers the others into believing that Gérard and Agathe love each other. When the net of lies finally tears, Paul takes poison and Elisabeth shoots herself. As she falls, she pulls down a screen that blocked the light, and the pale winter sun "turns the secret room into a theater open to spectators."¹⁰ The last vestiges of aesthetic autonomy have vanished.

The tragic result of Elisabeth's intrigues, motivated by her incestuous love-hate relationship with Paul, can no longer be couched in aesthetic terms: the narrator's comments and qualifications in the last chapters consistently support the title, namely that the children are *terrible*.

But why are these late-adolescents called "children" throughout the book? Does the "infantization" of adolescents not reinforce the initial notion of their "innocence," by exempting them of (legal) responsibility? Perhaps. Yet Cocteau's narrator does not intend to replicate the romantic myth of innocent children, for he writes, after all, about the evil within them. The survival of vocabulary cannot conceal the worn-out romantic juxtaposition of innocence and experience.

The childhood of Cocteau's "terrible" children is over. The metaphor of the room-ship setting out to sea implies cutting loose from the firm land of childhood identity and inherited values. The ship at sea permits its habitants an atavistic return to a primitive state where the moral and aesthetic values of civilization do not yet reign. Hall claims that identity formation begins anew during adolescence from such a precivilized state (see chapter 8), and he adds that some fixated youths never develop the new identity needed to function in civilization. Such, it seems, are Cocteau's "terrible children," whose fixation reflects the fascination of Cocteau's age and Cocteau's narrator with what was called primitivism. Instead of opposing adulthood to child-hood, the story contrasts adulthood with its "naked" state, its raw emotions stripped of their civilizing veneer. The narrator, Gérard, and Agathe are fas-cinated voyeurs, incapable of shedding their clothes in a similar way. The interference of the latter two, their complicitous participation in the siblings' primitive rituals, is what finally sinks the ship. There can be no autonomous adolescence in civilization.

SCHOOL

Educational institutions allow the adolescent subculture to crystallize, al-though (or perhaps because) its spaces are under adult control: the classroom, the hallway, the teachers' conference room, the dormitory, and the school yard become scenes of confrontations between adolescents and adults and enhance the coherence of the peer group. Although adult authority is only occasionally challenged directly (in *Stalky & Co.,* for example), the teachers cut a bad figure in most confrontations and become ridiculous in many of them: Stalky & Co. repeatedly outwits its elders (save the dictatorial Head); Tonio has a grotesque dance instructor; François's parents in *Le Grand Meaulnes* are kind but irrelevant; Törless's teachers are uncomprehending; the teachers in Wedekind's *Frühlings Erwachen,* who carry names like *Zungenschlag* (Mr. Stammer) and *Sonnenstich* (Mr. Sunstroke), avoid issues by arguing about open-ing the window; the director in *Les Enfants terrible* has pepper thrown in his face by Paul's mysterious friend Dargelos; most of Claudine's teachers in Wil-ly's and Colette's *Claudine à l'école* are assistants barely beyond adolescence, her principal is infatuated with one of them. Although the teachers may be pomp-ous, severe, sometimes even sadistic, their authority is often opposed with mar-tial cunning and wit. Whereas Thomas Mann's Hanno Buddenbrook enters school with a tragic sense of doom, the schoolboy in Frigyes Karinthy's brilliant series of interior monologues resourcefully redesigns his daily battle plans:

At eight, the day is still misty, and the chances and probabilities of the day ahead are taking shape, blurred and stumbling, in my sleepy head. Life is fraught with mortal dangers for the secondary-school boy, it is going to war that's renewed daily for eight consecutive years: at eight o'clock sharp every morning he dashes into the fluctuating battlefield of chance, among cunningly set traps, and fatal, decisive events. He sustains wounds and inflicts them. Sometimes he is left to bleed to death. Next day, he rises from the dead to start it all over again. . . .

This morning, his weapons are somewhat incomplete; therefore they have to be selected with much care.

First period—Mathematics. We have reached the subject of irrational equations, but have not yet got through the topic in the last lesson. Chances of being tested—25 to 27 per cent. This small percentage takes account of the fact that lots of boys haven't had a chance to better their bad marks yet, and that Fröhlich is an unstable character, an unequal-tempered, weak-willed person who yesterday may have believed sincerely that he would go on with his demonstration next time, but would now, all of a sudden, and without meaning it, begin to test the boys. You have to reckon with pathological symptoms like that, which are found in the hidden recesses of the human soul. (19–20)

In continental secondary schools, education was a protracted battle; school stories tend to depict the colorful clashes around the educational process, leaving the core unexamined, as if it were irrelevant. In fact, we do not see Stalky & Co., Tonio, Stephen, Demian, or the "terrible children" in class, for this is not where their existential soul searching takes place.

True learning happens elsewhere: its fictional genre is the bildungsroman, its modern classic Thomas Mann's *Magic Mountain,* in which a postadolescent youth is educated in a sanatorium in the shadow of death. Occasionally, a subject of reading or study may preoccupy an adolescent: imaginary numbers disturb Törless, Tonio empathizes with Schiller's figure of Philipp II, Stephen Dedalus formulates a Thomistic aesthetics, Silbermann brings Racine's verses to life, Bouteiller's pupils are fired up by Kantian ethics. But these are exceptions, deviations from rather than results of the school. In Thomas Mann's *Buddenbrooks,* Hesse's *Unterm Rad,* Kipling's *Stalky & Co.,* and elsewhere, school reduces literature and the arts to facts and rote memorizing.

Classrooms and schools provide educational value mainly as the setting in which socialization takes place. Törless's true education occurs in the secret attic room where the bullies Beineberg and Reiting torture Basini, and the dormitory where Basini slips into his bed. In the games, cliques, and fights of the school yard, adolescents learn the art of survival.

THE STREET

Like the secondary schools, the city streets were produced by industrialization and urbanization. Their literary image became as ambiguous as the portrayal of modern civilization in general.

At one end of the spectrum, the city was portrayed as hell. What Alain-Fournier's rural narrator reconstructs from Augustin's urban experiences is a counterpoint to rural purity. Keeping his weary watch under Yvonne's window in Paris, Meaulnes experiences urban hell: "In the twilight a policeman goes by. He is conducting to the nearest police station a miscreant who mutters all the insults and obscenities he can think of. The officer is furious, white-faced but silent. As they reach the corridor he begins to strike. Then he closes the door and is free to beat the poor devil at leisure . . . A horrible fancy takes hold of me: I have renounced heaven and stand impatiently at the gates of hell" (192, ellipses in original).

Meaulnes's later visit to Bourges, also reconstructed but this time told by François, reconfirms the urban alienation: the great cathedral lumbered above him "huge and indifferent," around him here and there was "a red lantern over a doorway, the sign of an equivocal hospitality." Amidst squalor and vice he had "a peasant's fear of, and a peasant's repugnance towards, this vast edifice where all the vices were carved in hidden corners, this church flanked by brothels and offering no remedy for the deep sorrows of a pure love . . ."

Meaulnes subsequently encounters two girls who provocatively stare at him and he accepts a rendezvous with one of them, "half disgusted, half reckless, as if to take revenge on his love or destroy it," in the Archbishop's garden, where Frantz once had a rendezvous with Valentine. To be sure, he fails to show up (200–201).

In other stories, city streets represent temptation, fascination, or simply spaces for socialization. And as social spaces, they are neither for the *flanneur* nor for the bourgeois family to promenade on Sundays; instead, they occasion adolescent conversations, as in *Tonio Kröger* or in *A Portrait,* where the city is an obsessive theme and the principal action, amidst conversation or revery, is walking (Levin 19, 43). Tonio and his fellow pupils in Molnár's Budapest may have to reverently lift their caps to their teachers, but they rarely meet policemen, who seem to protect rather than suppress them. The pupils in turn-of-the-century fiction rarely encounter the urban underworld and the urban vice that continuously lurk behind Dickens's boys. The relative safety of fictional adolescents starkly contrasts with the loud adult warnings against the corrupting influence of the cities in real life.

Indeed, city streets represent freedom for the boys of Pál Street when released from school: "All of them were ambling down the splendidly sunny street, tired and hungry. The haze that circulated in their heads dissolved only very slowly to reveal the many cheerful and life-signifying sights that the street offers. Like little prisoners who have just been released, they staggered in the plentitude of fresh air and sunshine; they rambled into this noisy, fresh, animated city, which was for them nothing but a disorderly medley of carriages, horse-drawn trams, streets, and shops through which they had to find their way home."[11]

But relative freedom from adult seductions and coercions does not make the streets safe for adolescents. Precisely because authority is barely visible on the street, the loners undergo traumatic clashes with other adolescents, whose size and strength often represent classes and forces outside the bourgeois order. Although Molnár's fictional Pál Street boys fought infinitely more gallantly than the real New York gangs described by Riis, the traumas were genuine. Hesse's Sinclair, it will be remembered, fell into the hands of Franz Kromer on the street, and Cocteau's *Les Enfants terribles* opens with a sinister snowball fight, in which Paul is severely wounded by a stone-filled snowball thrown by his adored friend Dargelos. Threats from within the peer group make the streets precarious.

CHAPTER FIVE

Literary Adolescence:
An Overview

Modern adolescence emerged from nineteenth-century social and institutional changes, but identity crises of youth, generational conflicts, processes of maturation, and initiation rites were traditional themes of literature well before adolescence as we know it emerged. Earlier literary portrayals of youth anticipate features I have been describing, but they differ in their narrative forms and in the institutional settings they depict.

Traditional literary elaborations on the "ages of man" inconsistently categorize the stages of youth. Shakespeare's Jacques sees the schoolboy suddenly mature into a lover:

> All the world's a stage,
> And all the men and women merely players.
> They have their exits and their entrances,
> And one man in his time plays many parts,
> His acts being seven ages. At first the infant,

Mewling and puking in the nurse's arms.
Then the whining schoolboy, with his satchel
And shining morning face, creeping like snail
Unwilling to school. And then the lover,
Sighing like furnace, with a woeful ballad
Made to his mistress' eyebrow.

(*As You Like It,* II, vii)

Although Shakespeare did not use the term and he described the age differently, he knew of an adolescent period in life. The shepherd in *The Winter's
Tale* fears what Jacques overlooks: "I would there were no age between ten
and three and twenty, or that youth would sleep out the rest. For there is
nothing in the between but getting wenches with child, wronging the an-
cientry, stealing, fighting" (III, iii). And, of course, Shakespeare knew of Romeo's and Juliet's passionate "mid-adolescence," so dominated by their first
love that they totally break with their families instead of passing through an
extended conflict between parental and peer-group loyalty (Dalsimer 77 ff.).
Shakespeare's most typical adolescents are Hamlet and Prince Hal: the former,
if we believe Freud, for struggling to overcome his Oedipal complex, the latter
for emancipating himself from Falstaff and his cohorts.[1] Last but not least,
pubescents and adolescents peopled Shakespeare's stage by enacting the female roles.

The first adolescents in Western fiction are the narrator-heroes of the
picaresque novels. Vagabond rogues like Lazarillo de Tormes (1554), Mateo
Alemán's Guzmán de Alfarache (1599–1604), Grimmelshausen's Simplicius
Simplicissimus (1669), Lesage's Gil Blas (1715–35) and Defoe's Moll Flanders
(1722) grow up by attempting to survive in hard times. In contrast to modern
literary adolescents, who are well provided for and preoccupied mostly with
internal problems and their peers, the picaros are without financial support,
formal education, and a "moratorium": they learn their lessons amidst war,
poverty, and social unrest. Picaro features reemerge in Cocteau's Thomas
(l'imposteur), Milords, the protagonist of Francis Carco's *Les Innocents,* and
other adolescents trying to survive World War I.

The youth of eighteenth-century literature includes Richardson's Pamela
and Clarissa Harlowe, Smollett's Roderick Random, Fielding's Joseph Andrews and Tom Jones, Rousseau's St. Preux, and Goethe's Werther. As Patricia Spacks has shown in her excellent chapter on English eighteenth-century
fiction (*Adolescent Idea* 89–118), their powerful passions repeatedly clash with
the social forces of control. In this they resemble their later descendants. But

whereas eighteenth-century English novelists "glorify maturity, as the social mythology of the age glorified it, yet try to imagine a mature mode that neutralizes the threat, without sacrificing the energies, of the dangerous age" (107), turn-of-the-century novelists may be said to participate in a new "social mythology," in which maturity is no longer the standard and adolescence is often the subject of glorification.

In the eighteenth-century novel, the adolescent years are marginal or absent, and the problems of youth differ from those of the modern adolescent: St. Preux and Werther experience adult insecurity due to their bourgeois birth and their hopeless love, the young English protagonists are usually struggling to pass from adolescence into marriage. Tom Jones's life between fourteen and nineteen is condensed into the short Book III; although the story ends before his twenty-first birthday, his amorous and other adventures would class him as postadolescent in turn-of-the-century literature. Eighteenth-century English youth of the more prosperous classes may have enjoyed a "psychosocial moratorium" (Spacks, *Adolescent Idea* 99), but there was no "peer group," and the crises could not fundamentally threaten their identity, for the "eighteenth-century fictional adolescents appear fixed . . . youth is already what he will become" (Spacks *Adolescent Idea* 112). This holds not only for the "ineluctably good" Tom and the "unalterably bad" Blifil, but also for the genuinely adolescent and permanently androgynous characters of eighteenth-century literature: Cherubin-Cherubino by Beaumarchais, da Porte, and Mozart, and Mignon in Goethe's *Wilhelm Meister's Apprenticeship* (1795–96). Goethe's novel marks the beginning of the bildungsroman, the novel of education, which is occasionally considered to cover the period of adolescence. But the distinguished German nineteenth-century bildungsromans, as well as some of George Eliot's novels and Flaubert's *Education sentimentale,* usually cover the heroes' postadolescent experiences outside educational institutions, involve an itinerant quest, and end with marriage.[2]

Whereas the bildungsroman explores the transition from late adolescence into adulthood, romantic literature focuses on the antecedent of adolescence, childhood. Romanticism sets the child as a symbol of innocence against adult corruption. In Blake's and Wordsworth's poetry, in Novalis's *Die Lehrlinge zu Sais* and other romantic works, children represent paradise and the golden age. As symbols, they tend to be fixed, although Blake's mythology and Tieck's subtle psychological novella *Der blonde Eckbert* contain frightening tales of puberty: the Fall into sin from the innocence of childhood. To the remaining youths in romantic literature we may apply Justin O'Brien's remark con-

77

cerning the adolescents in the stories of Chateaubriand, Musset, and Flaubert: their characterization strikingly omits "the intellectual awakening and the crisis of puberty—the two dominant characteristics of adolescence in all epochs" (4–5). Around midcentury, George Sand could still complain that poets and novelists had overlooked adolescence.[3]

Nevertheless, by midcentury, school experiences, postpubescent years, and adolescent friendships started to move from the fringes to the center of literature. The initial works are marginal in more than one sense. In some important works like Balzac's *Louis Lambert* and Dickens's *David Copperfield,* the protagonists' school experiences constitute a relatively brief episode within the depiction of their epic growth from early childhood into marriage and beyond; other works, like Flaubert's *Novembre* (1842) (first published in 1914) and Dostoevski's, *Netochka Nezvanova* (1849), are early novel fragments, marginal to the author's oeuvre. The third and largest "margin" constitutes a whole new literary genre, the English "public school story," which chose, for the first time, secondary schools as the locus of fiction and adolescents as protagonists. In contrast to Isabel Quigly, I shall exclude from this genre novels like Walpole's *Mr. Perrin and Mr. Traill* and G. F. Bradby's *The Lanchester Tradition,* which take place in public schools but focus on adults. My classification in terms of characters rather than place would go a long way to eliminate Quigly's problematic distinction between the popular and "the more adult, more individual" novels (Quigly 43–44), which (only) partly coincides with the line separating works with adolescent from those with adult readers. In fact, the classic school stories always had a mixed readership. My discussion of school stories includes books both about and for schoolchildren, regardless of whether these works also attracted adult readers. Because of its intended readers, this genre belongs in the fourth section of this chapter, but for comparative purposes I shall include it here and discuss in the later section only the stories serialized in magazines. To avoid duplicating Quigly's otherwise excellent discussion of these stories, I shall note only a few salient aspects of this genre that originates with Thomas Hughes's *Tom Brown's Schooldays* (1857) and includes Frederick Farrar's *Eric or Little by Little* (1858), Talbot Reed's *The Fifth Form at St. Dominic's* (1887), Kipling's *Stalky & Co.* (1899), the early works of Wodehouse, as well as the countless serialized stories.

Tom Brown's Schooldays unites two opposite elements that usually mix but often crystallize only in separate works: documentary and fantasy. To create a picture of Rugby and its great reformer Thomas Arnold, Hughes uses a fictional Tom, and the resultant work is partly a work of the imagination, partly a historical document. Whatever its shortcomings in either respect, it has become a classic literary evocation of the public schools that set a pattern for later works and that we may profitably compare with the (later) literary images of the German and French schools. The contrast is particularly striking if we keep the anguished school experiences in German literature in mind. Hughes considers school a social rather than academic experience: "The object of all schools is not to ram Latin and Greek into boys, but to make the good English boys, good future citizens; and by far the most important part of that work must be done, or not done, out of school hours" (63). Furthermore, this education for citizenship is largely carried out within the peer group, not only in the course of football and cricket games but also within the residential houses and in the hierarchical power structure of the forms (grades), whose cruel practices even Arnold was reluctant to reform from above. In comparison, academic questions are completely marginal and do not threaten the boys. Although Tom occasionally suffers from the injustice of his fellow schoolboys, suicide never enters his mind, and this remains true of the later schoolboys as well. The typical traumatic events of school stories—stolen exam papers, accidents out in nature, false accusations, intrigues—almost unfailingly find their happy resolution.

Although some new works did appear in the twenties, this genre essentially exhausted itself by the end of World War I, partly because of internal ossification, and partly because of increasing problems within the public schools themselves. The seventeen-year-old Alec Waugh wrote one of the last major works, the rather wooden *The Loom of Youth,* between January and March 1916 as a soldier in a camp. The war and the military changed his perspective on the public schools:

> I was in a nostalgic mood, but I was also in a rebellious mood. Intensely though I had enjoyed my four years at Sherborne, I had been in constant conflict with authority. That conflict, so it seemed to me, had been in the main caused and determined by authority's inability or refusal to recognise the true nature of school life. The Public School system was venerated as a pillar of the British Empire and out of that veneration had grown a myth of the ideal Public School boy—Kipling's Brush Wood Boy. In no sense had I incarnated such a myth and it had been responsible, I felt, for half my troubles. I wanted to expose it. Those moods of nostalgia and rebellion fused finally in an imperious need to relive my school days on paper, to put it all down, term by term, exactly as it had been, to explain, interpret, justify my point of view. (9–10)

The book did create considerable controversy, but Waugh's 1954 preface admits that the modern reader "will find nothing here to shock or startle" (12). Cheating at exams and excessive emphasis on sports are described but hardly criticized, and one finds here no impassioned or soul-searching exposition of the deepest moral dilemma, the pervasive homosexuality. Instead, it is only discreetly hinted at and shown to lead to expulsion if discovered.

Henry James draws the most subtle teenagers in turn-of-the-century English literature. After earlier figures like Nora Lambert in *Watch and Ward* (1878) and Pansy Osmond in *The Portrait of a Lady* (1881), James devoted the better part of a decade to writing about young girls (Shine vii), including Maisie Farange in *What Maisie Knew* (1897), the telegraphist of *In the Cage* (1898), and Nanda Brookenham in *The Awkward Age* (1899), his most thorough study of adolescence. James started from the romantic dichotomy between innocence and experience but concentrated on hesitant sensibilities in the obscure intermediary zone between them. Since his settings include no "moratorium," no school, and no peer group, adolescent socialization in his novels occurs through interaction with parents, governesses, and other adults. Nanda's taciturn personality is, for instance, conditioned by the absence of a peer group, and the emptiness of the adult discourse to which she is exposed when "sitting downstairs." The novel's famed attempt to convey a story almost exclusively by conversation, that is public language, served as a vehicle to communicate this typical predicament of Jamesian adolescence.

Dostoevski's *The Adolescent,* written during the period of his last, great novels in 1874, reveals what Dostoevski's oeuvre in general bequeathed to the novels of adolescence. Its protagonist, just out of school and seemingly on the threshold of adulthood, is still struggling to gain an identity, due to his unresolved Oedipal conflict. But early drafts of the novel portray a conflict between two life periods of a single person as well as a conflict between two brothers, indicating that the protagonist's problematic relation to his father is a symptom rather than the cause of the identity crisis. In Dostoevski's world, identity crises exist in many forms and in all ages: his characters are eternal adolescents, split figures without stability, eternally warring selves seeking in vain to secure an identity. Gide considered the "incoherence of the personality" and the "cohabitation of contradictory feelings" to be Dostoevski's great discovery (Massis, *Jugements* 2: 44); Alain-Fournier enthusiastically read *The Adolescent* while working on *Le Grand Meaulnes* (letter to Jacques Rivière, July 21, 1911).

Turning to the enormous body of adolescent literature around 1900 we note a remarkable divergence of national traditions. The English school story emerged early and showed great resilience, whereas German literary adolescence burst on the scene in the nineties after *Frühlings Erwachen*. Barrès's *Le Culte du moi* (1888–91), Mirbeau's *Sébastien Roch* (1890), and Gide's *Les Cahiers d'André Walter* (1891) also appeared in those years, although French schools and schoolboys entered literature only later, in passing with Barrès's *Les Déracinés* (1897), and as the central subject in Willy and Colette's *Claudine à l'école* (1900) and Larbaud's *Fermina Márquez* (1911). The number of French school stories remains relatively low when compared to English and German literature; a higher proportion of French adolescent literature deals with non-school experiences, including love. Almost every national literature produced boarding school stories. Examples from the smaller literatures are Lodewijk van Deyssel's Dutch novel, which carries the revealing title *De kleine republiek* (1889), and Zsigmond Móricz's *Be Faithful unto Death*.

To pinpoint a closure for literary adolescence is as difficult as to set a terminal date for adolescence itself: both extend themselves indefinitely and reemerge later. The great watershed of World War I did not diminish the literary concern with adolescence; instead, it refocused the theme by incorporating the war experience, as in the case of Hesse's *Demian,* Cocteau's *Thomas l'imposteur,* and Radiguet's *Le Diable au corps.*

But the postwar trends significantly differed in France, Germany, and England. In France, O'Brien observes, "it is during the ten or twelve years immediately following the World War that the literary exaltation of the adolescent reaches its height" (8). These were the years when works by François Mauriac, Lacretelle, Cocteau, and Radiguet appeared, together with Henry de Montherlant's *La Relève du matin* (1920), a work that O'Brien calls "the most articulate statement of the cult of adolescence" (38), Gide's *Les Faux-monnayeurs* (1925), and Jean Desbordes's *J'Adore* (1928), an apex of "the cult of spontaneity" according to O'Brien (42). Several of them received coveted literary prizes. Only around 1930 did Jaloux and others start to object to the surfeit of adolescents in fiction.

In contrast, few important English works on adolescence were published during the twenties; in Germany only Fleisser's merciless exposure of adolescent cruelty brought a new approach to the subject; elsewhere, the only outstanding new work on adolescence was Alberto Moravia's *Gli Indifferenti* (1929). *Neue Sachlichkeit* (new sobriety or objectivity), so powerfully represented by Fleisser, was generally unfavorable to the treatment of adolescence in the German-speaking countries. The contrast between the new climate and expressionism is well captured in the article "Männliche Literatur" ("Manly Literature," 1929) by Kurt Pinthus, a leading expressionist and editor of the famous anthology *Menschheitsdämmerung* (1919). By 1925, Pinthus suggested, the manliness of the *Neue Sachlichkeit* had replaced the "shouting, demanding, rebellious youth" of expressionism, where "the central figure was the young man, whose radiance illuminated all the other figures. The blaze and anger of this youth seems spent now . . . and from the ashes of the fallen triumphantly arises: man. . . . What matters now is not youth, but becoming or being man" (903, first ellipses in original).

Although not all the adolescents of the previous decades were "shouting, demanding, rebellious," a shift of interest from adolescence to sober adulthood was typical of German literature in the twenties. Not until Günter Grass's *Katz und Maus* (*Cat and Mouse,* 1961) does adolescence reappear in German literature.

QUESTIONS OF GENRE

O'Brien notes that "like the *chanson de gest,* the picaresque novel, the *drame bourgeois,* or the bildungsroman, the [French] novel of adolescence constitutes a literary tradition" (13). The statement holds true for German and English literature as well. But why are there no comparable traditions in poetry and drama? Why did fiction become the preferred medium for representing adolescence? Would it not be more logical to expect that lyric introspection and theatrical show, masks, and role playing would appeal most to adolescents as modes of self-expression?

A qualified negative answer must consider several different aspects. Poetry and the stage may indeed offer modes of expression to adolescents, but the main body of literature concerning adolescence was written by and for *adults,* who preferred subtle and form-conscious literature to emotions served raw. Adolescent anger or *Weltschmerz* are usually amateurish, and the fin-de-siècle climate was particularly unfavorable to them. The symbolist idiom disdained melodramatic romanticism and spoke by indirection and suggestion, through masks and intertexts, rather than personally. Modernism followed suit: Mallarmé's syntactic mannerisms, Laforgue's Pierot poems, Pound's imagism, Eliot's ironic intertextual weavings, Rilke's *Dinggedichte* (thing-poems), and Trakl's color-collages were ill-suited to reflect spontaneous bursts of adolescent expression. The stylistic reservations of the dominant taste are evident in the baroque turns of Mirbeau's preface to Francis de Croisset's collection of adolescent poems *Les Nuits de quinze ans* (1898): "If your *Nights* are not yet a masterpiece, they raise the hope for it, and that is much already, that is also very rare. They are so precious to me because they are very truly the cry and (in spite of their occasional artificiality) the spontaneous gushing of your youth, the occasionally naive expression (due to being insolently young) of your (and our) dreams of adolescence."[4] Only Hugo von Hofmannsthal's adolescent poems, Mauriac's *L'Adieu à l'adolescence* (1911), Radiguet's *Les Joues en feu* (1920), some poems written by Gide's fictional André Walter, Oskar Kokoschka's *Die träumenden Knaben* (see chapter 6), and a handful of expressionist poems escape being maudlin. Whether Stephen Dedalus's villanelle should be counted among them is a matter of scholarly debate.

Theater, at least in Germany, presents a different problem. Pathos-filled Oedipal conflicts are at the heart of Wedekind's *Frühlings Erwachen,* Max Halbe's *Jugend* (1893), Kurt Martens's *Wie ein Stahl verglimmt* (1895), Gerhardt Hauptmann's *Michael Kramer* (1900), Walter Hasenclever's *Der Sohn* (1914), Hanns Johst's *Der Junge Mensch* (1916), and Arnolt Bronnen's *Vatermord* (1920). Expressionist dramas developed new stage forms and a new language, but they remained schematic in characterization and their adolescent heroes were idealized models of the "new man" fighting against a corrupt father. Inner conflicts and the pressures of a cruel peer group appear only in Fleisser's *Fegefeuer in Ingolstadt* (*Purgatory in Ingolstadt,* 1926).

Father-son conflicts play a strikingly lesser role in fiction. In most narratives this conflict is simply absent; in some (*Tonio Kröger, Silbermann, The Counterfeiters*) it provides a subsidiary theme, but even when the tension between father and son appears as a central theme, as in Mauriac's *Le Désert de l'amour* (1925) and Franz Kafka's *The Judgment* (1913), the confrontation is more subtle. Perhaps only Oscar Thibault in Martin du Gard's family epic is truly comparable to the iron-fisted fathers of expressionist drama. But then, in *Les Thibaults*—as in Romain Rolland's *Jean Christophe,* Samuel Butler's *The Way of All Flesh,* Jules Vallès's *Jacques Vingtras,* and other family sagas and novels of education—adolescence appears as only one phase of an extended period. Novel cycles are not, strictly speaking, literature of adolescence.

Contrary to the received opinion that the theater is the most objective genre, expressionist theater tends to be a partisan glorification of rebellious youth, whereas the narrator's (let alone the author's) view of adolescence is often impossible to pinpoint in fiction. Turn-of-the-century fiction experimented with subtle modernist techniques by portraying the hidden recesses of fictional minds and employing multiple focalization. Novelists were attracted to the portrayal of adolescence because the subject demanded portrayals of inner lives and multi-perspectival representations. It was the ideal subject for portraying the loss of identity and the splitting of self that was Nietzsche's and Dostoevski's legacy to turn-of-the-century culture.

LITERATURE BY ADOLESCENTS

Adolescents incessantly speak and write about their problems, but very little of what they write becomes public. The "discovery" of adolescence at the end of the nineteenth century, however, aroused public interest in two traditionally private media: adolescent poetry and diaries.

Rimbaud appears to be the first prominent adolescent poet. The poets of the Sturm und Drang and romanticism wrote their first important works in their twenties. Their surviving juvenilia is unoriginal. The first great adolescent poets were Rimbaud (b. 1854), Hofmannsthal (b. 1874), and Paul Valéry (b. 1871). None of them made a smooth transition from adolescent poet into adult poet: Rimbaud abandoned literature altogether; Hofmannsthal—who recorded the crisis in the fictional "Lord Chandos" letter (*Ein Brief,* 1902)— turned to theater and prose; Valéry stopped writing poetry and resumed it only decades later by completing *La Jeune parque,* an abstract monologue of an adolescent consciousness. The burning out of adolescent poets was as typical of turn-of-the-century culture as was their very appearance.

The appearance of adolescent diaries, considered here as a form of literature, is no less curious than the appearance and disappearance of adolescent poets.[5] The urge to display oneself, warts and all, is a distinctly modern phenomenon, whose beginnings date from Rousseau's *Confessions* (1762). The flood of nineteenth-century autobiographical retrospectives was stimulated to no small degree by the rise of a reading public with ever greater appetite for the private lives of great men. Goethe's correspondence indicates how the expected publication of personal letters and diaries changed their tone; diaries by Gide, Valéry, and others reveal tensions between a private and a public stance.

That people with established reputations should consider even their most private experiences and communications a public matter was perhaps an inevitable consequence of the development of modern media. One would expect a different attitude in adolescent diaries, since their primary function has been to enhance self-expression and formation of identity, not communication with others. Nevertheless, some of the most important modern adolescent diaries were written with publication and ultimate fame in mind.

Anne Frank had distinguished predecessors. The first adolescent diary written with publication in mind (and perhaps the earliest published adolescent diary) was Marie Bashkirtseff's *Journal* (1887), written between the ages of twelve and twenty-four, in the shadow of death but in search of a posterity. As Marie wrote in her preface, she hoped to be remembered as a great artist, but if she were to die before having the chance to create great works of art, she wanted to have her journal published (5) to attain her dream "of glory, of celebrity, of being known everywhere" (17).[6] The still adolescent Hofmannsthal fittingly characterized the journal as "a coquettish and heartfelt letter to an unknown person" (121). Its charm derives partly from Marie's realization that the journal would only be published posthumously (207–8). Its publication was greeted enthusiastically by the hero of Barrès's *Le Cult du moi* (208); William Burnham, following Hall, considered it the best description of female adolescence and "of adolescent activity bordering on neurosis" (177–78).

Such public-oriented adolescent diaries differ from the majority, whose purpose is merely to cope with crisis through self-dialogue and search for expression. How common these diaries were in previous ages is difficult to say, for they remained private and did not survive. At the turn of the century, however, several older diaries were unearthed and published. In some cases (Michelet, for example) the publication may have been related to the author's later fame, or (in Bary's diary, for example) the historical events reported in the diaries, but even in these cases the newfound interest in adolescence was probably a motivating factor. In the first decades of the twentieth century a very large number of anonymous adolescent diaries were published with no other aim but to provide psychoanalysts, psychologists, and sociologists with raw material for studying adolescence.

Hall sought to stimulate writing by and on adolescents in the spirit of his "child study" (see chapter 8): "Many if not most young people should be encouraged to learn enough of the confessional private journalism to teach them self-knowledge, for the art of self-expression usually begins now if ever, when it has a wealth of subjective material and needs forms of expression peculiar to itself" (1: 589). In his enthusiastic preface to *A Young Girl's Diary* (1919), Freud claimed that it offered a hitherto unequalled insight into the emotional life of a pubescent. Charlotte Bühler, a pioneering psychologist of adolescence, considered the Freudian diary eccentric and unrepresentative and approached the matter differently. Seeking a more systematic base, she built up an archive of adolescent diaries in Vienna. By the mid-thirties this archive contained eighty-eight diaries, ranging from 1830 onward, as well as adolescent poetry and correspondence (preface to *Drei Generationen*). She published several of these in commentated editions, and she used them for her own work *Das Seelenleben des Jugendlichen,* for she was convinced that such spontaneous and unrehearsed diaries were the best source for studying adolescence.

But are such diaries ever "unrehearsed"? It is true that most of the ones Bühler used spontaneously and unabashedly report of ever new infatuations and little skirmishes, virtually ignoring social, economic, and national issues, including World War I. Yet their style as well as their values are evidently patterned after models taken as much from their readings as from their parents and schools. Siegfried Bernfeld, former editor of the school journal *Der Anfang* (see chapter 10), rightly set out therefore to study the ways in which traditional forms shape self-expression in adolescent diaries.[7]

LITERATURE FOR ADOLESCENTS

Adolescents consume more literature than they produce. Turn-of-the-century psychologists and pedagogues noted, with delight or concern, that the onset of puberty occasioned a veritable "reading craze" (*Lesewut*). Voracious reading satisfied curiosity, allowed the imagination to roam over exotic lands and possible worlds, and gave insight into the minds of others.[8]

Literature for adolescents appeared after the emergence of children's literature in the eighteenth century, but it is difficult to say just when writers started to write deliberately for an adolescent public. Much of the earlier literature that is now partly or mostly read by adolescents, including Defoe's *Robinson Crusoe* (1719) and Cooper's *The Last of the Mohicans* (1826), was originally intended for adults. In Germany, the first major book written for young readers is generally considered to be Joachim Jacob Campe's (1746–1818) adaptation, *Robinson der Jüngere* (*Robinson the Younger,* 1779). Campe, director of the Dessau Philanthropinum, an innovative gymnasium based on the ideas of Johannes Bernhard Basedow (1723–90), pursued highly didactic aims with his novel.

Not pedagogy but the commercial opportunities offered by the expanding young readership generated the upswing of adolescent literature in the nineteenth century. Authors started to write stories for adolescents, and specialists of the genre emerged, among them Jules Verne (b. 1828), Karl May (b. 1842), Johanna Spyri (b. 1829), and G. A. Henty (b. 1832).[9] The genre clearly divided along sex lines. Although girl's literature flourished, it was generally disdained, and in Germany it even acquired the derogatory name *Backfischliteratur* (literature for bobby-soxers).

Much of this literature first appeared in the magazines for youth that started to mushroom after midcentury. Verne's works were first serialized in the *Musée des familles* (1850–) and *Le Magasin d'éducation et de récréation* (1864–); in England, the popular "bloods" or "penny (later half-penny) dreadfuls" did a flourishing business with stories about Dick Turpin, Jack Sheppard, Sweeney Todd, and other criminals. When in the sixties it was discovered that adolescents avidly read the bloods, Edwin J. Brett, W. L. Emmett, and Charles Fox started magazines expressly for boys that often ran stories about such outlaws. Brett published the most successful "boys' journals," including *The Boys of England* (1866–), *Young Men of Great Britain* (1868–), and *Our Boys' Journal* (1876–), but he failed with *Our Girls' Journal* in 1882.

Commercial success was bought at the price of quality. In 1878 when William Sumner surveyed "What Our [American] Boys Are Reading" in magazines intended for the twelve-to-sixteen-year group, he found a limited stock of stories—neither "markedly profane" nor "obscene," merely "indescribably vulgar" (684)—most frequently featuring city youths, vagabonds, and imps. Their "moral," according to Sumner, was that boys ought to be strong and fight well, ought to cheat the "penurious father" who gives them less money than expected, and ought to drink according to "the bar-room code." Quiet home life was "stupid and unmanly," but one should remain cheerful under all circumstances (684).

Moral indignation aroused by such stories led the Religious Tract Society to start publishing in 1879 *The Boy's Own Paper,* which serialized Verne's *20,000 Leagues under the Sea,* Reed's *The Fifth Form at St. Dominic's,* stories by G. A. Henty, Conan Doyle, and many others. The journal looked for stories in which religion was a pervading spirit rather than a direct doctrinal teaching. Soon it became immensely popular, and by the mid-eighties over half a million copies were printed of each issue. A second "respectable" magazine, *Chums,* appeared in 1892; *The Captain,* which started in 1899, published a number of school stories by Wodehouse. Although these new magazines turned away from the underworld and the glorification of violence, they were by no means always innocent and untainted by ideology. Henty, who became the major writer of juvenile fiction in England after 1880, was particularly interested in the various wars within the empire, which he depicted from an imperialistic perspective. Karl May's ideological position is a matter of continued controversy.

In the nineties, a veritable flood of new magazines was started in England, including the *Halfpenny Wonder* (1892–), the *Halfpenny Marvel* (1893–), the *Boy's Friend* (1895–), *Pluck* (1894–), and *The Union Jack* (1894) by Alfred Harmsworth, who also initiated the detective serials on Sherlock Holmes (1887–), Sexton Blake ("the office-boy's Sherlock Holmes"), and Nick Carter (1900–). After setting up the Amalgamated Press (1902), Harmsworth initiated magazines that took life at the public schools as their subject. The key author of his *Gem* (1907–) and *Magnet* (1908–) became Charles Hamilton, who, it is estimated, wrote about a million-and-a-half words annually under diverse pseudonyms, including that of Frank Richards. The adventures of Billy Bunter at Greyfriars (*Gem*) and Tom Merry at St. Jim's (*Magnet*) turned public schools into mythic locales of games and intrigues. These works captured the imagination of all those who could not afford to get these experiences first-hand: the sons of shopkeepers, office employees, small business and professional men, even workers. Robert Roberts writes in recollecting slum life in Salford:

> Even before the first world war many youngsters in the working class had developed an addiction for Frank Richard's school stories. . . . With nothing in our own school that called for love or allegiance, Greyfriars became for some of us our true Alma Mater, to whom we felt bound by a dreamlike loyalty. . . . Over the years these simple tales conditioned the thought of a whole generation of boys. The public school ethos, distorted into myth and sold among us weekly in penny numbers, for good or ill, set ideals and standards. . . . In the final estimate it may well be found that Frank Richards during the first quarter of the twentieth century had more influence on the mind and outlook of young working-class England than any other single person, not excluding Baden-Powell." (161)

Not everybody was pleased to have such a national myth. George Orwell, who looked back with anger at his years at Eton, recalled in 1939 the serialized public school stories and attributed their unique success to English snobbism: "There are tens and scores of thousands of people to whom every detail of life at a 'posh' public school is wildly thrilling and romantic" (467). Orwell acknowledged that fat Billy Bunter was "a really first-rate character" (462) and found Frank Richard's style "extraordinary," though "artificial and repetitive," quite different from everything existing in English literature around

1940 (463). But he found the stories "fantastically unlike life" (464). Sex and religion were taboo, class frictions were absent, and foreigners were "funny." To a large proportion of adolescents, many of whom would later read only newspapers, these stories offered "a set of beliefs which would be regarded as hopelessly out of date in the Central Office of the Conservative Party" (482):

> The year is 1910—or 1940, but it is all the same. You are at Greyfriars, a rosy-cheeked boy of fourteen in posh, tailor-made clothes, sitting down to tea in your study on the Remove passage after an exciting game of football which was won by an odd goal in the last half-minute. There is a cosy fire in the study, and outside the wind is whistling. The ivy clusters thickly round the old grey stones. The King is on his throne and the pound is worth a pound. Over in Europe the comic foreigners are jabbering and gesticulating, but the grim grey battleships of the British Fleet are steaming up the Channel and at the outposts of Empire the monocled Englishmen are holding the niggers at bay. Lord Mauleverer has just got another fiver and we are all settling down to a tremendous tea of sausages, sardines, crumpets, potted meat, jam and doughnuts. After tea we shall sit round the study fire having a good laugh at Billy Bunter and discussing the team for next week's match against Rookwood. Everything is safe, solid and un-questionable. Everything will be the same for ever and ever. (473)

Frank Richards, whose identity with his other aliases was revealed to Orwell only later, replied that Orwell attributed to his "very innocent" stories "a fell scheme for drugging the minds of the younger proletariat into dull acquiescence in a system of which Mr Orwell does not approve" (485). In any case, Richards's reply made the implicit ultraconservative ideology of his own stories explicit. Concerning sex, the less an adolescent thought about it the better (486). The apparent snobbery in his stories was founded on the real distinction of the upper class: "The higher you go up in the social scale the better you find the manners, and the more fixed the principles" (488). As to politics: boys "ought not to be disturbed and worried" about it (492). They should feel as secure as possible in an insecure world, and not be forced to contemplate strikes, slumps, and unemployment. But the key to Richards's defense was his poetics:

> A boy of fifteen or sixteen is on the threshold of life: and life is a tough proposition; but will he be better prepared for it by telling him how tough it may possibly be? ... Happiness is the best preparation for misery, if misery must come.... Every day of happiness, illusory or otherwise—and

> most happiness is illusory—is so much to the good. It will help to give the
> boy confidence and hope. Frank Richards tells him that there are some
> splendid fellows in a world that is, after all, a decent sort of place. (490)

And yes, foreigners *were* funny, especially if they lacked a sense of humor.
Hitler, that "play-acting ass would be laughed out of existence" in England
(491).

Since Richards's rather spirited retort appeared in May 1940, during the
battle of Dunkirk, Orwell could have replied that Hitler was, after all, no
laughing matter, and the world at the time did not seem "a decent sort of
place." Was the myth of a safe and idyllic school the best preparation to fight
Hitler in anticipation of a better world? What sort of stories would be more
suitable? Orwell hoped for a left-wing, less illusion-filled boys' paper (483),
but he was quite cautious concerning its specific content. Indeed, he had
reason to be wary, for the Nazi pedagogues also demanded a "Primat der
Politik!" (Becker 151) and a "realistic" representation of the "volk" in adolescent literature. They too attacked the literature of "illusions" and
"escape."

Of course, Orwell and the Nazis attacked different forms of *l'art pour l'art*
literature, and they attacked them from different directions. Orwell, just back
from the Spanish civil war, wanted to reveal the reactionary ideology behind
Richards's apparently apolitical stories, whereas the Nazi ideologues attacked
the *Jugendschriftenbewegung* (youth literature movement), an aesthetics of youth
literature that harkened back to German classicism and idealism.

In the last decades of the nineteenth century, as German pedagogues began
to evaluate the existing literature for children and youth, Heinrich Wolgast
(1860–1920) started the journal *Jugendschriften-Warte* (1893–) in Hamburg.
This journal soon became the focal point of the *Jugendschriftenbewegung,* and
Wolgast's book *Das Elend unserer Jugendliteratur (The Misery of Our Youth Literature,*
1896) became its bible.

Ironically, Wolgast opposed youth literature as a species of writing: "If
you want to write for the young," said the motto he took from Theodor Storm,
"you must not write for the young." The implications of this were made
explicit in Wolgast's three interrelated critical postulates: (1) Poetic works
for youth (as distinguished from informative or didactic ones) must be works
of art (24); (2) literature specifically written for and serving solely the interest
of youth must disappear (24); and (3) literature for youth must neither be a
vehicle of knowledge or morality (21), nor offer mere entertainment.

By insisting that literature for youth should offer only aesthetic enjoyment, Wolgast followed Kant and Schiller: he believed in the autonomy of the aesthetic and demanded, in opposition to Enlightenment didacticism, that art teach only by indirection, namely by cultivating taste and creativity and by revealing the world in a new light (48). Can the didactic, moral, and aesthetic dimensions be separated in literature for youth? Is such a separation perhaps desirable? Wolgast's trenchant criticism of specific books for youth shows that his rigor was first and foremost directed against maudlin moralizing and not meant as a recipe for producing new books. He hated it when literary sugarcoating was used to make didactic messages palatable: "Books that offer in the external form of poetry the artifice of an impotent poetaster, or the didactic, moralizing, religious, or political utterances of an ideologist, must be strictly excluded from the reading of the young" (23 f.).[10]

Then what should adolescents read? The classics, Wolgast answered. Many applauded and followed Wolgast's movement, and the tenets of this movement came to dominate book reviews of literature for young people. But many remained skeptical, and their number increased with the passage of time. Although Wolgast's views dovetailed with the idealist-classical German tradition, they never became official dogma. Most parents and teachers, even Spranger (64), found the classics too sublime for adolescent consumption, and only such exceptionally mature adolescents as Karen Horney (*Adolescent Diaries* 66), preferred them to Backfischliteratur and adventure stories. Wolgast's followers defended a good cause in fighting the increasing tendency to impose an ideology on youth literature, but they were ineffectual. The Nazis and their fellow travelers violently condemned the *Jugendschriftenbewegung* because they could not tolerate its opposition to their ideology. They would have equally condemned Frank Richards's myth of the public school and Orwell's wished-for left-wing weeklies.

CHAPTER SIX

Visualizing Adolescence

Throughout the Middle Ages, children were portrayed in adult clothes (Ariès, *L'Enfant* 75), and adults were often shown playing children's games well into the seventeenth century (*L'Enfant* chap. 4). Velázquez still depicted the Infant Baltasar Carlos (1634) in full royal regalia on a horse, and Chardin still painted a postadolescent youth building a house of cards. Ariès sees in this an indication that the age groups were less sharply delineated in earlier ages (*L'Enfant* 29 ff.).

Delacroix's portrayal of Liberty leading the people in the 1830 revolution (*La Barricade* 1830) reveals another conception of childhood: a female personification of Liberty is flanked by a symbolic armed street urchin, indicating that for Delacroix and his romantic comrades-in-arms children appeared as emblems of both purity amid urban corruption and hope for a better future.

Adolescents begin to appear in the visual arts towards the end of the nineteenth century. Manet's *Breakfast in the Atelier* (1868) may be regarded as a forerunner, but, with the exception of Degas's dancers and Renoir's young girls, adolescents are still conspicuously absent from impressionist paintings.

In the 1880s and 1890s, Max Liebermann painted bathing boys as well as girls in the Amsterdam orphanage, and Félix Vallotton drew an adolescent self-portrait (1885) and produced several Jugendstil woodcuts of young people. Yet is was Munch who gave a decisive turn to the representation of adolescents around 1890.

EDVARD MUNCH

The young girl of Munch's *Puberty* (fig. 1)[1] projects the pain of transition. The observer's eye is led from the colorless skin of the pitifully emaciated figure to the anguished stare of the huge eyes that peer ahead. But where? The enigmatic answer is to be found behind, in the enormous dark shadow on the wall, which early critics already interpreted as male sexuality. Munch seems to have unintentionally followed Félicien Rops's illustration for Barbey d'Aurevilly's novella *Le plus bel amour de Don Juan* (Svenaeus 1: 93–95), which shows an adolescent with the open black cape of a towering Don Juan, instead of a black blotch, looming behind her. The bed dominates Munch's scene, but the girl, embarrassed by her nakedness, is hiding her genitals. The angular lines of her lean body conform to the harsh, geometric outline of the barren interior, which depersonalizes her distress. The title indicates that Munch's concern was with the phenomenon of puberty with its fears and even suicidal anxieties, rather than with the individual.

By the following decade Munch had shifted his attention from nude to dressed adolescents, from indoors to outdoors, and from individual to group portrayal. All of these changes serve to temper the dramatic power of the earlier works to a melancholy somberness. In a series of paintings, he depicts adolescent girls on a bridge, the symbol of transition, peering into dark waters below.[2] In the first version about 1901 (fig. 2) the railing diagonally dissects the painting, and the upper part is filled with the background, dominated by a huge circle-shaped tree and its dark reflection in the water, a mild reminiscence of the black shadow in *Puberty.* The anguished solitude of the earlier, exposed figure is replaced here by girls huddled against the subdued melancholy of the dusky landscape, but the broadened natural and human space does not relieve the sense of isolation. The girls face away, each contemplating for herself the water and the background, and the contrasting vivid blotches of their dresses moderate their physical closeness.[3] In a 1905 version the first girl turns to the viewer but her face is washed out. In a 1902 version the girls are grouped in conversation but moved into the background. The iso-

93

1. Edvard Munch, *Puberty,* 1895, Nasjonalgalleriet, Oslo, Norway.

lation of adolescents in this series strikingly contrasts with the social posture of young women on bridges in a parallel series, of which Revold (50) lists seven versions. When, in these years, Munch paints adolescents in blooming spring gardens, the efflorescence of nature overwhelms rather than supports the human figures. The stiff and forlorn adolescents of *Two Girls in a Garden* (1905) are dominated by a luxurious, oversized plant.

DIE BRÜCKE

The bridge became the emblem of a Dresden group formed in 1905 by Fritz Bleyl (b. 1880), Ernst Ludwig Kirchner (b. 1880), Erich Heckel (b. 1883), and Karl Schmidt-Rottluff (b. 1884).[4] The *Brücke* artists admired Munch's work and invited him, unsuccessfully, to join their Dresden exhibitions of 1906, 1908, and 1909 (Werenskiold 140–43), but their name does not seem to have been inspired by Munch's bridge paintings. What did the bridge emblematize? Was it a safe passage to firm ground, or a locus of suspension and a time of transition between "no longer" and "not yet"? Did it symbolize a revolutionary determination, like Delacroix's urchin, or an inner uncertainty, a confusion of identity? The canonized view of the Brücke, supported by the group's self-presentation, perceives them in a provocative, self-assertive posture against the bourgeois world of the father. In the presentation of adolescence, however, this challenging posture is repeatedly hollowed out by manifestations of self-doubt and inner division. Only by superposing self-doubt upon provocation do we get a full picture of the Brücke and the whole generation coming of age around 1900. Adolescents provided the Brücke with a theme to express its own inner divisions.

Conflicting comments by Brücke artists on their name supports this interpretation. On the one hand, a programmatic woodcut by Kirchner from 1906 says: "Believing in development, in a new generation of creators as well as art lovers we call upon all youth to gather. As harbingers of the future we want to create elbowroom and existential freedom against the settled older forces. Anyone who directly and authentically reproduces the creative urge within himself is one of us."[5] Similarly, when on February 4, 1906, Schmidt-Rottluff invited Nolde to join, he wrote that the name signified the desire "to attract all the revolutionary and surging elements" (Selz 84). Yet Heckel recalls that Schmidt-Rottluff chose the word by explaining that Brücke was a "multilayered word" that implied no program but suggested a transition "from one bank to another" (Elger 15), and Heckel commented later: "It was

2. Edvard Munch, *Girls on the Bridge,* about 1901, Nasjonalgalleriet, Oslo, Norway.

clear to us what we had to leave behind—where we would arrive at was, to be sure, less certain" (Felix 11). On the bridge, the inherited identity was discarded but no new one had yet been found.

Nietzsche was probably a key figure in shaping the diffuse identity of the Brücke. Heckel made a woodcut of him in 1905, and Kirchner recalls that Heckel loudly declaimed from Nietzsche's *Zarathustra* at their first encounter (Felix 17). According to Kirchner's *Chronik* (Selz 320), the joint diary of the group, now lost, carried the Ovidian title "Odi profanum vulgus" (I hate the vulgar crowd)—a title echoed in Nietzsche's self-critical introduction to *The*

Birth of Tragedy. Gordon (*Expressionism* 14) suggests that the name was chosen with the prologue to *Thus Spoke Zarathustra* in mind: "Man is a rope, tied between beast and Higher Man—a rope over an abyss. A dangerous across, a dangerous on-the-way, a dangerous looking back, a dangerous shuddering and stopping. What is great in man is that he is a bridge and not an end: what can be loved in man is that he is an *overture* and a *going under*" (14–15). Whatever the origin of the name, Nietzsche's preoccupation with the death of the common and rebirth of a higher man, and his attacks on metaphysical notions of identity, accompanied by a search for authenticity are surely pertinent to the adolescent confusion that the Brücke artists so obsessively portrayed.

Indeed, the rebellious, self-assertive innovations of the Brücke (as well as of Kokoschka and Egon Schiele) obsessively depicted diffuse identity in terms of double portraits, androgynous figures, the make-believe world of circus clowns and masks, the varieté, and the nightclub. Their striving for authenticity—and their almost masochistic obsession with fluid situations, unstable characters, and images of impermanence—had to lead them to adolescence, the central theme of their "authentic" style in 1909–1911.

That style emerged as a melding of several interrelated trends, all of them pertinent to adolescence: the expressive, emotional turbulence of Van Gogh, the fauvists, and Munch; the encounter with native art; the preoccupation with and open treatment of sexuality; and a yearning for nature that could not suppress a fascination with the closed spaces of rooms and cities. A juncture of all these elements marked the last Brücke exhibition in Dresden in 1910. By the following year all members had moved to Berlin and had turned to new subjects, most conspicuously to city streets.

Kirchner's first adolescent was the impressionistic *Schlafendes Mädchen* (1905–6).[6] In 1908 and early 1909 he discovered van Dongen's and Matisse's curvilinear, two-dimensional, and highly distorted rendering of female nudes, and he adopted the style in *Mädchenakt auf blühender Wiese* (Gordon no. 81) and, above all, in *Mädchen unter Japanschirm* (Gordon no. 57). Pechstein delightfully recalls the crucial recruitment of the twelve- to fourteen-year-old Fränzi and Marcella as models:

> We had known the landscape [near Dresden] for a long time, and we knew that we had the opportunity there to paint nudes undisturbed, in nature. . . . We had to find two or three people who were not professional models and would therefore guarantee us movements free of training [*Atelierdressur*]. I remembered my old friend, the concierge of the Academy . . .

and he immediately had not only good advice to offer but also somebody in mind and became our helper in need. He referred us to the widow of an artist and her two daughters. I presented her with our serious artistic intentions. She visited our workshop in Friedrichstadt and since she found there a familiar setting she consented that her daughters should set out with us to Moritzburg. . . . We painters left in the early morning, heavily loaded with our gear, while our models followed with pockets full of food and drinks. We lived in absolute harmony, and worked and swam. If a male model was missing as a counterpart, one of us three would fill in. Every now and then the girls' mother would appear as a worried mother-hen to ascertain that nothing evil was happening to her little ducklings swimming on the lake of life. (41–43)[7]

The idyll was brought to a temporary halt by the appearance of a local policeman who suspected immoral activities and confiscated Pechstein's painting. The group had to swim and wade with its gear to the nearest undisturbed island (Heckel drawing in Jähner, p. 48), until, three months later, Pechstein was summoned to appear in court. But the public prosecutor laughingly dismissed the case (Pechstein 43–44) and the group resumed its normal work.

What were the fruits of this unconventional, even antibourgeois undertaking? In a letter to Carl Hagemann on November 19, 1935, Kirchner recalls that "the close human relationship especially with the girls . . . resulted in paintings that revealed this wonderful unity among people" (Gordon, *Kirchner* 19). In his Davos diary of 1935, he also remarked that in his early years he had sought a modernism that could only be realized via "a pure, naive study of nature, without the glasses of style (*Stilbrille*)." At the lakes he resolved the problem of using new means to represent nudes outdoors: "The human bodies shine in the water or between trees in unbroken colors of blue, red, green and yellow."[8]

Based on an interview with Heckel on September 7, 1953, Selz derives important cultural implications from these recollections: "They were prompted by a desire to achieve new strength through a close link with the sources of nature—an impulse found contemporaneously in the German youth movement and in the nudist cult. It was a worship of the freely moving human body as a part of the total complex of nature. Groups like the Wandervögel and movements such as the Freiluftbewegung and Nacktkultur were widespread and popular among the younger generation, who were in revolt against the urban restrictions of the period and rejected the confinement of the body in the corset as much as the confinement of the spirit in a Prussian school system" (99).

Heckel suggests that the Brücke and the youth movement were motivated by a common worship of nature, and Kirchner asserts that a harmony among people and a "pure, naive study of nature" was achieved at the lakes. Indeed, the immediate record of these summers was a large body of drawings, watercolors, and etchings that capture Fränzi's and Marcella's fresh movements and unrehearsed postures. It is as if in and through these girls the Brücke had found that romantic phantom of childlike spontaneity, freedom, and innocence.

But the idealizing terminology makes these reports suspect. Would children, rather than awkward pubescent girls, not have suited better the Brücke's search for naturalness? The late recollections of the three participants evoke a hedonistic bliss but systematically ignore the profound sense of uncertainty and confusion that emanates from the major paintings and woodcuts of the girls. This duality runs through the artistic production of those summers, separating moments of youthful abandon from periods of ruthless self-searching that undermined the harmony and sought to penetrate to the heart of the matter, however painful and ugly. The ruthless scrutiny resulted in embarrassing rather than beautiful adolescent bodies. If the watercolors and drawings, as well as a few paintings, try to capture the glorious moments, the larger and more carefully constructed indoor paintings and woodcuts of Fränzi and Marcella seek authenticity, and they expose, as I shall show, a disturbed psyche rather than a harmonious body.

Kirchner's *Marcella* (fig. 3) is indebted to Munch's *Puberty* but painted in a colorful, two-dimensional fauvist style (Gordon, *Kirchner in Dresden* 353) that is enhanced by the bow in her hair, so that the total impression is more cheerful and friendly. Marcella hides her genitals nonchalantly, in an almost conversational posture. And yet her darkly shaded eyes express worry, and her face, which dominates the painting, is so constrained into a mask like triangle that her expression appears stiff and depersonalized. The angularity, reinforced by the right elbow, clashes with fauvist curvilinearity and reveals a third, powerful style that Kirchner appropriated in 1909–10, from African and South Sea Island carvings he encountered in the ethnological section of the Dresden museum. The angular delineations of the "Palau" Brücke style partly replaced the fluid fauvist lines, but enough of the latter survived to convey by means of clashing styles an underlying psychological conflict.

"Modernist primitivism," the modernist discovery and incorporation of native art, was a European trend of largely independent phenomena that included the works of Paul Gauguin and the fauvists (mid-1906), Kokoschka's

3. Ernst Ludwig Kirchner, *Marcella,* 1909–10, Moderna Museet, Stockholm, Sweden.

admiration for Polynesian masks (*Mein Leben* 51), the attention to folklore in the *Blaue Reiter,* the unearthing of buried folk music by Béla Bartók and Zoltán Kodály, and the reenactment of an ancient Russian puberty rite in Igor Stravinsky's *Le Sacre du printemps.*[9] The importance of primitivism for the visual arts is indicated by Rubin's catalogue for the large 1984 exhibition at the Museum of Modern Art in New York.

The search for natural spontaneity that is said to have inspired the Brücke at the Moritzburg lakes may thus appear to be linked to a widespread modernist attack on Western conventions. But Gordon rightly objects that a quasi-romantic naturalism, a "belief in a content beyond convention" was not, as some people claim, the essence of expressionism (Rubin 369 ff.). Could the Brücke artists have been fascinated by the Palau carvings because they expressed "an untutored" (*unverbildete*), original way of life that allowed an instinctive artistic creation, unencumbered by conventions" (Hegewisch 27)? Perhaps, for, as Jakobson notes, revolutionary artists may see the deformation of an existing convention as a step towards realistic (and hence convention-free) representation (381). Nevertheless, Kirchner and his friends could hardly have been unaware of the conventions governing the native carvings, however different these may have been from those they had inherited. I suggest that the angularity of the Palau beam-carvings (partly due to the difficulty of carving curvilinear shapes with a simple knife) attracted the Brücke artists because it suited their expressive needs. Like fauvist curvilinearity, these carvings represented stylization and convention.

The sharp, angular contours of Palau art better suited the Brücke than the color mosaic of the impressionists, the swinging lines of Jugendstil, and the soft compositions of Matisse. They were adopted not only to suit Fränzi's and Marcella's "lean, angular bodies" (Gabler 49–50). These adolescent bodies were usually rendered round and full in the sketches at the lakes, and became angular only in the more elaborate works prepared and portrayed indoors, in which the artists' own harsh, "angular," and troubled vision appropriated the subject. In a very un-Freudian manner, the deeper preoccupations surface not in the spontaneous sketches but in the carefully crafted constructions, in which we find instead of some loving and admiring vision of youth a distanced and almost ruthless exposure of frailty, instability, and even ugliness. The stylistic experimentation fits the subject matter: the mask like faces of the confused adolescents project the painters' troubled sense of identity in the parental matrix of Western tradition.

Native art, shown in the Marcella-picture as a wall decoration on the left side, becomes central to *Fränzi with Carved Chair* (fig. 4). The pink chair, which Kirchner carved himself following African models, confines Fränzi from the side and culminates in a threatening black head that towers over the seated girl and functions psychologically like the background shadow in Munch's *Puberty.* Unlike Munch, Kirchner paints the background with vivid colors that link up with the girl's dress, necklace, and lips but sharply contrast with her jaundiced face. Though the contour of her face is somewhat less angular than the face in *Marcella,* the seductively red lips and heavily shaded eyes in a still childish face are no less ambiguous. Heavy makeup and stylized primitivism emerge from the experience at the lakes, where the artists sought nature and spontaneity!

Sitting Child: Fränzi (fig. 5) shows the girl in a different posture but also confined, this time by the color of the sofa. As with the painting of Marcella, the heavily shaded eyes and the thick, painted lips charge the young girl with an eroticism far beyond her age. The sexual connotations are reinforced by the green decorative male figure in the upper left corner, executed in native style. This time, the dominant bed is neatly made.

Kirchner's adolescents are appealing, in spite of their threatened expression and their incongruous eyes and lips. In contrast, Heckel's woodcuts highlight the body so unfavorably that it causes distress. The harshness is not due to the medium, for Kirchner and Heckel could readily adopt the curved lines in earlier Jugendstil woodcuts.

Fränzi's pale and undeveloped body in Heckel's *Standing Child* (fig. 6) provides a poor contrast to the stylized colors of nature in the background; the swung eyebrows in the oversized head clash with the slit eyes and the angular, mask like face. *Fränzi Reclining* (fig. 7) ironically assumes a traditional elbow-supported Venus posture, but the body is undeveloped and molded by the "entombing" blocks of color. The ambiguous Venus-posture is repeated in *Girl (Fränzi) with Doll* (fig. 8), this time underscored by the ironic contrast between the doll covering her genitals and the male abdomen hovering in the upper left corner of the background. Finally, in Heckel's woodcut for the cover of the 1910 Brücke exhibition catalogue (fig. 9), made after a now lost Kirchner painting, the relaxed Venus-imitation turns into a tense and contorted posture. The arms that aggressively reach out for embrace clutch only the tiny, doll-like object that hides the genitals. The already familiar thick lips and dark eyes exude seductive, adult sexuality. Heckel consistently contrasts features of sexuality against signs of immaturity.

4. Ernst Ludwig Kirchner, *Fränzi with Carved Chair*, 1910, Thyssen-Bornemisza
Collection, Lugano, Switzerland.

5. Ernst Ludwig Kirchner, *Sitting Child: Fränzi,* 1910, The Minneapolis Institute of Arts, Minneapolis, Minnesota.

VIENNA

Turn-of-the-century Vienna has been the subject of several impressive studies and exhibitions in recent years. But why Vienna, rather than Paris, Berlin, Munich, or London? I shall focus on one among several possible answers: the unique relationship between the upcoming generations and their doomed cultural and political heritage.

May one apply to this phenomenon a key metaphor that emerged from that very culture, the Freudian oedipal relation between fathers and sons? Schorske has, indeed, described the emergence of *die Jungen* since the 1870s, first in politics and then in all fields of culture, as a "widespread, collective oedipal revolt" (*Fin-de-siècle* 212). Yet, although every new departure neces-

6. Erich Heckel, *Standing Child,* 1910, Folkwang Museum, Essen, Germany.

7. Erich Heckel, *Fränzi Reclining,* 1910, Brücke Museum, Berlin, Germany.

sarily involves an opposition to the parental tradition, turn-of-the-century Vienna displays surprisingly few oedipal conflicts amid its many "secessions." Schorske himself notes that Freud's metaphor cannot be applied unreservedly to the Viennese artists growing up at the beginning of this century, for the "metaphysical wrath of the Expressionists was perhaps too large to find focus in Oedipal revolt or generational resentment" ("Generational Tension" 120). Expressionist artists "often held their forebears in love and respect": filial attachment, not jealousy and hatred, was Arnold Schoenberg's attitude to Gustav Mahler, Schiele's to Gustav Klimt, and Adolph Loos's to Otto Wagner.

One may add that this filial respect usually extended to the literal fathers, and that literary portrayals of generational conflicts were comparatively rare and usually involved only subordinate themes. Oedipal conflict was not the essence of the youthful rebellion around 1900, only part of a more broadly conceived identity crisis. As Rolf-Peter Janz has suggested, this identity crisis is the "signature" of fin-de-siècle Vienna ("Identitätskrise" 170–74). I propose more concretely that the culture of the Viennese *Jungen* was *adolescent,* both in a literal sense, for its adolescent artists and its thematization of adolescence, and metaphorically, for displaying the typical oxymoron of adolescence, narcissism and ego diffusion.

This adolescent culture in turn-of-the-century Vienna spanned two generations, aptly characterized by Schorske as "transformation" of and "explo-

8. Erich Heckel, *Girl (Fränzi) with Doll,* 1910, Private Collection.

sion" in the garden (*Fin-de-siècle* 279 ff., 322 ff.). The generation growing up in the 1890s included Hofmannsthal (b. 1874), his friend, Andrian-Werburg (b. 1874), and schoolboys from the *Schottengymnasium,* who associated with the loose circle of somewhat elder literati in the Café Griensteidl, the so-called *Jung-Wien.* Arthur Schnitzler (b. 1862) appeared there, as did Richard Beer-Hoffmann (b. 1866), Hermann Bahr (b. 1863), Felix Salten (b. 1869), and the Viennese oddity Peter Altenberg, whose photo collection of females on the walls of his hotel room included many nude pubescent girls.[10] *Jung* here referred to a mental attitude rather than to chronological age.

The adolescent Hofmannsthal is remembered today for his brilliant poetry, but he also experimented with prose, and here he obsessively encircled adolescence. The fragment "Age of Innocence" (*Prosa* 1: 147–54) attempts to evoke the mind of a pubescent; other fragments (*Werke* 29: 44–47) present

9. Erich Heckel, woodcut after Kirchner's 1910 Brücke poster, Brücke Museum, Germany.

filial images of fathers: one adolescent separates himself from his consciously *Jung-Wien* peers (*Werke* 29: 45), another experiences deep compassion for his father, who seems to him "helpless in facing God and the world" (*Werke* 29: 44).

Hofmannsthal's essays were also preoccupied with adolescence: he reviewed Bashkirtseff's adolescent diary (*Prosa* 1: 121–28) and Barrès's *Le Culte du moi* (*Prosa* 1: 47–57), and he gauged the mood of his deeply self-divided adolescent generation in terms of lyric aestheticism, sublimated sexuality, and resigned narcissism: "We possess only sentimental memory, paralysed will, and an uncanny ability to duplicate ourselves. We are spectators of our own lives."[11] The remark fits Andrian-Werburg's *Der Garten der Erkenntnis,* which contains no generational conflict: Erwin's father dies before the boy reaches adolescence, the incapacity to act is due only to an inner irresolution.

Hence the "transformation of the garden"—the turn from its Voltairean moral cultivation to its aesthetic contemplation—involves no serious clashes with the parental order. The "explosion in the garden"—a prank by the adolescent Kokoschka that Schorske reads as a figure for the generation of the following decade—is more problematic. On the face of it, defiant challenges to the fathers' world replaced then passive contemplation. And yet, by Schorske's own admission, the outrage and provocation of the new art was not directed against the previous generation, which, as in the case of Klimt, was equally provocative. Schorske's phrase, "metaphysical wrath," indicates that the adolescent gesture of defiance and challenge was an expression of frustration and a way of coping with inner bewilderment. Like Kirchner and his friends, Kokoschka (b. 1886) and Schiele (b. 1990) sought spontaneity and authenticity but they created complex textures of provocation and self-questioning.

The quest for an authentic self often involved discovering art from abroad. Their incorporation at home helped shake off the inherited conventions, but the resultant works showed a new stylization rather than the absence of convention. Brücke art did not reach Vienna in its first decade, but Max Reinhardt brought his Berlin staging of *Frühlings Erwachen* to Vienna in 1907, and Ferdinand Hodler's *Spring* (*Frühling,* 1901), depicting an adolescent girl's ecstatic admiration for a disinterested boy, aroused much interest at the Secession exhibition of 1901.

The key gesture in Viennese representations of adolescents was taken from the *Kneeling Boy,* a sculpture by the Belgian artist George Minne. The arms of this remarkably elongated boy are folded over his chest in a self-embrace that seems to shield his body and soul just as the adolescents depicted by

10. George Minne, *The Fountain of Kneeling Boys,* 1901? Museum voor Shone Kunsten, Gent, Belgium.

Munch, Kirchner, and Heckel protect their genitals. Reiterating their plea for privacy, Minne's boy isolates himself for total introspection.

Minne made the streak of narcissism in the boy's gesture transparent in an elaboration on the theme: at Henry van de Verde's wish, he brilliantly intensified the hermeticism in the *Fountain of Kneeling Boys* (fig. 10), by placing five replicas of the youth around a fountain, whose marble version is in the Folkwang Museum of Essen. They face here not only their alter egos, but, as true embodiments of Narcissus, also their reflection in the water. Turning their back on the world around, and hermetically sealing themselves off, they seem to have achieved perfect identity—though they literally and figuratively divide into confronting selves. The sculpture, justly baptized "Narcissus Fountain" by the poet Karl van Woestijne, is a true image of adolescence, for it diffuses through multiplication a figure of self-absorption and identity.

This all but forgotten sculpture had an enormous impact in Vienna. When Ludwig Hevesi, the leading art critic, saw the fountain in the Eighth Secession exhibition in November 1900, he compared Minne's "scraggy, wiry, pointed sculptures of asceticism" to "Christian fakirs" and was struck by the incongruity between the "pitiful" bodies and the spirituality of expression. One had to be emaciated to embrace one's body like these poor boys who "can reach everywhere with their hands, even crosswise at their own shoulder-blades."[12] *Ver sacrum* dedicated its second issue of 1901 to Minne and reproduced the *Kneeling Boy,* the fountain, and two boys in bronze. Minne's lean adolescents and their self-embrace were adopted in Klimt's *Beethoven-frieze,* Wilhelm Lehmbruck's sculptures, and Schiele's figures; Kokoschka recalls that Minne's brittle and introverted figures moved him more deeply than the works of Van Gogh, Gauguin, and the fauvists, for they overcame the two-dimensionality of Jugendstil: "Under the surface, inside these young boys something was moving like the tension that controls, even creates, three-dimensional gothic space."[13]

Oskar Kokoschka

Minne's heritage lives on in Kokoschka's main contribution to the portrayal of adolescence, a longer poem entitled *The Dreaming Boys* (*Die träumenden Knaben,* 1907–8), illustrated with eight colored lithographs. Kokoschka used circus children as models and surmised later that Minne must have used similar ones. Like Minne, Kokoschka constructs a composite work out of the tension between identity and division, but he uses different parameters. Minne replicates spatially, Kokoschka gives a sequence of corresponding texts and images; Minne multiplies an autonomous figure, Kokoschka uses a single narrative voice that passes through different roles and moods, in accordance with the plural "boys" in the title. The shifts in role are marked by the refrain "and I fell down and dreamt" (und ich fiel nieder und träumte), which gives the sequence a dreamlike, surrealist quality.

The poem opens with the boy's warning to a red fish circling in the waters:

> rot fischlein, fischlein rot
> stech dich mit dem dreischneidigen messer tot
> reiss dich mit meinen fingern entzwei
> dass dem stummen kreisen ein ende sei (12)[14]

> red fishling, fishling red
> with a triple-bladed knife I stab you dead

with my fingers I rend you in two
to end this soundless circling.

The red fish (plural!) of the first lithograph are meant to threaten the encircled sleeping girl; the boy-speaker could be seen as her knightly defender. But the red fish also appear in the decidedly lyrical second lithograph, *Das Segelschiff.* The boy's verbal violence can only be justified if we assume that the folkloristic image refers to Goethe's poem *Heidenröslein.* The tenderly embracing elongated male figures in the foreground may represent Kokoschka and Klimt, to whom Kokoschka dedicated his work, but their identities are uncertain. In any case, the figures evidently represent two generations in delicate touch: the boy's hand seeks support on the shoulder of his elder, and his melancholy head seems about to find rest on it.

Subsequently, image and text go their own ways. In the text, the initial childlike savagery rises to an adolescent aggression against the world of the father. The rebel-werewolf threatens to break into the bourgeois gardens:

ich bin der kreisende wärwolf—

wenn die abendglocke vertönt
schleich ich in eure gärten
in eure weiden
breche ich in euren friedlichen kraal

mein abgezäumter körper
mein mit blut und farbe erhöhter körper
kriecht in eure laubhütten
schwärmt durch eure dörfer
kriecht in eure seelen
schwärt in euren leibern

aus der einsamsten stille
vor eurem erwachen gellt mein geheul

ich verzehre euch
männer
frauen
halbwache hörende kinder
der rasende liebende wärwolf in euch

und ich fiel nieder und träumte (16)

I am the encircling werewolf

when the evening bell dies off
I stalk into your gardens

into your pastures
break into your peaceful corral
my unbridled body
my body exalted with pigment and blood
crawls into your huts
swarms through your villages
crawls into your souls
festers in your bodies

out of the loneliest stillness
before your awakening my howling shrills forth

I devour you
men
women
drowsily hearkening children
the berserk loving werewolf within you

and I fell down and dreamt.

Yet the lithograph that accompanies this text, *Sailors Calling,* depicts distressed sailors in boats apparently calling for help instead of a savage werewolf distressed. The call for help belies the threatening shrill howl of the text. The howl drowns out the voice of helplessness but cannot blot out the image.

This emotional outburst is followed by passages of self-reflection, accompanied by images of folkloristic splendor entitled "The Distant Islands," "Confidential Conversations," and "The Dream Carriers." In the second part of the text the speaker metamorphoses into an adolescent lover addressing a girl called Li (although stylized in Kokoschka's autobiography into a Swede, she was a fellow student and sister of Kokoschka's friend Erwin Lang).

The seventh lithograph, *Eros,* rejoins the textual theme, but only in the final one, *The Girl Li and I* (fig. 11), do the lovers appear as naked Minne-like elongated and androgynous figures, separated by a flaming-red interspace (which some read as a phallic erection). Yet the eroticism is tender: the lovers, enclosed in their separate visual spheres, pensively gaze ahead rather than at each other, awkwardly posturing, seemingly embarrassed by their angular, sexually as yet indistinct, bodies. Her breasts are undeveloped and his arms are folded on his chest, clutching his shoulders as if he, not she, had something to hide. Every detail suggests identity diffusion.

Kokoschka's original assignment from the *Wiener Werkstätte* was to illustrate a book of fairy tales, but he quickly abandoned that project and started to experiment with modern verse and free-floating lyric imagery. His title was to indicate that the work became "a sort of report in word and image about

ich greife in den see und
tauche in deinen haaren
wie ein versonnener bin
ich in der liebe alles wesens/
und wieder fiel ich nieder
und träumte/
zu viel hitze überkam mich
in der nacht/ da in den wäl-
dern die paarende schlange
ihre haut streicht unter dem
heißen stein und der wasser-
hirsch reibt sein gehörn
an den zimmtstauden/ als
ich den moschus des tieres
roch in allen niedrigen
sträuchern/
es ist fremd um mich/ je-
mand sollte antworten/
alles läuft nach seinen eigenen fährten/ und die
singenden mücken über-
zittern die schreie/
wer denkt grinsende götter-
gesichter und fragt den sing-
sang der zauberer und alt-
männer/ wenn sie die boot-
fahrer begleiten/ welche
frauen holen/
und ich war ein kriechend
ding/ als ich die tiere suchte
und mich zu ihnen hielt/
kleiner/ was wolltest du
hinter den alten/ als du die
gottzauberer aufsuchtest/
und ich war ein taumelnder/
als ich mein fleisch er-
kannte/
und ein allesliebender/ als
ich mit einem mädchen
sprach/

dieses buch wurde geschrie-
ben und gezeichnet von
Oskar Kokoschka/ verlegt
von der wiener werkstätte/
gedruckt in den offizinen
Berger und Chwala/ 1908

11. Oskar Kokoschka, *The Girl Li and I,* from *The Dreaming Boys,* 1908.

the state of my soul then"[15] As Schorske remarks, Kokoschka "transformed
the childish dreams of fairyland so fashionable among his elders into adolescent nightmares" (*Fin-de-siècle* 330). In the words of the adolescent boy:

> nicht die ereignisse der kindheit gehen durch mich
> > und nicht die der mannbarkeit
> aber die knabenhaftigkeit
> ein zögerndes wollen
> das unbegründete schämen vor dem wachsenden
> und die jünglingsschaft
> das überfliessen und alleinsein
> ich erkannte mich und meinen körper (18)

> not the events of childhood move through me
> > and not those of manhood
> but boyishness

a hesitant desire
unfounded feeling of shame before what is growing
and the stripling state
the overflowing and solitude
I recognized myself and my body.

The adolescent moods of Kokoschka's poem run the gamut of self-assertion, violence, fear, and sexual yearning, evoking thereby the incoherence of
an adolescent consciousness in the manner of Lautréamont's *Maldoror,* Rimbaud's *Le Bateau ivre,* and Valéry's *La Jeune parque.* Joseph Lux reported that
Kokoschka was the wunderkind of the Kunstschau. The colorful intoxication
of Kokoschka's puberty legends reminded him of Rimbaud and his drunken,
unruly verses (50).

Kokoschka further accentuated the identity diffusion by stylistically and
thematically dissociating words and images. The tender, lyrical, and highly
decorative lithographs exude a fairy-tale atmosphere, into which the occasionally violent and always disjunctive text merges only at the beginning and
the end. The images exude the charm, the text mostly the violence, of fairy
tales. The joining of the disparate, backward- and forward-looking idioms of
the two media uniquely exemplifies modernist primitivism.

At the 1908 Kunstschau, Kokoschka also exhibited large drawings for a
gobelin entitled "The Dream Carriers" (perhaps an enlargement of the sixth
lithograph), which made Kokoschka's corner the Kunstschau's "Chamber of
Horror." Hevesi called Kokoschka *Oberwildling* (chief-savage) and noted that
Die träumenden Knaben was "no fairy-tale book for children of Philistines"
(kein Märchenbuch für Philisterkinder), but Max Mell, a young poet, reviewed
it with remarkable perception and enthusiasm. He thought that Kokoschka's
book was a "revision of childhood impressions undertaken by a young artist."
Hence "the manifold chaos that allows the images to disintegrate into groups;
a multiplication of motives and a resultant fragmentation of the totality, precisely the disorderly content of a youthful imagination, a richness that poetically furnishes the colorful dreams by means of orphic and demonic
monologues."[16]

Egon Schiele

Self-portraits and sketches of youths represented Schiele's debut when still
an adolescent.[17] He was soon considered too provocative: in 1911 he was
expelled from Krumau, his mother's Bohemian hometown, for painting nude
teenage girls, and when he moved to Neulengbach in the same year, he was

imprisoned because, to the consternation of his neighbors, he made porno-graphic drawings of pubescent girls he brought to his house.

Kokoschka and the Brücke artists set their adolescents against back-grounds, Klimt wrapped his figures in elaborate decoration. Schiele, however, suspended them in a vacuum, intensifying thereby their expression. Most of his drawings and sketches of adolescents uncompromisingly provoke by means of contorted bodies and shamelessly displayed genitals. In the 1910 sketches of a pubescent girl (1964 cat. nos. 94, 97, 115, and 126) Schiele's pencil outlines her undeveloped body with crinkled lines but uncanny assurance, setting the just-budding breasts against the adult lushness of the pubic hair. Her eyes are coquettish, and if she partly covers her genitals (1964 cat. no. 126), this is to suggest masturbation rather than shyness. The Brücke artists conveyed split identity by setting the darkened adult eyes and lips against genitals concealed by body position or a doll. Schiele's inverse approach is most evident in a 1910 study he made of his sister Gerti (*Nude Girl with Arms Crossed over her Breast,* fig. 12) for a painting now lost. The elongated body with the folded arms is reminiscent of Minne's boy, but the impact is totally dif-ferent, for the self-enclosing and self-protecting gesture of the arms, rein-forced by the face that gazes sideways as if ashamed, is negated by the lower part of the frontally placed adolescent body, which prominently exhibits her pubic hair. Mitsch notes the "shivering self-withdrawal and detachment" (*Schiele* [1974], 28) of the figure, but unexplainably ignores the provocative, unmitigated display of the abdomen, which seems to suggest that the mental attitude has no control over sexuality.

The Brücke artists portray sexuality using the face, whereas Schiele displays it at its very seat. Minne achieves an adolescent blend of narcissism and ego diffusion by means of quintuplicating self-absorbed figures around a fountain, whereas Schiele, who frequently used mirrors for his work, portrays it by masturbation (Gordon, *Expressionism* 143) and double figures that often suggest homoeroticism. In the painting *Selbstseher I (Self-Seer I)* of 1910, as well as in a preparatory sketch for it (fig. 13), ego diffusion is indicated by a double-portrait. In Schiele's usual style, the two selves stare at the viewer instead of facing each other. In the painting (Selz, plate 65), they are joined, however, by a hand that juts out of the drapery and seem to press the two figures together. The narcissism of this gesture is even more pronounced in Schiele's 1911 double-portrait, *Selbstseher II (Self-Seer II)* (Gordon, *Expressionism* 48), where the hand juts out from the genital area. Gordon (*Expressionism* 47) in-terprets the crossed arms, one of them only a handless stump, as a reference

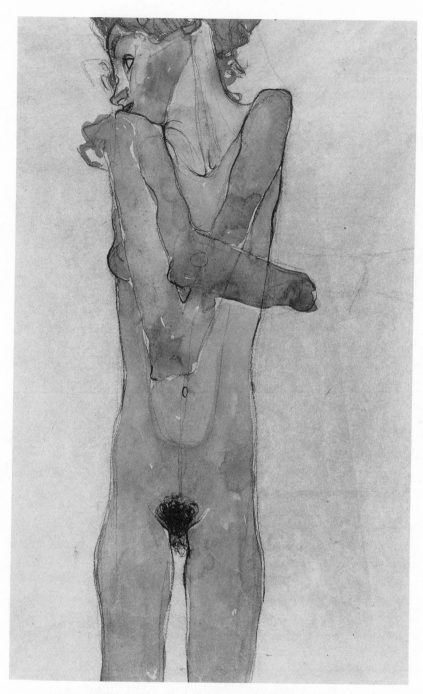

12. Egon Schiele, *Nude Girl with Arms Crossed in front of her Breast,* 1910, Graphische Sammlung Albertina, Vienna, Austria.

13. Egon Schiele, Sketch for the *Self-Seer I,* 1910, Graphische Sammlung
Albertina, Vienna, Austria.

to Christ's cross, which may imply compassion and charity. I tend to read the gesture as masturbatory and homoerotic, and the whole picture as a juncture of schizophrenic self-division and narcissistic self-enclosure. In a beautiful double-portrait drawn four years later (Mitsch, *Schiele* [1974], 85), the antagonism between the two selves gives way to a tender search for support.

Homoeroticism becomes prominent in Schiele's double-portraits of adolescent girls. What appears subdued in the 1911 painting of two embracing girls (Mitsch, *Schiele* 1974, 143) becomes unmistakable in the two 1915 versions of the theme: *Two Girls Lying Intertwined* (Mitsch, *Schiele* 1974, 85) and *Two Girls Embracing Each Other* (fig. 14). In the latter, the nude in the front is explicitly placed between the thighs of the other. Both works present the girls similarly: the nude displays its body and partially covers the clothed one, who has a stylized, mask like face. Their embrace suggests two intertwining selves: a naked "natural" one yoked to the masked social self.

ADOLESCENCE AND NATIONAL SOCIALISM

Whereas adolescence remains a literary theme even today, its representation in the fine arts essentially terminated with World War I, in Vienna as well as elsewhere. Munch, the Brücke artists (with the exception of Otto Mueller), and Kokoschka turned to other subjects; Schiele died in 1918. In the 1920s, neither the established nor the upcoming artists were interested in adolescents, save Chaim Soutine, who painted a few superb portraits of page boys and choir boys.

The war can only partly explain this shift in interest, for the crisis of Viennese culture, the motivation for its interest in adolescents, did not come to an end with the fall of the Hapsburg empire. It is true, however, that maturity and identity became prime concerns, as can be seen in Hofmannsthal's reaffirmation of tradition and the sober values of the *Neue Sachlichkeit* in the 1920s. Maturity was surely worth pursuing, yet when we weigh adult self-affirmation against adolescent self-division we should remember another member of Kokoschka's and Schiele's generation, who overcame his adolescent crisis by means of a belief in his historic mission. When Hitler (b. 1889) was rejected by the Art Academy, he went on to forge a new identity and took revenge by eliminating expressions of self-division as "degenerate art"

14. Egon Schiele, *Two Girls Embracing Each Other,* 1915, Szépmüvészeti
Múzeum, Budapest, Hungary.

(*entartete Kunst*). An identity crisis may be preferable to its unsatisfactory resolution.

Oskar Schlemmer's experiences with panel paintings for the now destroyed circular hall of Minne's fountain in the Folkwang Museum may serve as an epilogue to the visual preoccupation with adolescence.[18] The museum's director, Ernst Grosebuch, decided to provide decoration for the hall and chose the youth movement of the twenties ("Die jungmännische Bewegung unserer Zeit") as the theme. Later he specified that sport was to be included. Schlemmer, Willi Baumeister, and Heckel were invited to compete, and, as Schlemmer reported to Otto Meyer on September 11, 1928 (*Letters* 235), the commission went to Schlemmer.

The first two versions proved unsatisfactory, but Schlemmer finished and exhibited the final panels in 1930 (*Oskar Schlemmer* 6–10). The success was short-lived. Graf Baudissin, the new Nazi museum director, dismantled the panels in 1933 and announced a new competition in the spring of 1934. Schlemmer naively thought he could participate, and even tried to convince Baudissin that he too had ideas about the "new man" and the need to be part of a community. But Baudissin was quick to reply that these words had different meanings for the two of them. One of Schlemmer's panels was exhibited as degenerate art in the 1937 Munich show, and (in spite of Baudissin's promises to preserve them) all panels disappeared. The Nazis had their own ideas about adolescence.

CHAPTER SEVEN

The Adolescence of Psychoanalysis

As we move from fiction to its social and historical context, we pass through the intermediate zone of psychoanalysis, and particularly through Freud's "case studies," which are presented as nonfiction although they involve narration. The narrative and dramatic fabric of Freud's case studies requires that they be treated apart from other psychological theories of adolescence.

Psychoanalytic treatments involve constructing a biography with a therapeutic value. A biography is needed because Freud assigns a shaping force to infantile and childhood experiences. The aim of the treatment is to reconstruct the forgotten or suppressed early experiences that are coresponsible for the adult symptoms and attitudes.

Freud's claim that "sexual life does not begin only at puberty, but starts with clear manifestations soon after birth" (*Outline* 152), led him to a certain neglect of adolescence. He devoted to it only a rather slight contribution from 1914 to the fiftieth anniversary of his Gymnasium entitled *Some Reflections on Schoolboy Psychology,* in which he suggests that our affective disposition toward both sexes is determined during the first six years of life. Although these attachments can be developed and transformed later, the early attachments to parents and siblings are decisive, for all "later choices of friendship and love follow upon the basis of the memory-traces left behind by these first prototypes" (243). Later attachments are constrained by an "emotional heritage": the teachers as father substitutes reenact the oedipal conflict, whereas the peer group as a sibling substitute has, in Freud's view, a relatively minor role in shaping adolescence.

In the *Three Essays on the Theory of Sexuality* (1905) Freud distinguishes three stages in sexual development: object-directed infantile sexuality (originating in the attachment to the mother's breast), "auto-erotic" childhood sexuality, and object-directed genital sexuality reached during puberty (207). Since Freud considers female childhood auto-eroticism clitoral and of "a wholly masculine character," he finds the last, pubescent transition particularly problematic for girls (219). Reaching adult female sexuality implies a painful suppression of a masculine clitoral sexuality and a shift in erogenous zones, which become the source of a greater tendency in females to neuroses and hysteria, and a fundamental burden on femininity (221).

Adult, object-directed sexuality is for both sexes patterned after infantile sexuality, so that the child's sucking at the mother's breast becomes "the prototype of every relation of love. *The finding of an object is in fact a re-finding of it*" (222, my emphasis).[1]

Thus, according to Freud, puberty and adolescence usually replicate infantile experiences. Although the illness may appear only in adolescence, the analyst is "driven to trace back the patients' life history to their earliest years" (*Dora* 27). Therapy entails finding clues to those years through dreams, neurotic symptoms, and transference. A dream, according to Freud, "endeavours to re-shape the present on the model of the remote past. For the wish which creates the dream always springs from the period of childhood; and it is continually trying to summon childhood back into reality and to correct the present day by the measure of childhood" (*Dora* 71). Similarly, neurotic symptoms need "infantile prototypes" for "recollections derived from the impressions of later years do not possess sufficient force to enable them to establish themselves as symptoms" (*Dora* 103). Transference, finally, deroutes the analysis, because "the tendencies and fantasies" aroused and made conscious during analysis impose some earlier person upon the analyst, stamp him a "new edition" or a "facsimile" of the predecessor (*Dora* 116).[2]

As Karen Horney writes in *New Ways in Psychoanalysis,* Freud has a "theory of repetition compulsion" (45). He is "evolutionistic in his thinking, but in a mechanistic way," because he assumes "that nothing much new happens in our development after the age of five, and that later reactions or experiences are to be considered as a repetition of past ones" (44). The relationship between this preprogrammed life and the biography constructed during therapy is far from simple. Establishing a life history involves choices. As Roy Schafer writes, there is "no single, necessary, definitive account of a life history" (30), because we never possess all the facts and, more importantly, because the choice of relevant facts, the emphasis placed on them, and the connections between them inevitably depend on our interpretive stance. Freud's method involves using a set of postulated psychic structures and processes (ego, unconscious, libido, oedipal complex) by means of which one can select, give prominence to, and interrelate the "facts" in a patient's history. Therapy applies the investigator's assumptions "concerning the origins, coherence, totality, and intelligibility of personal action" (Schafer 30). The procedure resembles writing history rather than investigating something in nature, and it incorporates much that is essential to writing fiction.

To regard Freud's case histories as particular kinds of narratives is no imperial expansion of literary analysis and no attack on Freud's therapeutic method. Freud's approach to analysis was highly literary: he was a great stylist, he repeatedly drew upon his vast literary erudition to illustrate his points, gained fundamental concepts of his theory from literature, and, finally, wrote striking interpretations of literature and artworks.

But would Freud have been happy with a literary approach to his case studies? At unguarded moments he acknowledged the bold, imaginative character of psychoanalysis, yet he tended to present himself as a "biologist of the mind" (to use Frank Sulloway's title) who was extending science to a hitherto unmapped territory. He pleaded for the legitimation of psychoanalysis before the tribunal of his medical and scientific elders by claiming that psychoanalysis, like the nineteenth-century positivistic sciences, was on a fact-finding mission.

When making such pleas in search of scientific respectability, Freud took a rather condescending attitude towards the arts. Though he acknowledged their superior power to sublimate primal drives, he labeled them in *Civilization and Its Discontents* a "mild narcosis" that offers temporary relief but cannot obliterate "real misery" (*Civilization* 81). In *Dora*, Freud was so eager to distinguish his explanation from fiction that he introduced the concept of "over-determination" in a highly peculiar manner:

> I must now turn to consider a further complication to which I should certainly give no space if I were a man of letters engaged upon the creation

of a mental state like this for a short story, instead of being a medical man engaged upon its dissection. The element to which I must now allude can only serve to obscure and efface the outlines of the fine poetic conflict which we have been able to ascribe to Dora. This element would rightly fall a sacrifice to the censorship of a writer, for he, after all, simplifies and abstracts when he appears in the character of a psychologist. But in the world of reality, which I am trying to depict here, a complication of motives, an accumulation and conjunction of mental activities—in a word, overdetermination—is the rule. (*Dora* 59–60)

The passage is curious, because by proposing that psychological phenomena and symptoms are *over*determined, that is, traceable to alternative and complementary causes, Freud is actually taking a radical departure from mechanistic causality: overdetermination sets psychoanalysis apart from science rather than from fiction. Anticipating the criticism that overdetermination abandons determinism and turns psychoanalysis into speculation, Freud claims to follow "reality" and disclaims commonality with fiction writers, who, he says, postulate simple mechanical links between psychological cause and effect.

But surely, Freud's "complication of motives" could not persuade scientific positivists that psychoanalysis was a true science, and the condescending remark about literature is blind to the modernist use of multiple perspectives and conjectures. Or was Freud perhaps clouding the issue precisely because he recognized that over determination and modernist fictional techniques sought similar answers to positivism?[3]

FRAMING DORA

Dora's treatment took place between October and December 31, 1900, and Freud wrote it up in the first three weeks of January 1901.[4] The original title, "Dreams and Hysteria," indicates that he considered it an application of his *Theory of Dreams* (1900), but he published the study only in 1905, after thoroughly revising it, partly in light of the ideas on puberty developed in the *Three Essays on the Theory of Sexuality*. Dora's treatment and its write-up are thus embedded in important theoretical concerns, which become explicit in the text's lengthy generalizations and the cumbersome but scientifically honorable title, *Fragment of an Analysis of a Case of Hysteria*. Nevertheless, even though Freud took pains to present his text as a scientific study rather than an anecdote, analysis of its narrative mode may be illuminating. I hope to make a contribution to the already considerable literature on the narrative mode of Freud's case studies by linking my approach to the analyses of stories about adolescents in the previous chapters.[5]

Dora was an eighteen-year-old adolescent with a history of nervous cough, shortness of breath, and loss of voice. She had threatened her father's "friendly" relation with couple K. by accusing Herr K. of having proposi- tioned her and her father of having an affair with Frau K. When Herr K. flatly denied the accusation, Dora's father (who had previously been treated by Freud upon Herr K.'s recommendation!) brought Dora to Freud with the comment, "Suchen Sie sie jetzt auf bessere Wege zu bringen"—rather freely rendered in English as "Please try to bring her to reason" (*Dora* 26). Freud came to believe Dora's accusations (*Dora* 34) but labeled the girl's revulsion at Herr K.'s earlier attempted embrace hysterical, because he considered it abnormal that "an occasion for sexual excitement elicited feelings that were preponderantly or exclusively unpleasurable" (*Dora* 28)! The remark has been justly taken as a sign of Freud's insensitivity to the female adolescent psyche.

Freud's treatment, based mainly on ingenious analyses of Dora's dreams, led him to conclude that she had been in love with Herr K. and homosexually attracted to Frau K. Her illness was partly an expression of anger that both of them betrayed her: the husband by denying that he propositioned her, the wife by becoming her father's lover. But Freud's theory demanded that the recent events and symptoms be traced back to Dora's unresolved oedipal conflict, associated with childhood bedwetting and masturbation (*Dora* 78– 79). In this view, Dora feared that she might surrender to the father-substitute and summoned the prototype for protection, only to prove thereby her love for Herr K.: "You are summoning up your old love for your father in order to protect yourself against your love for Herr K. But what do all these efforts show? Not only that you are afraid of Herr K., but that you are still more afraid of yourself, and of the temptation you feel to yield to him. In short, these efforts prove once more how deeply you loved him" (*Dora* 70).

At first approximation, *Dora* is Freud's story about an adolescent girl. But Freud's text includes next to Dora's biography also the history of its making, the story of the sessions that included Dora's monologic free associations and dreams, Freud's interpretive comments, and dialogues between the two par- ticipants. In this sense, Freud's text consists of a double story, Dora's life and the history of her therapy. The pattern may be compared to a "framed" story, where the inner story emerges from an embedding conversation between the narrator and his protagonist. In this frame story Freud is an "inner narrator," one who participates in the story he tells, but he is decidedly not a "peer-group narrator," for none of those narrators we have encountered have the kind of superiority over their protagonists that age, sex, and professional status confer upon Freud when facing Dora.

Freud's interspersed theoretical disquisitions are to be read as the narrator's explanation why and how he constructed his story the way he did. Like Thomas Mann, Faulkner, and other modernists, Freud combines storytelling with reflections about it, and he interweaves story and reflection so artfully that the two plots (life story and its making) cannot be neatly separated. Contrary to Steven Marcus, I do not believe that the "Prefatory Remarks" (*Dora* 7–14) constitute in themselves "a kind of novelistic framing action" (Marcus 270). Indeed, Freud offers only glimpses of those "frame" conversations that constitute much of the life story's raw material, and the preface states explicitly that he will not reproduce "the process of interpretation to which the patient's associations and communications had to be subjected, but only the results of that process. Apart from the dreams, therefore, the technique of the analytic work has been revealed in only a very few places" (*Dora* 12–13).

We may now start to appreciate the essay's narratorial control. Is, then, Dora's contribution no more than what Meaulnes's letters and diaries are for François—material to be used freely? To a considerable extent this is so, for, as I shall show, Freud is quite dictatorial in constructing her story from what she offers. But the analogy with Alain-Fournier's story fails in one major respect: François does not write about writing the story. Presumably he is sitting alone, facing those letters and diaries instead of his live friend. The tension between the protagonist's fragmentary utterances and the narrator's interpretation remains hidden in *Le Grand Meaulnes* but constitutes the heart of the struggle between Freud and Dora. Freud must tell the story of that therapeutic struggle because only the incompleteness of the sessions can explain the fragmentariness of the biography.

Let us take a closer look. The story of the treatment (*Behandlungsgeschichte*) tells how Dora's life story is constructed out of an underlying subtext, a dramatic dialogue between Dora, who has to understand her life in order to get well, and Freud, who pieces together Dora's dreams and free associations with his interpretive "glue," in part, though surely not completely, to demonstrate the power of his theory. But the conversational partners have unequal rights in spinning the story, not only because Freud is the sole editor of the final text, but because his theory doubly condemns Dora to the role of an "unreliable narrator." First, according to the psychoanalytic covenant, she must tell her thoughts and feelings pell-mell, without reflection and without an Aristotelian organization into beginning, middle, and end. She may produce only fragments that escape the censuring mechanism as shards embedded in free associations, body language, and dreams. Freud decides what is of value in her outpouring. When treating hysteria, "everything that has to do with the clearing-up of a particular symptom emerges piecemeal, woven into various contexts, and distributed over widely separated periods of time" (*Dora* 12–13).

Second, and more important, Freud regards Dora as an "unreliable" narrator because her inner censorship erases part of her story, and distorts, condenses, inverts, and chronologically jumbles whatever is allowed to surface. Her story is untrustworthy, because patients "consciously and intentionally keep back part of what they ought to tell"; "part of the anamnestic knowledge, which the patients have at their disposal at other times, inadvertently disappears while they are actually telling their story;" and, finally, the true amnesias get filled up with pseudomemories (*Dora* 17). Only Freud, as omnipotent editor, can undo the censorship, fill in the missing parts and discover the hidden meaning in and behind the unreliable story.

In spite of these handicaps, Dora produces three coherent text-passages: the episode with Herr K., a report on her father's affair that contradicts what he said (*Dora* 32–34), and accounts of two dreams. Her remaining story fragments are often teased out of her by Freud's remarks and questions.

What does Freud do with Dora's story fragments? Her dreams are in themselves incoherent and become controversial only through Freud's interpretation, as part of the life story he constructs for her.[6] Dora's accounts of her father's affair and of the scene with Herr K. are more problematic because they contradict what others claim. Freud accepts these stories because he can "not in general dispute Dora's characterization of her father" (*Dora* 34). His trust could engender Dora's confidence in him and postpone the transference that later saddles him with a negative father image. But when Freud accepts Dora's story he tells her only that she is an unreliable narrator:

> When the patient brings forward a sound and incontestable train of argument during psycho-analytic treatment, the physician is liable to feel a moment's embarrassment, and the patient may take advantage of it by asking: "This is all perfectly correct and true, isn't it? What do you want to change in it now that I've told it you?" But it soon becomes evident that the patient is using thoughts of this kind, which the analysis cannot attack,

for the purpose of cloaking others which are anxious to escape from criticism and from consciousness. A string of reproaches against other people leads one to suspect the existence of a string of self-reproaches with the same content. All that need be done is to turn back each single reproach on to the speaker himself. (*Dora* 35)

Thus Freud *silently* accepts Dora's story ("could not in general dispute" suggests that he did not tell her so), but questions her motives and turns her story against her, instead of boosting Dora's self-confidence and her trust in him. We must remember that this is the crucial event in Dora's life and the only major story she tells about herself. Stories by neurotic and psychotic persons may be generally untrustworthy, but one may ask whether exceptions should not be awarded with an expression of trust.

On two occasions Freud switches from narratorial report to longer quoted dialogues: during the interpretation of Dora's first dream (*Dora* 64–67, 68–70, 71–73) and in reenacting the last session (*Dora* 105–8). Such enactments usually suggest objectivity and balance not to be found in the inherently subjective narratorial report. But here the dialogues reveal only Freud's role as stage director. Whenever he gains interpretive insights—for instance that Dora must have been disgusted by Herr K.'s erection (*Dora* 30), that she fell ill in order to separate her father from Frau K. (*Dora* 42), that her cough and genital infection were symptoms of sexual concerns (*Dora* 82–83), that Dora secretly wished Herr K. to be serious in approaching her (*Dora* 108)—he gauges his diagnostic success by the degree to which Dora responds with protest or initial silence. She must react negatively to correct findings because patients *invariably* "dispute the conclusiveness of circumstantial evidence" (*Dora* 81). We cannot expect "that the patient will come to meet the physician half-way with material which has become pathogenic for the very reason of its efforts to lie concealed; nor must the enquirer rest content with the first 'No' that crosses his path" (*Dora* 24). When Freud concludes that Dora tried to suppress her love for Herr K., he triumphantly reads her expected "most emphatic negative" response as an affirmation:

> The "No" uttered by a patient after a repressed thought has been presented to his conscious perception for the first time does no more than register the existence of a repression and its severity; . . . If this "No," instead of being regarded as the expression of an impartial judgement (of which, indeed, the patient is incapable), is ignored, and if work is continued, the first evidence soon begins to appear that in such a case "No" signifies the desired "Yes." (*Dora* 58–59)

Thus every "no" is a priori a "yes": when he tells her that she has in all these years been in love with Herr K., "she did not assent to it" (*Dora* 37); when he surmises that as a child she must have been utterly in love with her father, she replies ("of course") "I don't remember" but goes on "to tell me something analogous about a seven-year-old girl" (*Dora* 57), which Freud takes as a negation of the negation. When Freud concludes from the first dream that Dora was ready to surrender to Herr K., he adds, "naturally Dora would not follow me in this part of the interpretation" (*Dora* 70). When Dora flatly denies remembering childhood masturbation, Freud tells her that she is "masturbating" with her reticule while talking (*Dora* 76).

In all these cases, Freud's brilliant "detective work" overwhelms Dora. But when Freud proudly displays his interpretation of the second dream after only two sittings, Dora belittles the achievement: "Why, has anything so very remarkable come out?" (*Dora* 105). Freud misses the hostility in her voice and perceives in it "the advent of fresh revelations" yet to come from Dora. But in the next and last session she responds to Freud's new interpretations with an unexpected assenting nod and a quiet listening "without any of her usual contradictions" (*Dora* 108–9). Her spirit of negation dwindles, but only to signal her unwillingness to contribute further to *his* story of *her* life.

Freud probably incorporated in the text only illustrative samples of the clashes that accompanied his construction of her story. Getting her to accept (his version of) her story must have been considerably more problematic than the text suggests. The text does not tell us how difficult it was for her to accept Freud's interpretation, nor does it report her inner struggles, because the story of the therapy (the frame story) maintains the rules of scientific reporting and denies itself the kind of insight into the protagonist's mind that is the privilege of fiction writers. The method sharply contrasts with the quasi-omniscient narratorial position Freud assumes in constructing the psychohistory of Dora's life, for there he repeatedly claims to know what went on in her mind.

But the narratorial restraint in the frame story is perhaps no self-limitation at all, only an admission that the narrator is really ignorant of what Dora was thinking. How else to explain Freud's failure to anticipate her decision to terminate the treatment? Should he not have read her mind? Should he not have anticipated that she would sooner or later come to resent being given a merely negative role in writing the script of her life?

Freud writes that he did not succeed in "mastering the transfer in good time" and became the victim of Dora's thirst for revenge on Herr K. (*Dora*

118). This view fails to acknowledge Freud's active role in assuming the burden of fatherly roles: he denied her his trust the way her father and Herr K.
did. The disturbed adolescent was brought to him in order to restore her
healthy sense of identity. As Freud recognized, Dora was hurt by those she
loved most. Her father, Herr K., and Frau K. all demanded that she accept
"their stories"—which Dora knew to be lies. She was outraged that Herr K.
denied having propositioned her and that her father sided with him in order
to save his affair with Frau K.

Freud disbelieved Dora's father the way Dora's father probably disbelieved
Herr K.; yet neither of them acknowledged that Dora was right. Instead of
strengthening her ego by accepting her story, Freud proceeded to construct
his own complicated account of her life and forced her into a position of mere
negation. His proud excitement at a brilliant application of his dream theory
must have blinded him to what should have been evident, namely that by
constructing his version of her story he squandered her trust in him and
clubbed her already vanquished ego with additional crushing blows. Could
Dora overcome her adolescent identity crisis by accepting a life history that
was predetermined by childhood events and forced upon her by the analyst-
narrator? Was it not predictable that a life story built by an authoritarian
narrator out of ineluctable past events would seem like a straitjacket to her?

Dora's decision to terminate the treatment was violent but predictable.
She acquiesced in Freud's version of her story but paid him back by "dic-
tating" part of the other story, forcing the Freudian narrator to conclude with
a therapy scenario she wrote herself. Creating a life story for Dora cost Freud
the story of the treatment, and this ironically led to gaps in the biography
he wrote.

My critique of Freud's handling of the case differs from the accusations
that scientists and philosophers of science have leveled against it. Benjamin
Rubenstein and others have challenged psychoanalysis to deliver hard empirical evidence, they judge it against yardsticks that Freud himself applied by
virtue of his nineteenth-century scientific education. These yardsticks demand evidence on Dora's bedwetting and masturbation, on her father's impotence, and on Herr K.'s "true" designs. And we expect the analyst to pursue
such evidence with detachment and disinterestedness.

Pursuing such evidence is necessary, but much of it will continue to remain
elusive. The healing of the mind would be a hopeless enterprise if it depended
on acquiring all the relevant facts from the past. Besides, the possession of
all the pertinent facts does not guarantee a cure. Freud believed that the

psychologically suppressed facts would acquire healing power in the light of reason, but belief in the power of truth was a part of his heritage from the Enlightenment that his theory tended to negate.

What was to be done? Since Dora suffered from a "distorted," largely private vision of herself, she needed a life story that was if not wholly factual at least personally satisfying and at the same time intersubjectively credible. A self-image and the corresponding life can be "distorted" only against some standard, however tenuous the status of that standard may be, and in this sense it was quite appropriate that Dora forced the others to acknowledge the correctness of her story after the treatment (*Dora* 121). But to make Dora face the truth, and only the truth, would have been an impossible and therapeutically useless goal, for she needed an affirmative self-image. In any case, Freud sought something much more complex than "facts" and "truth," and the major problem was that he imposed it upon her.

Confused patients need a life story that can both strengthen their identity and allow its integration. To tell such a story well means not only adhering to evidence but also keeping an eye on the therapeutic end, which cannot be achieved if the analyst is the only narrator. Patients retain their weak identity if they have no role in (re)constructing their lives. In Dora's case, Freud missed *his* chance to succeed by denying *her* participation in the "story telling." She avenged her inferior role as unreliable narrator, patient, adolescent, and woman, by truncating Freud's treatment story and making it into just *A Fragment* of an analysis. Freud regretted it for the rest of his life.

To put the matter differently, psychoanalytic "stories" ought to redistribute the weight between the "frame" and the "inner story," and, as Schafer argues, perhaps give even greater emphasis to the "frame" than to the life story that emerges from it:

> [analysands] tell the analyst about themselves and others in the past and present. In making interpretations, the analyst retells these stories. . . . The end product of this interweaving of texts is a radically new, jointly authored work or way or working. One might say that in the course of analysis, there develops a cluster of more or less coordinated new narrations, each corresponding to periods of intensive analytic work on certain leading questions. Generally, these narrations focus neither on the past, plain and simple, nor on events currently taking place outside the psychoanalytic situation. They focus much more on the place and modification of these tales within the psychoanalytic dialogue. . . . The psychoanalytic dialogue is characterized most of all by its organization in terms of the here and now of the

psychoanalytic relationship. It is *fundamentally a dialogue concerning the present moment of transference and resistance.* (35–36, my emphasis)

A therapeutically valuable life story demands that the "frame" discussion be a genuine dialogue between two narrators, none of whom should a priori be labeled "unreliable."[7]

THE ADOLESCENCE OF KAREN HORNEY

Dora's dialogue with psychoanalysis was written by Freud. As a counterpart I want to look at Karen Horney's adolescent diaries, which speak about her youth and her encounter with psychoanalysis from the perspective of an adolescent.[8] In addition to five diaries (which cover the ages 13–15, 15–17, 18–19, 19–22, and 25–26), the published book also contains Karen's letters to her future husband, Oskar Horney, which partly bridge the gap between the last two diaries and function as a diary. The last diary, written when Karen was already beyond adolescence, records her reactions to therapy and revaluates her adolescent problems. The book thus allows one to compare the immediate adolescent records with their later analytic reassessment.

Karen's words to Oskar (Little Hornvieh) illuminate the continuity between her early diaries, the correspondence with Oskar, and the responses to the analysis: "I'm just writing away, whatever comes into my head, hardly realizing that someone else is to read it. Little Hornvieh functioning as Karen's diary!" (October 6, 1906: 169). A few months later she adds, probably responding to Oskar's comments on his "diary role": "Yes, I find it highly sensible, letters in diary form. The business has only one hitch: assume I am in a very pronounced mood one day and write it down. When I go at the letter again, perhaps I read over what I wrote. And the letter strays into the waste-basket. Anyway that's the way it will be mostly, and the more, the more unreservedly I had put down everything in the sense of my mood, i.e., the more valuable the letter was as a letter . . . ?" (March 24, 1907: 190). Though two weeks later she felt "almost safe just writing to you" (April 10, 1907: 199), the awareness of a reader, even herself, provided a censor.

Karen started her diaries simply to recall the days of her youth in later years (3). Sporadic entries during the first two years reflect a naive, well-intentioned *Backfisch* with typical crushes on male as well as female teachers. Although she occasionally chided herself for lacking religious feelings and violently rebelled against her authoritarian father, she held decidedly middle-class values and was deeply embedded in her cultural tradition. From a late twentieth-century vantage point she is a naive and emotionally underdeveloped pubescent.

The tone of the diary changes, however, at seventeen, when a conflict develops between her middle-class heritage and her adolescent desire for personal and "natural" values. If her first moral law, "Thou shalt not lie," reaffirms the parental world, her second one enjoins her to seek a personal identity: "Thou shalt free thy self from convention, from everyday morality, and shalt think through the highest commands for thy self and act accordingly. Too much custom, too little morality!" (82). Now she writes poetry, copies poems into the diary, is enchanted by the erotic poetry of Marie-Madeleine, and reads about adolescent rebellion in Max Halbe's drama *Jugend*.

But the voice that demands the right of self-determination incorporates the parental voice of the superego: the injunction against lying is both a condemnation of conventions that foster insincerity and a part of her heritage. Like her fellow adolescent, Kafka, Karen opposes not the traditional beliefs and rules themselves but their undermining through hypocrisy. First she rejects her father for disobeying his own religious values, then she condemns the "utilitarian morality" of her brother Berndt (98), and finally of her adored mother, who refuses to receive Karen's Jewish boyfriend in their home (124).

Yet Karen does not reject her parental world only because it surreptitiously undermines the principles it ostentatiously upholds. She rebels against these principles under the banner of authenticity, freedom, and nature, she is an adolescent of her age, part of the turn-of-the-century generation that turned against its parental world by seeking the authenticity of instinct and spontaneous emotion, the fresh air of outdoors, the freedom of the naked body, the simplicity of folklore, and the magic of exoticism.

Karen's case shows how deeply this rhetoric of freedom and authenticity was rent by contradictions. What she seeks is no libertine freedom from all constraint, but submission to the "higher," "purer," and more personal laws of her own femininity. But these laws are not "naturally" evident, they are elusive and the source of much inner turmoil.

Just what do they demand of her? At nineteen, Karen is inspired by the Swedish feminist Ellen Key, the "lustrous star" guiding her soul, the source of her "sacred flame of enthusiasm" (92). Key wants to balance the individual's demands for happiness with a concern for the species" (92–93), and she tells Karen that a woman's "individual freedom of mind" is circumscribed by the "demands of nature," the raising of children within stable marriages.

The diary notes: "We want this freedom for our emotional life and for its expression, freedom not license, for we feel bound to the demands of Nature. We want to achieve a new morality" (102).

This "new morality" is not just a warmed-up old-fashioned one, for it is designed to safeguard women's emancipation. How wanton sexuality can endanger that emancipation is brought home to Karen when she accidentally comes upon the following passage in a book: "Force me to my knees, dearest. For I am a woman. No good, shy little girl of the humble womanliness described in books—no, on the contrary. But just for this proud, free, independently thinking woman there is no sweeter lot than to be allowed to worship, to bow down in love. Oh, dearest—will you be my master?" (73). The corny crudity of the passage did not temper its impact. Karen was a "proud, free, independently thinking woman" who blazed the feminist trail by attending Gymnasium and medical school—and she was fully aware of it. But she concluded that she could not gain full independence and freedom if, like the fictional female, she remained a slave of sexuality and therefore a servant of her male masters. The only solution that seemed open to her, the "new morality" of Ellen Key and others, demanded that she suppress the elemental sexual desires that repeatedly welled up in her. But this "new morality" was actually more coercive than the old one: Ellen Key, the Wandervogel, the adolescent teetotalers, the vegetarians, and all the other moral reformers and prophets of a "new humanity" spoke of liberation but demanded abstinence. Their moral rigor appealed to the idealism of youth.

Karen wished to accept the rigor of the "new morality" though she could not live up to it. Occasionally she rebelled against it and thought that her "debased" physical craving had a beauty and justification of its own, but generally she accepted its principles and accused herself of "sinning" against it. The condemnation of sexuality by the "new morality" reinforced the traditional bourgeois injunction. Karen's fear of her own sexuality appears already in her early adolescence, prior to encountering Ellen Key. When reading the erotic poems of Marie-Madeleine her senses exult "in unbridled delight" but her intellect "turns away in disdain" (63). She feels compelled to conclude: "In my own imagination I am a strumpet!" (64) In a poem a few months later she celebrates her "success" at liberating herself from one of her first dominating lovers: "My pride has conquered love. . . . He treated me like a strumpet" (77).

Two years later, on March 29, 1905 Karen is still burdened with the image of the "strumpet":

> To be free of sensuality means great power in a woman. Only in this way will she be independent of a man. Otherwise she will always long for him and in the exaggerated yearning of her senses she will be able to drown out all feeling of her own value. She becomes the bitch, who begs even if she is beaten—a strumpet. . . . Otherwise eternal battling. And every victory of the senses a Pyrrhic victory, bought with loathing, ever deadly loathing afterwards. (104)

A person unfamiliar with the context could trace this sexual philosophy to Christianity or Schopenhauer. Karen was familiar with Nietzsche, but she did not adopt his critique of Christian and Schopenhauerian self-debasing. Her late-adolescent years became "eternal battles" between the intellectual demands of the "new morality," which she accepted but could not obey, and her "base" sexual cravings that either conquered and lowered her self-esteem or were suppressed at the price of neurotic distress. Unable to live up to the principle of purity she accepted, she was given to periodic self-castigations; possessed by Ellen Key's "deep moral earnestness," she could not understand, why "the most brutal naturalism" seemed equally "intelligible" to her (91).

As a result, Karen's adolescent love life pathologically reenacts a Tannhäuserian conflict between the higher and the lower, the heavenly and the earthly, the pure and the debased. On one side are the "deep," "pure," and intellectually satisfying relations that Karen wishes to keep sexually "uncontaminated": her friendship with the Jewish Rolf that had a decisive influence on her development (recorded in a lengthy retrospective: 120–46, 150–60), and the epistolary friendship with "little Hornvieh." The first diary entry concerning Rolf, made on August 11, 1904, foreshadows everything:

> I love you like a sister, Rolf, like a friend who only wants the best for you. You say that my love gives you peace. See, I come to lay my hand on your poor tormented heart. I am too young for other feelings not to be mixed in with this pure love. Then a consuming longing for you comes over me, a wild turmoil of my senses. But that is just like a foreign element that doesn't belong to me, and it soon disappears. (89)

Sexuality seems like an alien intruder into her "true" self, a contamination of her pristine love for an intellectual and moral tutor (129). When Rolf kisses her "quite gently, quite uncertainly" for the first time, Karen is "disconcerted and sad": "I had the feeling that now a shadow had fallen across our delightful relationship as friends" (133). His kisses leave her cold at the outset, later she accepts them "with a sort of passive well-being" (137), but she resents her sexual arousals and accuses him as well as herself: "All the hours in which our senses spoke loudest seem to me somewhat ugly, like a foreign body that had entered in and did not belong there. And that lies not only in the matter itself, but I believe that the spiritual part involuntarily appears higher and nobler than the physical" (143). When Rolf, the clumsy kisser and horrible dancer (143, 135), suddenly reappears in Karen's life, she happily reports to Oskar that Rolf now understands "the sensual incident" as "a foreign body in our relation, because sensually we do not suit each other" (223).

Sexual incompatibility with the man who brought Karen's "spiritual awakening" (185) was part of a larger pattern. Her review of the year 1906 notes the painful closure of the relationship with Rolf and records its metamorphosed rebirth:

> Correspondence with the little Hornvieh and the start of a friendship with him. And with that the taking up again of a thread that ran luminously through a year of my life, the friendship with Rolf. What Rolf awakened in me is being brought to life again by Hornvieh. How shall I say it briefly? The reflecting about myself perhaps, about the deeper springs of my ego, the search within. (149)

The theme of repetition and continuity had already appeared three weeks earlier, in a letter of December 11–12, 1906, to Hornvieh himself: the "finer language" of his letters reintroduced the possibility of "a life of a higher sort" that Rolf had shown her in her "petit-bourgeois family" (175 f.). Ominously she confides, however, on February 13, 1907: "Perhaps there is a bit of the hussy in all of us" (187).

For a while, the danger of sexual "contamination" seems to be absent. Karen gets to know Hornvieh when she is in love with a man called Ernst Losch, Hornvieh departs, and their contact is reduced to a correspondence, in which Karen freely analyzes her amours (for example, 209–11, 228) and Hornvieh (inasmuch as this can be deduced from her letters) reciprocates. But once the "epistolary episode" of their relationship is over, during their marriage and her psychoanalytic treatment, it becomes evident that Hornvieh has inherited not only Rolf's idealistic, noble function but also his inability to satisfy Karen's "base" sexual cravings: "In Oskar I found everything I consciously wished for—and behold: my instinctual life rebels. . . . Oskar is always self-controlled. Even when he forces me to submit to him—it is never savagery or animal brutality—he is at all times controlled, he is never elemental. For living together, certainly ideal—but something remains in me that hungers" (April 18, 1910: 238–39). In the following January, Karen notes that she has an increased capacity for sexual enjoyment (247) and that her "relation with Oskar has become sexually harmonious" (249), yet the diary ends with somber and perplexed remarks about her neuroses.

"Animal sensuality" (106) not only "contaminates" Karen's "higher" relations with men, it also leads to self-accusations when she is strongly attracted to men she does not respect morally or intellectually. In her "lower" relationship to Ernst and Karl, as in her "pure" ones to Rolf and Oskar, the intrusion of something elemental lowers her self-esteem and disturbs her emotional balance.

When she gets to know Ernst at the end of her friendship with Rolf, the senses run "ahead of love" (November 17, 1905: 107). The short-lived romance leaves her perplexed: she often remembers the moments of passion with Ernst ("the man I really loved"!) as "beautiful and precious," but she feels compelled to add immediately that this may be because "with him I did not have the finer feeling, but was blindly craving a sacrifice for my senses" (April 1906: 143). By the end of the year, the image of Ernst and her attachment to him become unequivocally negative: "Out of the blue I was seized by a senseless passion for someone else, who was built of a coarser stuff [than Rolf]" (letter to Hornvieh, December 11–12, 1906: 176). "Now at last I am free of him and at rest, for I have seen him too clearly for what he is. Him in his good-citizens's pettiness and cowardice, in his mendacity, in his brutality and his egoism. How could I ever have loved him so deeply, so passionately? Forever an open question" (January 3, 1907: 149).

The open question asks for restatement. Karl, whom she gets to know as Hornvieh's philosophizing friend (224–26), reappears during her marriage as the person to whom her "instinctual life" (not she herself!) is drawn "because it scents the beast of prey in him, which it needs" (April 18, 1910: 238). Seeing him again, Karen has a strong desire to throw her arms around his neck and kiss him (241), but Oskar observes the scene and remarks subsequently that "I had 'thrown myself away' because I had so conspicuously flirted with Karl" (242). She responds with exaggerated "spasms of sobbing" and a "deep depression" because the remark hit a raw nerve that gets lacerated each time she is unable to live up to the sexual principles of the "new morality." On these occasions she becomes that fictional intelligent and emancipated woman, whose "animal passion" makes her a slave to male masters. Lest she becomes a bitch, a hussy, a prostitute, she has to emancipate herself and suppress this animal sexuality, but she repeatedly fails and self-flagellations follow.

Karen Horney's adolescent diary shows that the "new morality" had extended the reign of bourgeois values by insisting that sexual cravings be suppressed. The demand acquired a special function in the emancipation of women, for, as Karen's diary shows, it implied that women could maintain their independence from dominating males only by curbing their sexual desire. For Karen, at any rate, the injunction had disastrous consequences, for she repeatedly "slipped" and bitterly came to accuse herself in the wake of it. Hence her melancholy conclusion about the "hussy" in her and perhaps in all women (186). To an article that Hornvieh sent her on the question of emancipation she responds: I doubt "that women will *ever* be able to achieve intellectually what men do. Lies in the nature of the matter—women are too involved in the sexual—children! etc. So that the woman question won't bring any direct advance in the life of the mind (science, art)" (January 13, 1907: 184).

Yet not all voices of turn-of-the-century culture preached this sublimation of female sexuality, and in view of Karen's career one is particularly interested to know whether psychoanalysis brought her alleviation. Did she fare better than Dora? Did she find a more sensitive response to the needs of her female adolescence than Dora had found with Freud? Could psychoanalysis help to convince her that accepting her sexual urges would be part of her emancipation and the foundation of a more "natural" and secure self-image?

The diary shows that this was not the case, even though she was treated by Karl Abraham, the pioneering Freudian analyst in Berlin and one of the outstanding leaders of the movement. Karen's disappointing first exposure to psychoanalysis must have played an important role in the development of her later theory. Whether the dark, somber mood of the last diary from 1910–1911 is due to the analysis and whether she entered therapy for professional or for personal reasons is unclear. But during her illness and self-doubt analysis undeniably addressed her with the same ego-destructive voice as her father and the "new morality." Commodore Berndt Wackels Danielsen, who thought that a girl need not attend Gymnasium, Ellen Key, who thought that women must sublimate their sexuality in order to emancipate themselves truly, and Karl Abraham, who thought that Karen's secret "prostitution wish" was a normal interest that all middle-class women took in prostitution (242)—all these paternal voices could not fail to humble her self-image.

The very first entry from Berlin, on April 18, 1910, picks up old problems and offers old answers couched in a new language. Karen's great attraction to "brutal and rather forceful men," her "wanting to blend in with the will of a man who has set his foot on my neck," her "overly strong attraction" to Ernst ("that clumsy, brutally egotistic, coarsely sensual fellow" 238) are, according to Abraham, inescapable because they derive from Karen's oedipal love for her father. Karen, who hoped to kill her passion for Ernst and his likes through analysis, learns only: "all his inferior characteristics, which I kept before my eyes, did not in the least quench my passion; no, on the contrary: the instincts in me wanted such a man—and my conscious I, seeking a man of fine intelligence and discerning kindness, resisted against this in vain" (238).

When Oskar accuses Karen of conspicuous flirting, Abraham reminds Karen of her old self-image as a "hussy": "I had taken it so hard because the rebuke had hit upon a repressed wish, namely the very wish to throw myself away, prostitute myself—give myself to any man at random. . . . In the prostitution wish there is always a masochistic wish hidden: to relinquish one's own personality, to be subject to another, to let oneself be used by the other" (242). Psychoanalysis, unlike the "new morality," did not say that the prostitution wish and the related sexual urges had to be suppressed or sublimated, but it placed these in such a light that their acceptance inevitably lowered Karen's self-image.

Abraham's ego-destructive analysis was reinforced by Karen's psychoanalytic readings, foremost among them Alfred Adler's writings. Fatigued after several months into her therapy, she adopts Adler's view that her shyness and her fear of not being able to do first-class work is justified for "the masculine protest is developed in every woman and makes her inwardly unfree." Every woman "feels herself to be primarily, as such, inferior to men" (251).

The last item in the *Adolescent Diaries* is a letter to Abraham, which Karen left in her diary and did not send off. On July 9, 1911, five months after the death of her mother and four months after the birth of her first child, she laconically remarks that "it is not going well at all" but thinks "it is probably expedient to continue the analysis." Whether it continued is unclear. But one may add that her adolescent crisis ended and her true emancipation started only later, when she turned against the father figures of Freud, Abraham, and Adler by working towards an alternative psychoanalysis of female sexuality. Like Dora, Karen was the victim of the adolescence of psychoanalysis.

CHAPTER EIGHT

The Psychology of Adolescence

1890–1925

Freud's curious distinction in *Dora* between literary and psychoanalytic explanations exemplifies a deep conflict between aesthetic and rational principles, not only in Freud but in the culture of his age as well. This conflict affected approaches to adolescence: its "discovery" meant developing a rationale for its "emancipation," which, however, had to be accommodated to the general economy and rational organization of society.

The case for emancipation was aesthetic, not because it pleaded for "art, legends, romance" (Hall, *Adolescence* 1: xvii), but rather because it demanded that adolescence be given autonomy, freedom to experiment, and a moratorium on contributing to society.[1] The same criteria of autonomy, freedom, and purposelessness were generally considered central features of aesthetic objects.

In practice, adolescence had no more freedom and autonomy than art itself. Even the most liberal plea to grant independence and freedom to adolescents ultimately subordinated these goals to the interests of the nation and future humanity. "Adolescence for adolescents' sake" was never more than a call to grant temporary and limited space for youth, justified in terms of adult designs. Repose, leisure, and art were needed so that youth "can enter the kingdom of man well equipped for man's highest work in the world" (Hall 1: xvii). Yet freedom and experimentation were tolerated only as long as they posed no threat to the existing economic and scientific order. Differences arose with respect to the precise location of these boundary lines, which claimed to be defined by natural or social laws but were actually dictated by ideology, personal idiosyncrasy, momentary mood, or sheer ignorance. Turn-of-the-century psychologists claimed to approach adolescence with scientific impartiality but were often guided by unexamined ideas and ruling norms.[2] When echoing Rousseau that "nothing human" should be alien to the formative stage of adolescence (*Emil* Bk. 4), Hall (2: 303) and his colleagues defined human nature in terms of their own restrictive values and opposed adolescent departures from them. This was the case with masturbation, homosexuality, and feminism, three issues I discuss in this chapter.

These conflicts are beautifully illustrated by *Vaters Kind (Father's Child)*, one of the stories in Lou Andreas-Salomé's volume on adolescent girls entitled *Zwischenland (No-Man's Land,* 1902). The story concerns the thirteen-year-old Ria, who comes into conflict with her adored father, a school principal dedicated to education and the betterment of mankind. On one level, the conflict is purely oedipal. Ria receives a little dog from a young admirer, but her father discovers the identity of the donor and compels her to return the gift. When the pet attempts to return to Ria, it is overrun by a car and "mercifully" shot by her father. Her pet's death and her father's brutality become a terrible trauma for Ria, which her jealous father belittles when with great relief he discovers that she mourns for the pet and not for the boyfriend.

Andreas-Salomé poses this conflict on a second, philosophical level as a clash between utilitarian and aesthetic values. Ria's sexuality is as yet dormant. Her love for the pet is part of her "childish" love for all things living. She enjoys flowers, animals, and the "wilderness" of their neglected backyard "for their own sake." Asked about Darwinism, she replies that she is sorry for the apes (not men!) for they are appreciated merely as "forerunners" and not for what they are (121). This "childish" respect for all things, whatever their rank in the hierarchy of beings, must be replaced by a "mature" utilitarian world view, exemplified by Ria's didactic father, who turns all purposeless things into means of improving mankind. The sincere and selfless pedagogue intends to sacrifice his backyard "wilderness" and his vacations in order to teach, without remuneration, neglected peasant children. He is an "enlightened despot" who does not understand Ria's love for a "beast" and demands that she surrender adolescent "leisure" for useful adult purposes. Ria reluctantly and temporarily submits, but the story concludes by indicating that her "childish" mentality may yet find a place in the adult world without surrendering to teleology and utilitarianism. Her unstructured love for all things living, which adumbrates contemporary preservationist concerns (inasmuch as they demand nature's preservation, even if it has no visible economic or health value), receives an explicitly aesthetic tint: in the last scene she encounters a painter who preserves the artistic image of ephemeral flowers and mushrooms for eternity.

The anti-utilitarian stance is worth contemplating, in spite of its all too evident fin-de-siècle aesthetic metaphysics: Ria may become an artist in order to preserve for herself and nature a degree of self-value, but her author is remembered as "Lou," the woman who entered the lives of famous men— Nietzsche, Rilke, and Freud—and not as an independent female writer.

THE PSYCHOLOGISTS

The conflict between aesthetic and purposive values is evident in Hall's study of adolescence. One side of his brain voraciously consumed and digested empirical data generated by his own team and others. The *Pedagogical Seminary,* which he founded in 1891, became a journal of empirical studies on youth that published articles by William Burnham (1891), E. G. Lancaster (1897), Edgar Swift (1901), and others.[3] Hall also initiated a "child study" movement and collected empirical material on the behavior of children and adolescents. As founder of what is now developmental psychology he gained considerable influence among educators.

But this voracious empiricism, which swelled Hall's book on adolescence to an unconscionable size, is governed by a thundering rhetoric that displays his speculative hypotheses and visions in purple prose and with quaint neologisms like "extravasation of thought" and "paleopsychic traits" (1: v, x). Hall's advocacy of adolescence had a touch of genius, but it spoke with a double tongue and for a split audience: it overwhelmed the scientific colleagues with empirical data and mesmerized the lay public with mysterious chants.

Hall's theory may be reduced to three basic principles: (1) acquired characteristics may be inherited, (2) individual development recapitulated the history of the species, and (3) acquiring inheritable traits was most likely to occur during adolescence (1: 50). The last principle was what made adolescence such an important developmental phase. For if the psyche shook off part of its heritage during adolescence and atavistically reverted to a more fluid state, experiences at that stage could leave deep imprints on the adult personality and its future inheritors: adolescence, "and not maturity as now defined, is the only point of departure for the superanthropoid that man is to become" (2: 94).

Hall's vision of a teleological evolution towards a "superanthropoid" was indebted to Darwin, Nietzsche, Spencer, and Haeckel and constituted a quasi-religious belief that many others shared around 1900. But the desire to reach for the "superanthropoid" hollowed out Hall's plea to grant adolescents "repose, leisure, art, legends, romance, idealization" (1: xvii). His liberal, youth-centered view of adolescence as an end in itself was negated by his teleological vision, which demanded that everything having a value in itself be turned into means to reach the final "superanthropoid." We recognize the conflict in Andreas-Salomé's story.

Was a Nietzschean "transvaluation of all values" necessary to reach Hall's "superanthropoid"?[4] As an advocate of adolescence, Hall questioned Victorian standards, and he believed that deviations from those standards could become norms in the future by means of a Lamarckian transference of acquired features. In contrast to infancy, which was just the birth of the "rudimentary physical and psychic traits," adolescence was a "new birth" (1: xiii), "the glorious dawn of imagination, which supplements individual limitations and expands the soul toward the dimensions of the race." Experiments during adolescence were nature's "stretching of the soul . . . to full-orbed perfection," they expanded and enriched the ego to open "the flood-gates of higher heredity." In contrast to the romantic adulation of the child as the embodiment of innocence (still evident in Andreas-Salomé's story), Hall regards childhood as egotistic and adolescence as the transition from egotism to altruism. If the first voice of adolescence affirms selfhood, the second voice says "renounce and serve, life is short, powers and opportunities are limited, suffering is needful to perfection, so obey, find the joy of sacrifice, get only to give, live for others, subordinate the will to live to love, or to offspring" (2: 302–3). In spite of his social Darwinism, Hall demands that individuals emerging from adolescence subordinate themselves to the "race": "The ulterior law of service and self-sacrifice, which seems at first to be contradictory of all that has preceded, begins to loom up, and the prolonged period of readjustments and subordinations begins. Henceforth the race, not the self, must become supreme" (2: 303).

Having traced a line of thought within Hall's book from individualism and freedom to renunciation, submission, and service to others, we are now poised at a watershed from where we can survey the repressive dimension of his thought, which often demanded surrender to existing social norms. Fearing that deviations may lead to a decline in rather than an improvement of mankind, Hall was quite reluctant to fully release adolescents. As a Victorian moralist indebted to German idealism, he regarded his own norms as natural and deviations from them as morally, intellectually, and physically "abnormal" or "remedial." Atavistic reversions to an "open" but savage state of adolescence threatened to bring about degeneracy. Adolescent mental and physical frictions may threaten the social order:

> Every step of the upward way is strewn with wreckage of body, mind, and morals. There is not only arrest, but perversion, at every stage, and hoodlumism, juvenile crime, and secret vice seem not only increasing, but develop in earlier years in every civilized land. . . . Sex asserts its mastery in field after field, and works its havoc in the form of secret vice, debauch, disease, and enfeebled heredity, cadences the soul to both its normal and abnormal rhythms, and sends many thousand youth a year to quacks, because neither parents, teachers, preachers, or physicians know how to deal with its problems. Thus the foundations of domestic, social, and religious life are oftenest undermined. (1: xiv–xv)

This atavistic, chaotic, and savage adolescence was precocious and had to be combated by enforcing a "*natural*" (!) pace of maturation. The study of adolescence was to find "*true norms* against the tendencies to precocity in home, school, church, and civilization generally, and also to establish criteria by which to both diagnose and measure arrest and retardation in the individual and the race" (1: viii, my emphasis). By now we perceive in Hall's theory a (literally) "conservative" approach to adolescence, which was motivated by his fear that urban civilization lured youth into "premature" adulthood:[5]

> Under these provocations, some instincts spring into activity with a suddenness that is almost explosive, and so prematurely, that as, e.g., with sex and drink, the strong and complex psychic mechanism of control has no time to develop and forbidden pleasures are tasted to satiety, till the soul

has sometimes not only lost its innocence before it understood what purity and virtue really mean, but life is *blasé,* a burnt-out cinder, admiration, enthusiasm, and high ambitions are weakened or gone, and the soul is tainted with indifference or discouragement. (1: 322)

We have come full circle: if at the outset adolescence seemed like a means to accelerate the teleological evolution towards the "superanthropoid," it now appears as precocious and therefore in need of a "retarding" force. In Hall's resultant double-edged educational policy the fight against precocity came to dominate.

As an American familiar with the "adult ways" of European culture (shades of Henry James!), Hall came to envision America as a precocious adolescent,[6] poised between childhood and chaos, promise and degeneration, millennial utopias and visions of doomsday: "a late, partial, and perhaps essentially abnormal and remedial outcrop of the great underlying life of man-soul" (1: vii). Precocious America had no genuine childhood and, showing a lessening sense for duty and discipline, it displayed "the haste to know and do all befitting man's estate before its time, the mad rush for sudden wealth and the reckless fashions set by its guilded youth":

We are conquering nature, achieving a magnificent material civilization, leading the world in the applications though not in the creation of science, coming to lead in energy and intense industrial and other activities; our vast and complex business organization that has long since outgrown the comprehension of professional economists, absorbs ever more and earlier the best talent and muscle of youth and now dominates health, time, society, politics, and law-giving, and sets new and ever more pervading fashions in manners, morals, education, and religion; but we are progressively forgetting that for the complete apprenticeship to life, youth needs repose, leisure, art, legends, romance, idealization, and in a word humanism, if it is to enter the kingdom of man well equipped for man's highest work in the world. (1: xvi–xvii)

This may indicate the missionary fervor of *Adolescence,* which brought a hitherto unfamiliar term into currency but left its outlines obscure. Hall assembled vast amounts of psychological, sociological, and anthropological data that did not cohere. The unity, inasmuch as there is one, is not theoretical and scientific but *narrative*: it is based on Hall's comprehensive recapitulatory meta-story, his notion that the trajectories of individual lives are patterned after mankind's evolution.

Hall is usually remembered today for having introduced Freud to America, but he was no Freudian—even though their ideas occasionally overlapped. Both of them considered adolescence a time of shifting from inner to outer direction (from egotism to altruism for Hall, from narcissism and autoeroticism to object-directed sexuality for Freud), and both of them viewed consciousness as a fragment of a sunken mass of the unconscious (Hall 2: 66). But whereas Freud posited in the unconscious mainly suppressed infantile experiences, Hall was more inclined to trace the line back into the biological past of the progenitors and to claim that this past became reactivated during adolescence. Freud worked with individuals, whereas Hall used questionnaires and sought to arrive at statistically significant data, partly by relying on the work of others. Hall cared little for introspective, individualized psychology, for he was primarily interested in global rather than individual history. The cultural pessimism of Freud's *Civilization and Its Discontents* starkly contrasts with Hall's biologistic and dynamic ideas that claimed we must "go back to Aristotle in rebasing psychology on biology, and realize that we know the soul best when we can best write its history in the world, and that there are no finalities save formulae of development. The soul is thus still in the making, and we may hope for an indefinite further development" (1: viii).

France took a leading role in early European psychological studies of adolescence. In addition to Gabriel Compayré and August Lemaître, who wrote up case studies of adolescent mental disorders in the early years of this century, Pierre Mendousse published a major and popular study (1909) that was republished as late as 1947. In England, no significant books appeared apart from John Slaughter's *The Adolescent* (1911). Somewhat surprisingly, the first major German studies by Eduard Spranger and Charlotte Bühler appeared only during and after the war.

Most of these early European studies of adolescence were indebted to Hall; Slaughter and Compayré admitted that their work was a digest of his lumbering study. For Compayré, it was a "marvellous collection of facts and ideas," a compendium of the physical and moral traits of adolescence (3).

Mendousse, Spranger, and Bühler deviated from Hall in two important ways. First, they were more interested in adolescents' social lives and souls than in their sexuality. Claiming a primacy of psychology over physiology, they deemphasized puberty and saw instead of a "saltatory" growth (1: xiii) a continuous development from childhood to adolescence (Compayré 167–68; Spranger 23, 106–8).

The second difference concerned evidence and method. The continental psychologists were fascinated by the questionnaire method used by Hall's team, and Mendousse even preferred it to the mathematical approach of his great compatriot, Binet, but they recognized that the answers depended on the questions. Compayré, Mendousse, and Bühler preferred diaries and other unsolicited adolescent expressions. As we saw, Bühler built an archive of these works in Vienna.

Spranger (b. 1882) observed the emergence of the German youth movement as a young scholar, and he followed its metamorphoses during and after the war. His ambition was to write a generally valid scientific study of *Jugendalter* (roughly covering the years of adolescence), but his experience made him aware of the social, cultural, and historical relativity of the phenomenon, and he could never resolve the tension between universality and relativity. Although he minimized class differences (28), he recognized national and racial ones, admitting that his generalizations were not fully valid for Jewish-German adolescents, and even less so for English, French, American, and Russian ones. He wished to speak of an epochal adolescence that stretched from the Enlightenment by way of nineteenth-century German idealism and English-French positivism into the twentieth century (28), but he ruefully admitted in the 1932 reprint of his book that even the experience of the early youth movement had become obsolete in the Weimar Republic (xiv). We shall see in the following sections how his striving for general norms seriously jeopardized his views.

ADOLESCENT IMAGINATION AND CREATIVITY

The treatment of the imagination is a touchstone for studies on adolescence. Witness the ambiguity that underlies Hall's glowing praise of it:

> Puberty is the birthday of the imagination. This has its morning twilight in reverie, . . . in many sane children, their own surroundings not only shrivel but become dim and shadowy compared with the realm of fancy. This age is indeed sadly incomplete without illusions, and if the critical faculties which are later to slowly decompose them are not developed, the youth is rapt, apart, perhaps oblivious of his environment, and unresponsive to its calls, because his dreams have passed beyond his nascent and inadequate power of control and become obsessions. Many states that become trancoidal and absorptive are best described as the drunkenness of fancy, a state which may become habitual and passionate, but which, true to its secret nature, is unrevealed to others save in certain katatonic attitudes and a clumsiness to mundane reactions, such as Plato ascribes to the true phi-

losopher. Here, near the verge of normality, belong many of the long-continued stories, imaginary companions, fancied but perhaps zoologically impossible animals, and romances. . . .

. . . There are dreams of leadership, victory, and splendor amid the plaudits of an admiring world. All these more or less flickering and iridescent trailing clouds of glory usher in a new inner dawn, when everything seems turning to gold at the touches of fancy, and that only poetry can ever describe. (1: 313, 2: 302)

The encomium is mixed with caveats, for Hall could tolerate the roaming of the imagination only as long as it did not venture off limits and delay the growth of altruism. Solitary reverie counteracted socialization, even if it did not involve the contemplation of lurid images.

This explains Hall's hesitant appreciation of the adolescent "reading craze." He approved of it inasmuch as reading helped to transcend personal experience and brought vicarious profit from the lives of fictional characters (2: 474). He even approved of reading "Captain Kidd, Jack Sheppard, Dick Turpin, and other gory tales" (1: 408), thinking that catharsis could arouse "the higher faculties which develop later." But he found many famous books detrimental to moral development: Werther engendered the psychosis of Wertherism; Stendhal almost reveled in murder as an indication of energy; Barrès eulogized "exalted and fierce, mystic and cruel" Spain (1: 387).

Hall's hefty but disappointing chapter on "Adolescence in Literature, Biography, and History" (1: 513–89) is a similarly pedestrian inventory. Its panoramic survey covers the adolescents in Plato's dialogues, the adolescent disciples of Jesus, the youth of Christian saints, the thirty adolescents in Shakespeare's theater (adopted from Libby's article), and recollections of adolescence by eminent people. Hall's promising suggestion that "ephebic literature should be recognized as a class by itself, and have a place of its own in the history of letters and in criticism" is unfortunately spoiled by the didactic addition: "Much of it should be individually prescribed for the reading of the young, for whom it has a singular zest and is a true stimulus and corrective" (1: 589). Even Compayré, who considered this chapter "the most pleasant and attractive" (65), had to admit that Hall's commentaries and conclusions were often banal (81).

Mendousse's more sensitive discussion starts from the premise that adolescents prefer imaginary objects because they have no control yet over the real ones (69–70). During adolescence, "dream substitutes for reality" and perception is dominated by two constructive mental powers, the imagination, and, to a lesser extent, logic (!) (70–71, 106, 141). Dreaming is selfish and dangerous, but those who do not dream during adolescence will never become creative (110).

The inner world is chaotic, adds Mendousse. The "anarchy of tendencies" in the pubescent body (189) is accompanied by a mental anarchy that results from the simultaneous pursuance of several incompatible goals (108). Adolescents proceed through "trial and error" (v), but they forget the results (205) and are blind to the contradictions between the different systems and people they associate with. Although they are prone to submit to ideas and people, they are obsessively preoccupied with themselves (46); their inability to make sustained commitments prevents them from true love or creativity (110). Like the dream image of Roman Rolland's adolescent Jean-Christoph (Rolland 347), which is split into several different personalities (208), adolescents are in a state of continual availability (*disponibilité*) and therefore inherently unstable. Following Hall (2: 75–88), Mendousse suggests that they oscillate between twelve basic oppositions, including hyperactivity versus exhaustion and egoism versus altruism (202–4).

For Spranger, self-discovery is a key feature of *Pubertätsalter,* and "anarchy of tendencies" a normal, even desirable state: the greater the storm and stress, the greater the potential range of the soul (38–39). Like Hall, he encourages experimental departure from the norm, but, as we shall see, his abstract liberalism becomes highly restrictive when dealing with homosexuality and feminism.

The postulated primacy of psychology over physiology leads Spranger to concentrate on adolescent reflection, introversion, and self-observation. But whereas Mendousse dwells on the "anarchy," Spranger focuses on its overcoming through self-expression and -discovery. In his view, self-discovery begins with a sense of alienation, the realization that one is divided by a deep gulf from others. This alienation may lead the isolated subject to fold upon itself and discover a universe inside (40–41). Diaries, letters, poems, and other forms of expression may then offer new avenues into the world, modes of self-objectification and even self-liberation (67).[7]

EROS AND SEXUALITY

Compayré, Mendousse, Bühler, and Spranger neglect the physiology of puberty and sexuality because they believe in the primacy of mental processes. All of them advocate the sublimation of sexual drives. According to Mendousse, it is degenerate and regressive to act upon "brute sensation"; mental and physical activities are needed to distract adolescents from obsession with sex (42). "Manly dignity" can be achieved only if the reproductive instinct is progressively raised to "the noble sentiment sung by poets." Apparently, Mendousse was not very up-to-date on his poets of decadence.

For Spranger, that "noble sentiment," that spiritual and aesthetic love, is eros. It is aesthetic in Kant's sense, because it seeks satisfaction through empathy and visual absorption (81–82), a union with images rather than with real people. Hänschen Rilow's "contemplation" (of Vecchio's *Venus* in the toilet) was, of course, "degraded eroticism" (119–21).

Spranger shares the German preoccupation with eros (see Blüher and Gustav Wyneken in the following chapters). Directly addressing Freud (129 ff.), he argues that eroticism is an independent disposition rather than a sublimation of sexuality. The latter always engenders guilt, not because it clashes with public morality but because it lowers one's self-image by showing that one does not live up to one's potential. A "sexualisation" of (aesthetic) eroticism destroys ideal love (84). Just such a sense of inadequacy was typical of Karen Horney's state of mind, though I tried to show that this sense was the product of the cultural environment rather than an inherent feature of the adolescent psyche.

Spranger admitted that eroticism and sexuality were usually intertwined, but considered them incompatible during adolescence: pure adolescent eroticism "knows nothing of sexuality but keeps away from it in fear, infinite shyness, and shame because this form and stage of unification could not satisfy its highest sense. . . . The body is not yet co-productive in the fullest sense" (134–35). Spranger appeals here, against his own principles, to physiology (adolescent bodies are sexually immature) in order to explain the culturally and historically conditioned adolescent fear, shyness, and shame in facing sexuality. As we shall see in chapter 10, most members of the youth movement shared Spranger's view, whereas today, only vanishingly few teenagers are ignorant of sexuality and the number of those that avoid it "in fear and infinite shyness" is not much larger.

Spranger admitted at least once that his view of eros applied only to Germans of his time and "cultural level" (85), but he repeatedly claimed natural and universal validity for it, and he insisted that the "higher" spiritual forces were not repressive and sublimatory but "normal" and natural. Since "nature's ways" were as yet physically and psychologically obscure during the chaos of adolescence, he allowed for some experimentation and deviation, arguing in a quasi-Darwinian way that nature itself seemed to experiment with many possibilities and selected, in happy cases, what was optimal for adulthood (110).

Hence Spranger took a liberal attitude towards adolescent masturbation, homosexuality, and other "deviations" as long as these experiments did not lead to adult "perversions." Experimentation was permissible during the "moratorium" of adolescence if it sought nature's "higher" intentions, but was prohibited if it threatened to lead to "unnatural" adult traits. The double standard (what is natural during adolescence is unnatural during adulthood) actually reduces to a single one: adolescent "deviations" from existing cultural values may never lead to the revision of adult norms, which unconditionally retain their primacy. In this sense, Spranger attributed natural power to his cultural values.

THE SECRET VICE

The opening chapter of Lodewijk van Deyssel's *De kleine republiek* describes little Willem's departure for a Catholic boarding school. At the end of a traumatic and exhausting day he falls on his cold and lonely bed, and "because he wanted to be near something that seemed just as if it did not belong to him, he put his right hand into his unbuttoned pants and enclosed his tender-soft sexual organ, rolling the warm, strange little mass of flesh in his hand and playing with it until he fell asleep."[8]

This poignant scene in an otherwise rather puritanical novel takes a uniquely touching and humane approach to a practice that educators, physicians, and parents either ignored or violently condemned—although they acknowledged its universality during adolescence. Masturbation was admitted into the discourse on adolescence around 1900 because authorities and quasi-racist theories like eugenics predicted physical and mental disasters if the practice was not curbed.

Hall's treatment of masturbation (1: 432–68) includes a survey of studies from Samuel Tissot's classic *L'Onanisme* (1760) to the works of Antoine Marro and Hermann Rohleder, which all evoke terrible masturbatory diseases and parade speculations, hearsay, and previous "findings" under the name of science and pedagogy. Various authorities blithely reconfirmed masturbation's disastrous moral, social, and physical consequences, bolstering the moral and social warnings with the authority of religion, and the physical predictions with that of science. Marro's work, which principally relied on inherited lore, became the canonized sourcebook for Hall, Mendousse, and others.

Hall concedes that the "terror," "shamefacedness," and "bashfulness" of masturbators are due to those horror stories (1: 439) he no longer fully believes in. Why then does he condemn masturbation as one of "the very saddest of all the aspects of human weakness" (1: 432) and perhaps "the most perfect type of individual vice and sin" (1: 452)?

The answer lies in Hall's fear of precocity and egotism. To begin with, masturbation signals a precocious imagination: "In bright, nervous children pubescence often dawns with almost fulminating intensity and suddenness, and sweeps the individual into pernicious ways long before moral or even intellectual restraints are operative" (1: 438). Such a premature, intellectually and morally uncontrolled imagination is prone to stimulate masturbation and foster the development of an indulgent personality that cannot resist sin. Like Mendousse, Hall believes that lack of self-control and willpower is likely to lead to loss of self-respect, fear, overworking, neurasthenia, underachieving, and premature aging (Mendousse 25, 27 ff.). Both Hall and Mendousse consider "self-abuse" worse than promiscuity, for it needs no partner and may lead to severe self-indulgence.

Worse still, a masturbatory imagination is narcissistic and hence asocial: "One of the most direct moral effects is lying, secretiveness, and hypocrisy which conceals or denies a whole area of interests very real to the subject, and this is closely connected with cowardice, timidity, egoism, and frivolity" (1: 443). Solitary pleasure could lead to mental isolation, hallucinations, and, in the worst case, to madness (Mendousse 31).

Like Edouard in *The Counterfeiters* (chapter 3), Hall recognizes that the imagination has analogous roles in masturbation and literature. The seductive power of the "morbidly intense and acute" adolescent imagination, the "marvellous intensity of the lascivious fancy," are best revealed when conjuring up for masturbatory purposes "the form, presence, or more often some particular object connected with the other sex," trumping thus reality with images. Hence one of the most "inviting" areas of the "new psychology" concerns the relationship between "mental masturbation" and perversions of the imagination in youth. Such studies can illustrate "how easily illusions and hallucinations may arise in this soil, where love and fancy normally celebrate their glorious nuptials" (1: 441).

The "new psychology" occasionally criticizes traditional condemnations of masturbation. Hall disagrees with two earlier French studies that painted in colors "truer to the needs of morality than to science" the terrible damages of self-abuse in "brain and cord, paralysis, dementia, blindness, tabes" (1: 432–33). He rejects the "exaggerated horror" of "the 'scare' and quack literature" (1: 432), because it overstates the physical effects: "the brain is not literally drained away; dementia, idiocy, palsy, and sudden death are not imminent, nor is there any peculiar infallible expression, attitude, or any other manifestation instantly recognizable by experts" (1: 439).

Nevertheless, Hall reverts to this view just a few pages later, by vividly painting the putative consequences named by earlier authorities. After casually referring to studies on masturbation's effect on metabolism and the heart (1: 442–43), he succumbs to the canonized wisdom that masturbation leads to senility, gray hair, baldness, "a stooping and enfeebled gait," and symptoms cropping out "in retina, in cochlea, in the muscular or nervous system, in the stomach" (1: 444). Still worse, masturbation very likely leads to sterility and feeblemindedness in the offspring (1: 444). The sober voice of the clinician is now drowned out by the thundering homily of the Victorian moralist who predicts that masturbating families and nations will be wiped out in the struggle for survival:

> The ascendant individual family or stock is the one that refuses to yield in excess to the temptation of the flesh, and the descendants are those whose instincts for selfish gratification preponderate over those of race-conservatism. These are the sins of the parents that are visited on their children, devitalizing, arresting their full development, and finally exterminating them. . . . The invective of a decadent son upon a sire but for whose private vice he might have been well born, is as haunting and characteristic a note of our modern culture as was the curse of Atreus's time for ancient Greece. (1: 438–39)

Spranger was slightly less severe on masturbation than Hall and Mendousse because he distrusted the statistics and the medical lore about the deleterious physical consequences. Like homosexuality, masturbation was normal for adolescents, though it degraded eros and the higher, spiritual self (119–21). Sooner or later it would lead to self-hatred.

Only Slaughter, a follower of Hall, took a more judicious approach to masturbation:

> Many an adolescent lives in terror of what he thinks is surely impending— insanity. The community in cynical, and even criminal negligence, allows

the press to be used by a host of quacks for the purpose of exploiting these fears in their own interest. . . . The harmful consequences have been enormously exaggerated and are in no case so calamitous as the morbid fear so commonly associated with them. Again, the relation of vice to insanity has never been established as causal, but is frequently consequential and symptomatic. . . . As to treatment, it may be pertinent to suggest that good results will come from closer adherence to the facts and somewhat less of the high pulpit method usually practised; for the rest, confidence must be placed in hygiene and in Nature's kindly periodicity. (68)

The quacks mentioned by Slaughter were authors of cheap pamphlets (often circulated in schools) that portrayed with lurid colors the terrible consequences of masturbation in order to peddle their "miracle" pills, ointments, and exercises—exclusively through the mail. In one of the pamphlets I found, a certain Dr. J. L. Curtis of London evoked mental and physical hell to extract the exorbitant sum of twelve Dutch guilders for a consultation and one hundred for a shipment of medicine. Another pamphlet from Berlin by a Dr. Miller offered "miracle patent medicine" against onanism, impotence, and discharges. One adolescent reported to Lancaster: "Got hold of a lot of quackeries about the danger of emissions, which frightened me almost to death. . . . I had first consulted medical companies, who all tried to make me think my condition was deplorable in the extreme. If ever a set of men deserved to go straight to hell, it is these companies. I often contemplated suicide" (95).

Robert Baden-Powell's handbook for boy scouts seems to tackle the problem with more subtlety. "Beastliness," as Baden-Powell preferred to call it, was no manly vice like smoking, drinking, and gambling because "men have nothing but contempt for a fellow who gives way to it." For the rest, Baden-Powell repeats conventional views: the habitual self-abuser "becomes feeble in body and mind, and often ends in a lunatic asylum" (*Scouting* 196–97); boys ought to fight beastliness by avoiding lurid books, indigestion, rich food, constipation, and hot beds; they were to sleep on their back, bathe in cold water, and exercise their upper body with arm movements as in boxing. But the conventionality of the text is deceptive. Tim Jeal reports that the original typescript spoke of "awful diseases," including one "that rots away the insides of men's mouths, their noses, and eyes." It was watered down when, after furious debates, the printer simply refused to print the "obscene" passage (106–7)! To the very end of his life, Baden-Powell continued to fulminate against masturbation in thousands of letters to boys who asked for his advice.

HOMOSEXUALITY

Hall thought that Plato's best dialogues "owe much of their charm to the noble love of adolescent boys" (1: 513)—but this is as far as he ventured in treating homosexuality. Others dared further—but not by very much.

That adolescents became temporarily infatuated with members of their own sex was generally known and tacitly tolerated, although educators and psychologists were uneasy about its relation to homosexuality, which was a crime. Attitudes varied according to the social and legal conditions of the country.

Homosexuality was rampant in the English public schools and present in scouting. Baden-Powell, who probably repressed his own strong homosexual tendencies (Jeal 74–109), had to quietly dismiss several pederast advisers (Jeal 509–10). School authorities, many of whom were also pederasts, preferred to ignore it whenever possible; delinquent boys had to be dismissed and the eventual publicity would have been disastrous for the school. The rough-and-tumble team sports encouraged male bonding, although they were often publicized as a means to sublimate sexual desire. Cyril Andrews challenged the common wisdom that sports were a way to combat homosexuality by showing that more than half of the "moral perverts" were good athletes and students, "not marked by any mental or physical weakness, but rather the reverse. The sad, dejected look which the moralists picture to us is conspicuous by its absence" (88). He claimed, furthermore, that none of the gifted adolescent perverts "had gone to an asylum or ended in conspicuous disaster" (87). At worst, they failed to live up to their potential. Andrew's view had far-reaching implications but did not seem to have made an impact.

Ennis Richmond feared that even in initially innocent friendships boys may carry "their intercourse with each other to the point of falling completely under the influence of what is sensuously evil in their fleshly natures" (169), yet he knew that this "most poisonous weed" existed in all schools and could not be extirpated.

Following Richmond, Mendousse warned against close relations if one of the boys was older and sexually mature (49), but he considered most adolescent homoerotic friendships harmless, hardly different from heterosexual love, and even useful: "a boy who is incapable of friendship during the years following puberty will have little chance ever to devote himself to one of those altruistic goals, which are the privilege of human conscience" (53).

In Germany, the youth movement and the beginnings of gay emancipation stimulated studies of adolescent homosexuality. Spranger's extensive treatment of the subject was a reaction to Blüher's *Wandervogel,* which interpreted the movement as homoerotic male bonding (chapter 10). Predictably, Spranger disagreed. He distinguished a transitory, aesthetic, and "normal" adolescent homoeroticism (89) from carnal homosexuality, which was either socially learned or a tragic inborn "inversion" (123–24). Homosexuality, he thought, should not be portrayed as attractive or inevitable, and he particularly opposed theories of inborn inversion, for he thought that such theories encouraged homosexuality by making socially conditioned practitioners believe in the inevitability of their condition. He admitted that homoeroticism may have existed in the youth movement as a minor strain, but he thought that Blüher's book encouraged adolescents to extend and rigidify their transitional homoeroticism into permanent adult homosexuality (126–27).

FEMALE ADOLESCENCE

A lengthy footnote to Spranger's critique of Blüher's theory of homoeroticism offers an instructive contrast between his views on homosexuality and feminism. The note concerns Elisabeth Busse-Wilson's book on women in the youth movement, which took issue with the traditional dictum, "Men are created for logos, women are tied to eros" (Busse-Wilson 14). She argued that logos and eros were reconcilable in a *Körperseele* (33, 96), and women could develop their artistic and intellectual talents if motherhood was freed from marital economic dependency (34–35). Once the responsibility for raising children was shared, women could become economically independent and raise themselves to a higher cultural level. Spranger rejected Busse-Wilson's argument by claiming that womanhood, unlike homosexuality, was not cultural but fixed once and for all. Her abstract notion of a "new woman" could never be realized because the "eternally feminine" (the phrase is Goethe's) was grounded in a "natural-metaphysical" order (Spranger 127).

Similar arguments were made by all opponents of coeducation, feminism, and the economic emancipation of women, even in America, where the public high schools were coeducational and girls entered secondary education in larger numbers than in Europe. Opponents of coeducation often presented themselves as defenders of women by charging that coeducation systematically ignored their specific needs. Such was the strategy of E. H. Clarke in *Sex in Education; or, A Fair Chance for the Girls* (1873). Clarke did not claim that girls were intellectually inferior, he merely argued that menstruation prevented girls from regular study and attendance and hence from successful competition with boys in coeducational high schools: "Boys must study and work in a boy's way, and girls in a girl's way" (18).

What seems like a plea to recognize physiological differences between the sexes, and a critique of a school system that endangered female health by neglecting "the peculiarities of a woman's organization," quickly acquires a different tone when it slides from demanding an "education *as* women" to "education *for* womanhood" (19). The argument that feminine biology demands a particular *organization* of instruction now turns into a claim that women's education should have *aims* consonant with their social roles. This latter claim, based on social considerations, appropriates the scientific authority of the biological argument by suggesting that modern women have "unnaturally" deviated from their natural being. Indeed, Clarke's ire is most cutting when it berates the newfangled "foolish" ideas of mothers and the vanity of daughters:

> An immense loss of female power may be fairly charged to irrational cooking and indigestible diet. We live in the zone of perpetual pie and doughnut; and our girls revel in those unassimilable abominations. Much also may be credited to artificial deformities strapped to the spine, or piled on the head, much to corsets and skirts, . . . leucorrhoea, amenorrhoea, dysmenorrhoea, chronic and acute ovaritis, prolapsus uteri, hysteria, neuralgia, and the like, are indirectly affected by food, clothing, and exercise. (22–23)

Clarke's book created a heated controversy but his leading assumptions were generally accepted (Kett, *Rites* 141–43). Hall's condescension towards girls, already amply evident in his chapter on "Periodicity" (1: 472–512), became even more explicit in *Youth: Its Regimen and Hygiene,* a shortened version of *Adolescence.* Here we rediscover Clarke's view that girls were incapable of serious intellectual work while they established their regular menstruation and Spranger's notion that eternal womanhood had "natural" boundaries. In Hall's view, women never achieved identity and self-knowledge, never outgrew their adolescence (*Youth* 293). Accordingly, he did not support coeducation, and he recommended an intellectually lightweight program of studies in girls' schools. Carol Dyhouse (128–33) has shown that Hall's views on girls had a strong impact.

The notion of an "eternal-feminine" is defended with still greater vehemence by Wolf, this time, primarily with social arguments. Modern education is to be blamed for the "degeneration" (*Entartung*) of women, because it does not prepare them for their predestined social roles: "The main functions of men are public affairs, the state, the production of art and science; those of women, the family and social life" (26).

Like Clarke, Marro, Hall, and others, Wolf offers advice to parents on dealing with the "secret vices" and "aberrations of the natural drive" of girls, which are, according to him, as prevalent among girls as among boys. Mothers should become their daughters' confidants but also the strict supervisors of their readings and activities, which are to be restricted to harmless entertainment and contemplation of noble matters. Sexual excitement could be prevented by avoiding coffee, tea, and sitting still, taking a nutritious but unspiced diet, eating lightly at dinner, and seeking regular bowel movements. Life should be spartan: a hard bed with light covers and without a pillow in an unheated bedroom, early bedtime and rising, and douses of cold water in the morning and the evening to control any upsurge in sexuality. Although Wolf considered discipline and medicine ultimately of little help, he recommended strengthening one's moral willpower and, above all, following the English model by steeling one's body through sports (41–42). Wolf thought that daughters of the higher classes learned about sex regrettably early and outside their home, from schoolmates or from the medical scare pamphlets. In an age of precocity, it was never too early to assume the painful task of communicating the facts of sexuality to girls, especially if they were suspected of "physically or morally damaging habits."

Were girls indeed precocious? The term has no fixed standard. By our standards, the surviving adolescent girls' diaries are anything but precocious, and many observers around 1900 would have agreed. *Frühlings Erwachen,* which appeared a year before Wolf's book and also pleaded for parental sexual enlightenment, indicates how sexually naive, rather than precocious, girls were at the time. Between 1895 and 1899 Wedekind also wrote a satire on girls' schools entitled *Mine-Haha,* in which girls are allowed to play crude sexual scenes on stage without understanding them. Upon graduation they still know nothing about the "facts of life." A postscript tells us that "Mine-Haha" means "Laughing Water" in an Indian language—but "Mine" is also a pun on the Middle High German concept of higher love, *Minne.*

CHAPTER NINE

Adolescence in School, Church, and Court

Adolescence was both a product of changing institutions and a force for institutional change. At first glance, the secondary schools seem to have been the crucible in which adolescence was formed, while the churches and courts responded (often reluctantly) to that new social formation. But secondary education was itself reconstituted in the process, and churches and courts contributed to the definition of adolescence: all institutions played both an active as well as a passive role in the process.

SCHOOLS

Aristotle suggested in Book 7 of his *Politics* that adolescents need special education. Locke, after giving detailed instruction for the selection of a private tutor who can provide such an education (§ 88–94, pp. 66–71), declared that during the "raw and unruly," "boiling, boisterous Part of Life" that stretches from sixteen to twenty-one tutors are insufficient to guide young men on their Grand Tour, for they then "think themselves to be too much Men to be governed by others, and yet have not Prudence and Experience enough to govern themselves" (§ 212, pp. 184–85). In Rousseau's *Emile* the private tutor becomes as it were the guardian of the future.[1]

In most European countries private tutors were gradually replaced by institutionalized secondary education in the early nineteenth century, but the form of these institutions, and hence adolescent experience, came to vary from country to country. A comprehensive history of European secondary education has yet to be written,[2] so I shall suggest five areas of comparison: (1) growth and homogenization, (2) curriculum, (3) administration, structure, location, and social function, (4) the images of school and school experience, and (5) educational experiments. Developments in the first two categories were largely similar throughout Europe, but national distinctions predominate in the last three areas.

Growth and Homogenization

The number of pupils and schools rapidly grew in all countries throughout the nineteenth century, although the rates of growth differed. In England, the percentage of fourteen-year-old boys attending secondary schools grew from 2 percent in 1870 to 9 percent in 1902; for the seventeen-year-old ones the growth rates were only 1 percent and 2 percent respectively (Gillis, *Youth* 135). As Albisetti notes, the number of schoolboys in French secondary education grew from 69,000 in 1842, to 113,000 in 1898, and to 120,000 in 1911, making the group proportionately smaller than in Germany (297).[3]

Growth produced age grading. In the early nineteenth century, secondary schools typically accommodated youths up to their middle twenties; in the second half of the century the range narrowed and classes became largely segregated by age. European schools were further homogenized by sex segregation. Girls were educated in smaller numbers, for a shorter time, and with a "feminine" curriculum, although the situation gradually improved towards the end of the century in all three respects, in spite of considerable opposition.

Curriculum

The great debate between Julian Huxley and Matthew Arnold exemplifies clashes that occurred in all countries between defenders of traditional humanistic curricula, with emphasis on the classics, and proponents of a modern education, with emphasis on mathematics, the sciences, and the modern languages. Should the prestigious classical education of the Gymnasium and the lycée include a modern branch? Should other secondary schools also be entitled to prepare for the university? How much attention should be given to the national language and history? Should physical education be expanded?

The answers differed from country to country. In France, the lycée maintained its prestige but technical studies became popular. Parity between scientific and classical education ("bifurcation") was established by the decree of August 30, 1852, but rescinded in 1864. The reform of 1872 reduced Latin and encouraged the modern languages; a track without Latin was introduced in 1902. By 1880 about half of the pupils in the collèges, and a fourth in the lycées attended the modern branches (Weill 181). They started to offer the baccalaureate in 1886 and were renamed modern secondary schools in 1891. Public outcry about overburdening (*surmenage*) in 1885–86 led to a sharp reduction of classroom hours in the lycée in 1890 (Weill 188–89). Nevertheless, Demons wrote, the French system continued to be burdened with the primary task of preparing civil servants and concentrated exclusively on examinations (*Anglo-Saxons* 4, 7).

In Germany the classical Gymnasium came under fire: the severity of its demands produced an unacceptable drop-out rate and its emphasis on the classical languages no longer seemed justifiable. Paulsen's history of German higher education (1885) asserted that the classical languages used to be mere tools to acquire other knowledge; to learn them for mental discipline was a questionable modern idea. Versions of the *Realschule* were created and gradually upgraded to satisfy modern demands, but only in 1900 were the *Realgymnasium* and the *Oberrealschule* granted the same rights to university admission as the classical Gymnasium.

Emperor Wilhelm II opened a Prussian conference on school reform in 1890 by declaring that the schools overburdened their pupils with useless knowledge, neglected the modern skills, and failed to prepare students for life. But his apparently liberal stance had nationalistic and conservative motives: he wanted citizens fit "for the struggle for existence," more precisely, fit for Germany's struggle against other nations. He wanted fewer bespectacled schoolboys (a goal he hoped to achieve with more physical education), and more attention to the German language and recent German history, even if this impinged on the teaching of the classical and foreign languages. He minced no words: "I need soldiers, I need a strong generation that is fit to serve its country" (Demolins, *Anglo-Saxons* 33).

The decree of 1892 enforced the emperor's requests by reducing Greek and Latin in the Gymnasium, raising somewhat the proportion of German in all schools, reducing the weekly load by two hours, and increasing physical education. Most other German states followed suit, but the reduction of Latin was partly undone in 1895, and many felt that the emperor's demands were not fully observed (Lietz, *Emlohstobba* 131).

In 1900 a second conference with a subsequent decree strengthened nineteenth-century German history in the curriculum. Albisetti concludes: "Educating a significantly larger portion of the population than the French or Russian secondary schools; sending more students on to the universities and possessing a much more solid tradition of modern schools than did England; even moving decisively, if belatedly, to open higher education to women—the Prussian schools had, after much debate and several false starts, adapted successfully to many of the 'demands of the present'" (Albisetti 313). The picture looks less rosy if we realize what the emperor meant by "demands of the present."

Physical education became a volatile issue in all countries. In the English public schools, sports were first extracurricular activities in the public schools, introduced partly to reduce the widespread hunting, chasing, and torturing of animals. After 1860 they gradually became part of the compulsory curriculum (Springhall, *Coming of Age* 116–19) and acquired a central role in "character building." By the end of the century, reformers like Cecil Reddie complained that the "athletic mania" and "*business* of football *war*" got out of hand: "The moral purpose of games has been forgotten, and even the mental and physical purpose of the game is fast getting lost sight of. Football tours suggest—not the revelling of young blood in the delights of Nature—but the hothouse, and crowds of bettings adorers of brute strength" (157–58). Reddie unfortunately spoiled his point by adding that "it would be a national benefit if this superfluous energy were drilled and disciplined by compulsory military service" (158).

Nevertheless, other countries looked with envy at the English sports facilities and programs. In Germany, team sports were all but unknown, and the main form of physical education was indoor gymnastics (*turnen*), which "Papa" Jahn (1778–1852) had started around 1810 in order to strengthen Prussian youth against Napoleon. By the end of the century, gymnastics instruction (in street clothes) amounted to a mere two hours per week. Lietz considered it a "grammatical" exercise (*Emlohstobba* 107), some authorities thought it was dangerous during periods of rapid growth (Mendousse 232), and most reformers, including Gurlitt, preferred games. However, the great Italian literary scholar Francesco de Sanctis, who also served as minister of education, vigorously argued for the incorporation of gymnastics into the Italian school curriculum in 1878.

Fears of national and racial degeneration made sports and physical education a hot issue. Those fears are evident in Hall's theory, the German emperor's speeches, various campaigns against alcohol and tobacco, Max Nordau's two-volume European best-seller *Degeneration,* French worries about British supremacy, and eugenics, "the science which deals with all influences that improve and develop the inborn qualities of the race" (Galton 82).

Vigorous physical exercise was supposed to compensate for the damages of urban life and extended learning, thus assuring the survival of the educated. In addition to improving the national arsenal of lungs and muscles, the sports were to serve national interests by cultivating competitiveness, cooperation, and fair play. Baden-Powell expected scouting to cultivate the virtues of sport among the less privileged and make "our nation entirely one of gentlemen, men who have a strong sense of honour, of chivalry towards others, of playing the game bravely and unselfishly for their side, and to play it with a sense of fair play and of happiness for all" (quoted by Rosenthal 294).

The French also praised sports, even though this meant praising the British. Games, Mendousse wrote, demanded "a harmonious contribution from all the faculties in a single operation," which was of great value in character building and training for citizenship (235–37). But he had to add that the French adolescents no longer knew how to play, and the new sport associations did not change the situation (238). Pierre de Coubertin, the initiator of international sporting competitions and the modern olympic games, started by strengthening physical education in the French schools. His multivolume book on the education of adolescents in the twentieth century begins, appropriately, with physical education.

But the blessings of sport and Coubertin's beautiful idea of friendly rivalry among nations were from the outset tainted with violence and chauvinism. As one French youth noted of his peers: their sense of equality, fraternity, and socialism quickly faded when driving the ball towards the goal "with a savage desire to reach it, whatever the cost." He added that the importation of boxing from England promoted not only courage, daring, and endurance among French youth but also their "scent of the prey" (*goût de sang*). Now they came to realize that "war was not stupid, cruel, and detestable, but quite simply 'sport for real'" (Agathon 143). Massis and de Tarde, editors of the survey, apparently shared the new mood, for they greeted the rage of soccer, motor racing, and aviation as means to further collective action, military virtues, and an *atmosphère belliqueuse*" (Agathon 35). Baden-Powell was concerned with sports as entertainment. He despised spectator sports because they produced "narrow-chested, hunched-up, miserable specimens, smoking endless cigarettes, numbers of them betting, all of them learning to be hysterical as they groan or cheer in panic-unison with their neighbors" (*Scouting* 292). Only his description of the body build seems erroneous.

Administration, Structure, Location, and Social Function

Substantive differences existed between nations and even within a single nation in the inner structure and the outer context of the schools. For purposes of comparison, I shall concentrate on the dominant prestigious schools: the British public school, the French lycée, and the German Gymnasium.

The British public schools were financially independent, mostly residential institutions, usually located in the countryside or small towns. Although these schools had social prestige in each country, Eton, Winchester, Harrow, Charterhouse (in London until 1872) and other leading public schools became "the bulwark of social stability and continuity" (Musgrove 47) and thus assumed a more important social function than the more intellectually oriented lycées and Gymnasiums.

Thomas Arnold, headmaster of Rugby in the 1830s and the adult hero in the background of *Tom Brown's Schooldays,* brought order to the chaos and brutality he found at the school and became the admired reformer of the nineteenth-century public schools. But his moral and religious earnestness left little room for leisure and "moratorium." Arnold found no value in "lingering wilfully in the evil things of childhood," and he argued in a series of sermons during August 1839 that education should hasten the transition from childish selfishness and thoughtlessness to adult altruism, wisdom, and thoughtfulness. Precocity of the mind was an aid to hasten growth and shorten adolescence (Findlay 145–55).

In spite of Arnold and in contrast to the continental institutions, the public schools became places of leisure and moratorium, a sheltered environment that segregated boys from adults as well as from girls. The master served in loco parentis but many daily affairs were regulated by semi-independent customs, hierarchies, and authorities among the boys. The resultant homoerotic bonds became models for adult male bonding in the military and the clubs.

In France, two major types of schools emerged: the lycée, financed by the central government and offering scholarships, and the collège, run by local governments and later also by the church. Boarding arrangements declined during the nineteenth century (Gerbod 99–100), further exposing French pupils to those temptations of the city that were mostly unknown and inaccessible to the English schoolboys.

The German Gymnasiums, like the French lycées, were state-controlled day schools, often complemented by boarding arrangements and usually located in cities. However, they were governed by the ministries of education in the separate states, and hence less centralized and more loosely linked to the universities than their French counterparts. Partly because of Germany's political and social decentralization, which changed only gradually after the unification in 1870, Germany had no national hierarchy, no elite schools comparable to those in France. This difference is of some importance for my topic: although the severity and general intellectual level of the gymnasiums were comparable to those of the lycées, they were lacking in that extra competitiveness that admission to and survival in the elite lycées required. It remains a puzzle, why, in spite of this additional pressure, there was less protest against the school system in France than in Germany.

The Image of Schools and School Experience

We have limited access to adolescents' school experiences. Some adolescent diaries describe schools directly, but what we know about schools comes mostly from statistics, which cannot capture the experience itself, and from adult recollections, educational tracts, and fiction, which portray the school experience from a distance.

Thus, we have to study and compare national *images* gleaned from literature as well as such other sources as memoirs, pedagogical tracts, political debates, and psychological treatises.[4] The *literary* image of the English public schools was, as we have seen, quite positive, often quasi-mythic until World War I. Even if we take into account that camaraderie, sports, and access to nature probably mitigated the pains of adolescence, it remains puzzling that the sentimental images of the school years in literature ignore or render harmless the pain caused by the separation from parents, the mechanized learning, the flogging by teachers, and the bullying by older boys.

The literary image was fairly faithfully duplicated by the image in personal recollections, until Orwell angrily exposed the dark side in his recollections. Still, the image remained gentle in Spender's description of the "innocent" English adolescent, and nostalgic-ironic in Connolly's well-worded description of "Permanent Adolescence":

The experiences undergone by boys at the great public schools, their glories and disappointments, are so intense as to dominate their lives and to arrest their development. From these it results that the greater part of the ruling class remains adolescent, school-minded, self-conscious, cowardly, senti-mental, and in the last analysis homosexual. Early laurels weigh like lead and of many of the boys whom I knew at Eton, I can say that their lives are over. Those who knew them then knew them at their best and fullest; now, in their early thirties, they are haunted ruins. (*Enemies* 271)

The positive pre–World War I image of the English schools contrasts with the very negative one of the Gymnasium and the rather vague and neutral one of the lycée.[5] The *Gymnasiast* and the *lycéen* both had a more difficult time than the schoolboy in England, because by attending a day school they had less chance to form cohort bonds, were more isolated, and were subjected to the double pressure of parents and teachers. In the lycée, competition was, if anything, keener, and supervision no less strict. And yet, literary and non-literary images of the French schools was considerably less negative than those of the German Gymnasiums.

In Germany, the Gymnasium came under heavy attack by artists, intellec-tuals, and even by pedagogues and politicians towards the end of the century, even though it was widely admired and imitated in Russia, the United States, and other countries. By the early years of this century, this critique inspired two crucial and interrelated movements: school reform and the youth move-ment. In France, school reform had a lesser impact and there was no youth movement to speak of. Why similar institutional conditions failed to produce comparable reform and youth movements in the two countries, seems to me a key question in a European history of education that has not yet been addressed.In this and the following chapters, I describe this contrast and suggest some tentative answers.

Educational Experiments

The Prussian reforms of secondary education were motivated by ruling economic and political interests, not by fresh visions. These reforms sought to adapt the schools to meet the national needs while leaving the authoritarian and mechanical teaching largely intact.

The more radical educational reformers took their cues from Nietzsche, Paul de Lagarde, and Julius Langbehn, whose general cultural critique is eclectic and ideologically difficult to categorize. Whereas German historians, peda-gogues, and philosophers emphasized these reformers' liberal message, Fritz

Stern, George Mosse, and others have argued that their conservatism, chauvinism, and anti-Semitism adumbrated Nazi ideology. The latter attacks rightly point out the distasteful and occasionally contemptible elements in the cultural-educational critique, but they often ignore or deny its liberal dimension (for example, Stern xv). Mosse, in particular, gives a strongly biased reading of German texts and all too readily regards chauvinism and anti-Semitism as specifically German and proto-Nazi (66). Yet Zeev Sternhell has shown in a series of books that similar ideas were powerfully expressed by French writers, journalists, politicians, and ideologues.

The highly popular, though obscurely written, *Rembrandt als Erzieher* (*Rembrandt as Educator,* 1890) is a case in point. Langbehn wanted to strengthen art and creativity in the curriculum as a way to cultivate individualism, which he regarded both as the highest good and the essential element of German culture (3). Science he considered authoritarian because it sought universal truths and left no space for the individual. Though this critique of science was one-sided and quite irrational, some of its elements anticipate the critique of instrumental reason in Adorno's and Horkheimer's *Dialectic of the Enlightenment.* Similarly, nationalist and pan-Germanic tendencies did not prevent Langbehn from including Rembrandt, Shakespeare, and (in spite of the addition of an anti-Semitic chapter in 1891) Spinoza among his cultural heroes and great educators.

Langbehn's ideas were instrumental in the "art education" (*Kunsterziehung*) movement, which sought to expand the role of creativity in the curriculum and to increase the appreciation for art by children and adolescents. Its leader, Alfred Lichtwark, director of the Kunsthalle in Hamburg, initiated museum visits by secondary school children. The aim of art education was to learn to observe rather than to acquire knowledge about art history. Franz Cizek, who taught at the Werkstätte in Vienna, was a pioneer in allowing children and adolescents to express themselves freely in art instead of copying models.[6] The Viennese Kunstschau exhibition of 1908 contained one room with art for children and another one with works produced by Cizek's children's class. A comment by one of the reviewers would have warmed Hall's heart: "Primitive art, lamented by many as vanished, flourishes here again. The childhood of nations (Völker) and the childhood of art atavistically repeat themselves in every human life" (Lux 53).

Gurlitt, whose family distinguished itself in the fine arts, strongly supported the art education movement. He belittled the value of his classicist profession, for he questioned the value of the past in resolving the problems of the present (*Schule* 64), and he was perhaps naively enchanted by Houston Stewart Chamberlain's praise of German culture (*Vaterland* 92). But to suggest that he was a "völkish" chauvinist (Mosse 157–59) is very misleading: *Der Deutsche und sein Vaterland* is a severe critique of German servility and bureaucracy and contains not a trace of anti-Semitism. It is a plea for liberal and pragmatic education, supported by a panegyric on English education and society. The 1902–3 addenda include praise for John Dewey, whose *The School and Society* (1899) was translated in 1905 by Else Gurlitt, Ludwig's sister (and Langbehn's wife!).

The German debate about schoolboy suicides lends further credence to Gurlitt's position. In 1893 Gustav Siegert conducted a study and discovered that only Denmark exceeded Prussia in numbers of suicides below the age of sixteen.[7] His recommendations included strengthening physical education and alleviating anxiety about exams and failing classes (91). A ministerial commission investigated the matter but exonerated the schools, and Baer (52–57) also concluded that heredity, social circumstances, and home education were to blame rather than the schools. Hall (*Adolescence* 1: 383) agreed.

Gurlitt mentioned the issue in 1902 (*Vaterland* 98) and returned to it in 1908, exploiting it for a frontal attack on the educational system. In Britain, he noted, adolescent suicides were unheard of; the success of the empire rested on "character building" in British schools (*Schülerselbstmorde* 11). If Germany declined, it would be due to militarism and the "castration" of its intellectuals in the Gymnasium (*Schülerselbstmorde* 58–59). Gurlitt was joined later by Wyneken (*Kampf* 55 ff.) and other reformers.

As far as I know, Albert Eulenburg, a physician, made the last contribution to the debate concerning adolescent suicides. Although his collection of newspaper reports showed that about 40 percent of the male adolescent suicides were explained by failure in school, he too exonerated the schools: "Out of excessive intellectualism on the one hand and morbid sentimentality on the other, we often pamper children, which undoubtedly results in ruinous consequences and specifically furthers the suicidal tendencies during childhood and adolescence. Even a brief survey of the long list of motives given above demonstrates how ridiculously trivial, at times even senseless, are the motives that led these *spoiled and miseducated, internally unstable and unresisting youths* to throw their lives away and take the step toward the terrible act of suicide" (33, my emphasis). Eulenburg's mentality unmistakably reflects the shadow of war.

Although the debate on school-age suicides was unique to Germany, school reform in general was not. In 1897 two important books on educational reform appeared, Edmond Demolin's *A quoi tent le supériorité des Anglo-Saxons* (*What is the Key to Anglo-Saxon Superiority?*) and Hermann Lietz's *Emlohstobba*. Both of them singled out Cecil Reddie's experimental public school in Abbotsholme (Emlohstobba in reverse) as their model, both placed education in a larger social and political context, both proposed a new type of education for their country that was subsequently put into practice by founding a school. These schools, in turn, stimulated new ones.

First to the model itself. Cecil Reddie opened his school in Abbotsholme, Derbyshire, in 1889, with a typically imperial and Darwinistic aim: "To help, in a humble corner, the creation of a nobler Englishman, to organise a nobler English-speaking Empire, to aid the Ascent of Man" (Reddie x).

Reddie was no iconoclast. He acknowledged that "alone of all schools in the world," the great English public schools "have aimed at cultivating, not merely the intellectual powers, but the physical, social, and moral nature of the youth as well" (22). But he regretted that leisure ("without which true education is impossible") had disappeared and the schools had become "steam-driven factories for turning out by the dozen hastily crammed candidates for examinations" (20). Relying on the educational notions of Carlyle, Ruskin, and Disraeli (11), Reddie wanted "to develop harmoniously all the powers of the boy—to train him in fact how to *live,* and become a rational member of society" (21). Accordingly, he designed a four-part general curriculum, consisting of a "1) physical and manual, 2) artistic and imaginative, 3) literary and intellectual, and 4) moral and religious" education (24). Specializations allowed for the development of individual talent. The curriculum involved manual labor and handicraft, the practice of music, poetry, and painting, the cultivation of English and modern languages (even at the cost of the classical ones), a stress on modern history (wherever possible in combination with geography), and teaching science through experience and observation.

Demolins, a respected sociologist, argued that England's success at educating self-motivated individuals was the key to the empire (a point *Stalky & Co.* made indirectly two years later). While France and Germany prepared unthinking bureaucrats, England trained for independence. Demolins buttressed his argument by comparing the German emperor's apparently modern ideas on education with the truly liberal principles of an English school, which, to the chagrin of the famous public schools, was the upstart Abbotsholme. *A quoi tient* became a best-seller, stirred up hefty discussions in England, and was favorably received in France by Jules Lemaître, George

Rodenbach, Edouard Drumont, Lucien Descaves, Francisque Sarcey, Paul Bourget, François Coppée, and Marcel Prévost (see Reddie's *Abbotsholme*). Hall called it "one of the most important of recent educational books" (*Adolescence* 2: 513).

Encouraged by the response, Demolins published his plan for an Abbotsholme-type school in France, *L'Education nouvelle,* the following year, and the Ecole des Roches opened its doors near Verneuil, Normandy, in 1899. By the time Demolins was buried there in 1907, more than half-a-dozen similar schools had sprung up in various parts of France (Röhrs 114).

Lietz taught with Reddie for a year, and *Emlohstobba* (an English translation of which is included in Reddie's book) is an enthusiastic report of what he saw in Abbotsholme: a mixture of intellectual, artistic, and physical activities; a collegial relationship between teachers and pupils; an absence of compulsion and corporal punishment; a cultivation of rugby and boxing; a selective, "edited" use of the Bible; and a prohibition against alcohol. Lietz discreetly overlooked the cult of nudity. The second part of *Emlohstobba* proposed that the authoritarian methods, rote memorizing, and abstract thinking in the traditional German *Unterrichtsschule* (school of instruction) be replaced by an Abbotsholme-type *Erziehungsschule* (school of education).[8] In 1898 Lietz opened a lower-level *Landerziehungsheim* ("country education home") in Ilsenburg, followed by a middle school in Haubinda (1901) and a high school in Bieberstein (1904).

Lietz followed the English pattern by settling in rural environments. What had been somewhat of a historical accident with the traditional public schools, and an educational principle with Reddie, now became the cornerstone of a Weltanschauung: Lietz believed that education *for* society had to be removed *from* it, for the parental home and the cities could no longer provide *Erziehung* (*Emlohstobba* 83). A cluster of "families," each containing ten boys and a teacher, formed Ilsenburg's "school-state," which cultivated moral, religious, and patriotic values in opposition to the "chaos," "dandyism," and "mammonism" of urban-scientific civilization (*Emlohstobba* 184). As the *Manchester Guardian* noted in a review of Lietz's book on July 6, 1897: "The author does not grapple with the real problem—whether Dr. Reddie's 'return to nature' is compatible with the demands of our complex civilisation" (Reddie 389).

But if Lietz's practical orientation involved a removal from society, and thus clashed with practicality and usefulness in the emperor's sense, it nevertheless involved a strong national component. Lietz was hostile to French culture (*Nationalschule* 36–37) and fearful of an invasion by "eastern hordes" (*Em-*

lohstobba 66). He advocated military training (*Emlohstobba* 185), and his contempt for modern life inclined him towards *völkisch* racism and anti-Semitism.[9] In Lietz's later notion of a "German National School" (*Die deutsche National-schule,* 1911) the reactionary elements of reform became predominant: physical fitness and artistic-manual skills were to serve a Christian nationalism, no foreign languages were to be taught in the lower levels, and mathematics was to become an "auxiliary science," for neither languages nor mathematics furthered a "genuine vigor and joy of living" (*Nationalschule* 40). Subjects without direct relevance to German national culture and contemporary life were now labeled "dead foreign bodies"; the Middle Ages, Antiquity, foreign countries and cultures, the Orient and the Mediterranean empires were to be dropped" (*Nationalschule* 45). By now, the practical orientation of Lietz's liberal education and the emperor's demand for well-trained citizens were difficult to distinguish.

Nevertheless, Lietz had started an important movement. Two of the other leading reformers, Gustav Wyneken and Paul Geheeb, began as teachers in Haubinda but broke with Lietz and founded the coeducational *Freie Schulge-meinde* (Free School Community) at Wickersdorf (1906) and the *Odenwaldschule* (1910) respectively.[10] Although from a pedagogical point of view, both men's theories merit equal attention, I shall focus on the ideas that Wyneken attempted to put into practice in Wickersdorf due to Wyneken's extensive writings and his participation in the youth movement (chapter 10).[11] This problematic interaction with the youth movement gave German school reform an importance that Demolins "pédagogie rocheuse" (Röhrs 114) did not acquire, since no youth movement developed in France.

Like Lietz's schools, Wyneken's Wickersdorf emphasized physical labor, vigorous exercise, and the arts, but it allowed greater pupil participation in school governance (except for the curriculum) and offered no religious education. Drawing on Hegel, Nietzsche, Darwin, and Dilthey, Wyneken saw history as the development of the human spirit by means of repeated self-improvement. Like Ria's father in Andreas-Salomé's story, Wyneken measured achievement in terms of a person's contribution to mankind's efforts to overcome the present (*Schule* 11). Like Barrès, he rejected the cult of the self (*Schule* 126), but sought to integrate the individual into a future community rather than a communal tradition. Anxious to protect his utopian experiment from encroachments by the present, he was even more insistent than Lietz that education had to be moved from the bosom of the family into rural educational "reservations" (Schule 13, 17). He resolutely refused to educate for the "demands of the present" and rejected Lietz's pragmatism.

Yet Wyneken's Freie Schulgemeinde had its dark side. First, the "pedagogical province" inevitably fostered a disdain for urban values and science, so that Wyneken's holistic progressivism became tainted with a conservative ruralism in the manner of Lietz and Barrès. Second, individual freedom within the school was circumscribed by the severe demands of Wyneken's vision of history: to liberate youth from the coercion and the conventions of Prussian society meant an ascetic submission to an idea. As an ardent idealist, Wyneken advocated a spiritual control of the body, a "coercion of nature," an overcoming of the beast in humanity (Schule 88). The school meetings were to inculcate "an understanding of the necessity to subordinate, even sacrifice the interests of the individual to the community" (Scheibe 128).

Wyneken's notions of sexuality similarly combined emancipation and suppression. He advocated a liberation of the body by means of dance, nudity, and rhythmic exercise (no soccer or boxing!), but this actually amounted to a sublimation of sexuality into eros, and a domination of the body by a "beautiful soul" (Schule 52–54). Masking and sublimating sexuality into a Socratic educational eros was Wyneken's way of coping with his homosexuality, but it did not protect him against charges of pederasty.

The idea of pedagogical eros received support from a theory of male bonding that Blüher developed from his experience in the youth movement (chapter 10). In Die Rolle der Erotik in der männlichen Gesellschaft (The Role of Eros in Male Society, 1917) Blüher distinguishes between two basic forms of education. In the first, traditional transmission of knowledge, boys are prepared for positions in life. Since the teachers represent the state, the boys cannot become their true friends. Educational confrontations forestall pederasty, enforce the cohesion of the peer group, and encourage teachers to marry. The second form, Socratic education, has no utilitarian value. It weakens the peer group by mobilizing an educational eros paidikos between master and disciple, and it allows for sexual inversion (Erotik 1: 223–24). Such an eros paidikos cannot flourish under coeducation, and Blüher regretted that Wyneken introduced it at Wickersdorf (Erotik 1: 225).

As a matter of practice, Wyneken's eros paidikos failed, not only because charges of homosexuality forced him out of Wickersdorf, but because it fomented favoritism and factionalism. He returned to Wickersdorf after the war but was charged with pederasty in 1921. Wyneken admitted to a naked embrace with two boys but explained it as a mythic-erotic bond: "If I translate the embrace into words . . . it says approximately: you threw yourself into my arms, you want to belong to me during your young years of seeking and learning. I, then, will also want to belong to you, a holy bond exists now between you and me . . . The ancient secret saying that disciples are given the master's body now unveils a new meaning."[12] Although Wyneken advocated that disciples submit to their Socratic educational *Führer,* with age he himself became, as Ebermayer movingly describes, sadly dependent on a series of boyfriends. His sublimation of homosexuality into an educational eros found little sympathy among those who sought gay liberation more openly.

I suggest, then, even before discussing the youth movement, that early twentieth-century reform pedagogy was strongest in Germany, in part because it became linked up with a host of broader issues, including that of adolescence. But why did things happen this way?

Part of the answer may lie in the different national expectations with respect to education. The English boarding schools aimed at "character building," which involved a comprehensive process of socialization and preparation for "citizenship." As day schools, the lycée and the Gymnasium were too much integrated into the fabric of society to carry out a broader moral and social education. Yet the idea of educating the "whole person" was at the heart of *Bildung* as conceived around 1800 by Schiller, Goethe, Humboldt, Kant, Fichte, Herbart, and the romantics. This holistic ideal, formulated by the great Germany cultural authorities, provided a critical and theoretical springboard from which the inadequacies of the existing secondary education could be attacked with increasing intensity during the nineteenth century, both in the bildungsroman and in essays by Nietzsche, Langbehn, and others.

Reddie must have become acquainted with these German holistic ideas while studying in Göttingen, and it seems likely that they contributed to shaping Abbotsholme. The reviewer of the *Lancashire Evening Post* perceptively remarked that the prospectus of Abbotsholme "more nearly resembles in its proposed aims and methods what Goethe pictured [in the utopian "pedagogical province" of Book 2, in *Wilhelm Meisters Wanderjahre*] than anything else to our knowledge now existing" (*Abbotsholme* 35). Whether Reddie had actually read Goethe is irrelevant; the point is that Lietz's import from England bore considerable resemblance to ideals in the native cultural tradition, and this tradition supported the creation of pedagogical islands or provinces. That France had no comparable educational ideals alive (Rousseau and Pestalozzi were Swiss and were followed more attentively in their native country) may help explain why her restrictive intellectual education came under lesser fire.

A second reason may be that Germany's long fragmentation, late industrialization, and slow urbanization made for a stronger artistic and intellectual attachment to rural life and values. The examples of Rousseau and Barrès show that such nostalgic attachments to rural values existed in France, but they were not strong enough among the bourgeoisie to provide significant support for country boarding schools, and they were not dominant among writers, who preferred Paris to the provinces. Flaubert's epochal *Madame Bovary* was ironically subtitled *Moeurs de province*. In Germany, on the other hand, romantic anti-urbanism and anticapitalist were stronger than in France, and these trends provided a fertile soil for the country boarding schools, as well as the youth movement. Although it is not true that German education and educational reform "pre-eminently institutionalized" *völkisch* ideology (Mosse 152), the existence of a conservative as well as a progressive, a nationalistic as well as a cosmopolitan, an irrational as well as an intellectual dimension in educational reform must be admitted.

A general point may deserve restatement in conclusion. As with professional psychology (chapter 8), the idea of a pedagogical island forms, paradoxically, part of a cultural network. I have tried to show that the images of education (in literature, psychology, philosophy, and pedagogy) were not simple reflections of the existing conditions but mental structures codetermined by tradition, contemporary artistic and intellectual currents, and forms of discourse. These images, in turn, codetermined institutional change. The formative idea of an educational province in Goethe's *Wilhelm Meisters Wanderjahre* may go a long way toward explaining why reform pedagogy became more important in Germany than in France.

CHURCH

Religious rites of passage indicate that in the mythic past adolescence was a single precise hurdle rather than a quagmire spreading between childhood and adulthood. Although rites of passage survive in most religions, the lengthening of adolescence in the nineteenth century required the development of more extensive activities and organizations.

The churches responded somewhat sluggishly. In 1844 the Young Men's

Christian Association (YMCA) was founded in London, mostly for postado-lescent, working youth. The bulk of church-sponsored adolescent organiza-tions emerged only towards the end of the century. According to Dehn, they were started even later in Germany, mostly to combat socialist influences among the young. I shall discuss a typical French Catholic reaction in the section on "Adolescent Jesus."

Adolescent Conversions

Kett suggests that teenagers became conspicuous in American history dur-ing the "Second Great Awakening" in the nineteenth century ("Adolescence" 289). Such awakenings, fostered by the revivalist churches, became of special concern to Hall and the psychologists around him. Hall's long and impassioned chapter on "The Adolescent Psychology of Conversion" (2: 281–362) starts from the premise that conversion, revival, and reawakening are forms of ad-olescent rebirth; they are "natural, normal, universal, and necessary" when life "pivots over from an autocentric to an heterocentric basis" (2: 301).

Starbuck, a student of Hall's, employed questionnaires to ascertain the "universal laws" of these conversions (16). He defined them as a "distinctively adolescent phenomenon," manifesting "apparently sudden changes of char-acter" (21) and occurring most frequently when growth is the fastest, be-tween 13 and 16 in females, and in males around 17 (28, 38). Sudden conversions and spontaneous awakenings are produced by longer subconscious processes (108) due to "the physiological and psychical readjustments incident on the transition from childhood to manhood and womanhood." As such, they are perhaps "the purest and most characteristic" phenomena of adoles-cence (224). Following Hall, Starbuck interpreted conversion as a surrender of the personal will and a shift to "heterocentricity": the "exalted" adolescent ego undergoes "unselfing," establishes a sympathetic relationship with the outside world (126–28), and awakens "into the larger life" (146–47).

Slaughter inverted the relationship: instead of assigning religion a role in adolescent rebirth he made the latter a cornerstone of religion. If religion is conceived according to its function rather than its dogmas, adolescent con-versions constitute "its highest justification," for the doctrine of regeneration is rooted in the growth of civilization as postulated by recapitulation theory: "regeneration marks off civilisation from savagery as well as adulthood from childhood" (46). In Slaughter's view, the rebirth of self during adolescence patterns human evolution and informs religious-metaphysical notions of re-birth, such as the doctrine of Christ and the idea of rebirth after death.

Starbuck surveyed different professions and geographic areas but had to admit that his "universal laws" were inductions from samples among "Protestant, American members of professedly Christian communities," where conversion was common (13; also 25, 186). Psychologists generally acknowledged that Hall and Starbuck identified something important, but they doubted the universality of Starbuck's findings and criticized his method. William James, a competitor of Hall's, noted in the chapter "Conversion" of *The Varieties of Religious Experience* that revivals were socially conditioned results of "suggestion and imitation." Other religions and countries coped differently with the adolescent disposition towards rebirth: "In Catholic lands, for example, and in our own Episcopalian sects, no such anxiety and conviction of sin is usual as in sects that encourage revivals" (200). James accepted Starbuck's view that conversion shortened the adolescent storm and stress but he maintained that such conversions were derivative and imitative within specific societal structures, rather than universally inherent to adolescence (199–201).

Mendousse (213) and Spranger (315) voiced similar objections. Focusing on the "varieties" rather than the "essence" this time, Spranger suggested that adolescent conversions could also be secular and could lead to worldly asceticism, introspection, and penitential exercises. Indeed, one frequently finds such secularizations of religious conversion in literature, for instance when Barrès's Philippe follows the exercises of Loyola, when Joyce's Dedalus moves from religious penitence and conversion to secular initiation and asceticism, or when Demian (and many expressionists) envisions a "new man" emerging from a cataclysmic destruction.

It is literature that reminds us how problematic and dangerous Hall's blithely hailed "heterocentric" rebirth is. For the surrender of the self to something larger than itself (whether religious or secular) does not always amount to a positive socialization in a "larger life." In the twentieth century, it has all too often meant narrowing one's horizon, joining a cause, falling prey to an ideology in Erikson's sense. Recurrent television images of fanatic youths remind us how far we are from understanding and coping with the "varieties" of conversion that occur during adolescence.

The Adolescent Jesus

Shifting the image of Jesus from an infant in the manger of Bethlehem to an adolescent in Nazareth was surely one of the strangest manifestations of cultivating adolescence. Creative writers, churchmen, and psychologists all participated in "revitalizing" the figure of Christ.

One of Hall's last books was a major psychological study of Jesus that related to *Adolescence* in a double sense: it regarded Jesus' spirit as the "consummation" of adolescence (*Jesus,* 1: xviii), and it considered Jesus' adolescent baptism as a historical conversion experience.[13] Hall's detailed reconstruction of that experience is nothing short of (rather good) fiction—justified (in an impossible sentence) by the view that "one very essential part, at least, of the psychological Jesus Christ that was, is, and is to be, is that which painting, sculpture, poetry, drama, and literature have made" (1: viii). Like nineteenth-century American conversions, Jesus' rebirth was grounded in the messianic spirit of his age (1: 302); it meant, in accordance with Hall's theory, that Jesus now turned towards others, that "his consciousness began the great work of bearing the sins of others in a vicarious way" (1: 300). In Hall's unabashed "narrated monologue," Jesus' mind becomes transparent, meditations in the desert on messianic self-assertion and self-sacrifice reveal themselves as an adolescent quest for identity:

> The Messianic idea was a hovering presence, marvellously calculated to appeal with tremendous energy to the inmost soul of ambitious and gifted young men. It had been Jesus' own most fondly cherished form of idealism, and from his earliest fancies had lain secretly very warm and close about his heart. . . . Could he, should he, accept, or rather, dare he refuse it, and what were all the implications involved? . . . The call seemed indubitable and straight from the All-Father of his own soul, and so to refuse it would be cowardice and treason to the Most High. To succeed would be joy and salvation to himself and all who would accept him. The summons was authentically divine, and so he could not fail. . . . He was born in very truth the Messiah. In this thought, indeed, he merely learned his own true identity like the real son of a king who has been reared in ignorance of who he is, yearning for some noble career and finding in maturity that a throne is his by right. Thus in solitude he discovered his real self, and inner oracles that could not be gainsaid awoke and spoke. (302)

In content and mode of presentation the passage is indistinguishable from the seaside initiation in Joyce's *A Portrait*: Hall and Joyce's fictional narrator speak the same language and conceive of calling in the same secularized psychological terminology.

An Abbé remarks in Montherlant's *Le Relève du matin*: "Jesus receives the adoration of the magi at his birth and the respect of the learned at twelve. But nobody visits him during his whole adolescence, he is abandoned, he is no longer of interest. And while he is adored sometimes under the strangest aspects today, nothing (or very little) by way of legend, cult, or fiction pertains to the adolescent Jesus" (18 f). The Catholic church, suspicious of ecstatic revivals, recognized that Jesus of Nazareth could become a model for the adolescents the church now tried to reach, and the Abbé Max Caron, perhaps Montherlant's model, undertook the task of superimposing upon the romantic image of a Christ-infant cradled in Bethlehem a fin-de-siècle adolescent in Nazareth.

Like Scharrelmann, who also fictionalized the adolescent of Nazareth, the Abbé fills the open spaces of the Bible: he touchingly evokes the clothes, the charm, the "supple and gracious" movements of a solitary adolescent Jesus (171) and holds up for emulation his exemplary charity, humility, patience, obedience, and industriousness.

Caron was originally inspired by an unfinished sculpture of the eighteen-year-old Jesus by François Bogino (Le Bas 81–82). He financed its completion, allowed its exhibition in the Salon of 1893, and had it transported to Nazareth, where the Salesian order opened an orphanage of the "Adolescent Jesus" in 1896. In 1901 Caron founded in Versailles an adolescent Society (*Confrérie*) of the Adolescent Jesus (Le Bas 219), and in 1905 he proposed building a basilica in Nazareth. The construction started in 1906, the inauguration took place on September 6, 1923, and Bogino's sculpture was placed on the top of the sanctuary. Sculpture and basilica of "Jesus the Adolescent" still overlook the city from their elevated vantage point, observing in these days the intifada of Palestine children and adolescents and still waiting for the world to grow up.

JUVENILE DELINQUENCY

Since crime was most frequent among those not fortunate enough to attend secondary schools, one might expect that the "invention" of adolescence had little effect on the judicial system. Yet this was not so. Although delinquency among schoolchildren was indeed less frequent than among disadvantaged youth, it was literally and figuratively "just around the corner." Adolescent theft, suicide, violence, and murder fill the pages of Musil's *Törless,* Huch's *Mao,* du Gard's *Les Thibaults* (in *Les Pénitencier*), Gide's *The Counterfeiters,* and Cocteau's *Les Enfants terribles.* It worried the psychologists and decisively affected educational policies and theories.

Hall noted that boys aged eleven to fifteen love "predatory" organizations like "bands of robbers, clubs for hunting and fishing, play armies, organized fighting bands between separate districts, associations for building forts" (*Ad-*

olescence 1: 360). His discussion relies on older treatments, including Jacob Iris's classic *How the Other Half Lives* (1890), a study of the New York tenements and its gangs named "hell's kitchen," "cop beaters and roasters," "hell benders," "sheeny skinners," "sluggers," and "junk club." According to Iris, who was for years a police reporter, "every corner has its gang, not always on the best of terms with the rivals in the next block" (143). Though the groups are deadly, the individual "is an arrant coward. His instincts of ferocity are those of the wolf rather than the tiger. It is only when he hunts with the pack that he is dangerous" (145).

The discovery of adolescence involved calling attention to these appalling urban conditions, fighting for change in the judicial treatment of minors, and setting up asylums and correctional institutions. The "child saving movement" established special educational, judicial, and correctional-protective institutions for youth between the ages of fourteen and twenty. Like Gillis ("Conformity" 252), one may regard this as a "segregation" and a deprivation "of civic, social, and economic status," but a more charitable view would have to acknowledge also the protective goodwill behind the movement. The "child savers" did not "invent delinquency" (as Platt's subtitle suggests), they merely reinterpreted the term from unspecified "dereliction" to specifically "juvenile" delinquency. "Juvenile" lumped children and adolescents together but distinguished both from adults by assigning them to special courts and correctional institutions.

Late nineteenth- and early twentieth-century studies offered three reasons for juvenile delinquency: (1) the removal of youth "from the health-giving influences of the country" into crowded cities, which caused "lapses into mischief and crime" (Barnett 1); (2) adolescent instability due to stress, hormonal imbalance, and generational conflicts, which, according to Gillis (*Youth* 171), became the dominant explanation around 1900; and (3) heredity—an explanation particularly prominent in the writings of Lombroso and his followers (Hall, *Adolescence* 1: 365).

These three explanations were not mutually incompatible. Hall, for instance, held that some delinquents, "inferior in body and mind" (1: 365, 401), were inborn; others came from a bad environment and were habituated (1: 325 ff). Most of them had simply not yet passed the threshold from egotism to altruism. In this light, adult criminals were "overgrown children—egoistic, foppish, impulsive, gluttonous, blind to the rights of others" (1: 338).

The chosen explanation implied the recommended treatment. When heredity was perceived as the cause of the rising crime rate, apprehension about "racial degeneration" led to demands to treat hereditary criminals harshly.

Slaughter, who was the secretary of the British Eugenics Society, held that since the community permitted the birth of inborn criminals it was also responsible for them, but he asked that they "be denied the privilege of propagating their kind" (77). As to those who were "rendered criminal by circumstance," he hesitated: boys' gangs, he thought, were "highly amenable to guidance" (77), but public education was too weak to exercise "civilising influences" on them (70). Hall was equally ambivalent: he agreed that guardians of the young "should cultivate an educative temper, and officers should, if possible, be parents" (1: 404), but he was against abolishing flogging (1: 402).

In spite of these differences and inconsistencies, all countries gradually liberalized the treatment of juvenile delinquents.[14] Here too, England served as an example. The first great crusader for juvenile penal reform, Mary Carpenter, argued that minors were not adults and ought to be penalized in a special way, by assignment to juvenile reformatories for corrective treatment. The first Youthful Offenders Act of 1854 allowed state approved and inspected but privately run reformatory schools, to which children under sixteen could be sent for up to five years. The Industrial Schools Bill of 1857 allowed the establishment of schools for vagrant children aged seven to fifteen with no criminal record. Urban "child saving" was initiated by the churches but involved many other organizations as well, including the public schools, which established mission settlements in urban lower-class neighborhoods (Springhall, *Coming of Age* 149–51). Eton started London's "Mallard Street Club" in 1880; Harrow, Charterhouse, Rugby, and others followed suit.

The number of juveniles in English prisons dropped by two-thirds towards the end of the century (Duprat 176), but it could not be proven that this was due to the reforms, nor was it evident that it meant a similar drop in crime (Morrison 9 ff). Nevertheless, the statistics aroused envy on the continent. Duprat praised the English reform schools for their educational approach (175 ff) and noted that their French equivalent, the *pénitenciers*, enforced harsh discipline, acquired a bad reputation, and decreased in number as well as in accommodated pupils by the end of the century (172–73). He pleaded for special prisons and quarters for juvenile delinquents (166) but noted with satisfaction that France, like the United States, already had Juvenile Courts (167).

In Germany, such courts were not formed until approximately 1910, and the *Jugendgerichtsgesetz*, the law for juveniles (aged fourteen to eighteen), was adopted only in 1923. This law was perhaps the last major European move to recognize adolescence as a legal category.

CHAPTER TEN

Youth Organizations
and Movements

Adolescence was "invented" with the intent of emancipating young people. But free adolescents like Tonio Kröger, Stephen Dedalus, Max Demian, and Augustin Meaulnes exist only in fiction, and even there only at the margins of society. The social emancipation of adolescence amounted to the formation of institutions that engaged them for communal purposes. Baden-Powell, Lietz, Wyneken, Barrès, and Massis, the Boy Scouts, the German youth groups, the reform schools, the religious youth organizations—all in their own way advocated loyalty, discipline, altruism, and the submission of the individual to a community or an ideal. The new adolescent institutions curbed individualism, cosmopolitanism, and liberalism, only the authority that was commanding the loyalty varied: Baden-Powell prepared "bricks" for the edifice of the empire, Barrès yearned to reroot himself in regional soil and tradition, the Catholic church sought the emulation of Jesus, and Wyneken educated for an ideal future humanity.

THE FRENCH ADOLESCENTS

France had no indigenous adolescent mass movement comparable to the Boy Scouts and the *Wandervogel,* and historians, to my knowledge, have not yet explored why this should have been so. The answer, I suspect, will point to the factors that were also responsible for the relative weakness of the French educational reform movement.

Nevertheless, there seems to have been a general conservative turn among the youth, and many young people became attracted to the ultra-right-wing *Action Française* of Charles Maurras. The new mood was registered in a series of surveys on youth conducted in 1912–13, the most important among them being Emile Henriot's *A quoi rêvent les jeunes gens (Of What Do Young People Dream?)* on young writers and one conducted by Henri Massis and Alfred de Tarde in the journal *L'Opinion,* which canvassed the mood at the elite secondary schools and universities. The summary of the latter was published under the pseudonym "Agathon" with the title *Les Jeunes gens d'aujourd'hui (Young People Today,* 1913). The subtitle summarized the findings: "Disposition toward Action, Patriotic Faith, Catholic Renaissance, Political Realism." The book was reprinted ten times within the first year and was crowned by the Academy with the Prix Montyon. The elite was obviously in tune with the nation's mood, and, as Massis and de Tarde had hoped, the book crystallized vaguely felt sentiments and swept large segments of the population along (v). The survey provides important evidence contradicting the view held by George Mosse and others that young conservatism was a uniquely German phenomenon (160).

The new generation, Agathon claimed, was seeking "a cult of character and personality, a taste for moral discipline" (65). This generation worked towards a Catholic and national renewal because it preferred passion and action to abstract ideas and systems. The French defeat in 1870–71 led to apathy, skepticism, aestheticism, and egotism (7), qualities that Agathon associates with Paul Bourget's *Le Disciple,* the journal *Mercure de France,* the writings of Amiel, and the philosopher Frédéric Rauh. The new generation, animated by *goût de l'action,* overcame doubt (16), disdained intellectual introspection (19), rejected pacifism, and prepared itself to regain Alsace and Lorraine. In the elite educational institutions, where antimilitarists and disciples of Jaurès used to predominate, "humanist doctrines no longer win followers" (28). A. M. Tourolle, president of the General Association of Students, reported that war no longer frightened him after the 1911 Moroccan conflict with Germany, for French youth responded en masse to the German insult (30). According to the editors, young people saw in war an occasion for the noblest and highest human virtues, namely "energy, control, and sacrifice for a cause that surpasses us" (32). An Alsatian youth rejected *la belle vie,* for his circle of friends wanted to be seized, body and soul, by an "immediate and practical action" that drove them to utter abandon. He added: "One event only will permit such an action: war. Hence we desire it . . . in camp life, at the camp fire, shall we witness the magnificent unfolding of French powers within us" (32–33).

This martial *goût de l'action* is not unrelated to the "spirit of adventure" in Alain-Fournier's *Le Grand Meaulnes* and Rivière's essay "Novel of Adventure," both of which were published the same year as Agathon's survey. But adventure for Alain-Fournier and Rivière was neither military nor communal, and if, like Agathon (47–48), they sought to overcome symbolist introspection, they continued to probe individual minds. Massis, a friend and patron of Alain-Fournier's, read *Le Grand Meaulnes* with enthusiasm and initially promised to publish it as a supplement to *L'Opinion,* of which he was the secretary. But having just published Ernest Psichari's *L'Appel des armes* to exemplify the patriotic spirit of the Agathon survey, the editors considered Alain-Fournier's "beautiful story woven of gold and silver" unengaged and rejected it (Massis, *Alain-Fournier* 8).[1] Indeed, Massis and de Tarde glorified adventurousness for fuelling patriotism (35), whereas *Le Grand Meaulnes* showed just how mercilessly the adventurous Meaulnes treated Yvonne. But then, the Yvonnes were left out of Agathon's all-male survey universe. The one respondent who considered the feminist movement worth mentioning thought that its consequences were sometimes salutary, mostly disastrous (169).

The new spirit was hostile not only to symbolism and l'art pour l'art (48) but to all literature and art. According to the editors, young people sought great men to satisfy their need "to touch *real* beings capable of responding and leading them" (44). Away, then, with books! Action, this "sure antiseptic of the mind," happily banished the ghosts of the literary imagination and the corruptions of abstract thought: "Action is the yardstick of morality" (51). Surely no adage derivable from *Le Grand Meaulnes.*

Action meant collective undertakings, for the new pragmatism embraced the traditional institutions of state, church, and family. The "disposition towards the definitive" meant avoidance of experimentation, a "horror" of anarchy (63), and (what else?) *precocious* choices for profession and family (61).

Visions of a pragmatic and action-hungry generation worried even some who hailed the new spirit, and one commentator of the survey noted, with words that ring familiar, that single-minded haste in choosing and practicing a profession would lead to a disdain for all distracting intellectual and moral issues. The new mentality echoed Louis-Philippe's "enrich yourself" (177) and swelled the academic programs in banking, commerce, and economy, while starving the humanities. The worried critic cited Poincaré: "I care little for these very precocious and enthusiastic vocational choices. I prefer to these hasty decisions the scrupulous hesitations of a conscience that interrogates itself, and, if necessary, the instinctive revolt of a curious and proud intellect against the yoke of premature specialization" (178). If Agathon was right, the French adolescents of 1910 revolted against their immediate elders by reaffirming their grandfathers under Louis-Philippe!

The religious revival—represented in literature by Paul Claudel, Charles Péguy, and Francis Jammes—was, according to the editors, no vague mysticism, pantheism, or humanism but a voluntary commitment to and an active support of the doctrines of the Catholic church (65). The "religious realism" of the new generation sought "religion in the form of an effective community and a stable tradition." Though it respected individual uniqueness, it considered "religious individualism" a contradiction in terms (92).

Massis and de Tarde claimed that the adolescent elite rejected the extreme chauvinism and monarchism of George Sorel, George Valois's *Cercle Proudhon,* and Charles Maurras's *Action Française.* The right-wing contested this interpretation, read the new mood differently, and drew much more radical conclusions from it. One officer remarked with satisfaction that "nebulous internationalism" and "disappointing humanism" had been replaced by "a healthy notion of the fatherland," which, for him, meant welcoming a war that would finally rid France of the Germans (188). Valois explained the conservative revolution with "the impudence of the Jewish and intellectual groups after the Dreyfus affair, the humiliation of France under the people who came to power under the Dreyfusian revolution, and the inability of socialism to resolve political and social problems" (234). He considered Sorel, Barrès, and Maurras the new leaders of youth.

The editors of the survey nevertheless believed that the continued vitality of democracy (104) among the elite youth would resist the royalist and chauvinist temptations of the *Action Française.* Considering Massis's own devotion to France and the church it seems surprising that he even detected a "mystique républicaine," an individual credo that rejected systematic constraints and eternal truths among the young (105). But this was at the heart of his nationalism, for he thought that the rightist dogma of abstract and timeless institutions (106) came from nineteenth-century Germany (Wundt, Wagner, Savigny, List) and merely muddled "the clear current of contemporary French thought" (107). The German view that legislation expressed a higher, self-justified will led to mysticism and dogmatic authoritarianism (107), whereas the French tradition, descending from Montesquieu, assumed that legislation was by and for the people. Massis and de Tarde welcomed the revival of French nationalism but rejected the glorification of the state as an alien import.

After the war, Massis saw matters differently. If in 1913 he thought that youth reaffirmed traditional French values, in 1924 he considered adolescence as "the irrational period in human life." Only a world that exalted the base human drives would erect literary monuments to the glory of puberty, "the age when we are led by our instincts and the will of others. The man of French classicism is free, ethical, and responsible for his action, and this is, perhaps, why children scarcely have a role in seventeenth-century literature" (*Jugements* 119). In Massis's eyes, prewar French adolescents seem to have turned into Germanic literary figures.

BOY SCOUTS

The Boys' Brigade, the Church Lads' Brigade, and the Boy Scouts in England, the German youth movement (*Jugendbewegung*), and the Woodcraft movement in the United States were the most important adolescent organizations emerging around the turn of the century. The only comparative study on the subject, Gillis's comparison of English and German youth, finds surprising similarities behind the apparently different scouting and Wandervogel movements: both held middle-class values concerning "youth's place in the economy, the polity, and the social order," both left the adolescents in "political passivity and social dependence." Initial differences due "to the way adults handled the first appearance of mass adolescence" became less pronounced as the two movements converged in the twenties ("Conformity" 250–51). This provides a useful corrective to Mosse and others who claim that the German development was unique but marginalizes the decisive initial differences that I now intend to discuss.

The Boy Scout movement is the only survivor of the many English youth organizations that started around the turn of the century and shared certain common traits. As Springhall writes, a "deep general undercurrent of imperialism" ran "through many of the more florid statements of their leadership" ("Boy Scouts" 16, 18). All of them were initiated by adults, mostly as an extension of existing adult ideas and organizations: "The development of 'character' and 'esprit de corps' found in the public schools was to be extended to the 'lower ranks' in society through the agencies of the various boys' brigades and, later, the Boy Scouts" (Springhall, *Coming of Age* 64). In all these features, as we shall see, the English youth organizations differ radically from the German youth movement.

The oldest English youth organization, the Boys' Brigade, founded by William Alexander Smith in Glasgow in 1883, reached a national membership of 55,000 by 1904. It sought to instill "manly" Christian virtues in boys, primarily by means of Bible classes and military drills. The Church Lads' Brigade, Smith's major rival, was launched in 1891 in association with the Church of England. It was militarized, nationalistic, and resolutely teetotaling (Springhall, *Youth* 40), though Roberts recalls that it attracted working-class boys on account of its "very cheap, sketchy uniform and the pleasure of marching through Sunday morning streets (cursed by late sleepers) to the sound of bugle and drum" (161). Although Smith refused to incorporate the Boys' Brigade into a national cadet force, the Church Lads' Brigade joined in 1911. The other, mostly short-lived, organizations that emerged in the 1890s included the Jewish Lads' Brigade, the Catholic Boys' Brigade, the nonmilitary Boys' Life Brigade, and several clubs founded to prevent juvenile delinquency by getting boys off the streets.

The Boy Scout movement, a somewhat late rival, soon surpassed these brigades in size and importance, thanks mainly to the genius of its by then somewhat aged founder, Robert Baden-Powell (1857–1941). "BP," as he came to be called, was himself formed by two typically English institutions of male camaraderie: the public school, where he was a mediocre pupil, and the imperial army, where he became a national military hero during the siege of Mafeking in the Boer war. The public schools contributed to scouting the ideals of honor, loyalty, and gamesmanship; the military provided the idea of scouting and some military trappings, although, it must be added, Baden-Powell successfully resisted the pressure to make drilling a part of scouting. There is perhaps no better example of Cyril Connolly's "permanent adolescent" than Baden-Powell, this "Boy-Man" (title of Tim Jeal's recent biography) who revived his adolescence by devoting his old age to boys.

Scouting was fed from the outset by incongruous ideas that pulled the movement in different directions. Most recent studies by historians (Springhall, Gillis, Morris, and Rosenthal) have focused on the conservative, imperialistic, and militaristic aspects, whereas Jeal's painstakingly careful biography tries to redress the balance by emphasizing its liberal and humanistic dimensions, as well as the context of the time. In the final analysis I find Jeal more balanced and considerate, though his contextual defenses do not always suffice to answer the charges from the other camp.

As Jeal admits, one impulse behind scouting was the fear that Britons were physically and mentally declining and would eventually lose their empire. Social Darwinism claimed that only the fittest of the nations would survive, and Baden-Powell, who observed a "softening" and "shirking" among the British, feared that "the same causes which brought about the fall of the great Roman Empire are working to-day in Great Britain" (*Scouting* 290). The decline and degeneration had to be combatted by physical fitness, the cultivation of team sports, and scouting: if Britons hold together, "then we shall remain strong and united, and there will be no fear of the whole building—namely, our Great Empire—falling down because of rotten bricks in the wall" (*Yarns* 182).

Michael Rosenthal's title aptly suggests that scouting was (not unlike the public schools) conceived as a "character factory" to produce good citizens. But Rosenthal somewhat one-sidedly understands this citizenship merely as serving the needs of the empire, neglecting thereby the social and humanistic aspects symbolized by the notion of a helping hand. Harmony between classes, between nations, and between man and nature was part of Baden-Powell's vision, though they often clashed with the more military aspects of scouting.

Baden-Powell considered the British government "the easiest and fairest for everybody" (*Scouting* 285), but he saw that it had to reduce class tension and strengthen the nation's cohesion in order to spread its blessings. His aim of sharing outdoor life with the children of the disadvantaged urban population, was designed, in part, to forge a new imperial consciousness that cut across class barriers: "A Scout is Loyal to the King, and to his officers, and to his parents, his country, and his employers. He must stick to them through thick and thin . . . he is to do his duty before anything else . . . A SCOUT IS A FRIEND TO ALL, AND A BROTHER TO EVERY OTHER SCOUT, NO MATTER TO WHAT SOCIAL CLASS THE OTHER BELONGS" (from the "Scout Law," *Scouting* 48–49). Nevertheless, the scouting officers were overwhelmingly drawn from the public-school-educated members of the middle class. As Robert Roberts recalls, the high price of a boy scout uniform already created a formidable barrier for lower-class boys (161).

The naturalist element in scouting was partly inspired by Ernest Thompson

Seton, who started a youth movement in the United States in 1902 and wrote a series of articles about it for the *Ladies Home Journal*. He encouraged playing "injun," and he introduced the boys to wood crafting, wildlife, and outdoor life in general. He employed tribal organizations, introduced games, and acquainted boys with primitive forms of survival. Baden-Powell adopted a number of games and outdoor activities from Seton (not always fully acknowledging his debt), but imposed a scouting discipline on them. The result was an amalgam of naturalism and militarism that left many naturalists within the movement uneasy and forced several of them to leave during and after the war. Seton, who became the United States' Chief Scout in 1910, was quietly dropped in 1915 when his condemnation of militarism in scouting became an embarrassment to the movement. His ideas influenced Earnest Westlake, a naturalist and scientist, who founded the "Order of Woodcraft Chivalry" in 1916, and John Hargrave, a young and popular scouting leader, who dedicated his first book to Seton. When Hargrave was expelled from scouting in 1921 for criticizing its militarism, he started the "Kindred of the Kibbo Kift" ("proof of great strength") movement, a mixture of Seton's naturalism and socialistic ideas. Later, Hargrave's authoritarian and populist ways drove the Kibbo Kift to the right, into the vicinity of fascism. Like Westlake, Hargrave sought to offer youth an escape from a collapsing civilization by offering training that started from a primitive state and recapitulated, according to Hall's theory, the stages of mankind's development (Wilkinson 20; Morris 189).

THE GERMAN YOUTH MOVEMENT

The youth movement in Germany had no Baden-Powell, though it too eventually came under adult control. The movement's initial spirit was closer to woodcrafting than to scouting. Initiated by young people who had no clear plans and visions, the youth movement lacked scouting discipline and was eulogized later as a spontaneous organization emerging from a free, communal interaction lacking structure, statutes, and elections (Spranger 163).

The Origins of the German Youth Movement

Despite this eulogy, internal strife was rampant during the early years of the Wandervogel (Migrating Bird), which began at the Gymnasium of Steglitz, at the edge of Berlin.[2] The key actors of its inauspicious beginnings were Hermann Hoffmann, a law student and instructor of an extracurricular short-hand course at the Gymnasium, who initiated excursions with his pupils in the spring of 1896; Karl Fischer, a schoolboy who joined in early 1897 and assumed the leadership of the flourishing hiking club when Hoffmann was drafted in 1900; Ludwig Gurlitt, still a teacher of classics but on his way to becoming a popular critic of the school system (he quit in 1907);[3] Robert Lück, the conservative director who resented Gurlitt's populist attacks on schools but generously supported the hiking club; and, finally, Hans Blüher, a younger schoolboy who later gave memorable renderings of Fischer, Gurlitt, Lück, and the early years of the whole movement.

The hikes, often several weeks long, were highlighted by campfires, singing, and sleeping in haystacks. Their popularity spread like wildfire, and Hoffmann agreed with Fischer in 1900 that clubs should be started at other schools. After graduating in 1901 Fischer founded the *Ausschuss für Schülerfahrten* (AfS), a committee of dues-paying adults that provided an official umbrella for the movement. Fischer appointed himself *Oberbachant* of the club (title of the leader among medieval traveling students), demanded from member-candidates an oath of absolute obedience to himself, and entered new *Scholaren* into a legendary membership book. In order to attain the rank of *Bursche,* such "scholars" had to submit an essay on a hike. The insignias, caps, and other trappings of medieval student life corresponded in function to the very different trappings of scouting.

The hiking movement quickly spread, but Fischer's authoritarian leadership led to a schism. On June 29, 1904 the *AfS* dissolved and was reconstituted as a local *Steglitzer Wandervogel e.V.* Gurlitt became the director; the Oberbachant was replaced by a democratic executive committee. In November 1904, Fischer's adherents founded the *Alt-Wandervogel,* which retained the insignias, caps, and the idea of traveling scholars. Nevertheless, Fischer became alienated from the leadership during his studies in Halle, and he resigned in 1906 to leave for China. By 1907 the Alt-Wandervogel had 122 local groups with 1,353 members (Ziemer and Wolf 121) and continued to grow much faster than its local rival. The youth movement spread to Austria and Switzerland and entered the universities (the *Akademische Freischar* was founded in Göttingen in 1906). New splinter-groups emerged, among them the *Wandervogel Deutscher Bund* (1907), the *Jung-Wandervogel* (1910), and the Hamburg *Wanderverein,* which gave more attention to urban living, art, and culture (Ahlborn in Ziemer and Wolf 105).

Hans Blüher's History and Theory of the Wandervogel

Instead of looking at the details of this kaleidoscopic movement, we may do well to concentrate on the figure of Fischer, for Fischer's role raises some fundamental questions about the movement and the nature of image formation in general. He is the tragic hero of Blüher's *Wandervogel* (1912–1913), the movement's first, brilliant but idiosyncratic history.

Blüher rightly claimed that his book gave the movement its first identity (*Werke* 181),[4] but one may also read that book as an account of its author's own struggle for identity (in 1912, he was only twenty-four), his coping with an Oedipal complex and with his sexuality. Blüher saw the Wandervogel as a rebellion without intellectual, political, or patriotic goals (*Wandervogel* 1: 90–91), a romantic rebellion of middle-class youth against incomprehending parents (1: 77) and servile teachers (1: 73). Fischer's charismatic personality substituted for the absent true fathers at home and in school (2: 22); his legendary room and the outdoors offered autonomous adolescent spaces, where boys could confide in each other (1: 126). In words reminiscent of Molnár's *Pál Street Boys,* Blüher evokes playing Indians and fighting at the "rauhe Berg" in Steglitz (1: 11). Fischer's Wandervogel would gather in the evenings at the abandoned plot of the "Veits Wiesen" to sing, but, Blüher adds darkening his idyllic portrait, going home Fischer would speak about the *völkisch* significance of his plans (1: 132). Blüher did not consider the Wandervogel as a hiking club or a flight back into nature. He saw it instead as a cohort socialization that involved both playing at traveling scholars or vagabonds (1: 115), and, occasionally, smoking, drinking, and associating with true vagabonds. Reverence for nature, prohibition of alcohol, and sexual abstention were introduced only later, in the newer groups.

Blüher was obviously infatuated with the somewhat older Fischer. In fact, one of the early crises of the movement erupted when Fischer resisted his subordinates' request to eject Blüher for unruly behavior. Fischer became Blüher's hero, but the book is an intellectual son's revenge on an erstwhile powerful father as well: Blüher exposes Fischer's hazy ideas on race and volk, his inarticulateness, and his provocative "Germanic" hikes into Bohemia and Poland (1: 143).[5] Blüher prefers charismatic leaders to democratic team leadership, but recognizes that "Caesarism" brought Fischer's downfall.

Blüher's image of Fischer has been severely criticized by Kindt, Ziemer, and especially Korth, but their correctives relate to Fischer's role in the movement rather than his personality. What kind of a person was he? Fischer himself wrote nothing substantial during the Wandervogel years; his brief recollections from the twenties, unearthed by Korth, reconfirm that he was power-hungry, ambitious, and ready to sell hiking for its disciplinary and military value (Korth 60–61). He claims he had envisioned a "schoolboys' state," a *"Lebensraum* where boys can be, are permitted, and must be boys, in order to become truly men" (Korth 127).

Testimonies by others add little to this picture. According to Breuer, Fischer told him in 1901 that the key to the success of hiking was "a great propagandizable (*propagandafähige*) idea": "The big city disfigures youth and perverts its instincts, alienates it evermore from a natural, harmonious way of life. Out of the great sea of houses rises a new ideal: save yourself, grab your traveling-staff, and seek out the man whom you have lost, the simple, plain, and natural one. In this, youth had found a new healing truth all by itself" (Korth 64; Ziemer and Wolf 73–75). This statement, contrary to Blüher, would affirm the naturalist impulse in hiking, but the authenticity of the remark is questionable.

Blüher highlighted Fischer's figure by ignoring Hoffmann's initial contributions to the movement. But the attempt by Korth and others to cleanse the movement of Fischer's ideologically ambiguous figure by positing Hoffmann's naturalism as its governing idea is equally questionable. To claim that "original elements [Hoffmann's ideas] in the movement constantly reasserted themselves against external, alien influences [Fischer's and other *völkisch* ones]" (Korth 135) is to invoke the suspicious metaphor of biological-organic purity. Better admit that the early youth movement was fed by heterogeneous and incompatible ideas. Although it differed from scouting in its original initiative and later governance, it too was torn between naturalist, social, and political aims, some liberal, many of them conservative.

The German youth movement had no clear "founding ideas," certainly none that persistently dominated. Blüher's thesis that the Wandervogel started as a rebellion against school and parents has been contested by many, including Fischer himself (Korth 195), who claimed that he respected his Gymnasium, did not rebel, and did not seek "Robinson-adventures." Hiking was for him a socially viable and permissible alternative to rebellion (Korth 192–95).

The debate on Blüher's image of Fischer cannot be separated from the truly provocative aspect of his book, the thesis of the third volume that the Wandervogel was held together by "erotic" male bonding. Did Blüher merely project his own attachment to Fischer onto the movement? Homosexuality did indeed become an public issue for the Alt-Wandervogel when Willi Jansen, a wealthy landowner, became president of its National Council on January 1, 1906. Blüher preferred Jansen's liberal camaraderie to Fischer's "Caesarism," but Jansen's disposition for naked swimming, sunning, and exercising soon got him into trouble: he was accused of homosexuality and expelled after severe internal crises. Blüher's defense of homoeroticism was a response to what he calls "inquisitional" persecution in the Alt-Wandervogel after Jansen's departure.

How could a persecution come about, if, as Blüher claimed, the Wandervogel was held together by a homoerotic bond? Blüher's answer made use of Freud's thesis that all neuroses resulted from the suppression of libidinal attachments to persons of the same sex (Freud, *Works* 5: 74–75; Blüher, *Wandervogel* 3: 127). Such an attachment to the same sex was, according to Blüher, neither abnormal nor perverse, but merely a creative and socially valuable "inversion" of heterosexuality.[6] The Wandervogel compensated for their disinterest in girls by developing temporary attachments to boys, attachments that usually merely postponed the transition to adult heterosexuality. But Blüher also recognized two types of leaders. The first, Jansen's type, extended its homoerotic stage and did not progress to heterosexual love. These *Männerhelden* (male heroes) were capable of special contributions to society and the state, because—in contrast to the inner-directedness of family—homoeroticism was intrinsically outer-directed. The second type suppressed its homoerotic inclination and became neurotic, which manifested itself in its persecution of the *Männerhelden* (3: 110 ff.).

This argument was an important, albeit strange contribution to gay emancipation, full of delicate and explosive issues. The Wandervogel officially ignored Blüher's work, but everybody read it, and with the passage of time most former leaders and members, including Fischer (Korth 195), came to deny that adolescent homoeroticism had a role in the movement. Erotic impulses, they claimed, were incompatible with their idealistic motivation (Ziemer and Wolf 421). Relying on Freud, Blüher responded that the denial was just another symptom of a suppressed inversion, but in *Die Rolle der Erotik* he admitted that the bulk of the movement, the *Metöken,* may not have been homoerotically inclined, merely swept along by the erotic power of a select few (2: 110, 112).

Feminism and Male Bonding

Die Rolle der Erotik, mentioned in the previous chapter, broadened the interpretation of the Wandervogel into a general theory of male societies. Blüher now recognized two basic social formations, the family, driven by heterosexuality, and the state, based on homosexual male bonding (1: 6–7). The "typus inversus" was a creative social force, particularly in statesmanship, and could rise to "male heroism" if it openly acknowledged its sexual preference. The second volume outlined the variety of male bonding found in cadet schools, the military, the order of templars, fraternities, clubs, and freemasonry. In all these formations, Blüher claimed, male bonding cut across peer groups, splintering their cohesion (2: 120).

Unlike some other early champions of homosexuality, Blüher was disparaging of and hostile to women. Although he claimed that European culture had been a gynarchy (*Wandervogel* 3: 159), he also asserted women's cultural inferiority. Reverting to the clichés that the spirit (*Geist*) was male and eros female (*Antifeminismus* 6–8), that all great cultural achievements were the products of men (*Antifeminismus* 17), and that male communities best advanced such achievements, he wanted women to be excluded from male schools, politics, and the youth movement, although he opposed the bourgeois antifeminism of the *Deutsche Bund,* which wanted to save the sanctity of marriage and brand children born out of wedlock.

Blüher argued for the recognition of male homoeroticism by combatting feminism, thus pouring oil on the already smoldering issue of women in the youth movement. Like Jews, women were held at bay. In 1905, the feminist and poetess Marie Luise Becker (wife of the writer and Wandervogel Kirchbach) petitioned that the hiking of women be permitted in the Alt-Wandervogel. When this was rejected, Becker organized an independent *Bund der Wanderschwestern* for women (Ras 22–23), which fizzled. But the inclusion of women continued to haunt the movement and was frequently raised, usually together with teetotalism. The Wandervogel feared women more than alcohol.

When in 1907 the petition of the Jena Alt-Wandervogel to admit women and to prohibit alcohol was rejected, the group made itself independent under the name of *Wandervogel Deutscher Bund* (WDB). In contrast to the Alt- and Jung-Wandervogel, where joint hikes were prohibited (Ziemer and Wolf 352), the WDB permitted them under the proviso of parental consent. Hans Breuer, who became the WDB's leader in 1910, wrote his famous *Teegespräch* on the subject in 1911: he was sympathetic to mixed hiking, but feared that girl hikers would turn into tomboys and the boys would become sissies (Ziemer and Wolf 223 ff.). In 1914 the first separate bond for girls was formed with questionable *völkisch* ideas (Ras 116–145). After the war, the sexes were formally separated into different organizations.

Girls' hiking formed part of a broader identity change among young women, which was only tangentially related to feminism. Ras identifies a new aesthetic and hygienic sense of the body as the core of changing identity, and she finds its symptoms in newer, looser clothing, the cult of nakedness, as well as eurythmics and dance. As we have seen in connection with Karen Horney, the new identity did not imply sexual emancipation. Preservation of purity (*Sittenreinheit*), abstinence, and sublimation were its guiding notions.

Elisabeth Busse-Wilson was an eloquent representative of this new mentality, though in some respects she went beyond it. She found the Wandervogel too spartan (Ras 53). Addressing Blüher as the *Antifeminist,* she argued that women were not constitutionally deprived of *Geist* but were prevented from contributing to culture because of their inferior social status. The youth movement did nothing to change the situation: it opposed the bourgeois double-standard of granting sexual license to men and allowing sex for women only in marriage, but merely demanding sexual abstinence from both sexes was hardly a solution. The Wandervogel idea of camaraderie rejected bohemian morality and safeguarded innocent hiking and fiddle-plucking, but this "ideology of chastity" (75 ff.) actually reaffirmed the bourgeois suppression of sexuality (78).[7] Adopting Kurella's notion of *Körperseele* (Kurella's *Die Geschlechterfrage*), Busse-Wilson sought a holistic union of body and soul.

Meeting on the Hohe Meissner

The youth movement's increasing puritanism in the prewar years was evident in the appearance of militant abstinence groups,[8] among them the *Vortrupp* (Vanguard), led by Hermann Popert, a judge in Hamburg. Brief remarks on Popert and the Vortrupp will indicate the ideological complexity of these currents.

In 1910, Popert published his immensely successful *Helmut Harringa,* a novel depicting a young Frisian judge's struggle with the sinister powers in and behind smoking, drinking, and prostitution. A *völkisch* perspective sets Frisianism against urban decadence. Upon learning that he has incurable venereal disease, Helmut's brother kills himself because his infected body would disgrace his ancestors:

> Our fathers rose over many thousands years, amidst struggle and dire need. Through primeval ice they fought their way, and then they struggled with hostile tribes and Friesland's avaricious sea for centuries. Their bones became powerful and their growth magnificent. They bequested to us their proud body for us to pass on to future generations. I lost that most precious

gift, lost it in the filthy double-intoxication of a quarter of an hour, and now I no longer dare to raise my eyes to my forefathers.[9]

Such racial consciousness (not so different from the awareness propagated by Hall) was compatible, however, with the idea of a Germanic alliance with Britain, as we have seen in the case of Reddie (chap. 9, n. 7). In *Helmut Harringa,* a certain Colonel Ellington recalls that while fighting rebels in India, he read a jingoist editorial in the *Times* that brought a paraphrase of Shakespeare to mind: "Be friends you Germanic fools; we have enough truck with the black, yellow, and brown fellows. If only you'd count!" (258).[10]

In 1912 when Popert started the journal *Vortrupp* as a "permanent continuation" of *Helmut Harringa,* the term *Rassenhygiene* (racial hygiene) made its ominous appearance (for example, 1.39, 1.645 ff.). As Paul Natorp noted at the time, anti-Semitic connotations of *Rassenhygiene* were hard to avoid in the prewar atmosphere (Kindt *Grundschriften* 141), but Popert, who was married to a Jew, meant by the term something ambiguous but more innocent, namely public health, the sustenance of the "genetic stock" through opposition to alcohol, tobacco, and promiscuity. In *Helmut Harringa,* as in much of the youth movement, the idealistic notion of purity was infected by the rejection of alien elements, which appear here as urban decadence and mobs, as well as the capitalist interests of the tobacco and liquor industries. It is difficult to say at what point Popert's fight for health became unhealthy. Although *Harringa* propagated a Teutonic myth, Popert's wartime diaries, *Tagebuch eines Sehenden 1914–1919,* strongly opposed the war.

Popert is even more difficult to place in an ideological spectrum if we consider that he co-edited *Vortrupp* with Hans Paasche, an undeservedly forgotten man, who started as a colonial officer, became a pacifist, environmentalist, and anticolonialist, and was finally murdered in 1920 by a rightist death squad.

We discover a totally different face of the *Vortrupp* if we consider what Paasche published in it under the name of Lukanga Mukara, a fictional African visitor to Germany. These fictional letters, completed with unpublished ones, appeared posthumously in 1921 under the title *Die Forschungsreise des Afrikaners Lukanga Mukara ins innerste Deutschland* and sold some sixty thousand copies. Recently they were republished in a series entitled "The Other Germany." The series title aptly characterizes Paasche, for his satire on industrialization, urban society, drinking, smoking, and gorging on food, which shares much of Popert's concern with "racial (public) hygiene," acquires a totally different tone when uttered by an African and placed in the light of anticolonialism and antiracism.

Lukanga Mukara's series of satires concludes with a glowing report on the meeting of the youth movement on the Hohe Meissner. Indeed, the *Meissnerfest* or *Freideutsche Jugendtag* of October 11–12, 1913, near Kassel was the high point of the youth movement. Proposed originally by Popert's outfit as a teetotalist counterdemonstration to the expected beer guzzling at the one hundredth anniversary of Napoleon's defeat at Leipzig (which furthered German unification), the gathering became a celebration of youth and a unification of the splintered youth movement into a *Freideutsche Jugend.*

Two central texts mark the event: the final call and the common platform (*Meissner-Formel*). The former hailed the dawn of self-consciousness in youth, the power of youth to shape its life free of conventions and according to its needs. It declared youth's readiness to defend the nation, although it rejected "cheap patriotism." The common platform was hammered out in complex negotiations and stated: "The Freideutsche Jugend wants to shape its life according to its own will, own responsibility, and inner truth. It will defend this inner truth under all circumstances in closed ranks." Upon Popert's insistence it declared: "All events of the Freideutsche Jugend are free of alcohol and tobacco."

Ironically, this celebration of independent youth was largely the work of adults. Wyneken (1875–1964) was thirty-nine, Popert (1871–1932) forty-three; the *Meissner-Formel* was penned by three university students, the final call bore Wyneken's imprint. The signatories included only the Austrian- and the Jung-Wandervogel; the Alt-Wandervogel stayed away, the *Bund Wandervogel,* the new umbrella organization, participated but did not sign. The rest were university groups and adult organizations like Wyneken's *Bund für Freie Schulgemeinden,* Popert's *Vortrupp,* and the *Serakreis* of the publisher Diederichs. The Hohe Meissner made explicit what slowly emerged with the passing of time, namely that the youth movement became an occasion for older men to celebrate their sentimental idea of youth. The phenomenon is delightfully highlighted in Blüher's malicious description of his own publisher, the aging Diederichs: crowned with ivy and garbed in clothes resembling those of a Balkan peasant, he would pass in a rattling, hand-drawn carriage through the streets of Jena, accompanied by (dominantly female) youth, heading to the hills to perform Dionysian rites.[11] Meanwhile, the Wandervogel would remain chaste.

The "Festschrift" of the Freideutsche Jugend (published at Diedrichs) gave the participating organizations an opportunity to present themselves, and the elders, among them Diederichs, Ludwig and Cornelius Gurlitt, Paul Natorp, Leonard Nelson, Ludwig Klages, Ludwig Thoma, Alfred Weber, sent their greetings. Several of them used the Festschrift and the preparatory meeting on October 11 to publicize their own causes. Fidus (see chapter 11) contributed his famous print *Hohe Wacht,* conveniently adding in the corner the address for mail orders.

The elders' high praise of youth could not conceal the fundamental differences among the participants. The two thousand young people who came to the Meissner engaged in sports, martial games, folk dances, and singing competitions, but they listened to speeches by adults. The only remarks made by young people, a greeting from the Austrian Wandervogel that spoke of "Slavic hordes" and a coming war against them, was not welcomed by the other speakers. The assembled youth, spoken at rather than speaking itself, danced through the speeches—to Wyneken's great consternation (Jantzen, *Jugendkultur* 24–25).[12]

Wyneken and the Culture of the Youth Movement

Predictably, the consensus of the Hohe Meissner was short-lived. When next January an anonymous pamphlet published in Munich attacked Wyneken, the Freideutsche Jugend, and the youth journal *Der Anfang,* the Bavarian legislator Schlittenbauer seized the opportunity and accused the Bavarian government of tolerating agitation against parents, schools, positive religion, and patriotism. Attacks in the press followed, and the Bavarian minister of culture immediately banned *Der Anfang.*

The youth movement counterattacked at a gathering in the Munich Tonhalle on February 9, 1914, and Wyneken defended himself with the pamphlet *Die neue Jugend.* But the accusations forced a wedge between the *völkisch* and apolitical factions on the one side and Wyneken's group on the other. At the Marburg meeting in March, several speakers, including Paul Natorp, warned against extremism and political involvement, and Wyneken felt compelled to dissociate himself.

The split was inevitable, in part, because Wyneken became enchanted with *an idea* of the youth movement rather than its reality. Since he never participated in the Wandervogel, he came to know about it from Blüher's book (Kindt, *Grundschriften* 84),[13] which depicted it as a momentous historical protest against the encrusted conventions of parents and schools. Wyneken immediately saw in this something akin to and useful for his own efforts. He thereby exploited for his own purposes the idea of "youth for youth's sake" (once more the topic of Andreas-Salomé's story!), but he also endowed the youth movement with an aura and excitement it would not have possessed without him. His dissociation became inevitable partly because his vision made excessive demands upon the mundane realities of the movement, partly because of blemishes in Wyneken's own vision. In light of his own and Blü-her's concept of youth culture (*Jugendkultur*) Wyneken found the Wandervogel culturally impoverished. He thought that their (or rather Blüher's) critique of the schools supported the new education he envisaged, but he considered it the task of Wickersdorf to raise the Wandervogel to the level of true youth culture.

Wyneken accused the Wandervogel of making no contributions to the cultural growth of the human spirit. Although he preferred the singing and dancing of the Wandervogel to the snobbism of urban high culture and the beer guzzling vulgarity of students, he asked for more: to stop with the instantaneous gratification of the senses and seek "higher style, introversion, greater severity" (*Kampf* 129). Spontaneous aesthetic excitement had to be morally scrutinized (*Kampf* 132), the "overman" was to sublimate the sensuality of singing and art appreciation into an art of "the great command, the law, the unconditional imperative." The great models were to be Shakespeare, Bach, Goethe, and Wyneken's admired classicistic contemporary, Carl Spitteler. In the realm of music he was advised by his brother-in-law, August Halm, who taught in Wickersdorf 1906–10 and 1920–29. Halm was an important theoretician of music, and, together with Heinrich Schenker, a founder of musical analysis, but he had little affinity with the modern music of his time, and as a believer in "absolute music" he wanted nothing to do with Wandervogel fiddling and singing.

Contrary to Mosse's claim (185–86), Wyneken was no friend of the expressionists. His heroic ethos did not sympathize with that expressionistic "chaotic individualism" (Mosse 187) that the Nazis later condemned as degenerate, and his classical taste led him to distrust the vulgar proto-Nazi type of "heroic" expressionism typical of Fidus, Johst, and others. He rightly objected that the Wandervogel's romantic revival of medieval garb and folklore represented an "escape from the age," an uncreative "borrowing of old forms" (*Kampf* 133), but he was naive enough to ask the "migrant birds" to submit to a rigorous education of taste. Still worse, his proposition to raise youth on a staple of canonized classics was artistically as dated as the Wandervogel taste. Although he criticized Wandervogel's rehashing of folklore, Wyneken overlooked the profound renewal of folklore and primitivism in the *Blaue Reiter,* the music of Stravinsky and Bartók, and the paintings of Brücke and fauvism. His demand that a "knightly service of the spirit" replace the Wandervogel's "cheap comfort, self-sufficiency, softness, precocious settling" (*Kampf* 136) would have befitted Gustav Aschenbach, Thomas Mann's ironically portrayed older artist in *Death in Venice.* But Tonio Kröger rejects it as a reductive resolution of the tensions between youth, society, artistry, and bohemianism.

Although Wyneken was unable to refine adolescent taste, he encouraged adolescent cultural criticism, and this was the major reason for his split with the youth movement. In 1913 he assumed legal responsibility for *Der Anfang* (*The Beginning*), a "journal of youth" edited by the still minor Georges Barbizon and Siegfried Bernfeld. It became the organ of left-wing adolescents, many of whom distinguished themselves later in life. Bernfeld himself became an eminent psychoanalyst; the anonymous contributors included Wieland Herzfelde, Carlo Schmid, Walter Benjamin (under the pseudonym "Ardor"), and Alfred Kurella.

Der Anfang published articles on education, schools, parents, adolescent sexuality, and religion. Although the opinions expressed were seldom revolutionary,[14] many adults found any criticism of authorities and institutions by schoolboys inadmissible, and the journal created an uproar, despite having only eight hundred subscribers.Since many of the contributors were Jewish, the reactions had an anti-Semitic undertone.

Der Anfang also initiated meetings (*Schülersprechsäle*) where pupils and students could air their concerns. In Vienna the participants included Norbert Elias, Paul Friedländer, and Paul Lazarsfeld. Further activities included the establishment of an Academic Committee for School Reform and an Archive for Youth Culture. These activities, probably more than the journal itself, were reasons for the *Freideutsche Jugend* to disavow Wyneken and the youth on the left.

But Wyneken's departure and the repudiation of *Der Anfang* notwithstanding, the political neutrality of the youth movement soon evaporated in the war hysteria. Many joined out of patriotism or in search of adventure; the few hesitants were accused by their Wandervogel journal of lacking solidarity and refusing their sole way to redemption (Karl 130). The emblem of this mentality became the Flemish village Langemarck, where waves and waves of German soldiers, many of them Wandervögel, stormed into their death, enthusiastically, unthinkingly, and with a song on their lips.

In a speech held on November 25, 1914, Wyneken surprisingly came out in support of the war (*Der Krieg und die Jugend*) and joined the Wandervogel in condemning those who shirked their "holy duty." Although he did not foment hatred of the enemy, he expected glorious deeds and sacrifices from the soldiers, as if "that incomprehensible, superhuman, almost supernatural" holy war (12) was another stage in the Hegelian march of the spirit. Like Hesse's Emil Sinclair, he saw the war's great payoff in the subsiding of social tension and the camaraderie in the trenches (19–20). The speech was dedicated to Wyneken's brother, who died in the first days of the war, and it cost Wyneken another comrade: on March 9, 1915, immediately after the publication of the speech, Benjamin "unconditionally" severed all ties with Wyneken, as a "final proof of loyalty" to the prewar stance of a man, who first introduced him "to the life of the mind."

"MIGRANT BIRDS" IN THE TRENCHES

Walter Flex's immensely popular *Der Wanderer zwischen beiden Welten* (*The Wanderer between both Worlds,* 1917) may serve as an epilogue and a symbolic summary of the history of prewar adolescence. The book sold millions of copies and became, together with Ernst Jünger's *In Stahlgewittern* and Remarque's *All Quiet on the Western Front,* one of the most popular German novels of World War I, but Flex was killed in 1917 and did not live to see the success of his story.

Der Wanderer is Ernst Wurche, who thought "that all the glory and health of future Germany came from the spirit of the Wandervogel." Looking back upon his friendship with Wurche who has been killed in the war, Flex adds: "And when I think of him, who embodied this spirit pure and bright, I believe he was right" (12). The "true story" that Flex tells hereafter offers a distressing example of the power of fiction and mythmaking.

What Flex intended as a monument to the Wandervogel can be read today as its symbolic history. The movement as well as Flex's story can be divided into two parts: an idyllic camaraderie in a seemingly safe natural island within chaos, and a subsequent expulsion, into the ugly realities of war, death, and mourning. For a reader today, it seems tragically ironic that neither the narrator-author, nor his editor (his surviving brother Martin Flex) understood the connection between the two contrasting scenes. Both remained prisoners of the prewar nationalistic discourse, deaf to the canons that punctured its rhetoric.

Wurche, a student of theology, carries in his knapsack a volume of Goethe,

Nietzsche's *Zarathustra,* and the New Testament. When asked how he can reconcile them, he laughingly answers: "All kinds of alien minds have been forced to become comrades in the trenches. Books are no different from people. Whatever their differences, they just need to be strong, honest, and able to assert themselves—that yields the best camaraderie" (8).

The answer typifies a prewar admiration of power, which subordinated the meaning and implications of an idea to the manner of its presentation. The tolerant camaraderie of Jesus and Zarathustra is possible only if one disregards what they represent. By accepting all "strong" leaders, no matter what they stand for, Wurche eschews choice. His admiration for power at the cost of intellectual and moral responsibility typifies a dangerous "aesthetic" stance in the prewar crusade against individualism in Germany as well as the rest of Europe. Its consequences are depicted in *Der Wanderer,* though it remains the reader's task to make them explicit.

The aestheticism appears harmless in the idyllic scenes of the first half of the novel. Flex watches with homoerotic admiration as his naked, sun-drenched friend emerges from a swim in the river, chanting now from Zarathustra, now from Goethe: "Wet from the water and glistening all over with sun and youth, the twenty-year-old stood there in his slender purity" (22). Not the distant rumble of the canons, but the transformation of the young Siegfried appears ominous: "The edge of his helmet surrounded the headstrong form of his willfully elongated and magnificently arched skull, and as he marched with expansive *(frei ausgreifendem)* steps towards the forests that faintly resounded with distant thunders, trembling with joy and power, he seemed to harken impatiently to the din of the future" (22–23).

The idyll and the martial joy soon come to an end. Before dying, Wurche will have to pass through the hell of the cold, wet, unsanitary, and inhuman war of the trenches. Yet the ensuing unheroic misery, and the loss of his admired friend never seriously dampen Flex's glorification of the hero and the war. He reemerges victorious after his agonizing crisis of mourning, reaffirming the myth of the hero, the nation, and the war. We see him at the end marching through burning Russian villages, singing about his readiness to die for Germany. The myth lives on despite the experience of war.

It must be added that the myth does not incite chauvinism or racial superiority. Neither Wurche nor Flex expect German supremacy from the war, for they perceive that history is cyclical and Germany's decline inevitable. But they conclude, that one must live one's "destiny" to the best of one's ability (34–36), not that the war was senseless and could have been avoided. Flex's last letter to his brother, which appears in the epilogue sums up this viewpoint:

> Today I am as ready to volunteer for the war as I was on the first day. My former and present readiness are due, not to a nationalist fanaticism, as many think, but to a moral one. . . . What I wrote about "the eternity of the German nation" and about the world-redeeming mission of the Germans has nothing to do with national egotism, but is a moral belief that can realize itself even in defeat, or, as Ernst Wurche would have said, in the heroic death of a nation. (100–101)

One is reminded of *Götterdämmerung,* although the mentality adumbrates the mind-set of all those non-Nazis who readily fought and died for Hitler. The myth of the unswerving hero throws an ironic light on Wurche's Wandervogel adage about growing up: "To remain pure and to become mature—that is the most beautiful and difficult art in life" (37).

CHAPTER ELEVEN

Adolescence:
The Fiction of Reality

LITERATURE AS SOCIAL DOCUMENT?

"The safety of thrones rests on poetry" says Flex's motto from the Prussian general Gneisenau. It is an odd view, which to us seems neither a recommendation for poetry nor an explanation for its social power, but having traced adolescence from its literary presentation to its social manifestations, we may ask whether some other ways to tie the end of the thread to its beginning are possible. Here is Oscar Wilde's solution:

> Life is Art's best, Art's only pupil. . . . Literature always anticipates life. It does not copy it, but molds it to its purpose. . . . The nineteenth century, as we know it, is largely an invention of Balzac. Our Luciens de Rubempré, our Rastignacs, and De Marsays made their first appearance on the stage of the *Comédie Humaine*. We are merely carrying out, with footnotes and unnecessary additions, the whim or fancy or creative vision of a great novelist. ("The Decay of Lying," 921–22)

Life imitates what geniuses create from nothing—Wilde's neoromantic aesthetics hardly seems an improvement over Gneisenau. But if we can no longer conceive of "Life" and "Art," we can see specific social formations and conceptions as patterns of artistic models. Although the nineteenth century as such was hardly Balzac's creation, the image of that century in Wilde's circle ("the nineteenth century, *as we know it*") probably was shaped by the *Comédie Humaine*. Since then, imperialist, positivist, Marxist, and Nietzschean "nineteenth centuries" have been invented by and for specific social groups.

A passage in *Le Grand Meaulnes* suggests a less exuberant perspective. Searching for the lost trail after Augustin's departure for Paris, François reaches for Meaulnes's lost "mysterious felicity" and something still more mysterious, namely "the path you read about in *books*. . . . But while intoxicating myself with these hopeful fancies I emerge, without warning, into a clearing which proves to be an ordinary field" (110–11).

A common experience and a commonplace view of literature's relation to life: reading raises unreasonable expectations, the "mysterious" path that the imagination projects leads only to "ordinary fields." Life, François seems to say, does not imitate art, and to believe that it does leads to inevitable disappointments. Although Meaulnes knows this, he continues to model his life according to images in his mind. He can do it, but only as long as he need not force others to conform to his vision. *Le Grand Meaulnes* is a juxtaposition of François's and Augustin's vision of the interplay between literature and life.

Which of these visions can help us conceptualize the relation between literary and social adolescence, if the mere literary thematization of social phenomena no longer seems worthy of our attention? As J. Hillis Miller writes: "The social, political, and historical 'backgrounds' or 'contexts' of a given work may indeed be studied. . . . The vagueness and ungrounded speculation, the unexamined *a prioris,* begin just at that place where the relation between the 'background' or 'context' and the literary text as such, the words on the page, is asserted" (6).

Although one may respond that Miller's proposed rhetorical study of literature will also have to step outside the text if it is to identify the forces that motivate the rhetoric, his skepticism is well founded. All newer theories that attempt to bridge the gap between literary text and context—among them reception theory, readers' response theory, New Historicism, neo-Marxism, Jonathan Culler's theory of literary conventions, Peter Bürger's theory of literary institutions, and Stanley Fish's interpretive communities—remain methodologically problematic. Fiction speaks with many voices, and, as LaCapra has persuasively argued, its use as social-historical documentation selects but one of the many voices and tends to advance the writer's personal choice as historical fact. Furthermore, literary mimesis involves as much the imitative repetition of earlier literary images as the faithful reflection of social experience—which makes it an unreliable social indicator. And yet, early psychological studies of adolescence routinely used fiction as evidence. Hall, it is true, indefatigably consumed scientific treatises rather than fiction. But Spranger and Bühler illustrated their point with fiction, and Mendousse literally studded his essay with literary references, often not merely to illustrate a point established independently but to provide the main evidence from which he deduced important theses.[1] It seems quite likely that Mendousse took the notion of different simultaneous personalities in adolescents from Bourget's *Le Disciple* and Barrès's *Le Cult du moi.*

But contemporary social scientists tend to object to the habit of their turn-of-the-century colleagues of indiscriminately relying on fiction rather than on empirical observations and more representative historical data.

Laslett notes that in Shakespeare's England marriages in the early teens were rare and in the late teens less common than today.[2] Hence the early marriage of Romeo and Juliet was untypical for Shakespeare's age, and literary evidence, which deviates from the norm, "may be systematically deceptive" (*World* 86):

> The outcome may be to make people believe what was the entirely exceptional, was in fact the perfectly normal. This is what seems to have happened with the Capulet ladies and the Elizabethan age of marriage. It is easy to see how a very similar distortion might come about if some future historian used *Lolita* or *West Side Story* as a source book for our own sexual habits, uncorrected by other evidence unliterary and statistical. (*World* 87)

Of course, Shakespeare's love story set in *Verona* was not intended to reflect the social habits of Elizabethan *England,* and furthermore, the play itself emphasizes the lovers' unusually young age. Nevertheless, Laslett's doubts concerning the historical validity of literary portrayals cannot be cast aside lightly.

Albisetti has similar concerns. He devotes part of his chapter on the Gymnasium to fictional and autobiographical reactions but quickly dismisses criticism in fiction:

> These authors were more interested in dramatic stories, however, than in presenting an accurate description of the schools. Thus the general picture that their works present must be taken with a grain of salt; if as many

schoolboys killed themselves as do in these novels and plays, the schools would have run out of pupils. The major characters—Törless, Hanno Buddenbrook, Hans Giebenrath in *Unterm Rad,* Heinrich Lindner in *Freund Hein*—are portrayed as being atypical pupils, in any event; they are outsiders, possessed of artistic sensitivities that make school particularly unbearable. (44)

Now schoolboy suicides were indeed more frequent in literature than in life, and one could accuse Gurlitt and the other reformers of giving too much credence to fiction, of adopting too readily the perspective of Tonio Kröger and other outsiders. Yet the truth of fiction cannot be gauged by some statistically ascertainable social reality, for the meaning of even "hard" data depends on social norms and values. There is no absolute statistical tolerance level for schoolboy suicides; tolerance is exceeded when the public raises its voice.

But who sways public opinion and who constitutes the public? What weight are we to give to writers and pedagogical reformers as compared with the emperor, the military officers, the aristocracy, the captains of industry, the professors, the physicians, and the statisticians? What a certain public of the past thought is always the historian's construct. My claim is that turn-of-the-century German fiction played a major role in lowering the tolerance level for adolescent suicides. Quite possibly, its role was even more pivotal, for *Frühlings Erwachen* and a number of other literary works on schoolboy suicides *preceded* the publication of Siegert's scientific study on the subject. Although I have no evidence to show that these works stimulated Siegert's undertaking, the literature did anticipate the scientific concern and significantly fashioned the way those (quite unreliable) statistics were perceived and understood.

Literary studies have started to investigate the role of literary forms in nonliterary texts. They have focused on the figurative and narrative elements in historiography, as well as on the metaphors, the rhetoric, and the stories in political speeches, newspaper articles, psychoanalysis, and even the language of science. Having examined the narrative form of *Dora,* the rhetoric and the meta-narrative of Hall's *Adolescence,* and the use of "narrated monologues" in his *Jesus,* I now want to go a step further and show how specific literary works on adolescence have shaped even social institutions. This may indicate that modern adolescence was the product not just of slow and blind changes in family structure, schooling, and medical care, but also of perception and discourse that were in turn patterned to no small degree by fiction.

One of the best formulations of the process I want to describe is to be found in Marx's famous opening of *The Eighteenth Brumaire of Louis Bonaparte,* which suggests that whenever people confront new situations they revert to familiar patterns adopted from fiction or from semifictional history:

> Hegel remarks somewhere that all facts and personages of great importance in world history occur, as it were, twice. He forgot to add: the first time as tragedy, the second as farce. . . . Men make their own history, but they do not make it just as they please; they do not make it under circumstances chosen by themselves, but under circumstances directly encountered, given, and transmitted from the past. The tradition of all the dead generations weighs like a nightmare on the brain of the living. And just when they seem engaged in revolutionizing themselves and things, in creating something that has never yet existed, precisely in such periods of revolutionary crisis they anxiously conjure up the spirits of the past to their service and borrow from them names, battle cries and costumes in order to present the new scene of world history in this time-honored disguise and this borrowed language. (320)

Do all revolutionaries (or only "farcical" imitators) speak with "borrowed language" and wear a "time-honored disguise" on history's stage? The passage seems ambiguous. But it is admirably applicable to the mental and institutional emergence of adolescence, which was dominated by patterns of repetition and revival. Consider Hall's theory of recapitulation, Freud's theory that adolescent attachments repeat childhood ones, Cizek's notion that children's art recaptures stages of the primitive (Lux 53), the gathering on the Hohe Meissner, which (commemorated and) repeated the battle of Leipzig, and the Wandervogel, which staged itself in the "borrowed forms" of romanticism (Wyneken, *Kampf* 133). Such repetitions never revive the past "as it was," only some quasi-mythical version of it, already fashioned by the interpreter's imagination and "will to power." In this sense, adolescence is both an invention and a revival of myths.

Of course, the origin of the myth or legend need not be history, it can just as easily be Indian lore, or as Roberts recalls, Frank Richards's imaginary public school:

> The standards of conduct observed by Harry Wharton and his friends at Greyfriars set social norms to which schoolboys and some young teenagers strove spasmodically to conform. Fights—ideally, at least—took place according to Greyfriars rules: no striking an opponent when he was down, no kicking, in fact no weapon but the manly fist. Through the Old School

we learned to admire guts, integrity, tradition; we derided the glutton, the American and the French. We looked with contempt upon the sneak and the thief. Greyfriars gave us one moral code, life another, and a fine muddle we made of it all. . . . One lad among us adopted a permanent jerky gait, this in his attempt to imitate Bob Cherry's "springy, athletic stride." Self-consciously we incorporated weird clang into our own oath-sprinkled ban-ter—"Yarooh!" "My sainted aunt!" "Leggo!" and a dozen others. The Famous Five stood for us as young knights, *sans peur et sans reproche.* Any idea that Harry Wharton could possibly have been guilty of "certain prac-tices" would have filled us with shame. He, like the rest, remained com-pletely asexual, unsullied by those earthly cares of adolescence that troubled us. And that was how we wanted it. (160)

The example of life imitating art would have warmed Oscar Wilde's heart, save two, more than incidental matters: he would not have regarded Richards's stories as "Art," and he would have been disturbed by Roberts's addition: "It came as a curious shock to one who revered the Old School when it dawned upon him that he himself was a typical sample of the 'low cads' so despised by all at Greyfriars. Class consciousness had broken through at last" (160). The urge to play self-chosen roles may come into conflict with the roles we are compelled to play.

In the remainder of this chapter I want to show that these patterns of repetition continually shaped individual lives and group behavior in the two most important new social movements of adolescence, the Wandervogel and the Boy Scouts. In the absence of a social precedent they structured them-selves by means of recourse to the imaginative products of literature, the arts, legends, and quasi-fictional history, either by retelling them as some exem-plary fiction, or by actually reenacting and staging them.

ONCE MORE WANDERVOGEL

The Wandervogel started without clear models, plans, and visions. Fischer, its first adolescent leader, spoke disparagingly in 1927 about the literature on the Wandervogel (probably thinking mainly of Blüher) and added: "Perhaps we Germans are particularly prone to confuse literature with life. At the beginning was not the book but the deed" (Korth 196).

It remains to be asked, pace Fischer, whether that primordial deed was not patterned after books and whether it was not designed for a stage, to be displayed and watched. Fischer himself passionately played theater as a child

(Korth 191), and he knew how to package the "deeds" of hiking with the-atrical images taken from literature, which gave luster to his vague ideas. Although Hoffmann organized unrehearsed excursions into the woods and the countryside, Fischer stylized the activities by imitating medieval vaga-bonds and wandering students, introducing a salutation, caps, and clothes, and reviving interest in folk songs and guitar playing. The *Wandervögel* avidly read Wickram's *Rollwagenbüchlein* (1555) (Blüher, *Wandervogel* 1:130), Grim-melshausen's *Simplicissimus* (1668), Seume's *Spaziergang nach Syrakus* (1803), and Brentano's *Aus der Chronika eines fahrenden Schülers* (1818)—the latter itself compiled from medieval manuscripts.

The more artistically oriented youth group of Hamburg had no charismatic Fischer, but its meetings usually started with the recitation of uplifting pas-sages by Carlyle (Ziemer and Wolf 181), and it was particularly interested in the concept of the hero that Carlyle developed in *Ueber Helden,* the anthology *Arbeiten und nicht verzweifeln,* and other works. The motto of *Helmut Harringa* stems from Carlyle, and Pross goes as far as to claim that Carlyle, more than any other thinker, inspired the Meissner manifesto (91–92).

This recourse to older literature and music is particularly remarkable in view of the Wandervogel's equanimity towards the contemporary arts. Heck-el's commentary (chapter 6) notwithstanding, the adolescent mass movement had little affinity with the artistic avant-garde,[3] for it did not recognize the link between its own protest against commercialism and industrialization and the formal experiments among modernist artists. The Wandervogel preferred the "transfiguration of sterility" in the Jugendstil: "The body is preferably drawn in forms that precede sexual maturity. This idea is related to a re-gressive interpretation of technology" (Benjamin 266). Benjamin's charac-terization perfectly fits Hermann Pfeiffer's androgynous silhouette for the Wandervogel songbook *Der Zupfgeigenhansl* (fig. 15).

The mythmaker and cult figure of the movement became Fidus (Hugo Höppener, 1868–1948) on account of his naked figures, now androgynous, now male and homoerotic (frequently featured in *Der Eigene,* the pioneering journal concerned with homosexuality). Working with the swinging lines of Jugendstil, he glorified the sun—his *Lichtgebet* was especially popular in the youth movement—the body, nature, mystic elemental powers, the Germanic past, and the coming *Übermensch.* His adulation of the "beautiful" body en-deared him to those, including the Nazis, who were disgusted by the ex-pressionist distortions of the body.[4] The *völkisch* element in the hostility to modern art is illustrated by George Otto Embden's 1912 remarks: "Painting

15. Hermann Pfeiffer, illustration from *Der Zupfgeigenhansl,* 1909.

should begin by stopping the pursuit of complicated problems. The new must first be digested thoroughly and reduced to simple, understandable formulae, from which German art will speak clear and pure to German hearts. Only in this way can we reestablish the contact between painting and the public."[5]

In the preface to the fifth edition of *Der Zupfgeigenhansl* (1911) Breuer condemned both urban capitalism and its bohemian critics by remarking that the Wandervogel became tired of "the chaotic potpourri of urban art and lifestyles" (Ziemer and Wolf 222). Order could only be regained by finding "a foothold on ancient solid ground." How this revivalism of folk art gradually slipped into more strident conservatism and nationalism is graphically illustrated in Breuer's later prefaces.

Although Breuer warned against mere revelry "in the role of the travelling bard and the roving knight" (9th edition), the songbook was clearly neo-romantic. In fact, it was a replay of Arnim's and Brentano's famous romantic folk song collection, *Des Knaben Wunderhorn* (1806–1808), and its patriotic role in the prewar years became comparable to that of the *Wunderhorn* during the Napoleonic wars. By reviving romanticism's revival, the *Der Zupfgeigenhansl* took recourse to a twice-mediated past.

Wyneken was not alone in criticizing this notion of creativity. In the introduction to the seventh edition (1911) Breuer had to defend *Der Zupfgeigenhansl* against the charge that the recycling of folk songs was a fanciful invention of a bygone romanticism, and in the tenth edition (1913) he had to answer the *Neutöner* (proponents of new sounds), who believed that modern life demanded new modes of expression. Breuer replied with increasing vehemence that the folk songs were means of cultivating a national tradition and of reintegrating the individual into his community. The collection should "strengthen us and elevate in our conscious feeling of what is German; may it contribute in its limited way to the inner striving of the nation, to the completion of Germanness" (ninth edition). Breuer conceded to the *Neutöner* in the tenth edition that the modern, divided mind could no longer assume the holistic spirit of the folk songs, but he thought that folk singing expressed a modern yearning for a lost unity, and he expected that "new war distresses, new national high tides will once more bring forth new folk songs." His last introduction, written in 1915, claimed that the war had justified the Wandervogel: "We must become evermore German. Wandering is the most German of all the inborn drives, it is our essence, the mirror of our national character altogether. And now, do not be misled. Now, more than ever, wander! Assume your German heritage by wandering."

Shortly after writing these lines in the trenches of the standing war near Badonviller, Breuer was killed.

ONCE MORE BOY SCOUTS

Baden-Powell had published *Reconnaissance and Scouting* (1885) and *Aids to Scouting for N.C.O.s and Men* (1899) before he made scouting into a game for boys. He became interested in education when he returned from Mafeking, but the idea of "boy scouts" was invented and introduced by magazines for boys. In 1900 the *True Blue War Library* started to serialize Harry St George's adventures, which included episodes like "The Boy Scout as Spy Tracker" and "The Boy Scout Joins B-P's Police" (Jeal 368). Later that year the *Boys of the Empire*—"arguably the most jingoistic of all the juvenile periodicals" (Jeal 367)—serialized Baden-Powell's *Aids to Scouting* and made further use of the term.

Once the organization was on its way, Baden-Powell filled his scouting handbook with exemplary anecdotes and stories, and he published "yarns" for Boy Scouts, which were to be spun at the campfire for the boys' edification. These stories illustrated the importance of path finding, the development of endurance and strength, the rise from poverty to a position of importance, and the art of gallantry. The stories enhanced the mystique of the campfires, propagated the scouting ideals, and showed their applications.

Baden-Powell traced the pedigree of the Boy Scouts back to King Arthur, the founder of the Knights of England. The seventh chapter of the *Handbook,* entitled "Chivalry of the Knights," contains several exemplary stories about the knightly virtues, a summary of their code (212), and a recommendation to read Cutler's *Stories of King Arthur* (219). The corresponding chapter in the *Yarns* (114–44), more explicitly entitled "The Knights of the Round Table," contains a twenty-five-page account of the legend. King Arthur is named "the founder of British Scouts" (117), the rules of chivalry are repeatedly described as the principles of scouting, and the oath of the knights to the king—a loose rendering of a passage in book 3, chapter 15 of Sir Thomas Malory's *Le Morte d'Arthur* (Rosenthal 296)—are claimed to be "much the same" as "the oath and duties of the Scouts" (120). Invoking the authority of his legend, Baden-Powell sent his scouts into the world as "knights seeking the Holy Grail," though he promised them only demythologized metaphors: "You are going about doing your duty, helping others, keeping straight and honest, cheery and brave, and, if you stick to that through thick and thin, you will see your Holy Grail—you will get your reward" (142).

The Everyman edition of *Le Morte d'Arthur* in 1906 had thus a direct link with the founding idea of the Boy Scouts. Baden-Powell turned to Malory for the same reason that Malory had turned to his French epic sources: both of them held up the shining example of a vanished knightly tradition to their own morally declining society.

If Malory's knightly code gave scouting a moral *raison d'être,* Sherlock Holmes offered it technique as well as popular appeal. Conan Doyle was a friend of Baden-Powell's and became a strong supporter of the Boy Scouts, for he shared Baden-Powell's fear of the physical and moral deterioration of British youth. Baden-Powell entitled the third chapter in the *Yarns* "Sherlock Holmes Work," because he regarded noticing, tracing, and interpreting small signs essential to crime detecting as well as scouting. In the fourth chapter of the handbook (*Scouting* 118–48), Baden-Powell discusses the methods of "tracking." He advises boys to observe details on the street, to deduce aspects of character from the way people wear their hats, and to learn to read tracks left by shoes, boots, bicycles, and horses. He not only gives many examples of what he calls "Sherlock Holmesism" (*Scouting* 141), he even recommends staging one: the instructor should arrange a room according to the story *The Resident Patient* in Conan Doyle's *Memoirs of Sherlock Holmes,* give each scout separately three minutes to observe it, and "go out and give in his solution, written or verbal, half an hour later" (*Scouting* 147–48). In general, "any one of Sherlock Holmes' stories makes a good play" (*Scouting* 148).

Sherlock Holmes knew all the tricks of the trade, but he was an adult professional, too awesome a model for identification. Baden-Powell found his needed adolescent model in Kipling's Kim, who exemplified "what valuable work a boy scout could do for his country if he were sufficiently trained and sufficiently intelligent" (*Scouting* 10).

The example is so well chosen that one cannot help but suspect that *Kim,* which appeared in 1901, was one of Baden-Powell's inspirations. Kipling's novel depicts intelligence gathering as a "Great Game," precisely in the manner in which a few years later Baden-Powell made military virtues and intelligence gathering into the "Great Game" of scouting. Baden-Powell and Kipling concur "that boys ultimately should conceive of life and empire as governed by unbreakable Laws, and that service is more enjoyable when thought of as similar less to a story—linear, continuous, temporal—than to a playing field—many dimensional, discontinuous, and spatial" (Said's introduction to Kim 14).

Both "Great Games" were based on powers of visual observation. Kim's first education under the British is the "Jewel Game" with Lurgan Sahib, in which he has to compete with the other players to list and describe with utmost precision "a half-handful of clattering trifles" of jewelry (204). Kipling immediately indicates the practical implications of this playful training of vision, by describing how at the end of each day Kim and a Hindu boy are asked to give a detailed account of the people who entered Lurgan Sahib's shop, "of all that they had seen and heard—their view of each man's character, as shown in his face, talk, and manner, and their notions of his real errand" (206–7). The power of sharp observation was, of course, already at the heart of Baden-Powell's concern with adult scouting, but its value for judging character came into the foreground only once scouting was "marketed" as a useful training of boys in peacetime. Jeal calls attention to Baden-Powell's "Cultivating Habits of Observation," a speech from July 9, 1902, to schoolteachers in Johannesburg, in which he stresses the educational value of observation. He emphasizes in Hall's and Mendousse's sense that observation of others can divert adolescents from introspection and selfishness: "By personal study of the little characteristics of one's fellow-men one develops sympathy with them. . . . This kind of sympathy or love . . . is the one great principle for which we ought to live" (quoted by Jeal 365).

It will not surprise us therefore that Kim and his adventures are described at length in the first chapter of the *Handbook* entitled "Scoutcraft" (*Scouting* 7–10). It is a prime example of how literature was "operationalized" in scouting. Baden-Powell stresses Kim's Irish parentage and British ties. Although he mentions that Kim "became great friends with an old wandering priest who was tramping about India," he marks the beginning of Kim's education with his capture by the British and his enrollment in a British school. Of Kim's services to the Government Intelligence Agency, Baden-Powell describes two episodes: how Kim disguises and saves a wounded native member of the agency on a train, and how, with the help of a Babu, he intercepts two Russian spies in the Himalayas and cheats them of their highly important secret papers.

Baden-Powell's summary systematically underrepresents Indian culture and Kim's debt to it. For Baden-Powell, Kim is just an Irish boy, lost, found, and educated in an alien land. What he omits is the weightier half of the book. At the outset, Kim is a street urchin, surviving in the street-jungle of Lahore. He will retain a love for the bustle and noise, as well as the hearty meals of commonplace India, a country where only the fittest survive. More important, the Orient is the locus of spirituality in Kipling's book. Kim's Indian companion, the "old wandering priest," is not "tramping about India," he is a Tibetan lama engaged in a holy "Search" for the place where the Lord's arrow came down. There, a river must have sprung that washes away "all taint and speckle of sin" (58). Although the book pokes fun at Indian superstition, it shows greatest respect for the lama's integrity and quest. Kim becomes his "chela," his attendant, and the lama, who seems quite lost in the world but knows something about the right life, takes charge of Kim's moral education and even secures the money for Kim's British education. There is a fundamental difference, however, between the British and the Buddhist education. Whereas the latter is a true *culte du moi,* the former is utilitarian. English education prepares Kim for spying and trains people in general to become part of an enormous, efficiently functioning, imperial bureaucratic machine. It is an education that also produces trains (which even the lama admires), spectacles, telegraphs, and other technological achievements, including the photographs and other museum pieces that the curator shows to the admiring lama at the outset of the story. At the end of that encounter symbolic exchanges occur: the lama invites the curator to cut himself loose and join him in his Search. The curator declines, for he is "bound" by the bureaucratic network, but he offers the lama his lightweight and unscratchable spectacles with the remark: "May they help thee to thy River" (60). The lama gratefully accepts them, but of course they are useless in finding the "River of the Arrow." Spectacles can improve scouting or the skills in the Jewelry Game, but a Quest demands a different kind of vision—a vision to which Baden-Powell is blind.

There is then no confrontation of cultures in Baden-Powell's summary. That *Kim* portrays an adolescent divided between two cultures, that some of the book's most poignant passages describe the hero's brooding over his split identity—this, and much more, Baden-Powell omits, for it does not suit his purpose of providing an example of *British* physical and moral strength.

Ironically, Baden-Powell did not merely distort by omission a rich and ambiguous novel, he praised unknowingly a model that was unfit to serve the scouting aim of saving children from urban squalor and moral degradation, of offering the disadvantaged city children what Charterhouse offered Baden-

Powell. Could Kim serve as a model in this sense? Consider the scene where he encounters the Irish regimen:

> Kim flitted into the dusk. He knew that in all probability there would be sentries round the camp, and smiled to himself as he heard the thick boots of one. A boy who can dodge over the roofs of Lahore city on a moonlight night, using every little patch and corner of darkness to discomfit his pursuer, is not likely to be checked by a line of well-trained soldiers. He paid them the compliment of crawling between a couple . . . (131)

Kipling pokes fun at the British soldiers, who eventually catch Kim but never quite domesticate him. They are outwitted here by one who was educated in the jungle of Lahore. Indian culture offers Kim not just the passive, contemplative wisdom of his teacher but also practical skills for survival. Ironically, Baden-Powell intends to lure children from urban temptations to nature by showing them a streetwise urchin of India:

> [Kim] executed commissions by night on the crowded housetops for sleek and shiny young men of fashion. It was intrigue, of course,—he knew that much, as he had known all evil since he could speak,—but what he loved was the game for its own sake—the stealthy prowl through the dark gullies and lanes, the crawl up a water-pipe, the sights and sounds of the women's world on the flat roofs, and the headlong flight from housetop to housetop under cover of the hot dark. (51)

By discreetly overlooking this urban-immoral part of Kim's education Baden-Powell misses one of the greatest celebrations of the urban scene in English literature (A. Wilson 130).

I have indicated how Kipling's text became an institutional instrument, but I must admit that my bridge from literature to social institutions terminates in midair, or, more precisely, in that part of the institution of Boy Scouts that Baden-Powell's text constitutes. Although such a "textualized" form of social context may be all we can get hold of, it is hardly sufficient, for it raises a host of additional and more important questions. However important Baden-Powell was for the scouting movement, he was not the movement itself. His reading of *Kim* is only partly representative, and it would be important to know how his text was received and interpreted. How often was the story told and discussed around the campfire? Did the scout officers notice the bias in Baden-Powell's interpretation? Did they notice that the divided and doubting Kim could not serve as a model for scouts, who were to become individuals with strong religious, moral, and patriotic sentiments? Did they notice that Kim, this glorious free spirit, was unsuited to becoming a "brick" in the wall of the empire or a cogwheel in its machine? How many scouts were led to the book after listening to its biased summary? Did they notice the discrepancy after reading the book? And if so, in what ways did this change their views on scouting and the Imperium? In sum, what role did Baden-Powell's interpretation play in the boy-scout reception of *Kim,* and what impact did this reception have on the lives of readers? Only by answering these questions could we complete the bridge from literature to social history. Unfortunately, we shall never be able to answer these questions for lack of relevant information.

Let us consider then another framework for Kipling's *Kim* and Baden-Powell's reading of it, namely a biographical one. The convergence of Baden-Powell's and Kipling's private lives and opinions belies the differences we observed between the novel and its interpretations. Baden-Powell and Kipling were ideological comrades who extended their youth into a permanent male adolescence. Kipling started from India but also had ties to South Africa. After strongly supporting the British in the Boer War, he spent a good part of the following decade in that colony and became a friend of both Baden-Powell's and of Cecil Rhodes's, the apostle of imperialism. Kipling's ill-famed "White Man's Burden" (1898), as well as some of his other poems, reveal an imperial vision comparable to Baden-Powell's, much of Kipling's work exudes the spirit of Baden-Powell's *Kim*-interpretation.

In fact, Kipling's contributions to scouting were considerable: he visited one of the early scouting camps in 1909, wrote "A Boy Scouts' Patrol Song" (1913), called himself a "Commissioner of Boy Scouts," and compiled later the *Land and Sea Tales for Scouts and Guides* (1923), a rather mediocre medley of older and more recent stories. Lines of Kipling's "The Feet of the Young Men" customarily opened the scouting campfire sing-alongs in the early twenties (Jeal 415), and, above all, Baden-Powell made, with Kipling's consent, heavy use of the *Jungle Books* in the *Wolf Cubs' Handbook* (Jeal 500). We may assume that Kipling would not have given his consent had he been dissatisfied with Baden-Powell's use of *Kim,* about which he surely knew.

And yet, *Kim* does not conform to the imperial ideology that Kipling shared with Baden-Powell; it is richer, more encompassing than the explicit ideological commitments held by its author. Such "polyphonic" works may be put to operational uses in society by those, like Baden-Powell, who seek action, but as instruments of an ideology they inevitably become "monophonic." The clarity is paid for by reduction.

To be sure, not all literature is polyphonic, and even *Kim* omits, as Said (24 ff) reminds us, the anti-British and female voices. Still, *Kim* is different from Kipling's "White Man's Burden," Flex's *Der Wanderer zwischen beiden Welten,* and so much of ideologically inspired literature that we now find offensive. But ideology cannot be eliminated from literature. Like adolescent minds, texts speak with many voices; again and again they also bombard us with saving messages from the soapbox.

1881   Vallès, Jules. *Jacques Vingtras: Le Bachelier.*

1882   Anstey, F. *Vice Versa.*
        Barbey d'Aurevilly, JulesAmédée. *Le Plus Bel Amour de Don Juan.*
        France, Anatole. *Les Désirs de Jean Servien.*

1883   Bonnetain, Paul. *Charlot s'amuse . . .*

1885   France, Anatole. *Le Livre de mon ami.*
        Margueritte, Paul. *Tous quatre.*

1886   Bourget, Paul. *Un Crime d'amour.*
        Mirbeau, Octave. *Le Calvaire.*

1887   Bashkirtseff, Marie. *Journal.*
        Bourget, Paul. *André Cornelis.*
        Prévost, Marcel. *Le Scorpion.*
        Reed, Talbot Baines. *The Fifth Form at St. Dominic's.*

1888   Ajalbert, Jean. *Le P'tit.*
        Barrès, Maurice. *Sous l'oeil des barbares.*

1889   Barrès, Maurice. *Un Homme libre.*

Bourget, Paul. *Le Disciple.*
Charpentier, Armand. *L'Enfance d'un homme.*
Deyssel, L. van. *De kleine republiek.*

1890 [Bary, Emile]. *Les Cahiers d'un rhétoricien de 1815.*
Estaunié, Edouard. *Un Simple.*
Loti, Pierre. *Le Roman d'un enfant.*
Mirbeau, Octave, *Sébastien Roch.*
Rod, Edouard. *Les Trois coeurs.*

1891 Barrès, Maurice. *Le Jardin de Bérénice.*
Burnham, William H. "The Study of Adolescence."
Gide, André. *Les Cahiers et les poésies d'André Walter.*
Hermant, Abel. *Serge.*
Hofmannsthal, Hugo von. "Maurice Barrès."
Wedekind, Frank. *Frühlings Erwachen.*

1892 Barrès, Maurice. *L'Ennemi des lois.*
Wolf, Max. *Die physische und sittliche Entartung des modernen Weibes.*

1893 Adam, Paul. *Les Images sentimentales.*
Berenger, Henri. *L'Effort.*
Halbe, Max. *Jugend: Ein Liebesdrama*
Hofmannsthal, Hugo von. "Tagebuch eines jungen Mädchens."
Siegert, Gustav. *Das Problem der Kinderselbstmorde.*
Wildenbruch, Ernst von. *Das edle Blut.*

1894 Meredith, George. *Lord Ormont and His Aminta.*
Renard, Jules. *Poil de Carotte.*

1895 Andrian-Werburg, Leopold v. *Der Garten der Erkenntnis.*
Bölsche, Wilhelm. "Mädchenlektüre."
Gide, André. *Paludes.*
Martens, Kurt. *Wie ein Strahl verglimmt.*

1896 Estaunié, Edouard. *L'Empreinte.*
Morrison, William Douglas. *Juvenile Offenders.*
Sigaux, Jean. *Au printemps de la vie.*
Wolgast, Heinrich. *Das Elend unserer Jugendliteratur.*

1897 Barrès, Maurice. *Les Déracinés.*
Bierbaum, Otto. *Stilpe.*
Demolins, Edmond. *A quoi tient la supériorité des Anglo-Saxons.*
Gide, André. *Les Nourritures terrestres.*
James, Henry. *What Maisie Knew.*
Lancaster, E. G. "The Psychology and Pedagogy of Adolescence."
Lietz, Hermann. *Emlohstobba: Roman oder Wirklichkeit?*
Mack, Louise. *Teens.*

Marro, Antoine. *La Puberté.*

Wassermann, Jakob. *Die Juden von Zirndorf.*

1898   Aicard, Jean. *L'Ame d'un enfant.*

Demolins, Edmond. *L'Education nouvelle.*

Dujardin, Edouard. *Initiation au péché et à l'amour.*

Juhellé, Albert. *La Crise virile.*

Kipling, Rudyard. *Stalky & Co.* (serialized 1898–99)

1899   Bertrand, Louis. *Le Sang des races.*

France, Anatole. *Pierre Nozière.*

Gide, André. *Le Prométhée mal enchaîné.*

Hélie, Jean. "Le Vagabondage des mineurs."

James, Henry. *The Awkward Age.*

Le Roux, Hughes. *Jeune amours, mémoires d'un adolescent.*

Starbuck, Edwin Diller. *The Psychology of Religion.*

1900   Daudet, Alphonse. *Premier voyage, premier mensonge.*

Juhellé, Albert. *Les Pécheurs d'hommes.*

Reddie, Cecil. *Abbotsholme.*

Richmond, Ennis. *Through Boyhood to Manhood.*

Willy and Colette. *Claudine à l'école.*

1901   Adam, Paul. *L'Enfant d'Austerlitz.*

Baer, Adolf. *Der Selbstmord im kindlichen Lebensalter.*

Binet-Valmer, H. G. *Le Gamin tendre.*

Ebner-Eschenbach, Marie von. *Der Vorzugsschüler.*

Forbush, William Byron. *The Boy Problem.*

Hofmannsthal, Hugo von. *Ein Brief.*

Kaiser, Georg. *Der Fall des Schülers Vehgesack.*

Key, Ellen. *Das Jahrhundert des Kindes.*

Kipling, Rudyard. *Kim.*

Libby, M. F. "Shakespeare and Adolescence."

Swift, Edgar James. "Some Criminal Tendencies of Boyhood."

Willy and Colette. *Claudine à Paris.*

1902   Andreas-Salomé, Lou. *Im Zwischenland.*

Brand, Franz. *Die Zukunftslosen.*

Gurlitt, Ludwig. *Der Deutsche und sein Vaterland.*

Hollaender, Felix. *Der Weg des Thomas Truck.*

Rilke, Rainer Maria. *Die Turnstunde.*

Strauss, Emil. *Freund Hein.*

1903   Brulat, Paul. *La Gangue.*

Geiger, André. *André.*

Mack, Louise. *Girls Together.*

Mann, Thomas. *Tonio Kröger.*
Régnier, Henri de. *Les Vacances d'un jeune homme sage.*
Wedekind, Frank. *Mine-Haha, oder Über die körperliche Erziehung der jungen Mädchen.*
Wodehouse, P. G. *A Perfect Uncle.*
Wodehouse, P. G. *The Tales of St Austin's.*

1904   Hall, Granville Stanley. *Adolescence.*
Rodes, Jean. *Adolescents (moeurs collégiennes).*
Sageret, Jules. *La Jeunesse de Paul Méliande.*

1905   Ferri-Pisani. *Les Pervertis, roman d'un potache.*
Freud, Sigmund. *Drei Abhandlungen zur Sexualtheorie.*
Freud, Sigmund. *Bruchstück einer HysterieAnalyse.* [Dora.]
Gurlitt, Ludwig. *Der Deutsche und seine Schule.*
Puffer, J. Adams. "Boys' Gangs."
Rolland, Romain. "L'Adolescent." Pt. 3 of vol. 1 of *Jean Christophe.*
Wodehouse, P. G. *The Head of Kay's.*

1906   Hall, Granville Stanley. *Youth. Its Regimen and Hygiene.*
Hesse, Hermann. *Unterm Rad.*
Marc-Elder. *Une Crise.*
Musil, Robert. *Die Verwirrungen des Zöglings Törless.*

1907   Adelswärd-Fersen, Jacques d'. *Une Jeunesse.*
Gide, André. *Le Retour de l'enfant prodigue.*
Huch, Friedrich. *Mao.*
Molnár, Ferenc. *A Pál utcai Fiúk.*
Wodehouse, P. G. *The White Feather.*

1908   Baden-Powell, Robert S. S. *Scouting for Boys.*
Ernst, Otto. *Semper der Jüngling.*
Gurlitt, Ludwig. *Schülerselbstmorde.*
Kokoschka, Oskar. *Die träumenden Knaben.*
Lux, Joseph August. "Wiener Kunstschau."
Margueritte, Paul. *Les Jours s'allongent.*
Mell, Max. "Chaos der Kindheit."
Miomandre, Francis de. *Ecrit sur de l'eau.*
Rouquès, Amédée. *Le Jeune Rouvre.*

1909   Baden-Powell, Robert S. S. *Yarns for Boy Scouts.*
Compayré, Gabriel. *L'Adolescence.*
Duprat, G.-L. *La Criminalité dans l'adolescence.*
Gide, André. *La Porte étroite.*
Mendousse, Pierre. *L'Ame de l'adolescent.*
Wodehouse, P.G. *Mike and Psmith.*

Wodehouse, P. G. *Mike at Wrykyn.*

Der Zupfgeigenhansl.

1910   Lemaître, August. *La Vie mentale de l'adolescent et ses anomalies.*

Lietz, Hermann. *Die deutsche Land- und Erziehungs–Heime.*

Popert, Hermann. *Helmut Harringa.*

Rilke, Rainer Maria. *Die Aufzeichnungen des Malte Laurids Brigge.*

Tarkington, Booth. *Penrod and Sam.*

1911   Beresford, John D. *The Early History of Jacob Stahl.*

Caron, Max. *Jésus et les adolescents.*

Hirsch, Charles-Henry. *L'Amour en herbe.*

Larbaud, Valery. *Fermina Márquez.*

Lietz, Hermann. *Die deutsche Nationalschule.*

Mauriac, François. *L'Adieu à l'adolescence.*

Slaughter, John W. *The Adolescent.*

1912   Andrews, Cyril, Bruyn. *An Introduction to the Study of Adolescent Education.*

Der Anfang.

Blüher, Hans. *Wandervogel.*

Burte, Hermann. *Wiltfeber der ewige Deutsche.*

Lafon, André. *L'Élève Gilles.*

1913   Agathon [Henri Massis and Alfred de Tarde]. *Les Jeunes gens d'aujourd'hui.*

Alain-Fournier. *Le Grand Meaulnes.*

Barnett, Mary G. *Young Delinquents.*

Freideutsche Jugend.

Freideutscher Jugendtag 1913.

Henriot, Emile. *A quoi rêvent les jeunes gens.*

Kafka, Franz. *Das Urteil.*

Lunn, Arnold. *The Harrowians.*

Mackenzie, Compton. *Sinister Street.*

Mauriac, François. *L'Enfant chargé de chaînes.*

Walpole, Hugh. *Fortitude.*

Wodehouse, P. G. *The Little Nugget.*

Wyneken, Gustav. *Schule und Jugendkultur.*

1914   Andreas-Salomé, Lou. "Kind und Kunst."

Eulenburg, Albert. *Kinder- und Jugendselbstmorde.*

Frank, Leonhard. *Die Räuberbande.*

Freud, Sigmund. *Zur Psychologie des Gymnasiasten.*

Gide, André. *Les Caves du Vatican.*

Giese, Fritz. *Das freie literarische Schaffen bei Kindern und Jugendlichen.*

Guiard, Amédée. *Antone Ramon.*
Hasenclever, Walter. *Der Sohn.*
King, Irving. *The High-School Age.*
Mauriac, François. *La Robe prétexte.*
Moselly, Emile. *Les Etudiants.*
Nescio. *Titaantjes.*
Tarkington, Booth. *Penrod.*
Wyneken, Gustav. *Die neue Jugend.*

1915 Richardson, Dorothy M. *Pilgrimage I: Pointed Roofs, Backwater, Honeycomb.*
Morgan, Jean. *Un Enfant dans la foule.*
Tarkington, Booth. *Seventeen.*

1916 Blüher, Hans. *Der bürgerliche und der geistige Antifeminismus.*
Carco, Francis. *Les Innocents.*
Johst, Hanns. *Der junge Mensch.*
Joyce, James. *A Portrait of the Artist as a Young Man.*
Karinthy, Frigyes. *Tanár úr kérem.*
Neveu, Pol. *La Douce enfance de Thierry Seneuse.*

1917 Blüher, Hans. *Die Rolle der Erotik in der männlichen Gesellschaft.*
Flex, Walter. *Der Wanderer zwischen beiden Welten.*
Hall, G. S. *Jesus, the Christ, in the Light of Psychology.*
Reuter, Gabriele. *Die Jugend eines Idealisten.*
Valéry, Paul. "La Jeune parque."
Waugh, Alec. *The Loom of Youth.*

1918 Blüher, Hans. *Familie und Männerbund.*
Blüher, Hans. *Führer und Volk in der Jugendbewegung.*
France, Anatole. *Le Petit Pierre.*
Giraudoux, Jean. *Simon le pathétique.*
Hirsch, Charles-Henry. *"Petit" Louis, boxeur.*
Jaloux, Edmond. *Fumées dans la compagne.*
Wells, H. G. *Joan and Peter.*

1919 Béhaine, René. *Si jeunesse savait!*
Carco, Francis. *Bob et Bobette s'amusent.*
Dehn, Günther. *Grossstadtjugend.*
Galzy, Jeanne. *La Femme chez les garçons.*
Hesse, Hermann. *Demian.*
Kaiser, Georg. *Rektor Kleist.*
Loti, Pierre. *Prime Jeunesse.*
Sinclair, May. *Mary Olivier.*
Wyneken, Gustav. *Der Kampf für die Jugend.*

1920   Beresford, John D. *An Imperfect Mother.*

Bronnen, Arnolt. *Vatermord.*

Busse-Wilson, Elisabeth. *Die Frau und die Jugendbewegung.*

Chadourne, Louis. *L'Inquiète adolescence.*

Dell, Floyd. *Moon-Calf.*

Lacretelle, Jacques de. *La Vie inquiète de Jean Hermelin.*

Mauriac, François. *La Chair et le sang.*

Montherlant, Henry de. *La Relève du matin.*

Móricz, Zsigmond. *Légy jó Mindhalálig.*

Obey, André. *L'Enfant inquiet.*

Radiguet, Raymond. *Les Joues en feu.*

Scharrelmann, Wilhelm. *Jesus der Jüngling.*

1921   Blüher, Hans. *Der Charakter der Jugendbewegung.*

Braun, Otto. *Aus nachgelassenen Schriften eines Frühvollendeten.*

Bühler, Charlotte. *Das Seelenleben des Jugendlichen.*

Cazin, Paul. *Décadi ou la pieuse enfance.*

Cremieux, Benjamin, *Le Premier de la classe.*

Drieu La Rochelle, Pierre. *Etat Civil.*

Ferber, Edna. *The Girls.*

Jouhandeau, Marcel. *La Jeunesse de Théophile.*

Mauriac, François. *Préseances.*

Maus, Octave. *Les Préludes, impressions d'adolescence.*

Prellwitz, Gertrud. *Drude.*

Rolland, Romain. *Pierre et Luce.*

Tarkington, Booth. *Alice Adams.*

Wyneken, Gustav. *Eros.*

1922   France, Anatole. *La Vie en fleur.*

Lacretelle, Jacques de. *Silbermann.*

Leslie, Shane J. R. *The Oppidan.*

Martin du Gard, Roger. *Les Thibault,* vol. 1.

Morgan, Jean. *Les Jeux du printemps.*

Thierry, Albert. *Le Sourire blessé.*

Werth, Léon. *Dix-neuf ans.*

1923   Betz, Maurice. *Rouge et blanc.*

Cocteau, Jean. *Le Grand Ecart.*

Cocteau, Jean. *Thomas l'imposteur.*

Colette. *Le Blé en herbe.*

Etiveaud, Raymond d'. *Une Jeunesse, témoignage contemporain.*

Fabre, Lucien. *La Jeunesse de Rabevel.*

Fleisser, Marieluise. *Die Dreizehnjährigen.*

Foerster, Fr. W. *Jugendseele, Jugendbewegung, Jugendziel.*

Gabory, Georges. *Les Enfants perdus.*

Jolinon, Joseph. *Le Jeune Athlète.*

Kipling, Rudyard. *Land and Sea Tales.*

Lacretelle, Jacques de. *La Mort d'Hippolyte.*

Maurière, Gabriel. *Le Bel Age.*

Ptaschkina, Nelly. *The Diary of Nelly Ptaschkina.*

Radiguet, Raymond. *Le Diable au corps.*

Renaitour, Jean-Michel. *L'Enfant chaste.*

Renaud, Jean. *La Jeunesse de Prosper Bourasset.*

1924 Arland, Marcel. *Etienne.*

Barbey, Bernard. *Le Coeur gros.*

Béhaine, René. *La Conquête de la vie.*

Bernier, Jean. *Tête de melée.*

Carco, Francis. *Rien qu'une femme.*

Delarue-Mardrus, Lucie. *La Mère et le fils.*

Lemonnier, Leon. *La Maîtresse au coeur simple.*

Piéchaud, Martial. *La Romance à l'étoile.*

Sedgwick, Anne. *The Little French Girl.*

Spranger, Eduard. *Psychologie des Jugendalters.*

Van Offel, Horace. *Les Deux Ingénus.*

1925 Aichhorn, August. *Verwahrloste Jugend.*

Anet, Claude. *Adolescence.*

Bashkirtseff, Marie. *Cahiers Intimes. Inédits.*

Bost, Pierre. *Homicide par imprudence.*

Bunin, Ivan. *Mitina ljubov.*

Duhourcau, François. *L'Enfant de la victoire.*

Gide, André. *Les Faux-monnayeurs.*

Mauriac, François. *Le Désert de l'amour.*

INTRODUCTION

1 "Wendla: 'Jedenfalls steht mir mein Prinzesskleidchen besser als diese Nacht-schlumpe.—Lass mich's noch einmal tragen, Mutter! Nur noch den Sommer lang. Ob ich nun vierzehn zähle oder fünfzehn, dies Bussgewand wird mir immer noch recht sein'" (*Werke* 2: 97).

2 These include Halbe's *Jugend* (1893), Ernst's *Flachsmann als Erzieher* (1901), Heinrich Mann's *Professor Unrat* (source for the film *The Blue Angel*), Ebner-Eschenbach's *Der Vorzugsschüler* (1901), and Dreyer's *Der Probekandidat* (1900).

3 "Es hängt das zusammen mit der wissenschaftlichen Erkenntnis von aller Entwicklung und allem Wachstum der Seele, mit der neuen Lehre, dass jedes Lebensalter gleichen Lebenswert habe und dass der Erwachsene eigentlich gar nicht das Vorbild der Jugend ist, sondern sich zu dieser verhält wie die Frucht zur Blüte" (198).

4 Freeman charges that Mead set out to prove her point instead of subjecting the hypothesis to tests of falsification, but this charge cannot be substanti-ated. Neither is it true (Freeman 316 and, following him, Springhall, *Coming*

of Age 31–32) that Mead wanted to disprove Hall's biological interpretation of adolescence. She knew that he believed in its cultural dependence. Mentioning Hall and the theory that adolescence was universal, Mead writes: "The careful child psychologist who relied upon experiment for his conclusions did not subscribe to these theories. He said, 'We have no data.' . . . But the negative cautions of science are never popular. If the experimentalist would not commit himself, the social philosopher, the preacher and the pedagogue tried the harder to give a short-cut answer. They observed the behaviour of adolescents in our society, noted down the omnipresent and obvious symptoms of unrest, and announced these as characteristics of the period" (2–3). This last sentence does not, in my opinion, refer to Hall anymore.

5 E. T. A. Hoffmann uses *Lümmeljahre* in *Lebensansichten des Katers Murr* (3: 217); on *Flegeljahre* see Jean Paul's novel of the same title. *Pubertätsalter* ("puberty-age"), *halbwüchsig* ("half-grown"), and, above all, *Jugendalter* ("youth age") are the most common terms today.

CHAPTER 1: (METAPHORIC) IDENTITY

1 Chester G. Anderson finds three types of answers: (1) Stephen is "an autobiographical hero who triumphs over his tawdry environment . . . there is little 'distance' between the painter and his portrait"; (2) "Joyce sees Stephen as an autobiographical representation of the author, a 'portrait of the artist' drawn 'as a young man' by an older man. Joyce asks the reader to join him in seeing Stephen as a priggish, narcissistic young egoist" (Joyce, *Portrait* 447–49); (3) "Joyce's view of his own past in Stephen is mixed, both ironic and romantic or sympathetic" (Joyce, *Portrait* 451).

2 In this view, the reduction of commentary impoverished *A Portrait*: "Joyce himself judged his hero's theory in greater detail than we could possibly infer from the final version alone" (335). Readers cannot infer from *A Portrait* Joyce's private judgments, "We should never come to as rich, as refined, and as varied a conception of the quality of Stephen's last days in Ireland as Joyce had in mind" (336). But surely, no text fully replicates its author's intentions, and seeking solely to recover these we may impoverish our reading. Besides, recovering "effaced" intentions from an early draft assumes that the final version retained the narrator's earlier view of the protagonist.

3 In fact, Riquelme reads *A Portrait* as a double autobiography, "the author's autobiographical fiction and the autobiography of the fictional character" (51).

4 In contrast to Virginia Woolf's *Mrs. Dalloway* and other modernist narratives where the narrator shares narrated monologues with several fictional char-

acters, the narrators of *A Portrait* and *Tonio Kröger* read only the mind of their protagonist. This creates a special relation between them.

5 "Die Wintersonne stand nur als armer Schein, milchig und matt hinter Wolkenschichten über der engen Stadt. Nass und zugig war's in den giebeligen Gassen, und manchmal fiel eine Art von weichem Hagel, nicht Eis, nicht Schnee" (273).

In preparing this and the following translations I have consulted that of H. T. Lowe-Porter in Thomas Mann, *Death in Venice and Seven Other Stories*. New York: Vintage, 1958. 76–134.

6 Tonio "ging nachlässig und ungleichmässig, während Hansens schlanke Beine in den schwarzen Strümpfen so elastisch und taktfest einherschritten . . ." (274).

7 "Tonio Kröger. Manche gehen mit bewusster Nothwendigkeit in die Irre, weil es einen richtigen Weg für sie überhaupt nicht giebt" (Wysling 49).

8 "Er ging den Weg, den er gehen musste, ein wenig nachlässig und ungleichmässig, vor sich hin pfeifend, mit seitwärts geneigtem Kopfe ins Weite blickend, und wenn er irreging, so geschah es, weil es für etliche einen richtigen Weg überhaupt nicht gibt. Fragte man ihn, was in aller Welt er zu werden gedachte, so erteilte er wechselnde Auskunft, denn er pflegte zu sagen (und hatte es auch bereits aufgeschrieben), dass er die Möglichkeiten zu tausend Daseinsformen in sich trage, zusammen mit dem heimlichen Bewusstsein, dass es im Grunde lauter Unmöglichkeiten seien" (290 f.).

9 "Denn etliche gehen mit Notwendigkeit in die Irre, weil es einen rechten Weg für sie überhaupt nicht gibt" (335).

10 "Damals lebte sein Herz; Sehnsucht war darin und schwermütiger Neid und ein klein wenig Verachtung und eine ganze keusche Seligkeit" (283).

11 "Und er umkreiste behutsam den Opferaltar, auf dem die lautere und keusche Flamme seiner Liebe loderte, kniete davor und schürte und nährte sie auf alle Weise, weil er treu sein wollte. Und über eine Weile, unmerklich, ohne Aufsehen und Geräusch, war sie dennoch erloschen" (290).

12 "Sehnsucht ist darin und schwermütiger Neid und ein klein wenig Verachtung und eine ganze keusche Seligkeit" (341). The heart metaphor shows that the story is both incremental and circular, for Tonio returns to an earlier position after assuming a mistaken identity: he resolves his adolescent confusion by adopting the professional, bohemian artistic conventions, but he finally returns to his adolescent "intermediacy." His final identity is, paradoxically, an extended or permanent adolescence. Siegfried Bernfeld ("Typische Form" 187) has suggested that creative people never end their adolescence.

13 "[Ich bin] ein Bürger, der sich in die Kunst verirrte, ein Bohemien mit Heimweh nach der guten Kinderstube, ein Künstler mit schlechtem Ge-

wissen. . . . Ich stehe zwischen zwei Welten, bin in keiner daheim und habe es infolgedessen ein wenig schwer." (340)

14 "Tonio Kröger stahl sich fort, ging heimlich auf den Korridor hinaus und stellte sich dort, die Hände auf dem Rücken, vor ein Fenster mit herabgelassener Jalousie, ohne zu bedenken, dass man durch diese Jalousie gar nichts sehen konnte, und dass es also lächerlich sei, davorzustehen und zu tun, als blicke man hinaus.

Er blickte aber in sich hinein, wo so viel Gram und Sehnsucht war. Warum, warum war er hier? . . . Nein, nein, sein Platz war dennoch hier, wo er sich in Inge's Nähe wusste, wenn er auch nur einsam von ferne stand und versuchte, in dem Summen, Klirren und Lachen dort drinnen ihre Stimme zu unterscheiden, in welcher es klang von warmem Leben. Deine länglich geschnittenen, blauen, lachenden Augen, du blonde Inge!" (288)

15 A summary of the discussion on language in *Törless* may be found in Varsava. Elisabeth Stopp (107) rightly argues that Törless's problems with articulation are not simply signs of an epochal "language crisis" such as Hofmannsthal exemplified in *Ein Brief.* The narrator's lush figural language indicates that Törless's inarticulateness is a specifically adolescent problem. Nevertheless, it may be symptomatic of a language crisis that Musil and so many others chose adolescents as their heroes. See also Hoffmeister and Kühne.

CHAPTER 2: THE OTHER

1 The late nineteenth-century fictional diaries and autobiographies on adolescence include Dostoevsky's *The Adolescent,* Anatole France's *La Vie en fleur,* Gide's *Les Cahiers d'André Walter,* and Colette's and Willy's *Claudine à l'école.* *André Walter* differs from the others in having temporal depth, for the diary on the present incorporates older diary segments.

2 Later examples of this genre, often called "witness narratives," include Thomas Mann's *Doktor Faustus* (1949) and Günter Grass's *Katz und Maus* (1961).

3 On *Fermina Márquez,* see also Brown and Simon.

4 "Son égoïsme s'amollissait, et il avait envie de dire à Fermina tous ses secrets et toutes ses espérances . . . ces projets de séduction paraissaient si lointains! . . . quel enfantillage, mon Dieu! il en avait honte, maintenant" (71–73).

5 "Et lui, qui avait pensé trouver, à défaut d'une amante, au moins une amie, une camarade à qui il pourrait tout dire, une égale! *Une égale!*—Bon! il retombait encore dans ses théories sur la bêtise des gens. Il lui avait déplu, et voilà tout" (97).

6 "En somme, toute son éloquence revenait à ceci: 'Entre Santos Iturria et

moi, vous avez choisi. C'est bien. Mais sachez donc qui vous avez rejeté et regrettez-moi!'" (125).

7 "C'était l'époque où je me récapitulais mon année, me félicitant de n'avoir pas mérité une seule punition; car j'étais moi aussi, un très bon élève" (146).

8 On *Le Grand Meaulnes* see Cancalon, Gibson, Goldgar, Gross, Husson, Jones, Loize, Rabine, and Sorrell. References to *Le Grand Meaulnes* will pertain to the English translation of Frank Davison.

9 In later sections of the book, the fusion of then and now, of experience and writing, is frequently achieved by switching to the present tense.

10 Alain-Fournier wrote to Jacques Rivière on April 4, 1910: "The hero of my book is a man whose childhood was too beautiful. He drags it along during his whole adolescence" (le héros de mon livre est un homme dont l'enfance fut trop belle. Pendant toute son adolescence, il la traîne après lui). Meaulnes returns from his adventure in the lost domain "as a mysterious and insolent young god" but "he is in the world as somebody who is going to depart. This is the secret of his cruelty" (Il est dans le monde comme quelqu'un qui va s'en aller. C'est là le secret de sa cruauté). On September 28, 1910, he writes to Rivière again: "Only the women who loved me can know how cruel I am. Because I want everything. I don't even want that one lives that human life. You see here the hero of my book, Meaulnes" (Seules les femmes qui m'ont aimé peuvent savoir à quel point je suis cruel. Parce que je veux tout. Je ne veux même plus qu'on vive dans cette vie humaine. Vous voyez d'ici le héros de mon livre, Meaulnes).

11 Sorrell, for instance, calls François a "co-author" (79) and Gross thinks that his "complicated pattern of representations and misrepresentations" purposefully obscures his "genuine demonism" (626).

12 References refer to the English translation made by Michael Roloff and Michael Lebeck.

13 Like Musil's narrator, Sinclair repeatedly describes the adolescent relationship between feelings and their articulation. Although he admits he could not have perceived things so clearly then (45), he insists that his unarticulated feelings were intense (49).

14 "Moi, je l'écoutais fixement, frappé par une soudaine découverte. Ces mots assemblés, que je reconnaissais pour les avoir vus imprimés et les avoir mis bout à bout, mécaniquement, dans ma mémoire, ces mots formaient pour la première fois image en mon esprit.... Je n'avais pas cru jusqu'ici que cette représentation vivante et sensible d'une tragédie classique fût possible.... il me fit songer, avec son teint jaune et sous le bonnet noir de ses cheveux frisés, au magicien de quelque conte oriental qui détient la clef de toutes les merveilles" (21–23).

15 "Il était petit et d'extérieur chétif. Sa figure ... était très formée, mais

assez laide, avec des pommettes saillantes et un menton aigu. . . . L'ensemble éveillait l'idée d'une précocité étrange; il me fit songer aux petit prodiges qui exécutent des tours dans les cirques" (11–12).

16 "Dans l'instant, je songeai à tout ce que comportait l'amitié de Philippe: un sentiment doux et bien réglé, des joies faciles et approuvées . . . Devant ces images aimables, je fus près d'abandonner Silbermann. Mais, de l'autre côté, se présentait une tâche ardue; j'entrevis une destinée pénible; et exalté par la perspective du sacrifice, je répondis d'un souffle irrésistible:—Lui" (48, ellipses in original).

17 "Maintenant, je suis sorti de mes rêves. En Amérique, je vais *faire de l'argent*. Avec le nom que je porte, j'y étais prédestiné, hein! . . . David Silbermann, cela fait mieux sur la plaque d'un marchand de diamants que sur la couverture d'un livre!" (109, ellipses in original).

18 Although the narrator usually treats his friend as an individual, the stereotype emerges early in his mind. He comments on Silbermann's mocking reaction to his injury: "That clowning displeased me. Words of the Bible occurred to me: 'Disbelieving and perverse race . . .' Be quiet I said to him impatiently. That was the first time that I treated him brusquely" (64, ellipses in original).

19 "J'avais compris, en reconnaissant la fragile matière de ce pur visage [of the mother], qu'il n'est point d'âme, toute vertueuse et toute tendue à la sainteté qu'elle est, qui puisse s'élever hors de l'imperfection humaine" (119). As in *Törless,* the parental image slides here from saintly purity to tainted humanity, though the events are very different. Törless's parents committed no "sin," their changed image results from their son's experience with other people. In *Silbermann,* the image of the tainted parents allows the narrator to accept his own impurity.

20 Philippe's "visage était gai et serein. Il semblait se tenir sur une route bien plus facile, où étaient ménagés des biais commodes, des sauvegardes propices, et qui côtoyaient les abîmes sans s'y perdre jamais.

   J'eus le sentiment que j'étais placé devant ces deux chemins et que mon bonheur futur était suspendu au choix que j'allais faire. J'hésitais . . . Mais tout d'un coup le paysage du côté de Philippe me parut si attrayant que mon être se détendit; et faiblement, je laissai échapper un sourire" (124, ellipses in original).

21 "Je me retournai vers la caricature de Silbermann et, après un effort, je dis sur un petit ton moqueur dont le naturel parfait me confondit intérieurement:—C'est très ressemblant" (124).

22 "I savored a delicious feeling. 'I offer everything to him' I said to myself, 'the affection of my friends, the will of my parents, and even my honor'" (Je savourais un sentiment délicieux. "Je lui offre tout," disais-je intérieure-

ment, "l'affection des mes amis, la volonté de mes parents et mon honneur même" [91]). See also pp. 69, 78, and 79.

23 "Je tombai dans une profonde désolation. Ni sa personne même ni la fin de notre amitié n'en étaient cause. Je souffrais de ne plus recevoir, chaque matin, à mon réveil, en même temps que la première flèche du jour, l'inspiration de cette tâche glorieuse" (111).

CHAPTER 3: GROUPS

1 Mme Sophroniska, who gives a detailed account of free association and dream analysis (176–80), is highly critical of Boris's mother for having tried to suppress his masturbation by instilling fear and guilt in him. Boris came to believe that his sinful masturbation caused his father's death (208). Gide himself was expelled from the Ecole Alsacienne for masturbating in class, and the problem, related to his homosexual inclination, haunted him throughout his life. The struggle to overcome the desire to masturbate was, according to him, one of the true subjects of *Les Cahiers d'André Walter,* Gide's first book (*Si le Grain ne meurt* 242).

2 Molnár (1878–1952) later emigrated to the United States and wrote such successful Broadway plays as *The Swan, The Play's the Thing,* and *Liliom* (source of *Carousel*).

3 "Úgy kiáltották, hogy: 'Éljen a grund!'—mintha azt kiáltották volna, hogy 'Éljen a haza!' " (35).

4 "Notre morale, notre religion, notre sentiment des nationalités, sont choses écroulées, constatais-je, auxquelles nous ne pouvons emprunter de règles de vie, et, en attendant que nos maîtres nous aient refait des certitudes, il convient que nous nous en tenions à la seule réalité, au *moi*" (18).

5 "Premier principe: Nous ne sommes jamais si heureux que dans l'exaltation. Deuxième principe: Ce qui augmente beaucoup le plaisir de l'exaltation, c'est de l'analyser. . . . Conséquence: Il faut sentir le plus possible en analysant le plus possible" (136).

A variation of the first principle appears in Gide's *Les Cahiers d'André Walter*: "To multiply the emotions. Not to lock oneself up in one's own life, in one's own body only; to make one's soul the hostess of several emotions" (Multiplier les émotions. Ne pas s'enfermer en sa seule vie, en son seul corps; faire son âme hôtesse de plusieurs [50]). Both remarks were preceded by Nietzsche's key statement on perspectivism in *On the Genealogy of Morals,* where the maximizing of emotions is made into an epistemological issue: "There is *only* a perspective seeing, *only* a perspective 'knowing'; and the *more* affects we allow to speak about one thing, the *more* eyes, different eyes, we can use to observe one thing, the more complete will our 'concept' of this thing, our 'objectivity' be" (Third essay, section 12, p. 119).

6 "Courons à la solitude! Soyons des nouveau-nés!" (138).

7 "Mon *moi du dehors,* que me fait! Les actes ne comptent pas; ce qui importe uniquement, c'est mon *moi du dedans*! le Dieu que je construis" (215).

8 "Mon âme mécanisée est toute en ma main, prête à me fournir les plus rares émotions. Ainsi je deviens vraiment un homme libre" (164). "Je me suis morcelé en un grand nombre d'âmes" (248). "Les émotions que nous connûmes hier, déjà ne nous appartiennent plus. Les désirs, les ardeurs, les aspirations sont tout; le but rien" (250).

9 "Dès mes premières réflexions d'enfant, j'ai redouté les barbares qui me reprochaient d'être différent; j'avais le culte de ce qui est en moi d'éternel, et cela m'amena à me faire une méthode pour jouir de mille parcelles de mon idéal. C'était me donner mille âmes successives; pour qu'une naisse, il faut qu'une autre meure; je souffre de cet éparpillement. Dans cette succession d'imperfections, j'aspire à me reposer de moi-même dans une abondante unité. Ne pourrais-je réunir tous ces sons discords pour en faire une large harmonie?" (289).

10 "Les individus, si parfaits qu'on les imagine, ne sont que des fragments du système plus complet qu'est la race, fragment elle-même de Dieu. Echappant désormais à la stérile analyse de mon organisation, je travaillerai à réaliser la tendance de mon être" (206–7).

11 "Je suis un jardin où fleurissent des émotions sitôt déracinées. Bérénice et Aigues-Mortes ne sauront-ils m'indiquer la culture qui me guérirait de ma mobilité? Je suis perdu dans le vagabondage, ne sachant où retrouver l'unité de ma vie" (294).

12 "Cultiver son moi, ce n'est pas le libérer, le précipiter en des folles aventures, mais retrouver en lui les énergies de sa race, de ses morts et l'élargir dans le sens de son destin" (Agathon 15).

13 "Isolés de leurs groupes de naissance et dressés seulement à concourir entre eux, des adolescents prennent de la vie, de ses conditions et de son but la plus pitoyable intelligence" (13).

14 "Nomadic" harks back to "barbarian" in the first trilogy. It has been recently used by Gilles Deleuze in precisely the same sense, albeit positively: "Pensée nomade" is Deleuze's study of Nietzsche's rootless and centerless philosophy.

15 "Chaque individu est constitué par des réalités qu'il n'y a pas à contredire; le maître qui les envisage doit proportionner et distribuer la vérité de façon que chacun emporte sa verité propre" (23).

16 The English translation incorrectly says "nostalgia for my *former* self," confusing thus the childhood self with the future authentic self, which can also be an object of nostalgia since it is the "true home."

CHAPTER 4: ADOLESCENT SPACES

1 "Über ihm glühten und tosten die Blätter eines ungeheuren Baumes, schwangen in Feuerkreisen, schwarze Früchte platzten und barsten auseinander und schossen den goldenen, leuchtenden Staub zahlloser Funken nieder auf die alte Heimat.
Da klang, sprang und zerriss eine ungeheure Harfe.
Arbeiter fanden ihn am andern Morgen im Abgrund, tot, im fahlen Frühlicht" (168).

2 "Hát kellett ennél gyönyörűbb hely a mulatozásra? Nekünk, városi fiúknak bizony nem kellett. Ennél szebbet, ennél indiánosabbat mi el se tudtunk képzelni. A Pál utcai telek gyönyörű sík föld volt, s ez volt az, ami az amerikai prériket helyettesítette. . . . A grund . . . Ti szép, egészséges alföldi diákok, akiknek csak egyet kell lépnetek, hogy künn legyetek a végtelen rónán, . . . ti nem is tudjátok, mi a pesti gyereknek egy üres telek. A pesti gyereknek ez az alföldje, a rónája, a síksága. Ez jelenti számára a végtelenséget és a szabadságot. Egy darabka föld, melyet egyik oldalról düledező palánk határol, s melynek többi oldalán nagy házfalak merednek az ég felé. Most már a Pál utcai grundon is nagy, négyemeletes ház szomorkodik, tele lakóval, akik közül talán egy se tudja, hogy ez a darabka föld néhány szegény pesti kisdiáknak a fiatalságát jelentette. . . . Ez a kis darab terméketlen, hepehupás pesti föld, ez a két ház közé szorított kis rónaság, ami az ő gyereklelkükben a végtelenséget, a szabadságot jelentette, ami délelőtt amerikai préri volt, délután Magyar Alföld, esőben tenger, télen az Északi-sark, szóval a barátjuk volt, s azzá változott, amivé ők akarták, csak hogy mulattassa őket" (21–22, 20, 87).

3 "Dès que j'eus une chambre, je ne me reconnus plus. D'enfant que j'étais la veille, je devins un jeune homme. Mes idées, mes goûts s'étaient formés en un moment. J'avais une manière d'être, une existence propre. . . . J'eus une vie intérieure. Je fus capable de réflexion, de recueillement. . . . Elle me séparait de l'univers, et j'y retrouvais l'univers" (334–36).

4 "Das war bis jetzt der einzige Segen, den ihm die Examengeschichte gebracht hatte—das eigene kleine Zimmer, in dem er Herr war und nicht gestört wurde. . . . Hier hatte er aber auch die paar Stunden gehabt, die ihm mehr wert waren als alle verlorenen Knabenlustbarkeiten, jene paar traumhaft seltsamen Stunden voll Stolz und Rausch und Siegesmut, in denen er sich über Schule, Examen und alles hinweg in einen Kreis höherer Wesen hinübergeträumt und gesehnt hatte" (17).

5 "Sans les lits, on l'eût prise pour un débarras. Des boîtes, du linge, des serviettes éponge jonchaient le sol. . . . Des punaises fixaient partout des pages de magazines, de journaux, de programmes, représentant des vedettes de films, des boxeurs, des assassins" (27–28).

6 "Ces montagnes de linge, étaient la ville du malade et son décor. Elisabeth se délectait de détruire des points de vue essentiels, d'écrouler des montagnes sous prétexte de blanchisseuse et d'alimenter à pleines mains cette température d'orage sans laquelle ni l'un ni l'autre n'eussent pu vivre" (51).

7 "Car c'était bien un chef-d'oeuvre que créaient ces enfants, un chef-d'oeuvre qu'ils *étaient,* où l'intelligence ne tenait aucune place, et qui tirait sa merveille d'être sans orgueil et sans but" (58).

8 "Son envergure était plus vaste, son arrimage plus dangereux, plus hautes ses vagues. Dans le monde singulier des enfants, on pouvait faire la planche et aller vite. Semblable à celle de l'opium, la lenteur y devenait aussi périlleuse qu'un record de vitesse" (74).

9 "C'était à cette inconscience primitive que la pièce devait uns jeunesse éternelle. Sans qu'ils s'en doutassent, la pièce (ou chambre si l'on veut) se balançait au bord du mythe" (78).

10 "faisant de la chambre secrète un théâtre ouvert aux spectateurs" (176).

11 "A kapun csak úgy dűlt kifelé a sok gyerek. Fele jobbra, fele balra oszlott. És tanárok jöttek köztük, és ilyenkor lerepültek a kis kalapok. És mindnyája fáradtan, éhesen ballagott a ragyogóan napfényes utcán. Egy kis kábultság járt a fejükben, mely csak nagy lassan oszladozott a sok vidám és életet jelentő látványra, amit az utca nyújt. Mintha kiszabadult kis rabok lettek volna, úgy támolyogtak a sok levegőn és a sok napfényben, úgy kószáltak bele ebbe a lármás, friss, mozgalmas városba, amely számukra nem volt egyéb, mint kocsik, lóvasutak, utcák, boltok zűrzavaros keveréke, amelyben haza kellett találni" (9).

CHAPTER 5: LITERARY ADOLESCENCE: AN OVERVIEW

1 On Shakespeare's "adolescents" see Libby.

2 Hicks claims that the German school novel developed continuously "from *Wilhelm Meister* via the novels of Hölderlin, Jean Paul, Gottfried Keller, Wilhelm Raabe" down to the teacher and schoolboy novels (77) yet he excludes the bildungsromans of these authors from his study because schools are marginal to them!

3 "Je trouve que les poètes et les romanciers n'ont pas assez connu ce sujet d'observation, cette source de poésie qu'offre ce moment rapide et unique dans la vie d'un homme. Il est vrai que, dans notre triste monde actuel, l'adolescent n'existe pas, ou c'est un être élevé d'une manière exceptionelle" (1: 76). Sand subsequently sketches a remarkable picture of an awkward adolescent, deformed by a detestable education.

4 "Si vos *Nuits* ne sont pas encore un chef-d'oeuvre, elles en donnent l'espé-
rance, et c'est déjà beaucoup, et c'est aussi très rare. Elles ont ceci de
précieux pour moi qu'elles sont bien réellement le cri et malgré l'artifice ici
et là, le jaillissement spontané de votre jeunesse, l'expression naïve quelque-
fois, à force d'être insolemment jeune, de vos rêves—et de nos rêves—
d'adolescent" (1).

5 See *A Young Girl's Diary,* Bary, the works of Bashkirtseff, Braun, Bühler's
publications, Heym, Horney (*Diaries*), Ptaschkina, and *Tagebuch.* A heavily
revised version of Jules Michelet's account of his childhood and adolescence,
written at age twenty-two in 1820, was published by his second wife and
dedicated to the youth in 1884.

6 Like Rousseau, Marie promised unprecedented honesty: "This journal is the
most useful and the most instructive of all writings that have or will be.
This is a woman with all her thoughts and her hopes, disappointments,
meanness, beauties, chagrins, and joys" (59).

7 "Was veranlasst den heutigen Jugendlichen, das heutige Kind, den litera-
rischen Brauch 'Tagebuch' für sich anzunehmen; wie weit gleicht er sein
Tagebuchaufschreiben einer Norm an; was veranlasst diese Formübernahme;
was bedeutet ihm die Form und ihre Übernahme psychisch?" (Bernfeld, *Trieb*
3)

8 The reading craze was probably unique for the late-nineteenth and early-
twentieth centuries. In earlier ages there was no publishing industry to serve
the reading-hunger, whereas the amount of time for reading has drastically
diminished recently through the appearance of television.

9 In its entry on teenage novels, *The Oxford Companion to Children's Literature*
writes that "until the middle of the 20th century children who grew out
of juvenile books were expected to read popular classics, such as the works
of Dickens and Scott, before graduating to more demanding adult novels."
Accordingly, the *Companion* lists the virtually unavailable and unknown *Teens*
by Louise Mack (1897) as the "first and almost isolated" English adolescent
novel. That date seems much too late to me and conflicts with the *Companion*'s
own detailed account of the nineteenth-century school stories.

10 Hence Wolgast (47–48) opposed the suggestion that "large areas of school
instruction, for instance almost all of history and geography, major parts of
physics, and several other fields could be based almost completely on reading,
or reading aloud, exciting historical stories and travel narratives" (Bölsche
574).

CHAPTER 6: VISUALIZING ADOLESCENCE

1 The original painting of 1886 was destroyed by fire. During his stay in Berlin
(1893–94), Munch prepared two new versions as well as a lithograph. There

is also an etching from 1902. *The Voice* (1893), originally entitled *Summer Night's Dream,* shows a somewhat older pubescent girl with an indistinct face in a moonlit forest. Her pose suggests "both sexual self-display and doubtful withdrawal" (Reinhold Heller, *Munch: The Scream* 46).

Munch's own adolescence was marked by encounters with death: in 1877, at the age of thirteen, he became seriously ill, and his fifteen-year-old sister Sophie died the same year.

On Munch see Eggum, Reinhold Heller, Hodin, Langaard, Moen, Revold, Svenaeus, Weisner, and Werenskiold.

2 Of the eleven versions listed by Revold (50), nine were made between 1899 and 1912. Krieger (98) mentions yet another one made in 1907.

3 I have difficulty understanding how Eggum could consider the bridge "one of Munch's most harmonic and lyrical motives," and a convincing representation "of the children's communal spirit and their communal experience of nature" (Weisner 169).

4 In 1906 they were joined by Max Pechstein (b. 1881) and, temporarily, by Emil Nolde (b. 1867); Otto Mueller (b. 1874) joined them in 1910. Bleyl left the group in 1907.

5 "Mit dem Glauben an Entwicklung, an eine neue Generation der Schaffenden wie der Geniessenden rufen wir alle Jugend zusammen und als Jugend, die die Zukunft trägt, wollen wir uns Arm- und Lebensfreiheit verschaffen gegenüber dem wohlangesessenen älteren Kräften. Jeder gehört zu uns, der unmittelbar und unverfälscht das wiedergibt, was ihn zu schaffen drängt" (Elger 20).

6 Kirchner systematically predated his paintings. Gordon, who has rectified much of it, assigns only *Girl on a Divan* (oil, 1906) and the lithograph *Girl in Bathtub* (1908) prior to 1909 (Dresden 362). According to the most recent dating, Heckel, Pechstein, and Schmidt-Rottluff did not depict any young girls prior to 1909.

7 This seems to have taken place in 1910 and not, as Gordon believes, in 1909. Although Kirchner and Heckel went to the lakes in 1909, Pechstein (and hence the two girls) joined them only in 1910. See Reidemeister (Moritzburg) and Lucius Grisebach.

8 "Diese stete Arbeit brachte schliesslich als Resultat die Lösung des Problems, nackte Menschen in freier Nature mit neuen Mitteln darstellen zu können. In ungebrochenen Farber, blau, rot, grün, gelb, leuchten die Körper der Menschen im Wasser oder zwischen Bäumen."

But Kirchner adds that these "styleless" representations revealed new "forms and laws" when moved indoors: "oder in Räumen, die Kirchner mit einfachsten Mitteln, mit Kistenmöbeln und bemalten Stoffen den neu gefundenen Formen und Gesetzen der Bilder wieder anzugleichen suchte" (Grisebach 85).

In Kirchner's case, spontaneity and originality have become indecipherable because he reworked his Dresden paintings.

9 *Le Sacre* contains a dance of adolescents in Part 1 and ends with the self-sacrifice of an adolescent girl, who dances unto death. Adorno (135–37) notes that in both *Petruschka* and *Le Sacre* the sacrifice of the individual for the collective is affirmed by the victim and portrayed with detached music. Following Cocteau, Adorno also notes the link between the fauvists and *Le Sacre;* he criticizes Stravinsky's "virtuoso piece of regression" (137) and modernist primitivism in general. He points out, however, that the Nazi barbarians could not tolerate modernist barbarism, whose roots were liberal.

10 The exhibition catalogue *Traum und Wirklichkeit—Wien 1870–1930* includes some of Altenberg's photos, among them one of Lilith Lang, the "Li" in Kokoschka's *Die träumenden Knaben.*

11 "Wir haben nichts als ein sentimentales Gedächtnis, einen gelähmten Willen und die unheimliche Gabe der Selbstverdoppelung. Wir schauen unserem Leben zu" (*Prosa* 1: 171).

12 "Die fünf Männer, die auf jenem Brunnenkranze knien und in das geweihte Wasser hinunterstarren, gleichen christlichen Fakiren. Seit dem Mittelalter ist keine solche dürre, grätige, eckige Asketenplastik gemacht worden. Diese Menschen sind mit der Milch der sieben mageren Kühe gesäugt, sie bestehen grösstenteils us Röhrenknochen und Muskelschwund. Nur bei solcher Ausmergelung ist es möglich, dass einer sich selbst in der Weise umarmt, wie diese armen Leute. Sie können in der Tat mit den Händen überallhin langen, sogar kreuzweise an ihre eigenen Schulterblätter. Und im Knien sind sie Spezialisten, sie sind dazu geboren und stammen von Büssern ab, die auf den Knien heilige Berge emporrutschen. Und dennoch sind es keine Karikaturen. In diesen Jammergestalten liegt eine Inbrunst und Geistigkeit, wie man sie erst wieder in unseren Tagen darzustellen weiss. Eine ausdörrende Glut der Andacht, Theologie mit Osteologie gepaart" (Hevesi 293–94).

13 "Unter der Oberfläche bewegte sich im Inneren dieser Knabenfiguren etwas wie die Spannung, die in der Gotik den Raum beherrscht, ja, den dreidimensionalen Raum erst schafft" (*Mein Leben* 56).

14 In preparing the translation of *Die träumenden Knaben,* I have consulted Schorske's in *Fin-de-siècle Vienna.* I have followed the typographical arrangement of the poem used in the 1959 edition. However, in the original edition each stanza was pressed into a column, so that the lines were not kept.

15 "eine Art Bericht in Wort und Bild über meinen damaligen Seelenzustand" (*Mein Leben* 52).

16 "Die träumenden Knaben" sind die Revision der Kindheiteindrücke, die ein junger Künstler vornimmt. Daraus erklärt sich das vielfach Chaotische, das

die Bilder in Gruppen zerfallen lässt; eine Häufung von Motiven und damit ein Zersplittern des Ganzen, eben der noch ungeordnete Besitz der jugendlichen Phantasie, ein Fülle, die durch orphische und dämonische Monologe die farbigen Träume auch dichterisch ausgestaltet" (251).

17 On Schiele see Borowitz, Comini's works, Kallir's works, Leopold, Mitsch's works, Nebehay, and the exhibition catalogues *Egon Schiele: Paintings . . . , Europäischer Expressionismus,* and *Egon Schiele in der Albertina.*

18 See Herzogenrath, Schlemmer, and *Oskar Schlemmer,* the Schlemmer catalogue of 1971.

CHAPTER 7: THE ADOLESCENCE OF PSYCHOANALYSIS

1 Freud added in 1915 that not all sexual objects are found through an imitation of early infantile models. One may also find one's own self in the other, which frequently leads to pathological consequences (222).

2 Next to *reprints,* transference may also produce *revised editions* of some earlier key figure (usually the father), in which case the image of the analyst may incorporate some "real" features.

3 Steven Marcus rightly calls the passage on over determination an "elaborate obfuscation" (272), but he is wrong to suggest that Freud imperceptibly slides from "being the nineteenth-century man of science to being the remorseless 'teller of truth,' the character in a play by Ibsen" (296–97). The Ibsenian hero, like the nineteenth-century scientist (and often Freud himself), was a seeker of truth and certainty. With overdetermination, Freud is moving into the realm of conjecture and interpretation.

4 Of the enormous literature on Dora's case, I have primarily made use of Bernheimer and Kahane, Cixous, Cohen and Laudan, Deutsch, Glenn, Hertz's works, Marcus, Muslin and Gill, Ramas, and Rubenstein.

5 Recent interest in the fictional status of Freud's case studies started with Steven Marcus's 1974 essay on Dora. Marcus saw Freud as a great modernist artist, and *Dora* as an experimental novel of "virtual Proustian complexity" with involuted and multidimensional representation and embedded theoretical passages (280). Marcus also reads *Dora* as a series of plays by Ibsen, where Freud is both the author and "one of the characters in the action" (264). Neil Hertz in the opening pages of his essay, "Dora's Secrets," makes a revealing comparison between the narrative perspectives in *Dora* and in James's *What Maisie knew.* Peter Brooks compares analysts and patients to narrators and narratees, whereas I shall consider *Dora* in terms of two competing narrators. Susan Suleiman suggests that Freud himself offered two competing love stories: a heterosexual one and a later and not fully developed lesbian one of Dora's attachment to Frau K. (94–95). She speaks in this

context of a conflict between Freud's desire to achieve a Balzacian narrative mastery and his susceptibility to hysterical discourse.

6 Freud regarded the patient's dreams as texts that needed analytic dream work in order to become meaningful. Dreams were easier to interpret than transference because in the former case "the patient himself will always provide the *text*," whereas in the latter the patient gives no assistance (*Dora* 116, my emphasis).

7 Freud's concern to distinguish his discourse, and consequently his identity, from hers, is the main subject of Hertz's article.

8 The diaries have received regrettably little attention, and my efforts to find a German publisher for the original have so far been unsuccessful. Yvon Brès ("Horney" 60–62) considers them irrelevant to psychoanalysis and to Karen's later theories. Contrary to Brès, I believe they are of interest on account of Karen's career and for the light they throw on early twentieth-century feminism and psychoanalysis.

CHAPTER 8: THE PSYCHOLOGY OF ADOLESCENCE

1 Unless otherwise noted, all references to Hall in this chapter refer to his *Adolescence*.

2 My discussion is based on texts by Blüher, Bühler, Burnham, Clarke, Compayré, Duprat, Hall, William James, Lancaster, Lemaître, Marro, Mendousse, Puffer, Slaughter, Spranger, Swift, and Wolf.

3 These first systematic studies of adolescence adopted Hall's assumption that individual growth recapitulated the history of mankind, as well as his methodological preference for working with questionnaires. Swift, for instance, suggested that truancy recapitulated the age of migrations (66) and that the "criminal instincts of children are the racial survivals of acts that in past ages fitted their possessors to survive" (86). In the life of every normal boy there comes a point "when primitive impulses, the reverberation of savage life, carry him on, with almost resistless fury, toward a life of crime," from which only the right environment can save him (89).

Burnham had bad luck and received very few responses, but the "syllabus on Adolescent Phenomena in Body and Mind" by Lancaster and Hall was answered by 827 persons. Swift asked "upright" men to report on their juvenile pranks. Puffer questioned boys entering the Lyman School about their gang affiliations. I shall discuss Starbuck's questionnaires on religion in chapter 9.

4 Hall considered Nietzsche's "will to power" an ideology of adolescence. It represented a "crass reversion to the egoism of savagery. Lust of power is glorified to the point of tyranny and to the actual disparagement of tender-

ness and humanity. Whatever truth there is in this view, it has its best outcrop in this age"—namely adolescence (2: 82).

5 This conservatism does not mean, however, as Spacks (*Adolescent Idea* 235, 250, 255) believes, that Hall sought to preserve adolescence and its values.

6 Hall also speaks of non-Western "adolescent races" and treats them, in terms of his Darwinian and recapitulatory vision of history, with condescension. His last chapter labels them atavistic rather than precocious, and it is unclear just what role they are to have in the future of mankind. The "lower races," he notes, were never perhaps "being extirpated as weeds in the human garden, both by conscious and organic processes, so rapidly as to-day. In many minds this is inevitable and not without justification" (2: 651). Hall attributes the idea of "extirpation" to Nietzsche and does not say what he himself thinks of it.

7 During adolescence, Spranger adds, stories, sand castles, and building with "real materials" are replaced by poetry, music, dance, theater, and other art forms of empathy and expression. This classification of the arts seems reductive. After all, reading travel and adventure stories need not involve identification with the heroes or villains, and construction with "real materials" may be expressive.

8 "Om dat hij met iets wilde zijn, dat net was als of het niet tot hem zelf behoorde, deed hij zijn rechter hand van voren tusschen zijn opengeknoopte broekgulp en nam er zijn week mollig geslachtsdeel in, het warme rare vleeschkokertje draayend in zijn hand en er meê spelend tot hij insliep" (19).

CHAPTER 9: ADOLESCENCE IN SCHOOL, CHURCH, AND COURT

1 Like most poor German graduates of the university, Hölderlin, Hegel, Herbarth, Lenz, and Jean Paul became tutors first. Lenz attacked the institution in *Der Hofmeister,* whereas Jean Paul provided a handbook for it in *Levana.* See Fertig. According to Musgrove (37 ff.), "domestic education" by fathers flourished within the upper and professional classes in early nineteenth-century England. Concerns about precocity strengthened public education, which was considered to extend adolescence (54).

2 Comparative studies on school reform have been published by Röhrs. Some comparisons are also made by Albisetti and Gillis. On French education see Gerbod, Mendousse (128–41), Prost, and Weill; on Germany see Albisetti, Cauvin, Flitner and Kudritzki, Gillis (*Youth*), Kunert, Paulsen, and Scheibe; on Great Britain see Chandos, Connolly (*Enemies*), Dyhouse, Gillis (*Youth*),

Honey, and Spender; on the United States see Clarke, Hall (*Adolescence*), and Kett (*Rites*).

3 The first public high school in the United States opened in 1821 in Boston. There were 40 public high schools by 1860, almost 800 in 1880, and 6,005 with 519,251 pupils in 1900. This number represented 12 percent of the age group, far more than in countries with elite secondary education (Hall, *Adolescence* 2: 503)

4 Hugo Dyserinck has developed a methodology for such a study of literary images.

5 The German schools were unequivocally criticized and condemned in the works of Wedekind, Wildenbruch, Halbe, Bierbaum, Ebner-Eschenbach, Rilke, Strauss, Thomas and Heinrich Mann, Huch, Musil, Ernst, Hesse, and Kaiser. I know of no positive literary images. In contrast, schools are less frequently portrayed in French literature and, when they are depicted, the portraits tend to be less critical. In the works of Mirbeau, Larbaud, Lacretelle, Gide, Cocteau, and Alain-Fournier schools provide a neutral background rather than targets of criticism. Only in Barrès's *Les Déracinés* and Colette's *Claudine à l'école* is the school itself attacked. The phenomenon is surprising if one considers that a number of French writers, including Gide and Alain-Fournier, had bad experiences at school.

6 Cizek's class was attended by children between the ages of seven and fourteen (*Franz Cizek* 32). On children's art see also Bühler ("Kunst und Jugend"), and Andreas-Salomé ("Kind und Kunst").

7 Durkheim's epochal study *Le Suicide* (1901) barely mentions school-age suicides, although it contains a comparative table showing that the suicide rate for 16 to 20 year olds was highest in Saxony, followed by Prussia. The rates were much lower for Italy and France. Mendousse (218–20) reproduces the table but is content to note that adolescents in all countries are less suicide-prone than adults.

8 In his preface to *Emlohstobba* Reddie pleaded for an alliance between the "two chief branches of the great Teutonic family" and a combination of "the best German school-*instruction* with the best all-round English school-*life*" (381, 383).

9 Lietz's chauvinism and anti-Semitism is a moot point. A Dutch observer noted in 1898 that Lietz "still dreams of a *national education,* of a Pan-Germanism" and that he follows his "Pedagogue on the Throne," who expects that the schools "shall furnish *soldiers for him* to combat social Democracy" (Reddie 566). Indeed, military training was dear to Lietz's heart (*Emlohstobba* 184), and Wyneken (*Kampf* 32–33) sharply criticized him for it.

Andreesen, Lietz's Nazi student and biographer, stresses Lietz's anti-Semitism, but Lietz claims in *Von Leben und Arbeit* that his liberalism was put to the test by a disproportionate number of Jewish boys in his school who did not relish physical work and rural values. When Theodor Lessing, a Jewish teacher, defended the Jewish pupils, Lietz dismissed him in 1903. Hereafter his prospectuses stressed that his schools had a "German-national and a Germanic character" and would accept only a few "foreigners and Israelites" (*Leben* 187). Lietz undoubtedly grew more chauvinistic and anti-Semitic, but Mosse's categorical condemnation (164–67) is blind to Lietz's liberal side. Although Mosse acknowledges that Andreesen published an expurgated and slanted version of Lietz's recollections, he claims that "Andreesen only fulfilled the ideological presuppositions upon which the country-boarding-school movement was founded" (167). This is patently wrong.

10 Both schools appear in thinly disguised fiction: Wickersdorf (during the twenties) in Erich Ebermayer's *Odilienberg*; the Odenwaldschule in Gertrud Prellwitz's *Drude*. Klaus Mann gives an affectionate picture of the Odenwaldschule and Geheeb in *The Turning Point*.

11 On Wyneken see Ebermayer, Geissler, Maasen, Panter, and Scheibe. According to Mosse, "Most of the schools that adopted a boarding-school format and a revolutionary educational methodology were accompanied by a Volkish emphasis" (168), with the exception of Geheeb and Wyneken, who disdained "narrow nationalism and Volk interests." This seems to me unfair to the bulk of the boarding schools and, as I shall show, somewhat too generous with respect to Wyneken.

12 "Übersetze ich die Umarmung in Worte . . . so sagt sie etwa: Du hast dich in meine Arme geworfen, willst in den jungen Jahren deines Suchens und Lernens mir angehören, in meiner Sphäre leben; so will ich auch dir gehören, zwischen dir und mir besteht jetzt ein heiliger Bund; . . . aus meinem tiefsten und persönlichsten Leben sollst du schöpfen und will ich dich nähren. Das alte geheimnisvolle Wort von dem Leib des Meisters, der für die Jünger gegeben wird, enthüllt einen neuen Sinn" (*Eros* 64).

13 I could find no evidence, however, that Jesus became a "kind of adolescent superman" (Ross 418) for Hall.

14 On juvenile delinquency, see Duprat, Morrison, Hélie, Platt, and Springhall (*Coming of Age*).

CHAPTER 10: YOUTH ORGANIZATIONS AND MOVEMENTS

1 Massis adds that the journal soon recognized its mistake and subsequently published another "unengaged" work about adolescence, Jean Giraudoux's *Simon le pathétique*. When *Le Grand Meaulnes* missed the Prix Goncourt, Massis

warmly praised the novel as an expression of the new generation, without associating it, however, with the ideology of his survey.

2 The literature on the *Wandervogel,* much of it now published with the help of the movement's archives in Ludwigstein, is enormous. See *Der Anfang,* Borinski and Milch, works by Blüher, Busse-Wilson, Flex, Gerber, Helwig, Jantzen, Karl, the collections of Kindt, Korth, Kurella, Laqueur, Mosse (171–89), Jakob Müller, Pross, Ras, Rosenbusch, Rügg, and Ziemer and Wolf. Kindt, Ziemer and Wolf, and other archival collections are invaluable but they marginalize the negative aspects, which, in turn, are exaggerated by Mosse and Pross.

3 Gurlitt supported the establishment of an adult umbrella organization for the club. In 1902 he became a member and in 1904 president of the directorate of the *Steglitz Wandervogel.* His memorandum to the Prussian Ministry of Education in 1903 led to the authorization to recruit Wandervögel in all Prussian Gymnasiums (Korth 80). That the Wandervogel grew out of his classes (as cited in Rosenbusch 23) is surely an exaggeration.

4 Blüher's life and work were shaped by his Wandervogel experience. He was a Prussian conservative, an elitist antidemocrat, and an arrogant "antifeminist," although he rejected chauvinism (*Wandervogel* 1: 162–83) and was too aristocratic, Prussian, and intellectual to become a Nazi. Indeed, as early as 1918 in *Führer und Volk* he declared that the German nationalism of the early Wandervogel was passé (32); in *Deutsches Reich* he rejected *völkisch* culture as barren, pointed to an analogy between the fate of Jews and Germans and expressed his admiration for Zionism and individuals like Freud, Fliess, Einstein, Gustav Landauer, and Martin Buber. But he disliked leftist Jewish literati like Tucholsky and Kurt Hiller (*Werke* 95), and he thought, as late as 1953, that "the mixing of German and Jewish blood was ruinous" (*Werke* 235). He was a subtle psychologist, an original thinker, and a brilliant stylist. The vignettes in his *Werke und Tage* on teachers, writers, and intellectuals of his age are gems. But he vastly overestimated his own philosophical importance and can be read today (a frustrating as well as an invigorating experience) mainly as a commentary on and a symptom of an age.

5 Fischer, a "romantic Prussian" (Gerber) with *völkisch* leanings, was, according to Blüher (*Wandervogel* 1: 98), no anti-Semite, although he associated with Paul Förster, a leader of the *völkisch Alldeutscher Verband,* and participated in this group's summer solstice festivities in 1902 and 1903. Fischer apparently had a "separate but equal" view of Jews and hence he preferred separate youth groups for Jews. See Mosse 180–84 on Wandervogel and anti-Semitism.

6 Blüher adopted Freud's term *inversion* but did not regard it as a deviation, and attributed to it an "independent natural meaning and cultural value." Freud respected Blüher's works and published his article on bisexuality in Jakobsen's novel *Niels Lyhne* in *Imago* (Blüher, *Werke* 258–59).

7 Curiously, Busse-Wilson brought grist to Blüher's mill by noting that the absence of heterosexuality in the youth movement was partly due to the career-mindedness of the women who joined. The youth movement was inundated by "masses of uncourted girls," who de-sexed themselves (*Selbstentweibung*) and accepted the company of tame men: neutralized girls, the natural complement to unaggressive men, "found men, if not *a* man in the movement" (87). The dilemma Busse-Wilson attributes to the women in the youth movement is that of Karen Horney: how to achieve intellectual and economic emancipation without remaining sexually dependent.

The archives of the youth movement in Burg Ludwigstein preserve witty satires of Wyneken and others that were most likely written by Busse-Wilson (Ras 51–53).

8 Many adult-directed youth organizations emerged around 1910. Scouting, introduced in 1909, compensated for its foreign origin by emphasizing military readiness and the pursuit of national goals (Karl 89). The churches and political parties also entered the field of *Jugendpflege* (youth care), but the formation of political youth groups was outlawed on April 8, 1908, for fear of the socialists. The *Wehrkraftverein,* a military youth organization, was set up with state support in 1910. Prussia decreed on January 18, 1911, that the promotion of youth was a concern of the state.

9 "Durch tausend, tausend Jahre sind unsre Väter emporgewachsen in Kämpfen und Not. Und haben sich durchgesetzt gegen das Eis der Urzeit, haben dann durch viele Jahrhunderte siegreich gerungen mit Frieslands gieriger See und mit feindlichen Menschen. Ihr Mark ist kräftig geworden und herrlich ihr Wuchs. Der Leiber stolzen Bau haben sie uns vermacht, dass wir ihn weiter geben sollen an die fernsten Geschlechter. *Ich* habe ihr bestes Geschenk verloren, verloren in einer Viertelstunde schmutzigen Doppelrausches und mag nicht mehr den Blick erheben zu meinen Ahnen" (172).

10 "Seid Freunde, ihr Germanischen Narren; wir haben schwarze, gelbe und braune Händel genug, wenn ihr nur zu rechnen wüsstet"—a paraphrase of "Be friends, you English [Welsh, Irish, Scotch] fools, be friends. We have French quarrels enow" in act IV, scene 1 of Shakespeare's *King Henry V.* It must be added that the colonel opposes the jingoism.

11 In Blüher's scintillating German: Diederichs was slightly ridiculous when "in einem Aufzuge, den man etwa als balkanische Bauerntracht bezeichnen konnte, mit dem Thyrsostab in der Hand und Epheu im Haar auf einem klappernden Leiterwagen, umgeben von Jugend bevorzugt weiblichen Ge-

schlechts, durch Jenas Strassen in die Berge fuhr, um dort kultische Bege-
hungen dionysischer Art zu betreiben" (*Werke* 343).

12 By 1916 Wyneken explained the Meissner dancing as an expression of a new
body-feeling, but he still considered it a shocking "inanity" (Kampf 152 f.).
Wyneken continually wavered about dancing, partly because he disliked the
dances of his time. Whenever he considered dance, sport, and eurhythmics
as a means towards sexual emancipation, he really meant an aesthetic sublimation of sexual drives, a cult of the beautiful body: "For us the purpose
of sport and all physical exercise can only be the production of a beautiful
and controlled body" (*Schule* 53). He disdained soccer as a "materialist"
form of body building, and advocated gymnastics for he thought it would
"give an opportunity for the mind to penetrate and rule the body" (*Schule*
133). He probably thought of Jacques-Dalcroze's rhythmic gymnastics,
started in Dresden-Hellerau, 1911–12, and Rudolf Steiner's eurhythmics.

For Wyneken, sport had a subliminatory function (*Jugend* 43 ff.). He
greeted the new body-feeling as an inevitable historical event (*Kampf* 154)
that would convert sexuality into eros: "We must rehabilitate eros in public
thinking before we can consider the purification and ennobling of instinct"
(*Kampf* 157).

13 Blüher also influenced Wyneken's more outspoken views on Socratic homoeroticism in *Eros*. Blüher initially admired Wyneken as the last example of
the Fischer-type of charismatic leader (*Führer und Volk*), but he became disappointed when Wyneken participated in the revolution as a democrat and
mounted "the rainwater barrel" to preach to the masses (*Werke* 247). In the
1924 preface to *Führer und Volk* he admitted his mistake.

14 The Bavarian clerics would surely have trounced on anything offending belief
or public taste. But the articles advocated merely camaraderie instead of
sexual license (80–88) and confirmation instruction instead of religious education (93–95). Wyneken did not have to face lawsuits on this account.

CHAPTER 11: ADOLESCENCE: THE FICTION OF REALITY

1 The many literary examples in Mendousse include Barrès (63, 211), Loti
(57, 91, 93 209), Chateaubriand, Bourget (22, 210), Ferri-Pisani (22, 50,
132, 181), Goethe, Rousseau, and Romain Rolland (208).

2 According to Stone (*The Family* 49), around 1600 the average age at which
women of the aristocracy were married was slightly below twenty; the average age for first-born men twenty-two, and for all men twenty-four.

3 As so often, Mosse carries the contrast to a grotesque extreme by suggesting
that love of polyphonic music (I presume he means singing in canon) was a
"further reflection of the young people's desire to achieve unity in a common

cause . . . For their songs, the Wandervögel went back to earlier centuries, rejecting contemporary and romantic tunes, which were generally scored for one voice only" (175).

4 Margarete Buber-Neumann recalls that her local youth group was greatly disappointed, when, during a visit to the revered master "the creator of these heroic figures revealed himself as a slight, hardly imposing little man. He led us through his elaborately equipped atelier, which was dominated by a stuffy, erotic atmosphere instead of the expected crystal-clear mountain air. We left for home with one ideal less" (27).

5 "Die Malerei sollte vorerst das Verfolgen komplizierter Probleme aufgeben, sie muss zunächst das Neue gründlich verarbeiten und auf einfache, verständliche Formeln bringen, aus denen deutsche Kunst klar und rein zu deutschem Herzen spricht. Nur so kann der Kontakt zwischen Malerei und Publikum wieder hergestellt werden" (*Vortrupp*, 1: 296).

BIBLIOGRAPHY

Adam, Paul. *L'Enfant d'Austerlitz*. 1901. 4th ed. Paris: Ollendorff, 1902.

—————. *Les Images sentimentales*. 1893. 4th ed. Paris: Ollendorff, 1907.

Adorno, Theodor W. *Philosophie der neuen Musik*. 1949. In *Gesammelte Schriften,* vol. 12. Frankfurt/M.: Suhrkamp, 1975.

Agathon [Henri Massis and Alfred de Tarde]. *Les Jeunes Gens d'aujourd'hui. Le Goût de l'action la foi patriotique—Une Renaissance catholique le réalisme politique*. 1913. 6th ed. Paris: Plon, 1913.

Ahlborn, Knud. "Das Meissnerfest der Freideutschen Jugend (1913)." In *Grundschriften der deutschen Jugendbewegung,* ed. Werner Kindt. Düsseldorf: Diederichs, 1963. 105–15.

Aichhorn, August. *Verwahrloste Jugend*. 1925. 3d ed. Bern: Huber, 1951.

Alain-Fournier. *Le Grand Meaulnes*. 1913. In *Le Grand Meaulnes; Miracles*. Paris: Garnier, 1986. 159–381.

—————. *Le Grand Meaulnes*. Trans. Frank Davison. Harmondsworth: Penguin, 1966.

Albisetti, James, C. *Secondary School Reform in Imperial Germany.* Princeton: Princeton University Press, 1983.

Alden, Douglas. *Jacques de Lacretelle.* New Brunswick: Rutgers University Press, 1958.

Anderson, Chester G., ed. *James Joyce: A Portrait of the Artist as a Young Man: Text, Criticism, and Notes.* Harmondsworth: Penguin, 1977.

Andreas-Salomé, Lou. *Im Zwischenland: Fünf Geschichten aus dem Seelenleben halbwüchsiger Mädchen.* 1902. 2d ed. Stuttgart: Cotta, 1902.

————. "Kind und Kunst." *Das literarische Echo* 17 (1914): cols. 1–4

Andrews, Cyril, Bruyn. *An Introduction to the Study of Adolescent Education.* London: Rebman, 1912.

Andrian-Werburg, Leopold v. *Der Garten der Erkenntnis.* Berlin: Fischer, 1895.

Anet, Claude. *Adolescence.* Paris: Cité des livres, 1925.

Der Anfang: Zeitschrift der Jugend. Ed. Georges Barbizon and Siegfried Bernfeld. 1913–14. Selections ed. Eckart Peterich. Lauenburg/Elbe: Saal, 1922.

Anstey, F. *Vice Versa.* London: Smith, 1882.

Ariès, Philippe. *Centuries of Childhood: A Social History of Family Life.* New York: Vintage, 1962.

————. *L'Enfant et la vie familiale sous l'Ancien Régime.* 1960. Rev. and abbr. ed. Paris: Seuil, 1975.

Aristotle. *Politics.* Oxford: Oxford University Press, 1948.

Arland, Marcel. *Etienne.* Paris: Gallimard, 1924.

Arnim, Achim von, and Clemens Brentano. *Des Knaben Wunderhorn.* 3 vols. 1806–8. Munich: Winkler, 1957.

Aufmuth, Ulrich. *Die Wandervogelbewegung unter soziologischem Aspekt.* Göttingen: Vandenhoeck, 1979.

Baden-Powell, Robert S. S. *Aids to Scouting.* London: Gale, 1899.

————. *Reconnaissance and Scouting.* 1885. 2d ed. London: Clowes, 1891.

————. *Scouting for Boys: A Handbook for Instruction in Good Citizenship.* 1908. 7th enl. and rev. ed. London: Pearson, 1914.

————. *Yarns for Boy Scouts.* London: Pearson, 1909.

Baer, Adolf. *Der Selbstmord im kindlichen Lebensalter.* Leipzig: Thieme, 1901.

Balzac, Honoré. *Louis Lambert.* 1832–33. Paris: Corti, 1934.

Barbey d'Aurevilly, Jules-Amédée. *Le Plus Bel Amour de Don Juan.* In *Les Diaboliques,* with nine illustrations by Félicien Rops. Paris: Lemerre, 1882.

Barbey, Bernard. *Le Coeur gros.* Paris: Grasset, 1924.

Barnett, Mary G. *Young Delinquents: A Study of Reformatory and Industrial Schools.* London: Methuen, 1913.

Barrès, Maurice. *Le Culte du moi* (*Sous l'oeil des barbares* 1888; *Un Homme libre* 1889; *Le Jardin de Bérénice* 1891). 1892. Paris: Union générale d'éditions, 1986.

————. *Les Déracinés.* 1897. Paris: Union générale d'éditions, 1986.

[Bary, Emile]. *Les Cahiers d'un rhétoricien de 1815.* Paris: Hachette, 1890.

Bashkirtseff, Marie. *Cahiers Intimes: Inédits.* Ed. Pierre Borel. Vol. 1. Paris: Editeurs Associés, 1925.

————. *Journal de Marie Bashkirtseff.* 2 vols. Paris: Charpentier, 1887.

Becker, Jörg, ed. *Die Diskussion um das Jugendbuch.* Darmstadt: Wissenschaftliche Buchgesellschaft, 1986.

Benjamin, Walter. *Briefe.* Ed. Gershom Scholem and Theodor W. Adorno. 2 vols. Frankfurt/M.: Suhrkamp, 1966.

————. *Illuminationen.* Frankfurt/M.: Suhrkamp, 1961.

Bernfeld, Siegfried. *Trieb und Tradition im Jugendalter: Kulturpsychologische Studien an Tagebüchern.* Leipzig: Barth, 1931. Reprint. Frankfurt/M.: päd.-extra, 1978.

————. "Über eine typische Form der männlichen Pubertät." *Imago* 9 (1923): 169–88.

Bernheimer, Charles, and Claire Kahane, eds. *In Dora's Case: Freud-Hysteria-Feminism.* New York: Columbia University Press, 1985.

Bertrand, Louis. *Le Sang des races.* 1899. 7th ed. Paris: Ollendorff, n.d.

Bierbaum, Otto. *Stilpe.* Berlin: Schuster, 1897.

Blos, Peter. *On Adolescence.* Glencoe: Free Press, 1962.

————. *The Adolescent Passage.* New York: International University Press, 1979.

Blüher, Hans. *Der bürgerliche und der geistige Antifeminismus.* Berlin: Blüher, 1916.

————. *Der Charakter der Jugendbewegung.* Lauenburg: Saar, 1921.

————. *Deutsches Reich Judentum und Sozialismus.* Munich: Steinicke, 1919.

————. *Familie und Männerbund.* Leipzig: Der Neue Geist, 1918.

————. *Führer und Volk in der Jugendbewegung.* 1918. Jena: Diederichs, 1924.

————. *Die Rolle der Erotik in der männlichen Gesellschaft.* 2 vols. 1917. Jena: Diedrichs, 1919.

————. *Wandervogel. Geschichte einer Jugendbewegung.* 3 vols. 1912–13. Frankfurt/M.: Dipa, 1976.

————. *Werke und Tage: Geschichte eines Denkers.* Munich: List, 1953.

Booth, Wayne. *The Rhetoric of Fiction.* Chicago: University of Chicago Press, 1961.

Bölsche, Wilhelm. "Mädchenlektüre." *Die Zukunft* 13 (1895): 572–76.

Bonnetain, Paul. *Charlot s'amuse . . .* 1883. 2d ed. Brussels: Kistenmaeckers, 1885.

Borinski, Fritz, and Werner Milch. *Jugendbewegung: Die Geschichte der deutschen Jugend 1896–1933.* 1967. 2d ed. Frankfurt/M: Dipa, 1982.

Borowitz, Helen O. "Youth as Metaphor and Image in Wedekind, Kokoschka, and Schiele." *Art Journal* 33 (1974): 219–25.

Bost, Pierre. *Homicide par imprudence.* Paris: Fast, 1925.

Bourget, Paul. *André Cornelis.* Paris: Lemerre, 1887.

————. *Un Crime d'amour.* Paris: Lemerre, 1886.

————. *Le Disciple.* 1889. Paris: Plon, 1911.

Bradby, G. F. *The Lanchaster Tradition.* London: Smith, 1913.

Braun, Otto. *Aus nachgelassenen Schriften eines Frühvollendeten.* Ed. Julie Vogelstein. Leipzig: Insel, 1921.

Bréal, Michel. *Quelques mots sur l'instruction publique en France.* Paris: Hachette, 1872.

Breicha, Otto. *Oskar Kokoschka: Vom Erlebnis im Leben.* Salzburg: Welz, 1976.

Bremner, Robert H., ed. *Children and Youth in America: A Documentary History.* 3 vols. Cambridge: Harvard University Press, 1970–74.

Brentano, Clemens. *Aus der Chronika eines fahrenden Schülers.* 1818. In *Werke,* 4 vols. Munich: Hanser, 1963–68. 2: 597–635.

Brès, Yvon. "A propos des journaux d'adolescence de Karen Horney." *Ecrire* 4, no. 1 (1986): 59–62.

Brion-Guerry, L., ed. *L'Année 1913: Les Formes esthétiques de l'oeuvre d'art à la veille de la première guerre mondiale.* 3 vols. Paris: Klinsieck, 1971–73.

Bronnen, Arnolt. *Vatermord.* 1920 [written 1915]. In *Stücke.* Kronberg: Athenäum, 1977. 1–53.

Brooks, Peter. "Constructions psychanalytiques et narratives." *Poétique* 61 (1985): 63–74.

Brown, John. *Valery Larbaud.* Boston: Hall, 1981.

Brücke 1905–1913: Eine Künstlergemeinschaft des Expressionismus. Exh. Cat. Essen: Museum Folkwang, 1958.

Buber-Neumann, Margarete. *Von Potsdam nach Moskau.* Stuttgart: Deutsche Verlags-Anstalt, 1957.

Buchheim, Lothar-Günther. *Die Künstlergemeinschaft Brücke.* Feldafing: Buchheim, 1956.

Bühler, Charlotte. "Kunst und Jugend." *Zeitschrift für Ästhetik und allgemeine Kunstwissenschaft* 20 (1926): 288–306.

————. *Das Seelenleben des Jugendlichen.* 1921. 5th ed. Jena: Fischer, 1929.

————. *Tagebuch eines jungen Mädchens.* Jena: Fischer, 1922.

————, ed. *Drei Generationen im Jugendtagebuch.* Jena: Fischer, 1934.

————, ed. *Jugendtagebuch und Lebenslauf: Zwei Mädchentagebücher.* Jena: Fischer, 1932.

————, ed. *Zwei Knabentagebücher: Mit einer Einleitung über die Bedeutung des Tagebuchs für die Jugendpsychologie.* Jena: Fischer, 1925.

————, ed. *Zwei Mädchentagebücher.* Jena: Fischer, 1926.

Bunin, Ivan. *Mitja's Love.* First Russian ed., 1925. New York: Holt, 1926.

Burke, Kenneth. "Three Definitions." *Kenyon Review* 13 (1951): 173–92.

Burnham, William H. "The Study of Adolescence." *Pedagogical Seminary* 1 (1891): 174–95.

Burte, Hermann. *Wiltfeber der ewige Deutsche: Die Geschichte eines Heimatsuchers.* 1912. Leipzig: Sarasin, 1916.

Busse-Wilson, Elisabeth. *Die Frau und die Jugendbewegung: Ein Beitrag zur weiblichen Charakterologie und zur Kritik des Antifeminismus.* Hamburg: Saal, 1920.

Butler, Samuel. *The Way of All Flesh.* 1903 [written 1872–84]. Harmondsworth: Penguin, 1971.

Cancalon, Elaine D. *Fairy-Tale Structures and Motifs in "Le Grand Meaulnes."* Bern: Lang, 1975.

Carco, Francis. *Bob et Bobette s'amusent.* Paris: Michel, 1919.

————. *Les Innocents.* 1916. Paris: Ferenczi, 1924.

————. *Rien qu'une femme.* Paris: Michel, 1924.

Carlyle, Thomas. *Arbeiten, nicht Verzweifeln!* Düsseldorf: Langewiesche, 1902.

————. *Helden, Heldenverehrung und das Heldenthümliche in der Geschichte.* Berlin: Decker, 1853.

Caron, Max. *Jésus et les adolescents.* 1911. 2d ed. Paris: Haton, 1915.

Cauvin, Marius. *Le Renouveau pédagogique en Allemagne de 1890 à 1933.* Paris: Colin, 1970.

Chandos, John. *Boys Together: English Public Schools 1800–1864.* London: Hutchinson, 1984.

Cixous, Hélène. "Portrait of Dora." *Diacritics* 13 (1983): 2–32.

Clarke, Edward Hammond. *Sex in Education; or, A Fair Chance for Girls.* 1873. 5th ed. Boston: Osgood, 1874.

Cocteau, Jean. *Les Enfants terribles.* 1929. Paris: Livre de poche, 1959.

————. *Le Grand Ecart.* Paris: Stock, 1923.

————. *Thomas l'imposteur.* 1923. Paris: Gallimard, 1987.

Cohen, Robert S., and L. Laudan, eds. *Physics, Philosophy and Psychoanalysis: Essays in Honor of Adolf Grünbaum.* Dordrecht: Reidel, 1983.

Cohn, Dorrit. *Transparent Minds: Narrative Modes for Representing Consciousness in Fiction.* Princeton: Princeton University Press, 1978.

Colette, Sidonie-Gabrielle. *Le Blé en herbe.* 1923. Paris: Flammarion, 1969.

Comini, Alessandra. *Egon Schiele's Portraits.* Berkeley: University of California Press, 1974.

————. *Schiele in Prison.* Greenwich, Conn.: New York Graphic Society, 1973.

Compayré, Gabriel. *L'Adolescence: Etudes de psychologie et de pédagogie.* 1909. 2d ed. Paris: Alcan, 1910.

Connolly, Cyril. *Enemies of Promise.* 1938. Rev. ed. Harmondsworth: Penguin, 1961.

Connolly, Thomas, ed. *Joyce's Portrait: Criticisms and Critiques.* New York: Appleton, 1962.

Coubertin, Pierre de. *L'Education des adolescents au XXe siècle.* [*I. Education physique: La Gymnastique utilitaire (Sauvetage, Défense, Locomotion).* (1905); *II. Education intellectuelle: L'Analyse universelle.* (1911); *III. Education morale: Le Respect mutuel.* (1915).] 3 vols. Paris: Alcan, 1905–15.

Croisset, Francis. *Les Nuits de quinze ans.* Paris: Ollendorff, 1898.

Curtis, J. L. *Manbaarheid, de oorzaken van haar ontijdig verval en wenken om dat volmaakt te genezen.* Rotterdam: Stoeller, n.d.

Dalsimer, Katherine. *Female Adolescence: Psychoanalytic Reflections on Literature.* New Haven: Yale University Press, 1986.

Davis, Natalie Zemon. "The Reasons of Misrule." In *Society and Culture in Early Modern France.* Stanford: Stanford University Press, 1975. 97–123.

De Sanctis, Francesco. "L'Insegnamento della ginnastica nelle scuole secondarie, normali e magistrali." In *Opere.* 24 vols. Ed. Carlo Muscetta. Turin: Einaudi, 1951–73. 16: 249–67.

Dehn, Günther. *Großstadtjugend.* Berlin: Heymann, 1919.

Deleuze, Gilles. "Pensée nomade." In *Nietzsche aujourd'hui?* vol. 1: *Intensités.* Paris: Union générale d'éditions, 1973. 159–74.

Demolins, Edmond. *L'Education nouvelle. L'Ecole des Roches.* Paris: Firmin-Didot, 1898.

————. *A quoi tient la supériorité des Anglo-Saxons.* Paris: Firmin-Didot, 1897.

Demos, John, and Virginia Demos. "Adolescence in Historical Perspective." *Journal of Marriage and Family* 31 (1969): 632–38.

Desbordes, Jean. *J'Adore.* Paris: Grasset, 1928.

Deutsch, Felix. "A Footnote to Freud's 'Fragment of an Analysis of a Case of Hysteria.'" *Psychoanalytic Quarterly* 26 (1957): 159–67.

Dewey, John. *Schule und öffentliches Leben*. First Eng. ed., *The School and Society*, 1899. Trans. Else Gurlitt. Introd. Ludwig Gurlitt. Berlin: Walther, 1905.

Deyssel, Lodewijk van. *De kleine republiek*. 1889. Amsterdam: Scheltema, 1920.

Dickens, Charles. *David Copperfield*. 1849–50. Harmondsworth: Penguin, 1966.

Dostoevski, Fedor. *The Adolescent*. 1874. Trans. Andrew R. MacAndrew. New York: Norton, 1981.

————. *Netochka Nezvanova*. 1849. Trans. Jane Kentisch. Harmondsworth: Penguin, 1985.

Doyle, Arthur Conan. *The Memoirs of Sherlock Holmes*. London: Newnes, 1894.

Dreyer, Max. *Der Probekandidat*. Leipzig: Meyer, 1900.

Drieu La Rochelle, Pierre. *Etat civil*. 1921. Paris: Gallimard, 1977.

Dube [Heynig], Annemarie. *E. L. Kirchner: Graphik*. Munich: Prestel, 1961.

Dube, Annemarie, and Wolf-Dieter Dube. *Erich Heckel: Das Graphische Werk*. 3 vols. New York: Rathenau, 1964.

————. *Ernst Ludwig Kirchner: Das Graphische Werk*. 2 vols. Munich: Prestel, 1967.

Duhourcau, François. *La Voix intérieure de Maurice Barrès d'après ses cahiers*. Paris: Grasset, 1929.

Dujardin, Edouard. *L'Initiation au péché et à l'amour*. Paris: Mercure de France, 1898.

Duprat, G.-L. *La Criminalité dans l'adolescence*. Paris: Alcan, 1909.

Durkheim, Emile. *Le Suicide*. Paris: Alcan, 1897.

Dyhouse, Carol. *Girls Growing Up in Late Victorian and Edwardian England*. London: Paul, 1981.

Dyserinck, Hugo. "Komparatistische Imagologie: Zur politischen Tragweite einer europäischen Wissenschaft von der Literatur." In *Europa und das nationale Selbstverständnis*. Ed. Hugo Dyserinck and Karl Ulrich Syndram. Bonn: Bouvier, 1988. 13–38.

————. "Zur Entwicklung der komparatistischen Imagologie." *Colloquium Helveticum* 7 (1988): 19–41.

Ebermayer, Erich. *Gustav Wyneken*. 1969. Frankfurt/M: Dipa, 1982.

————. *Odilienberg*. 1929. Frankfurt/M.: Ullstein, 1964.

Ebner-Eschenbach, Marie von. *Der Vorzugsschüler*. 1901. In *Das Gemeindekind, Novellen, Aphorismen*. Munich: Winkler, 1978. 515–54.

Ecrire. Special issue of *Adolescence* 4 (1986).

Eggum, Arne. *Eduard Munch: Paintings, Sketches and Studies*. First Norwegian ed. 1983. New York: Potter, 1984.

Egon Schiele 1890–1918. Exh. Cat. Munich: Haus der Kunst, 1975.

Egon Schiele in der Albertina. Exh. Cat. Vienna: Graphische Sammlung Albertina, 1990.

Egon Schiele: Paintings, Watercolours and Drawings. Exh. Cat. London: Malborough, 1964.

Der Eigene: Ein Blatt für männliche Kultur. 1896–1931. Selections ed. by Joachim S. Hohmann. Berlin: Foester, 1981.

Eildermann, Wilhelm. *Jugend im ersten Weltkrieg: Tagebücher, Briefe, Erinnerungen.* Berlin: Dietz, 1972.

Elger, Dietmar. *Expressionismus.* Cologne: Benedikt, 1988.

Elias, Norbert. *The Civilizing Process.* Trans. Edmund Jephcott. 2 vols. Oxford: Blackwell, 1978–82.

Ellmann, Richard. *James Joyce.* 1959. New York: Oxford University Press, 1965.

Erich Heckel: Gemälde, Aquarelle und Zeichnungen im Besitz der Staatlichen Kunsthalle. Karlsruhe: Staatliche Kunsthalle, 1968.

Erikson, Erik. *Childhood and Society.* 1950. 2d, enl. ed. New York: Norton, 1963.

———. *Identity. Youth and Crisis.* New York: Norton, 1968.

Ernst Ludwig Kirchner, 1880–1938. Exh. Cat. Berlin: Nationalgalerie, 1980.

Ernst Ludwig Kirchner: Zeichnungen Pastelle Aquarelle. Exh. Cat. Aschaffenburg: Aschaffenburg Museum, 1980.

Ernst, Otto. *Flachsmann als Erzieher.* Leipzig: Staackmann, 1901.

———. *Jugend von Heute.* Leipzig: Staackmann, 1899.

———. *Semper der Jüngling: Ein Bildungsroman.* Leipzig: Staackmann, 1908.

Estaunié, Edouard. *L'Empreinte.* 1896. Paris: Perrin, 1912.

Eulenburg, Albert. *Kinder- und Jugendselbstmorde.* Sammlung zwangsloser Abhandlungen aus dem Gebiete der Nerven- und Geisteskrankheiten, vol. 10, no. 6. Halle: Marhold, 1914.

Europäischer Expressionismus. Exh. Cat. Munich: Haus der Kunst, 1970.

Fabre, Lucien. *La Jeunesse de Rabevel.* Paris: Nouvelle Revue française, 1923.

Farrar, Frederick William. *Eric or Little by Little: A Tale of Roslyn School.* Edinburgh: Black, 1858.

Félicien Rops: L'Oeuvre graphique complète. Ed. Jean-François Bory. Paris: Hubschmid, 1977.

Felix, Zdenek, ed. *Erich Heckel, 1883–1970: Gemälde, Aquarelle, Zeichnungen und Graphik.* Exh. Cat. Essen. Munich: Prestel, 1983.

Fertig, Ludwig. *Die Hofmeister: Ein Beitrag zur Geschichte des Lehrerstandes und der bürgerlichen Intelligenz.* Stuttgart: Metzler, 1979.

Findlay, J. J. *Arnold of Rugby.* Cambridge: Cambridge University Press, 1897.

Fishman, Sterling. "Suicide, Sex, and the Discovery of the German Adolescent." *History of Education Quarterly* 10 (1970): 170–88.

Flaubert, Gustave. *L'Education sentimentale.* 1869. In *Oeuvres.* 2 vols. Paris: Gallimard, 1979. 2: 31–457.

————. *Madame Bovary.* 1857. In *Oeuvres,* 1: 291–611.

————. *Novembre.* 1914 [written 1842]. In *Premières Oeuvres.* 4 vols. Paris: Fasquelle, 1925. 2: 309–401.

Fleisser, Marieluise. *Gesammelte Werke.* Ed. Günther Rühle. 3 vols. Frankfurt/M: Suhrkamp, 1972.

————. *Die Dreizehnjährigen.* 1923. In *Gesammelte Werke,* 3: 7–17.

————. *Fegefeuer in Ingolstadt.* 1926. In *Gesammelte Werke,* 1: 62–125.

Flex, Walter. *Der Wanderer zwischen beiden Welten: Ein Kriegserlebnis.* München: Beck, 1917.

Flitner, Wilhelm, and Gerhard Kudritzki, eds. *Die deutsche Reformpädagogik.* 2 vols. Düsseldorf: Küpper, 1961–62.

Foerster, Fr. W. *Jugendseele, Jugendbewegung, Jugendziel.* Munich: Rotapfel, 1923.

Forbush, William Byron. *The Boy Problem.* 1901. Boston: Pilgrim, 1913.

France, Anatole. *Les Désirs de Jean Servien.* 1882. In *Oeuvres.* 2 vols. Paris: Gallimard, 1984– . 1: 335–427.

————. *Le Livre de mon ami.* 1885. In *Oeuvres,* 1: 431–583.

————. *Le Petit Pierre.* Paris: Calmann-Lévy, 1918.

————. *La Vie en fleur.* 1922. Paris: Gallimard, 1983.

Frank, Leonhard. *Die Räuberbande.* Munich: Müller, 1914.

Franz Cizek: Pionier der Kunsterziehung (1865–1946). Exh. cat. Vienna: Historisches Museum der Stadt Wien, 1985.

Frecot, János, Johann Friedrich Geist, and Diethart Kerbs, eds. *Fidus 1868–1948.* Munich: Rogner, 1972.

Freeman, Derek. *Margaret Mead and Samoa: The Making and Unmaking of an Anthropological Myth.* 1983. Harmondsworth: Penguin, 1984.

Freideutsche Jugend: Zur Jahrhundertfeier auf dem Hohen Meissner 1913. Ed. Arthur Kracke. Jena: Diederichs, 1913.

Freideutscher Jugendtag 1913: Reden von Bruno Lemke, Gottfried Traub, Knud Ahlborn, Gustav Wyneken, Ferdinand Avenarius. Ed. Gustav Mittelstrass. 1913. Hamburg: Saal, 1919.

Freud, Sigmund. *The Standard Edition of the Complete Psychological Works.* Ed. James Strachey. 24 vols. London: Hogarth, 1953–66. Reprint New York: Norton, 1976.

————. *Civilization and Its Discontents (Das Unbehagen in der Kultur).* 1930. In *Standard Edition,* 21: 64–145.

————. *A Fragment of an Analysis of a Case of Hysteria (Bruchstück einer Hysterie-Analyse)*. [Dora.] 1905. In *Standard Edition*, 7: 7–122.

————. *An Outline of Psychoanalysis (Abriss der Psychoanalyse)*. In *Standard Edition*, 23: 144–207.

————. *Some Reflections on Schoolboy Psychology (Zur Psychologie des Gymnasiasten)*. 1914. In *Standard Edition*, 13: 241–44.

————. *Three Essays on the Theory of Sexuality (Drei Abhandlungen zur Sexualtheorie)*. 1905. In *Standard Edition*, 7: 130–243.

Gabler, Karlheinz. "Erich Heckels Zeichnungen und Aquarelle." In *Erich Heckel, 1883–1970*, ed. Zdenek Felix. Exh. Cat. Essen. Munich: Prestel, 1983. 41–54.

Galton, Sir Francis. "Eugenics: Its Definition, Scope and Aims." *Nature* 70 (1904): 82.

Galzy, Jeanne. *La Femme chez les garçons*. 1919. 7th ed. Paris: Rieder, 1924.

Gearhart, Suzanne. "The Scene of Psychoanalysis: The Unanswered Questions of Dora." *Diacritics* 9 (1970): 114–26.

Geissler, Erich E. *Der Gedanke der Jugend bei Gustav Wyneken*. Frankfurt/M.: Diesterweg, 1963.

Gerber, Walther. *Zur Entstehungsgeschichte der deutschen Wandervogelbewegung*. Bielefeld: Deutsche Heimat, 1957.

Gerbod, Paul. *La Vie quotidienne dans les lycées et collèges au XIXe siècle*. Paris: Hachette, 1968.

Gibson, Robert. *The Land without a Name: Alain-Fournier and His World*. London: Elek, 1975.

Gide, André. *Romans, récits et soties, oeuvres lyriques*. Paris: Gallimard, 1964.

————. *Les Cahiers et les poésies d'André Walter*. 1891. Ed. Claude Martin. Paris: Gallimard, 1986.

————. *The Counterfeiters*. New York: Random House, 1973.

————. *Les Faux-monnayeurs*. 1925. In *Romans*, 931–1248.

————. *Le Retour de l'enfant prodigue*. 1907. In *Romans*, 473–91.

————. *Si le grain ne meurt*. 1926. Paris: Gallimard, 1959.

Giesbers, Johannes. "Cecil Reddie and Abbotsholme: A Forgotten Pioneer and His Creation." Ph.D. diss., University of Nijmegen, 1970.

Giese, Fritz. *Das freie literarische Schaffen bei Kindern und Jugendlichen*. Leipzig: Barth, 1914.

Gillis, John R. "Conformity and Rebellion: Contrasting Styles of English and German Youth, 1900–33." *History of Education Quarterly* 13 (1973): 249–60.

————. *Youth and History: Tradition and Change in European Age Relations 1770-Present*. New York: Academic Press, 1974.

Giraudoux, Jean. *Simon le pathétique*. Paris: Grasset, 1918.

Glenn, Jules. "Freud's Adolescent Patients: Katharina, Dora and the 'Homosexual Woman.'" In *Freud and His Patients,* ed. Mark Kanzer and Jules Glenn. New York: Aronson, 1980. 23–47.

Goethe, Johann Wolfgang. *Sämtliche Werke.* 22 vols. Munich: Hanser, 1985– .

————. *Wilhelm Meisters Lehrjahre.* 1795–96. In *Sämtliche Werke,* vol. 5.

————. *Wilhelm Meisters Wanderjahre.* 1829. In *Sämtliche Werke,* vol. 17.

Goldgar, Harry. "Alain-Fournier and the Initiation Archetype." *French Review,* Special issue no. 1 (1970): 87–99.

Goldknopf, David. *The Life of the Novel.* Chicago: University of Chicago Press, 1972.

Gordon, Donald E. *Ernst Ludwig Kirchner: Mit einem Katalog sämtlicher Gemälde.* Munich: Prestel, 1968.

————. *Expressionism: Art and Idea.* New Haven: Yale University Press, 1987.

————. "German Expressionism." In *Primitivism in 20th Century Art,* ed. William Rubin. 2 vols. New York: Museum of Modern Art, 1984. 369–403.

————. "Kirchner in Dresden." *Art Bulletin* 48 (1966): 335–61.

Gorham, Deborah. *The Victorian Girl and the Feminine Ideal.* London: Croom Helm, 1982.

Grass, Günter. *Katz und Maus.* Hamburg: Rohwolt, 1961.

Greenblatt, Stephen. *Shakespearean Negotiations.* Oxford: Oxford University Press, 1988.

Grimmelshausen. *Der abenteuerliche Simplicissimus.* 1668. Munich: Winkler, 1956.

Grinder, Robert. E. "The Concept of Adolescence in the Genetic Psychology of G. Stanley Hall." *Child Development* 40 (1969): 355–69.

Grisebach, Lothar, ed. *E. L. Kirchners Davoser Tagebuch: Eine Darstellung des Malers und eine Sammlung seiner Schriften.* Cologne: DuMont, 1968

Grisebach, Lucius. "Erich Heckel und die 'Brücke.'" In *Erich Heckel, 1883–1970,* ed. Zdenek Felix. Exh. Cat. Essen. Munich: Prestel, 1983. 9–24.

Grohmann, Will. *E. L. Kirchner.* Stuttgart: Kohlhammer, 1958.

Gross, Ruth V. "The Narrator as Demon in Grass and Alain-Fournier." *Modern Fiction Studies* 25 (1979–1980): 625–39.

Gurlitt, Ludwig. *Der Deutsche und sein Vaterland: Politisch-pädagogische Betrachtungen eines Modernen.* 1902. 2d ed. Berlin: Wiegandt, 1903.

————. *Der Deutsche und seine Schule: Erinnerungen, Beobachtungen und Wünsche eines Lehrers.* 1905. 2d ed. Berlin: Wiegandt, 1906.

————. *Schülerselbstmorde.* Berlin: Concordia, n.d. [1908]

Halbe, Max. *Jahrhundertwende: Erinnerungen an eine Epoche.* 1935. 2d ed. Munich: Mueller, 1976.

Halbe, Max. *Jugend: Ein Liebesdrama.* Berlin: Fischer, 1893.

Hall, Granville Stanley. *Adolescence: Its Psychology and Its Relations to Physiology, Anthropology, Sociology, Sex, Crime, Religion and Education.* 2 vols. New York: Appleton, 1904.

————. *Jesus, the Christ, in the Light of Psychology.* 2 vols. New York: Doubleday, 1917.

————. *Youth: Its Regimen and Hygiene.* New York: Appleton, 1906.

Hasenclever, Walter. *Der Sohn.* Leipzig: Wolff, 1914.

Hassan, Ihab H. "The Idea of Adolescence in American Fiction." *American Quarterly* 10 (1958): 312–24.

Hauptmann, Gerhart. *Michael Kramer.* 1900. In *Sämtliche Werke,* 11 vols. Frankfurt/M.: Propyläen, 1966–74. 1: 1111–72.

Hegewisch, Katharina. "Einst ein Kommender vor Kommenden—Erich Heckel in seiner Zeit." In *Erich Heckel, 1883–1970,* ed. Zdenek Felix. Exh. Cat. Essen. Munich: Prestel, 1983. 25–40.

Hélie, Jean. "Le Vagabondage des mineurs." Ph. D. diss., Sorbonne, 1899.

Heller, Arno. *Experiments with the Novel of Maturation: Henry James and Stephen Crane.* Innsbruck: Innsbrucker Gesellschaft zur Pflege der Geisteswissenschaften, 1976.

Heller, Reinhold. "Edvard Munch, die Liebe und die Kunst." In *Edvard Munch. Liebe, Angst, Tod,* ed. Ulrich Weisner. Exh. Cat. Bielefeld: Kunsthalle, 1980. 297–306.

————. "Edvard Munch's 'Night,' the Aesthetics of Decadence and the Content of Biography," *Arts Magazine* 53, no. 2 (1978): 80–105.

————. *Munch: His Life and Work.* Chicago: University of Chicago Press, 1984.

————. *Munch: The Scream.* New York: Viking Press, 1973.

Helwig, Werner. *Die Blaue Blume des Wandervogels.* Gütersloh: Mohn, 1960.

Henriot, Emile. *A quoi rêvent les jeunes gens. Enquête sur la jeunesse littéraire.* Paris: Champion, 1913.

Hertz, Neil, ed. "Dora's Secrets, Freud's Techniques." *Diacritics* 13 (1983): 65–76.

————. *A Fine Romance: Freud and Dora. Diacritics,* Spec. ed. (Spring 1983).

Herzogenrath, Wulf. *Oskar Schlemmer: Die Wandgestaltung der neuen Architektur. Mit einem Katalog seiner Wandgestaltungen 1911–1942.* Munich: Prestel, 1973.

Hesse, Hermann. *Gesammelte Werke.* 12 vols. Frankfurt/M: Suhrkamp, 1970.

————. *Demian.* Trans. Michael Roloff and Michael Lebeck. New York: Bantam, 1970.

——. *The Prodigy* (Trans. of *Unterm Rad*). Harmondsworth: Penguin, 1973.

——. *Ein Stückchen Theologie*. 1932. In *Werke*, 10: 74–88.

——. *Unterm Rad*. 1906. In *Werke*, 2: 5–178.

Hevesi, Ludwig. *Acht Jahre Sezession (März 1897–Juni 1905): Kritik—Polemik—Chronik*. Vienna: Konegen, 1906.

Heym, Georg. "Tagebücher." In *Dichtungen und Schriften*. 3 vols. Ed. Karl Ludwig Schneider. Hamburg: Ellermann, 1960–64. 3: 6–176.

Hicks, W. R. *The School in English and German Fiction*. London: Socino, 1933.

Hodin, J. P. *Edvard Munch*. London: Thames, 1972.

Hoffmann, E. T. A. *Werke*. 4 vols. Frankfurt/M.: Insel, 1967.

Hoffmann, Edith. *Kokoschka: Life and Work*. London: Faber, 1947.

Hoffmeister, Werner. *Studien zur erlebten Rede bei Thomas Mann und Robert Musil*. The Hague: Mouton, 1965.

Hofmannsthal, Hugo von. *Prosa*. 3 vols. Frankfurt/M.: Fischer, 1950–52.

——. "Age of Innocence: Stationen der Entwicklung." Ms. 1891? In *Prosa*, 1: 147–54.

——. *Ein Brief*. 1901. In *Prosa*, 2: 7–22.

——. "Maurice Barrès." 1891. In *Prosa*, 1: 47–57.

——. *Sämtliche Werke. Kritische Ausgabe*. 38 vols. planned. Frankfurt/M.: Fischer, 1975–.

——. "Tagebuch eines jungen Mädchens." 1893. In *Prosa*, 1: 121–28.

——. "Wie mein Vater . . ." In *Prosa*, 1: 157–61.

Hölderlin, Friedrich. *Hyperion*. 1797–99. In *Sämtliche Werke*, 6 vols. Stuttgart: Kohlhammer, 1958–59. 3: 1–305.

Hollaender, Felix. *Der Weg des Thomas Truck*. 1902. 9th ed. Berlin: Fischer, 1910.

Honey, John Raymond de Symons. *Tom Brown's Universe: The Development of the English Public School in the Nineteenth Century*. New York: Quadrangle/New York Times Book Co., 1977.

Horney, Karen. *The Adolescent Diaries of Karen Horney*. New York: Basic, 1980.

——. *New Ways in Psychoanalysis*. 1939. New York: Norton, 1966.

Howard, Jane E. "The New Historicism in Renaissance Studies." In *Renaissance Historicism*, ed. Arthur F. Kinney and Dan S. Collins. Amherst: University of Massachusetts Press, 1987. 3–33.

Huch, Friedrich. *Mao*. Berlin: Fischer, 1907.

Hughes, Thomas. *Tom Brown's Schooldays*. 1857. Oxford: Oxford University Press, 1989.

Husson, Claudie. "Adolescence et création littéraire chez Alain-Fournier." *Revue d'histoire littéraire de la France* 85 (1985): 637–66.

Jähner, Horst. *Künstlergruppe Brücke.* Stuttgart: Kohlhammer, 1984.

Jakobson, Roman. "Über den Realismus in der Kunst." 1921. In *Texte der russischen Formalisten,* ed. Jurij Striedter, vol. 1. Munich: Fink, 1969. 372–91.

Jaloux, Edmond. *Fumées dans la campagne.* 1918. Lyon: Lardanchet, 1925.

———. "L'Esprit des livres." *Les Nouvelles Littéraires,* Jan. 4, 1930, p. 3.

James, Henry. *The Awkward Age.* 1899. Harmondsworth: Penguin, 1966.

———. *In the Cage.* 1898. In *In the Cage and Other Tales.* London: Hart-Davis, 1958. 174–226.

———. *What Maisie Knew.* 1897. New York: Anchor, 1954.

James, Williams. *The Varieties of Religious Experience.* 1902. New York: Longmans, 1907.

Jantzen, Hinrich. *Jugendkultur und Jugendbewegung: Studie zur Stellung und Bedeutung Gustav Wynekens innerhalb der Jugendbewegung.* Frankfurt/M: Dipa, 1963.

Janz, Rolf-Peter. "Die Faszination der Jugend durch Rituale und sakrale Symbole. Mit Anmerkungen zu Fidus, Hesse, Hofmannsthal und George." In *"Mit uns zieht die neue Zeit,"* ed. Thomas Koebner, Rolf-Peter Janz, and Frank Trommler. Frankfurt/M.: Suhrkamp, 1985. 310–37.

———. "Identitätskrise als Signatur des Wiener Fin de Siècle." In *Arthur Schnitzler: Zur Diagnose des Wiener Bürgertums im Fin de Siècle,* ed. Rolf-Peter Janz and Klaus Laermann. Stuttgart: Metzler, 1977. 170–74.

Jary, Jacques. *Essai sur l'art et la psychologie de Maurice Barrès.* Paris: Emile-Paul, 1912.

Jeal, Tim. *The Boy-Man: The Life of Lord Baden-Powell.* New York: Morrow, 1990.

Jean Paul. *Werke.* 6 vols. Munich: Hanser, 1959–63.

———. *Flegeljahre.* 1804–5. In *Werke,* 2: 567–1065.

———. *Levana.* 1807. In *Werke,* 5: 515–874.

Johst, Hanns. *Der junge Mensch. Ein ekstatisches Szenarium.* 1916. 2d ed. Munich: Delphin, 1919.

Jones, Louisa. "Window Imagery: Inner and Outer Worlds in Alain Fournier's 'Le Grand Meaulnes.'" *Symposium* 27 (1973): 333–51.

Jouhandeau, Marcel. *La Jeunesse de Théophile.* Paris: Nouvelle Revue française, 1921.

Joyce, James. *A Portrait of the Artist as a Young Man.* 1916. Ed. Chester G. Anderson. Harmondsworth: Penguin, 1977.

———. *Stephen Hero.* 1944. London: Granada, 1977.

Jünger, Ernst. *In Stahlgewittern.* Leipzig: Meier, 1920.

Kafka, Franz. *The Judgment.* 1913. In *The Penal Colony: Stories and Short Pieces.* New York: Schocken, 1961. 49–66.

Kaiser, Georg. *Werke.* Ed. Walther Huder. 6 vols. Frankfurt/M: Propyläen, 1971.

————. *Der Fall des Schülers Vehgesack.* Ms. 1901. In *Werke,* 1: 41–116.

————. *Rektor Kleist.* 1903, 1917–19. In *Werke,* 5: 223–73.

Kallir, Otto. *Egon Schiele: Das druckgraphische Werk.* Vienna: Zsolnay, 1970.

————. *Egon Schiele: Oeuvre-Katalog der Gemälde.* 2d ed. Vienna: Zsolnay, 1966.

Karinthy, Frigyes. *Please Sir!.* First Hungarian ed., *Tanár úr kérem,* 1916. Budapest: Corvina, 1968.

Karl, Willibald. *Jugend, Gesellschaft und Politik im Zeitraum des Ersten Weltkriegs.* Munich: Wolfle, 1973.

Keniston, Kenneth. "Psychological Development and Historical Change." *Journal of Interdisciplinary History* 2 (1971–72): 329–45.

Kenner, Hugh. *Dublin's Joyce.* London: Chatto, 1955.

Kett, Joseph. "Adolescence and Youth in Nineteenth-Century America." *Journal of Interdisciplinary History* 2 (1971–72): 283–98.

————. *Rites of Passage: Adolescence in America 1790 to the Present.* New York: Basic, 1977.

Key, Ellen. *Das Jahrhundert des Kindes.* First Swedish ed., 1901. Rev. and abbr. ed. Berlin: Fischer, 1907.

Kiell, Norman. *The Adolescent through Fiction.* New York: International Universities Press, 1959.

————. *The Universal Experience of Adolescence.* New York: International Universities Press, 1964.

Kindt, Werner, ed. *Grundschriften der deutschen Jugendbewegung.* Düsseldorf: Diederichs, 1963.

————, ed. *Die Wandervogelzeit: Quellenschriften zur deutschen Jugendbewegung 1896–1919.* Düsseldorf: Diederichs, 1968.

King, Irving. *The High-School Age.* Indianapolis: Bobbs-Merrill, 1914.

Kipling, Rudyard. *Kim.* 1901. Harmondsworth: Penguin, 1987.

————. *Land and Sea Tales.* 1923. In *Writings in Prose and Verse,* 38 vols. London: Macmillan, 1897–1938. 34: 1–220.

————. *Stalky & Co.* 1899. London: MacMillan, 1982.

————. *Verse.* Definitive Edition. London: Hodder, 1940.

Koebner, Thomas, Rolf-Peter Janz, and Frank Trommler, eds. *"Mit uns zieht die neue Zeit": Der Mythos Jugend.* Frankfurt/M.: Suhrkamp, 1985.

Kokoschka, Oskar. *Mein Leben*. Munich: Bruckmann, 1971.

———. *Die träumenden Knaben*. 1908. In *Die träumenden Knaben und andere Dichtungen*. Salzburg: Welz, 1959.

Korth, Georg. *Wandervogel 1896–1906. Quellenmässige Darstellung nach Karl Fischers Tagebuchaufzeichnungen von 1900 und vielen anderen dokumentarischen Belegen.* 1967. 2d ed. Frankfurt/M: Dipa, 1978.

Krieger, Peter. *Der Lebensfries für Max Reinhardts Kammerspiele: Edvard Munch*. Berlin: Mann, 1978.

Kühne, Jörg. *Das Gleichnis: Studien zur inneren Form von Robert Musils Roman 'Der Mann ohne Eigenschaften'*. Tübingen: Niemeyer, 1968.

Kunert, Hubertus. *Deutsche Reformpädagogik und Faschismus*. Hannover: Schroedel, 1973.

Die Künstlergruppe "Brücke" und der Deutsche Expressionismus. 2 vols. Exh. Cat. Feldafing: Buchheim, 1973.

Kurella, Alfred. *Die Geschlechterfrage der Jugend*. Hamburg: Saal, 1919.

LaCapra, Dominick. *Rethinking Intellectual History: Texts, Contexts, Language*. Ithaca: Cornell University Press, 1983.

Lacretelle, Jacques de. *Silbermann*. 1922. Paris: Gallimard, 1983.

———. *La Vie inquiète de Jean Hermelin*. 1920. Paris: Fayard, 1935.

Lafon, André. *L'Elève Gilles*. 1912. Paris: Perrin, 1915.

Lagarde, Paul de. *Deutscher Glaube Deutsches Vaterland Deutsche Bildung*. Ed. Friedrich Daab. Jena: Diederichs, 1913.

Lancaster, E. G. "The Psychology and Pedagogy of Adolescence." *Pedagogical Seminary* 5 (1897–98): 61–128.

Langaard, Johan H. "Edvard Munch 'Twee meisjes in een tuin.'" *Bulletin Museum Boymans–van Beuningen* 8 (1957): 51–57.

[Langbehn, Julius]. *Rembrandt als Erzieher: Von einem Deutschen*. Leipzig: Hirschfeld, 1890.

Laqueur, Walter Z. *Young Germany: A History of the German Youth Movement*. London: Routledge, 1962.

Larbaud, Valery. *Fermina Márquez*. 1911. Paris: Gallimard, 1979.

Laslett, Peter. "Age at Menarche in Europe since the Eighteenth Century." *Journal of Interdisciplinary History* 2 (1971–72): 221–36.

———. *The World We Have Lost*. New York: Scribner's, 1965. 2d ed. London: Methuen, 1971.

Lautréamont. "Les Chants de Maldoror." 1869. *Oeuvres complètes*. Paris: Gallimard, 1970. 41–252.

Le Bas, Maurice. *Monseigneur Caron (1845–1929)*. Paris: Bonne, 1945.

Lejeune, Philippe. *Le Pacte autobiographique*. Paris: Seuil, 1975.

Lemaître, August. *La Vie mentale de l'adolescent et ses anomalies*. St. Blaise: Foyer Solidariste, 1910.

Leopold, Rudolf. *Egon Schiele*. Salzburg: Residenz, 1972.

Le Roux, Hugues. *Jeunes Amours*. Paris: Calmann-Lévy, 1899.

Leshko, Jaroslaw. "Oskar Kokoschka: Paintings, 1907–1915." Ph. D. diss., Columbia University, 1977.

Leslie, Shane J. R. *The Oppidan*. New York: Scribner's, 1922.

Levin, Harry. *James Joyce*. 1941. Rev. ed. New York: New Directions, 1960.

Libby, M. F. "Shakespeare and Adolescence." *Pedagogical Seminary* 8 (1901): 163–205.

Lietz, Hermann. *Die deutsche Land- und Erziehungs-Heime: Gedanken und Bilder*. Leipzig: Voigtländer, 1910.

———. *Die deutsche Nationalschule*. 1911. 2d ed. Veckenstedt: Land-Waisenheim, 1920.

———. *Emlohstobba: Roman oder Wirklichkeit?* Berlin: Dümmler, 1897.

———. *Von Leben und Arbeit eines deutschen Erziehers*. Veckenstedt: Land-Waisenheim, 1922.

Locke, John. *Some Thoughts concerning Education*. 1693. Cambridge: Cambridge University Press, 1934.

Loize, Jean. *Alain-Fournier, sa vie et 'Le Grand Meaulnes'*. Paris: Hachette, 1968.

Loti, Pierre. *Prime Jeunesse*. Paris: Calmann-Lévy, 1919.

Lunn, Arnold. *The Harrowians*. London: Methuen, 1913.

Lux, Joseph August. "Wiener Kunstschau." *Deutsche Kunst und Dekoration* 23 (1908–9): 33–77.

Maasen, Thijs. "De Pedagogische eros in het geding. Gustav Wyneken en de pedagogische vriendschap in de Freie Schulgemeinde Wickersdorf tussen 1906–1931." Ph. D. diss., Vrije Universiteit, Amsterdam, 1988.

Mack, Louise. *Girls Together*. London: Pilgrim, 1903.

———. *Teens*. 1897. London: Melrose, 1903.

Mackenzie, Compton. *Sinister Street*. 2 vols. London: Secker, 1913.

Major, Jean-Louis. *Radiguet, Cocteau 'Les Joues en feu'*. Ottawa: University of Ottawa Press, 1977.

Malory, Sir Thomas. *The Book of King Arthur and His Knights of the Round Table*. Ed. Rhys. 2 vols. London: Dent, 1906.

Mann, Heinrich. *Professor Unrat*. 1905. Hamburg: Rohwolt, 1951.

Mann, Klaus. *The Turning Point*. New York: L. B. Fischer, 1944.

Mann, Thomas. *Buddenbrooks.* 1901. Frankfurt/M.: Fischer, 1961.

————. *Doktor Faustus.* Stockholm: Bermann Fischer, 1947.

————. *Tonio Kröger.* 1903. In *Gesammelte Werke in Einzelbänden: Frühe Erzählungen.* Ed. Peter Mendelssohn. Frankfurt/M.: Fischer, 1981. 273–341.

Marcus, Steven. *Representations.* New York: Random, 1975.

————. "Freud and Dora: Story, History, Case History." In *Representations,* 247–310.

————. "Stalky and Co." 1962. In *Representations,* 61–75.

Marro, Antoine. *La Puberté.* First Italian ed., 1897. Paris: Schleicher, 1902.

Martens, Kurt. *Wie ein Strahl verglimmt.* Leipzig: Wild, 1895.

Martin du Gard, Roger. *Le Cahier gris—Le Pénitencier—La Belle Saison.* Vol. 1 of *Les Thibault.* 8 vols. 1922–40. Paris: Gallimard, 1972.

Marty, P., et al. "Le Cas Dora et le point de vue psychosomatique." *Revue française de psychanalyse* 32 (1968): 679–714.

Marx, Karl. *The Eighteenth Brumaire of Louis Bonaparte.* 1852. In *Marx and Engels: Basic Writings on Politics and Philosophy,* ed. Lewis S. Feuer. New York: Doubleday, 1959.

Massis, Henri. *Alain-Fournier sans Goncourt.* Liège: Dynamo, 1963.

————. *La Pensée de Maurice Barrès.* Paris: Mercure de France, 1909.

————. *Jugements.* 2 vols. Paris: Plon, 1924.

————. "Histoires de Collégiens." In *Jugements,* 2: 125–34.

————. "Le Romantisme de l'adolescence." In *Jugements,* 2: 108–24.

Mauriac, François. *Oeuvres romanesque et théâtrales complètes.* 4 vols. Paris: Gallimard, 1978–85.

————. *L'Adieu à l'adolescence.* 1911. Paris: Stock, 1984.

————. *Le Désert de l'amour.* 1925. In *Oeuvres romanesque,* 1: 737–862.

Max Liebermann en Holland. Exh. Cat. The Hague: Staatsuitgeverij, 1980.

Max Liebermann in seiner Zeit. Exh. Cat. Berlin: Nationalgalerie, 1979.

Mead, Margaret. *Coming of Age in Samoa.* 1928. New York: Quill, 1973.

Mell, Max. "Chaos der Kindheit." *Die Zukunft* 64 (1908): 250–52.

Mendousse, Pierre. *L'Ame de l'adolescent.* 1909. 5th ed. Paris: Presses Universitaires, 1947.

Meredith, George. *Lord Ormont and His Aminta.* 1894. London: Constable, 1916.

Michelet, Jules. *Ma Jeunesse.* Paris: Calmann-Lévy, 1884.

Miller, J. Hillis. *The Ethics of Reading: Kant, de Man, Eliot, Trollope, James, and Benjamin.* New York: Columbia University Press, 1987.

Minder, Robert. "Kadettenhaus, Gruppendynamik und Stilwandel von Wildenbruch bis Rilke und Musil." In Minder, *Kultur und Literatur in Deutschland und Frankreich*. Frankfurt/M.: Insel, 1962.

Mirbeau, Octave. *Le Calvaire*. 1886. Paris: Union générale d'éditions, 1986.

―――. *Sébastien Roch*. 1890. Paris: Union générale d'éditions, 1977.

Mitsch, Erwin. *Egon Schiele*. Salzburg: Residenz, 1974.

―――. *Egon Schiele: Zeichnungen und Aquarelle*. 1961. 4th ed. Salzburg: Welz, 1972.

Moen, Arve. *Edvard Munch: Ein Bilderwerk*. 3 vols. Munich: Bruckmann: 1956–58.

Molnár, Ferenc. *A Pál utcai fiúk* (The Pál Street boys). 1907. Budapest: Móra, 1985.

Montherlant, Henry de. *La Relève du matin*. 1920. Rev. ed. Paris: Grasset, 1933.

Moravia, Alberto. *Gli indifferenti*. 1929. Milan: Bompiani, 1949.

Móricz, Zsigmond. *Be Faithful unto Death*. Budapest: Corvina, 1962.

―――. *Légy jó mindhalálig* (Be Faithful unto Death). 1920. In *Regények,* 4 vols. Budapest: Szépirodalmi, 1975–76. 2: 263–514.

Morris, Brian. "Ernest Thompson Seton and the Origins of the Woodcraft Movement." *Journal of Contemporary History* 5 (1970): 183–94.

Morrison, William Douglas. *Juvenile Offenders*. London: Unwin, 1896.

Moss, Robert, F. *Rudyard Kipling and the Fiction of Adolescence*. London: Macmillan, 1982.

Mosse, George L. *The Crisis of German Ideology: Intellectual Origins of the Third Reich*. New York: Grosset, 1964.

Mühlestein, Hans, and Georg Schmidt. *Ferdinand Hodler: Sein Leben und sein Werk*. 1942. Zurich: Unionsverlag, 1983.

Müller, Dr. *Zwakte tvestand: Onanie, geslachtelyke uitspattingen, Impotenz en hunne genezing*. Berlin: Stahn, 1881.

Müller, Jakob. *Die Jugendbewegung als deutsche Hauptrichtung neukonservativer Reform*. Zurich: Europa, 1971.

Musgrove, F. *Youth and the Social Order*. London: Paul, 1964.

Musil, Robert. *Die Verwirrungen des Zöglings Törless*. 1906. In *Gesammelte Werke*, ed. Adolf Frisé, 9 vols. Hamburg: Rowohlt, 1978. 6: 7–140.

―――. *Die Vollendung der Liebe*. 1911. In *Gesammelte Werke,* 6: 156–94.

―――. *Young Törless*. Trans. Eithne Wilkins and Ernst Kaiser. New York: New American Library, 1966.

Muslin, Hyman, and Merton Gill. "Transference in the Dora Case." *Journal of the American Psychoanalytic Association* 26 (1978): 311–28.

Muus, Rolf E. *Theories of Adolescence*. 1962. 3d ed. New York: Random, 1974.

Myers, Bernard S. *The German Expressionists: A Generation in Revolt.* New York: Praeger, 1966.

Nebehay, Christian M. *Ver Sacrum 1898–1903.* Vienna: Tusch, 1975.

Nescio [J. H. F. Grönloh]. *Titaantjes.* 1914. In *De uitvreter; Titaantjes; Dichtertje; Mene Tekel.* The Hague: Nijgh, 1983. 43–75.

Neveu, Pol. *La Douce enfance de Thierry Seneuse.* 6th ed. Paris: Fayard, 1916.

Nietzsche, Friedrich. *On the Genealogy of Morals.* Trans. Walter Kaufmann. New York: Vintage, 1967.

———. *Thus Spoke Zarathustra.* Trans. Walter Kaufmann. Harmondsworth: Penguin, 1978.

Nordau, Max. *Entartung.* 2 vols. Berlin: Puncker, 1892–93.

Novalis. *Die Lehrlinge zu Saïs.* 1802. In *Schriften,* 5 vols. Stuttgart: Kohlhammer, 1960–88. 1: 79–109.

O'Brien, Justin. *The Novel of Adolescence in France.* Oxford: Oxford University Press, 1939.

Orwell, George. "Boys' Weeklies." 1940. In *Collected Essays, Journalism and Letters.* 4 vols. London: Secker, 1968. 1: 460–93.

Oskar Kokoschka. Schriften 1907–1955. Ed. Hans Maria Wingler. Munich: Langen, 1956.

Oskar Schlemmer: Aquarelle, Pastelle, Zeichnungen. Exh. Cat. Essen: Museum Folkwang, 1971.

Otto Müller. Das graphische Gesamtwerk: Zum hunderdststen Geburtstag. Berlin: Galerie Nierendorf, 1974.

Oxford Companion to Children's Literature. Ed. Humphrey Carpenter and Mari Prichard. Oxford: Oxford University Press, 1984.

Paasche, Hans. *Die Forschungsreise des Afrikaners Lukanga Mukara ins Innerste Deutschland.* 1921. Bremen: Donat, 1988.

Panter, Ulrich. *Gustav Wyneken: Leben und Werk.* Weinheim: Beltz, 1960.

Paulsen, Friedrich. *Geschichte des gelehrten Unterrichts auf den deutschen Schulen und Universitäten.* 1885. 2d ed. 2 vols. Leipzig: Veit, 1896–97.

Pechstein, Max. *Erinnerungen.* Wiesbaden: Limes, 1960.

Pechter, Edward. "The New Historicism and Its Discontents: Politicizing Renaissance Drama." *PMLA* 102 (1987): 292–303.

Perrot, Michelle. "Journaux intimes: jeunes filles au miroir de l'âme." *Ecrire* 4, no. 1 (1986): 29–36.

Pinthus, Kurt. "Männliche Literatur." *Das Tagebuch* 10 (1929): 903–11.

Platt, Anthony. *The Child Savers: The Invention of Delinquency.* 1969. 2d, enl. ed. Chicago: University of Chicago Press, 1977.

Popert, Hermann. *Helmut Harringa*. 1910. Dresden: Köhler, 1919.

————. *Tagebuch eines Sehenden 1914–1919*. Hamburg: Jansen, Vortrupp-Verlag, 1920.

Prellwitz, Gertrud. *Drude*. 3 vols. Oberhof: Maien, 1921–26.

Prévost, Marcel. *Le Scorpion*. 1887. Paris: Lemerre, 1903.

Pross, Harry. *Jugend Eros Politik: Die Geschichte der deutschen Jugendverbände*. Bern: Scherz, 1964.

Prost, Antoine. *Histoire de l'enseignement en France 1800–1967*. Paris: Colin, 1968.

Psichari, Ernest. *L'Appel des armes*. Paris: Oudin, 1913.

Ptaschkina, Nelly. *The Diary of Nelly Ptaschkina*. Trans. Pauline de Chary. London: Cape, 1923.

Puffer, J. Adams. "Boys' Gangs." *Pedagogical Seminary* 12 (1905): 175–212.

Quigly, Isabel. *The Heirs of Tom Brown: The English School Story*. 1982. Oxford: Oxford University Press, 1984.

Rabine, Leslie W. "Meaulnes' Search; François' Research." *Michigan Romance Studies* 2 (1982): 101–38.

Radiguet, Raymond. *Le Diable au corps*. 1923. Paris: Grasset, 1983.

————. *Les Joues en feu*. Paris: Bernouard, 1920.

Ramas, Maria. "Freud's Dora, Dora's Hysteria: Negation of a Woman's Rebellion." *Feminist Studies* 6 (1980): 472–510.

Ras, Marion E. P. de. "Körper, Eros und weibliche Kultur: Mädchen im Wandervogel und in der bündischen Jugend 1900–1933." Ph. D. diss. Universiteit van Amsterdam, 1988.

Reddie, Cecil. *Abbotsholme*. London: Allen, 1900.

Reed, Talbot Baines. *The Fifth Form at St. Dominic's*. London: Religious Tract Society, 1887.

Régnier, Henri de. *Les Vacances d'un jeune homme sage*. Paris: Nilsson, 1903.

Reidemeister, Leopold. *Künstler der Brücke-Gemeinschaft der Dresdner Jahre*. Berlin: Brücke-Museum, 1973.

————, ed. *Künstler der Brücke an den Moritzburger Seen 1909–1911: Erich Heckel, Ernst Ludwig Kirchner, Max Pechstein*. Berlin: Brücke-Museum, 1970.

Remarque, Erich Maria. *Im Westen nichts Neues*. Berlin: Propyläen, 1929.

Renard, Jules. *Poil de Carotte*. 1894. Paris: Gallimard, 1979.

Renner, Ursula. *Leopold Andrians 'Garten der Erkenntnis': Literarisches Paradigma einer Identitätskrise in Wien um 1900*. Bern: Lang, 1981.

Rentsch, Arno. *Fiduswerk*. Dresden: Schönheit, 1925.

Reuter, Gabriele. *Die Jugend eines Idealisten*. Berlin: Fischer, 1917.

Revold, Reidar. "Over een motievengroep van Edvard Munch." *Bulletin Museum Boymans–van Beuningen* 11 (1960): 49–66.

Richardson, Dorothy M. *Pilgrimage I: Pointed Roofs, Backwater, Honeycomb.* 1915–17. London: Dent, 1938.

Richmond, Ennis. *Through Boyhood to Manhood.* London: Longmans, 1900.

Riis, Jacob A. *How the Other Half Lives: Studies among the Tenements of New York.* 1890. Reprint. Cambridge: Harvard University Press, 1970.

Rilke, Rainer Maria. *Sämtliche Werke.* 6 vols. Frankfurt/M.: Insel, 1955–66.

————. *Die Aufzeichnungen des Malte Laurids Brigge.* 1910. In *Werke,* 6: 709–946.

————. *Die Turnstunde.* 1902. In *Werke,* 4: 601–9.

Riquelme, John Paul. *Teller and Tale in Joyce's Fiction: Oscillating Perspectives.* Baltimore: Johns Hopkins University Press, 1983.

Rivière, Jacques. "Le Roman d'aventure." *Nouvelle Revue Française* 9 (1913): 748–65, 914–32; 10 (1914): 56–77.

Roberts, Robert. *The Classic Slum: Salford Life in the First Quarter of the Twentieth Century.* 1971. Harmondsworth: Penguin, 1973.

Rohleder, Hermann. *Die Masturbation.* 1898. Berlin: Fischer, 1921.

Röhrs, Hermann. *Die Reformpädagogik: Ursprung und Verlauf in Europa.* Hannover: Schroedel, 1980.

Rolland, Romain. "L'Adolescent." Pt. 3 of vol. 1 of *Jean-Christophe.* 1904–12. 3 vols. Paris: Livre de Poche, 1983.

Rosenbusch, H. *Die deutsche Jugendbewegung in ihren pädagogischen Formen und Wirkungen.* Frankfurt/M.: Dipa, 1973.

Rosenthal, Michael. *The Character Factory: Baden-Powell and the Origin of the Boy Scout Movement.* New York: Pantheon, 1986.

Ross, Dorothy. *G. Stanley Hall: The Psychologist as Prophet.* Chicago: University of Chicago Press, 1972.

Roters, Eberhard. "Beiträge zur Geschichte der Künstlergruppe 'Brücke' in den Jahren 1905–1907." *Jahrbuch der Berliner Museen* 2 (1960): 172–210.

Rothe, Friedrich. *Frank Wedekinds Dramen: Jugendstil und Lebensphilosophie.* Stuttgart: Metzler, 1968.

Rousseau, Jean Jacques. *Emile.* 1762. London: Dent, 1963.

Rubenstein, Benjamin. "Freud's Early Theories of Hysteria." In *Physics, Philosophy and Psychoanalysis,* eds. Robert S. Cohen and L. Laudan. Dordrecht: Reidel, 1983. 169–90.

Rubin, William, ed. *Primitivism in 20th Century Art: Affinity of the Tribal and the Modern.* 2 vols. New York: Museum of Modern Art, 1984.

Rügg, Walter, ed. *Kulturkritik und Jugendkultur.* Frankfurt/M.: Klostermann, 1974.

Sand, George. *Histoire de ma vie.* 1854. In *Oeuvres autobiographiques,* 2 vols. Paris: Gallimard, 1970–71. Vol. 1 and 2: 1–461.

Schafer, Roy. "Narration in the Psychoanalytic Dialogue." *Critical Inquiry* 7 (1980): 29–53.

Scharrelmann, Wilhelm. *Jesus der Jüngling.* Leipzig: Quelle, 1920.

Scheibe, Wolfgang. *Die Reformpädagogische Bewegung 1900–1932.* Weinheim: Beltz, 1969.

Schlemmer, Oskar. *The Letters and Diaries of Oskar Schlemmer.* Ed. Tut Schlemmer. Trans. Krishna Winston. Middletown: Wesleyan University Press, 1972.

Scholes, Robert. "Stephen Dedalus, Poet or Aesthete?" *PMLA* 89 (1964): 484–89.

Schorer, Mark. "Technique as Discovery." *Hudson Review* 1 (1948): 67–87.

Schorske, Carl E. *Fin-de-siècle Vienna: Politics and Culture.* New York: Knopf, 1980.

―――. "Generational Tension and Cultural Change: Reflections on the Case of Vienna." *Daedalus* (Fall 1978): 111–22.

Schweiger, Werner J. *Der Junge Kokoschka.* Vienna: Brandstätter, 1983.

Sedgwick, Anne Douglas. *The Little French Girl.* Boston: Houghton, 1924.

Selz, Peter. *German Expressionist Painting.* Berkeley: University of California Press, 1957.

Seume, Johann Gottfried. *Spaziergang nach Syrakus im Jahre 1802.* 1803. In *Prosaschriften.* Cologne: Melzer, 1962. 155–597.

Shakespeare, William. *As You Like It.* In *Complete Works,* ed. G. B. Harrison. New York: Harcourt, 1948. 777–808.

―――. *Winter's Tale.* In *Complete Works.* 1429–70.

Shine, Muriel G. *The Fictional Children of Henry James.* Chapel Hill: University of North Carolina Press, 1968.

Siegert, Gustav. *Das Problem der Kinderselbstmorde.* Leipzig: Voigtländer, 1893.

Simon, John Kenneth. "Valery Larbaud's 'Fermina.'" *Modern Language Notes* 83 (1968): 543–64.

Sinclair, May. *Mary Olivier.* 1919. New York: Dial, 1982.

Slaughter, John W. *The Adolescent.* 1911. 4th ed. London: Allen, 1917.

Sologub, Fyodor. *The Petty Demon.* First Russian ed., *Melkii bes,* 1907. Ann Arbor: Ardis, 1983.

Sorrell, Martin R. M. "François Seurel's Personal Adventure in 'Le Grand Meaulnes.'" *Modern Language Review* 69 (1974): 79–87.

Spacks, Patricia Meyer. *The Adolescent Idea: Myths of Youth and the Adult Imagination.* New York: Basic, 1981.

————. *The Female Imagination*. New York: Knopf, 1975.

Spender, Stephen. "The English Adolescent." *Harvard Educational Review* 18 (1948): 228–39.

Spranger, Eduard. *Psychologie des Jugendalters*. 1924. 16th ed. Leipzig: Quelle, 1932.

Springhall, J. O. "The Boy Scouts, Class Militarism in Relation to British Youth Movements 1908–30." *International Review of Social History* 16 (1971): 125–58.

————. *Coming of Age. Adolescence in Britain 1860–1960*. Dublin: Gill, 1986.

————. *Youth, Empire and Society: British Youth Movements, 1883–1940*. London: Croom Helm, 1977.

Staley, Thomas. "Strings in the Labyrinth: Sixty Years with Joyce's 'Portrait.'" In *Approaches to Joyce's "Portrait": Ten Essays,* ed. Thomas F. Staley and Bernard Benstock. Pittsburgh: University of Pittsburgh Press, 1976. 3–24.

Starbuck, Edwin Diller. *The Psychology of Religion: An Empirical Study of the Growth of Religious Consciousness*. 1899. 4th ed. London: Scott, 1914.

Stern, Fritz. *The Politics of Cultural Despair: A Study of the Rise of Germanic Ideology*. Berkeley: University of California Press, 1961.

Sternhell, Zeev. *La droite revolutionnaire, 1885–1914: Les Origins françaises du fascisme*. Paris: Seuil, 1978.

————. *Maurice Barrès et le nationalisme français*. 1972. Brussels: Complexe, 1985.

————. *Ni droit ni gauche: L'ideologie fasciste en France*. Paris: Seuil, 1983.

Stone, Lawrence. "Family History in the 1980s." *Journal of Interdisciplinary History* 12 (1981): 51–87.

————. *The Family, Sex and Marriage in England 1500–1800*. London: Weidenfels, 1977.

Stopp, Elisabeth. "Musil's 'Törless': Content and Form." *Modern Language Review* 63 (1968): 94–118.

Strauss, Emil. *Freund Hein*. 1902. Berlin: Fischer, 1911.

Suleiman, Susan Rubin. *Subversive Intent: Gender, Politics, and the Avant-Garde*. Cambridge: Harvard University Press, 1990.

Sulloway, Frank. *Freud, Biologist of the Mind*. New York: Basic, 1979.

Sumner, William Graham. "What Our Boys Are Reading." *Scribner's Monthly,* March 1878, 681–85.

Svenaeus, Gösta. *Edvard Munch: Im männlichen Gehirn*. 2 vols. Lund: New Society of Letters, 1973.

Swift, Edgar James. "Some Criminal Tendencies of Boyhood: A Study of Adolescence." *Pedagogical Seminary* 8 (1901): 65–91.

Tagebuch und dichterische Versuche eines Jugendlichen (16.-18. Lebensjahr) verfasst 1916–1918. Ed. Rudolf Mehnert. Leipzig: Leiner, 1930.

Taine, Hyppolite. *Etienne Mayran.* Ed. Paul Bourget. [written 1861–62]. Paris: Hachette, 1910.

Tarkington, Booth. *Alice Adams.* New York: Grosset, 1921.

————. *Penrod.* 1914. Bloomington: Indiana University Press, 1985.

————. *Penrod and Sam.* New York: Grosset, [1910?].

————. *Seventeen.* New York: Harper, 1916.

Tieck, Ludwig. *Der blonde Eckbert.* 1797. In *Werke,* 4 vols. Munich: Winkler, 1964. 2: 9–26.

Tissot, Samuel A. A. D. *L'Onanisme.* Lausanne, 1760.

Toller, Ernst. *Die Wandlung.* 1919. In *Prosa, Briefe, Dramen, Gedichte.* Hamburg: Rowohlt, 1961. 235–85.

Traum und Wirklichkeit—Wien 1870–1930. Exh. Cat. Vienna: Viennese Museums, 1985.

Turner, Ernest Sackville. *Boys Will Be Boys.* London: Joseph, 1948.

Valéry, Paul. "La Jeune parque." 1917. In *Oeuvres,* 2 vols. Paris: Gallimard, 1968–71. 1: 96–110.

Vallès, Jules. *Jacques Vingtras: Le Bachelier.* 1881. Paris: Charpentier, 1916.

Varsava, Jerry A. "Törless at the Limits of Language: A Revised Reading." *Seminar* 20 (1984): 188–204.

Vergo, Peter. *Art in Vienna 1898–1918: Klimt, Kokoschka, Schiele and Their Contemporaries.* London: Phaidon, 1975.

Vogt, Paul. *Erich Heckel.* Recklinghausen: Bongers, 1965.

Der Vortrupp: Halbmonatschrift für das Deutschtum unserer Zeit. Ed Hermann M. Popert and Hans Paasche. 1912–20.

Walpole, Hugh. *Mr. Perrin and Mr. Traill.* London: Mills, 1911.

Wassermann, Jakob. *Die Juden von Zirndorf.* 1897. Berlin: Fischer, 1906.

Waugh, Alec. *The Loom of Youth.* 1917. London: Richards, 1955.

Wedekind, Frank. *Gesammelte Werke.* Ed. Arthur Kutscher and Richard Friedenthal. 9 vols. Munich: Müller, 1912–21.

————. *Frühlings Erwachen.* 1891. In *Gesammelte Werke,* 2: 93–174.

————. *Mine-Haha, oder Über die körperliche Erziehung der jungen Mädchen.* 1903. In *Gesammelte Werke,* 1: 317–81.

Weill, Georges. *Histoire de l'enseignement secondaire en France 1802–1920.* Paris: Payot, 1921.

Weisner, Ulrich. ed. *Edvard Munch. Liebe, Angst, Tod. Themen und Variationen: Zeichnungen und Graphiken aus dem Munch-Museum, Oslo.* Exh. Cat. Bielefeld: Kunsthalle, 1980.

Werenskiold, Marit. "Die Brücke und Edvard Munch." *Zeitschrift des deutschen Vereins für Kunstwissenschaft* 28 (1974): 140–52.

Wickram, Jörg. *Das Rollwagenbüchlein*. 1555. In *Sämtliche Werke*, 13 vols. Berlin: de Gruyter, 1973. Vol. 7.

Wilde, Oskar. "The Decay of Lying." 1889. In *Works*. London: Collins, 1948. 909–31.

Wildenbruch, Ernst von. *Das edle Blut*. 1893. Berlin: Grote, 1903.

Wilkinson, Paul. "English Youth Movements, 1908–1930." *Journal of Contemporary History* 4, no. 2 (1969): 3–23.

Willy and Colette. *Claudine à l'école*. 1900. Paris: Michel, 1983.

————. *Claudine à Paris*. 1901. Paris: Michel, 1983.

Wilson, Angus. *The Strange Ride of Rudyard Kipling*. London: Secker, 1978.

Wingler, Hans Maria. *Oskar Kokoschka: Das Werk des Malers*. Salzburg: Welz, 1956.

Wodehouse, P. G. *The Gold Bat and Other School Stories*. Harmondsworth: Penguin, 1986.

————. *The Pothunters and Other School Stories*. Harmondsworth: Penguin, 1985.

————. *The Head of Kay's*. 1905. In *The Gold Bat*.

————. *The Little Nugget*. 1913. Harmondsworth: Penguin, 1988.

————. *Mike and Psmith*. 1909. Harmondsworth: Penguin, 1990.

————. *Mike at Wrykyn*. 1909. Harmondsworth: Penguin, 1990.

————. *A Perfect Uncle*. 1903. In *The Pothunters*, 123–241.

————. *The Tales of St Austin's*. 1903. In *The Pothunters*, 243–380.

————. *The White Feather*. 1907. In *The Gold Bat*.

Wolf, Max. *Die physische und sittliche Entartung des modernen Weibes*. Leipzig: Schupp, 1892.

Wolgast, Heinrich. *Das Elend unserer Jugendliteratur*. 1896. 4th ed. Hamburg: Wolgast, 1910.

Woolf, Virginia. *Jacob's Room*. 1922. London: Grafton, 1976.

Wucherpfennig, Wolf. *Kindheitskult und Irrationalismus in der Literatur um 1900: Friedrich Huch und seine Zeit*. Munich: Fink, 1980.

Wyneken, Gustav. *Eros*. Lauenburg: Saal, 1921.

————. *Der Kampf für die Jugend*. 1919. 2d, enl. ed. Jena: Diederichs, 1920.

————. *Der Krieg und die Jugend: "Öffentlicher Vortrag gehalten am 25. November 1914*. Munich: Steinicke, 1915.

————. *Die neue Jugend*. 1914. 3d ed. Munich: Steinicke, 1919.

————. *Schule und Jugendkultur*. 1913. 3d ed. Jena: Diederichs, 1920.

Wysling, Hans. "Dokumente zur Entstehung des 'Tonio Kröger.'" In *Quellenkri-*

tische Studien zum Werk Thomas Manns, ed. Paul Scherrer and Hans Wysling. Bern: Francke, 1967. 48–63.

A Young Girl's Diary. Trans. Eden and Cedar Paul. First German ed., 1919. London: Allen, 1921.

Ziemer, Gerhard, and Hans Wolf, eds. *Wandervogel und Freideutsche Jugend.* Bad Godesberg: Voggenreiter, 1961.

Ziolkowski, Theodore. *The Novels of Hermann Hesse: A Study in Theme and Structure.* Princeton: Princeton University Press, 1965.

Der Zupfgeigenhansl. Ed. Hans Breuer. 1909. 10th ed. Leipzig: Hofmeister, 1913.